D1525877

The Army of the Potomac in the
Overland and Petersburg Campaigns

Melanie + Charles,

   Thanks for all your support through the years. I hope you enjoy the book.

                    Steve

THE ARMY OF THE POTOMAC
IN THE
OVERLAND & PETERSBURG
CAMPAIGNS

Union Soldiers and Trench Warfare, 1864–1865

STEVEN E. SODERGREN

LOUISIANA STATE UNIVERSITY PRESS

BATON ROUGE

Published by Louisiana State University Press
Copyright © 2017 by Louisiana State University Press
Manufactured in the United States of America
First printing

Designer: Barbara Neely Bourgoyne
Typeface: Whitman
Printer and binder: McNaughton & Gunn, Inc.

Library of Congress Cataloging-in-Publication Data

Names: Sodergren, Steven E., author.
Title: The Army of the Potomac in the Overland and Petersburg Campaigns :
    union soldiers and trench warfare, 1864–1865 / Steven E. Sodergren.
Description: Baton Rouge : LSU Press, 2017. | Includes bibliographical references
    and index.
Identifiers: LCCN 2016027500| ISBN 978-0-8071-6556-0 (cloth : alk. paper) |
    ISBN 978-0-8071-6557-7 (pdf) | ISBN 978-0-8071-6558-4 (mobi)
Subjects: LCSH: Petersburg (Va.)—History—Siege, 1864–1865. | Overland
    Campaign, Va., 1864. | United States—History—Civil War, 1861–1865—Trench
    warfare. | United States—History—Civil War, 1861–1865—Social aspects. |
    United States. Army of the Potomac.
Classification: LCC E476.93 .S63 2017 | DDC 973.7/37—dc23
LC record available at https://lccn.loc.gov/2016027500

For Mom and Dad

Contents

Contents

Illustrations follow page 112

Maps and Tables

Acknowledgments

This project is the result of more than ten years of research and writing, including visits to archives and libraries across the country. Thus, one finds it incredibly difficult to distribute appropriate praise after so long a project, but I shall give it my best effort.

The bulk of the research for this project would not have been possible without the financial and archival assistance of multiple organizations. The General and Mrs. Matthew B. Ridgeway Military History Research Grant from the Military History Institute (now part of the United States Army Heritage and Education Center) enabled me to visit their beautiful facility in Carlisle and obtain access to a wealth of unpublished material. Once there, Richard Sommers unleashed his encyclopedic knowledge of Civil War matters and made my time there all the more productive. In 2005 the United States Army Center of Military History generously awarded me their dissertation fellowship to work on this project, and the staff there was very gracious with their time as I took advantage of their resources. Thanks are also due to the friendly and knowledgeable staffs at the Massachusetts Historical Society, the Library of Congress, the Old Military and Civil Records Branch of the National Archives, the David M. Rubenstein Rare Book & Manuscript Library at Duke University, the Southern Historical Collection at the University of North Carolina–Chapel Hill, the Delaware Public Archives, and the Spencer Research Library at the University of Kansas.

At the University of Kansas, Ted Wilson has been my guide in this endeavor from day one, and without him, none of what follows would have been possible. Thank you, Ted, for your continued counsel throughout; I fondly recall the hours spent in your Wescoe office chatting about history matters of various and sundry. Phillip Paludan, Jonathan Earle, and Christopher Gabel were all supporters of my work, and their comments were very useful in the early days of this project. Jennifer Weber, Ray Hiner, and Robert Baumann also kindly provided their assistance back in the initial stages of the research. Doug Harvey, Jeff Bremer, Becky Robinson, and other members of the Kansas University dissertation reading group reviewed drafts of several chapters, and their comments successfully kept my work in the realm of common sense.

The faculty and staff of Norwich University were exceptionally helpful with their time and resources as I refined and expanded the manuscript. Particular thanks go to Dave Westerman, Lea Williams, and the Office of Academic Research for their unflagging support. Additional praise must go to the helpful staff at the Kreitzberg Library along with the Archives and Special Collections department at Norwich. Thanks also to my colleagues Reina Pennington and Emily Gray for their comments on portions of the manuscript.

At Cornell College, Phil Lucas convinced me that I was on the right path and kept me focused on it. Craig Allin and Richard Thomas made my time there all the more rewarding and productive. Also, the Milts performed magnificently at offering counsel and distraction just when it was needed most.

At Louisiana State University Press, thanks go to Rand Dotson for his help pulling this manuscript together. Earl Hess reviewed multiple versions of the manuscript and provided many helpful comments along the way. Thanks also to Lee Sioles and Neal Novak at LSU Press, and to Gary Von Euer and David denBoer for being so meticulous with their work.

On a personal note, I have to thank my family for being extraordinarily patient with me as I plowed through year after year of this project and may not have been the friendliest person at times because of it. In addition, Cynthia's wisdom and friendship helped to make the hard times easier. Most importantly, thank you, Mary, for sticking with me throughout and understanding why this needed to get done.

I am sure that I have omitted many, and for that I apologize. The longer I worked, the more I realized how this was the product of a shared experience and not just my own individual effort. I thank all of those who contributed to that experience.

A Note on Sources

The literacy of Civil War soldiers varied widely, so it is no surprise to find their letters, diaries, and even some of their memoirs riddled with grammatical and spelling errors excessive even for their own time. Due to the uneven education of soldiers in both the North and South, men adopted a rather liberal use of the English language as they framed their words for family or themselves. In addition, life in camp or the trenches rarely proved amenable to those who wished to jot down a few lines about their day. Most letters were no doubt written on a soldier's knee or haversack, thus making accurate translation of their handwriting all the more difficult. In respect to the creativity of and difficulties faced by Union soldiers as they offered their thoughts on the world around them, little effort has been made here to alter the grammar or punctuation of their words beyond what is necessary to convey their meaning and intent. Thus, the use of [*sic*] has generally been omitted from the text. Bracketed corrections of quotations have been kept to a minimum, being employed only if included in a transcribed version of the soldier correspondence or if a correction was necessary to clarify the original intent of the author.

When a particular soldier is mentioned in the text, an effort is always made to include their full name, rank, and the regiment they were a part of at the time of speaking. However, due to source limitations, in a few cases rank and/or unit information is missing, and for at least one soldier included in this study, the name is missing as well.

Given the preponderance of infantry units, it should be assumed that a soldier's regiment is infantry unless otherwise stated.

The Army of the Potomac in the
Overland and Petersburg Campaigns

Introduction

SPRING 1864

There surely never was such a record of this in the annals of history! What army ever wrote such sublime, heroic sentences, such high-toned sentiments as will be found in this, our citizen soldiers' record?

—*Soldiers' Letters: From Camp, Battle-field, and Prison, 1865*

Spring in the Virginia countryside is a pleasant time, with warm weather, leafed-out shrubbery, and perhaps the occasional cool rain or thunderstorm drifting across the landscape. In March and April of 1864, as the warm air began to saturate the Virginia lowlands and the American Civil War entered its fourth year, the uniformed men of the Army of the Potomac braced for another campaign season. Spring found them encamped primarily along the Rappahannock River near Brandy Station, Virginia, a location far from the political heart of the Union war effort but quite close to the battlefields of previous years and the tortured memories that they evoked. While the previous year witnessed perhaps the greatest and bloodiest victory of the war for Union forces at Gettysburg, the fighting dragged on with few signs of impending conclusion. This continued indecision had only been confirmed in the months following Gettysburg with the so-called Mine Run campaign, a maneuver contest at the end of November between General George Meade's Army of the Potomac and General Robert E. Lee's Army of Northern Virginia. While Union commanders deserve credit for balking when it came time to throw their forces against a strong Confederate position across the uneven banks of Mine Run (no doubt stirring memories of the futile assaults against Marye's Heights at Fredericksburg less than a year earlier), it was only delaying the inevitable. Some soldiers marching through the crisp, cold night back to their camp at the end of the campaign were greeted with a rough sign drawn up by their comrades, proclaiming "The great moral show advertised by Lee and Meade has been indefinitely postponed."[1] The respite was welcome, for the coming months brought a mutual pause to the struggle as both sides settled in to the familiar tedium of winter quarters.

While the cold and damp brought a seasonal halt to active operations, the Union men of the Army of the Potomac spread out in the fields and meadows surrounding Brandy Station and indulged in the advantages of their winter quarters: crudely constructed wooden and mud huts that, while not the acme of comfort, offered a welcome change from the usual cloth tents and bedrolls that provided shelter on the march. These quarters, coupled with an uninterrupted supply line that kept the men well fed and provided with news and mail from the North, ensured an upbeat feeling in the ranks as spring dawned. Corporal Samuel Clear of the 116th Pennsylvania certainly displayed contentment when he reported in his diary on April 1, 1864, that "we are taking things easy, we have plenty to eat, wear and have a good warm place to sit and write to our friends."[2] Private Daniel Faust of the 96th Pennsylvania went further, reassuring his mother that he was "comfortable enough" and speculating that "I am as safe here as I am at home."[3] "I am *very comfortable indeed*," proclaimed English-born artilleryman James Horrocks in an April letter to his parents back in England, "I get the *best* of everything in the *edible* line that can be got here."[4] The advantages of relaxation, full stomachs, and of course, no imminent threat of death, were sometimes overshadowed by a larger, if somewhat unexpected, threat: tedium. To avoid allowing the men to lose their fighting edge, and to facilitate the continual integration of replacements into the ranks in the form of new volunteers and draftees, men were set to training and drilling for the inevitable campaigns of 1864. The repetitiveness of this process wore thin for many of the men; as in the previous several weeks, Private Francis Waller of the 6th Wisconsin could find little to note in his diary on April 16 other than "Same old story. *Drill.*"[5]

Despite the tedium and impending arrival of further bloodshed, many of these young men had already dedicated themselves to staying in the ranks and seeing out the struggle. The Northern government had taken steps to curb the possible manpower crisis expected that summer, when the three-year enlistments of tens of thousands of soldiers, the patriotic volunteers of 1861, were due to expire. By offering large bounties and short furloughs for those men who decided to reenlist, along with additional incentives for whole units that joined up for three more years, the Army of the Potomac managed to reenlist nearly 27,000 of their veteran '61 soldiers by the end of March, or nearly half of those whose enlistments were scheduled to expire.[6] Thousands of other soldiers were either in the middle of their enlistments or had only recently joined the army, such as in the case of Sergeant Clear, who enlisted in February 1864 because "I did not feel that I was doing my duty to stay at home when nearly all my comrades and friends was leaving for the seat of war."[7] Private Faust, who had been in the army for twenty months by April 1864 and had previously seen fighting at Gettysburg, echoed Clear's sentiment: "I think I wouldent [*sic*] be satisfied if I was home as long as the war lasts."[8] Reasons for enlisting in the first place or staying in after a long service were diverse: patriotism, money, boredom, peer pressure; but most merely stayed in or continued on because they legitimately felt that the end was near and did not want to miss it. By the end of April, Lieutenant Elisha Hunt Rhodes of the 2nd Rhode Island found himself dismissing those around him who spoke eagerly of returning to their homes. Having already reenlisted along with most of his regiment, Rhodes confided in his diary, "I want to see the end of the war as I saw the beginning."[9]

Some part of Rhodes's confidence in anticipating the imminent demise of the Confederacy stemmed from the new general-in-chief of Union forces, General Ulysses S. Grant. Grant, "the herow of Vicksburgh," carried a reputation for success and "unconditional surrender" hard earned in the western theater, from the opening of the Mississippi River to the liberation of Chattanooga in the foothills of Appalachia.[10] The citizens of the Union had great expectations for this new military chieftain, and the men of the Union's largest field army were no different. The soldiers' response to Grant's ascendancy to command on March 9 was mixed, but most expressed hope that his arrival would herald the much sought after victory over the Army of Northern Virginia. The men got their first look at the victorious western general in April, and some focused upon his appearance as a hopeful sign for victory. "Lieutenant Gen. Grant if not a good looking officer is a determined looking man," was Corporal Frederick Pettit's report after the first sight of his new commander.[11] Lieutenant Rhodes's comments in his diary on Grant were equally mixed, yet hopeful: "I was a little disappointed in the appearance, but I like the look of his eye."[12] Many soldiers shared Rhodes's dismay at the scruffy appearance of their new commander (who had never sought the kind of vainglorious image promoted by some general officers in the past) and instead focused on his record in battle as a positive indication. "Lee has Grant to face now, and if he is not careful, Grant will serve him worse than he did Pemberton at Vicksburg," was the opinion offered by Private Horace Paret of the 124th New York, while Captain Mason Tyler of the 37th Massachusetts praised the "prestige of success" surrounding Grant's arrival.[13] Grant brought with him to the East an unmatched list of Union victories, which had propelled him to the top of the Union command structure, and the soldiers of the Army of the Potomac shared the great expectations of their president and the nation.

For many of those in the Army of the Potomac, the West was a largely unknown world; those who had faced off against the already legendary figures of "Stonewall" Jackson and Robert E. Lee found it easy to question Grant's success in far off frontiers. While few were openly hostile toward Grant, several expressed an indifference born of a long series of commanding generals and disastrous campaigns stretching back three years. This lack of enthusiasm, still strong many years after the war, was captured in Private Frank Wilkeson's memoirs of his time in the 11th New York Artillery as he described his conversation with veteran soldiers regarding the promotion of Grant: "Well, let Grant try what he can accomplish with the Army of the Potomac. He cannot be worse than his predecessors."[14] Most held out hope that Grant would live up to his hype, but recognized that having Grant in command meant fighting, and soon. Only days before the opening of the Overland campaign, Private John Haley of the 17th Maine assessed the status of the Army of the Potomac in his diary and admitted with a slight sense of dismay that "no doubt that Grant will give them [the Confederates] as hot a fight as they have ever engaged in."[15] "We may expect hard work soon I suppose," wrote Major Howard Smith of the 1st New York Dragoons to his future wife, Mary, on April 3, adding "We all have great confidence in General Grant though the responsibilities that he assumes are very great."[16] The men knew what Grant was there to do and they held on to their hopes that he would bring victory, but as April dragged on the men were forced to wait until the army was ready to advance.

By the middle of the month, it became readily apparent that the waiting would soon be over. On April 7, 1864, General George Meade, still in operational command of the Army of the Potomac, issued General Orders No. 17, calling for the removal of all unnecessary civilians (specifically sutlers, independent salesmen who followed the army selling various supplies), along with unnecessary property to the rear.[17] Private Julius Ramsdell of the 39th Massachusetts packed up and sent off his winter gear, but complained to his aunt that still having to carry "our blouses, blankets, shelter tents and shirts . . . will make a pretty heavy load, especially in hot weather."[18] New volunteer Private Robert Ekin McBride of the 190th Pennsylvania dutifully packed up his baggage to be sent to the rear, never to lay eyes on it again once it vanished into the bureaucratic void.[19] Veteran soldiers knew that baggage to the rear meant a forward movement soon, and as their excess belongings disappeared northward to an uncertain fate, the men bided their time and girded themselves for the inevitable. As early as April 12, Captain James Latta of the 119th Pennsylvania penned in his journal his guess that "the general packing up of baggage on all sides favor strongly of an early move."[20] Corporal Cyrille Fountain of the 77th New York heard the order for the removal of sutlers and recognized immediately that "it looks goodeel like a move."[21] Down with the Army of the James on the Peninsula, Lieutenant Joseph Scroggs's Fifth United States Colored Troops was also preparing to advance on the same day that Grant was planning to put the Army of the Potomac in motion. On May 1, right before boarding transports headed to City Point, Virginia, Scroggs noted in his diary, "Ordered to prepare two days cooked rations, which looks like moving."[22] By May 4, the Army of the Potomac and the Army of the James were ready to advance on their mutual objective of Richmond, with the real intention of drawing out Lee's army to where it could be destroyed.

Thus commenced the fifth Union drive on the Confederate capital at Richmond in a little over three years of war. Despite the repetitive frustration of these efforts, soldiers in both the Army of the Potomac and the Army of the James expressed confidence in approaching victory. In the Army of the Potomac alone, close to 120,000 men set off on May 4 to face Lee's Confederates.[23] Being part of this immense military force was enough for some men to take heart that the end of the rebellion was within reach. Corporal Anson Shuey of the 93rd Pennsylvania was clearly impressed, writing to his wife in April, "I think the army is larger than it ever was before, I think we will be able to clear Virginia."[24] After the long stay in the camps over the winter, the men were eager to go, and reports from both within and without the Army of the Potomac indicate that the force that set out on May 4 was in excellent condition. Captain George Washington Whitman anticipated a forward movement in a late April letter to his poet brother Walt, praising Grant and proclaiming that "everyone seems to be in good spirits and hopefull."[25] Civilian Sylvanus Cadwallader, a *New York Herald* reporter who followed the army on the campaign and frequently found himself in close contact with private soldiers and general officers alike, noted in his wartime reminiscences that "never since its organization had the Army of the Potomac been in better spirits, or more eager to meet the enemy."[26] The feelings within the ranks, however, were best expressed by Private Austin Kendall, an enlisted man in the 117th New York Infantry, who wrote in a letter to friends that "as a Regiment we was never in better order to march and endure hardships than we are now. . . . there are but few sick and all seem anxious to go ahead and do all they can to wipe out this unholy rebellion. We all have great confidence in our leader Lieut. General Grant and we believe he will lead us on to victory."[27]

The new campaign season and fair Virginia weather carried with it sanguine expectations for an end to the civil struggle that had ravaged the country for years. Few anticipated the nightmares that lay ahead, and those who did worked hard to keep them from their mind. Victory was less than a year away for the Union forces, but that year would be filled with weeks upon weeks of battle beyond the keen of even the most veteran troops, followed by months of frustrating indecision amidst some of the most sophisticated trench systems devised during the nineteenth century. How these men survived, endured, and achieved ultimate victory is a compelling tale of how American men steeled themselves against the worst that the Civil War had to offer.

———

The final year of the American Civil War witnessed unprecedented bloodshed as combat reached its highest level of ferocity and constancy. Beginning with the Overland and Atlanta campaigns in the spring of 1864, Union armies grabbed hold of their rebel opponents and never let go, breaking the previous years' tradition of epic battles separated by weeks and months. General

Ulysses Grant's strategy was to keep the pressure on the Confederacy until it collapsed, and the result was the bloodletting of the Overland campaign of May and June 1864 that produced nearly 55,000 Union casualties in the span of six weeks.[28] It was during this campaign that soldiers then and historians since determined that the war had reached a new level, when men witnessed as never before "the full panoply of war in its most brutal manifestations."[29] Following on the heels of the Overland campaign was another new experience for the soldiers of the East: the investment of the city of Petersburg and more than nine months buried deep in a sophisticated network of earthworks while suffering through what has been labeled "constant, grinding, all-destroying warfare."[30] Petersburg involved the largest use of trench warfare during the war, and continued the trend of campaigns becoming lengthy struggles of attrition rather than intermittent set-piece battles.

Despite the changing circumstances of the war, authors rarely mention how a variation in the actual methods of warfighting may have had corresponding effects on the men charged with the prosecution of such warfare. Historians of both the Civil War combat soldier and the Overland and Petersburg campaigns have neglected this aspect of the wartime narrative, a surprising omission given the emphasis that many have placed on the ferocity and changing nature of these operations. Several works have tackled these campaigns in detail, some of the most recent and thorough efforts being from historians Gordon Rhea and Noah Andre Trudeau, but they typically fall into the realm of what John Keegan described as "the typical 'battle piece,' with its reduction of soldiers to pawns, its discontinuous rhythm, its conventional imagery, its selective incident and its high focus on leadership."[31] Earl Hess recently broke this trend with a series on the advent of field fortifications during the Civil War, a rich contribution to a poorly understood element of the conflict. While Hess's research is meticulous, his target is not men but earth; precisely tracking and mapping the disruptions in the ground erected either with haste or deliberation in an effort to save men's lives.[32] Authors such as Rhea, Trudeau, and Hess typically include an impressive amount of source material from those in the ranks in each of their studies, but such material is used primarily to develop the course of the battle or campaign and highlight tactical conditions on the ground, not to offer any sort of systematic analysis of the soldier's experience. When insight is offered into the combat experience, it is to present a bleak picture of combat conditions that make it appear impossible that anyone could have survived in such an environment, such as Gerald Linderman's assessment of trench life at Petersburg as a "mole-like existence [that] had strained and broken not only men's bodies but their allegiance to many of the ideas with which they had begun the war."[33] Such a presentation of men in combat presents the soldier more as a victim, with those exposed to the horrendous conditions of combat (modern or otherwise) being overwhelmed by the experience yet somehow managing to muddle through to victory. This does little justice to those men who struggled so valiantly to survive long enough to see that victory. By examining the specific conditions of some of the most horrific and varied combat environments of the war, while placing them in the context of evolving methods of warfare, one can truly appreciate how and why soldiers were able to endure.

Perhaps the most extensive work on the particular subject of soldiers in the last year of the Civil War has been performed by J. Tracy Power, who presented an analysis of the final year in the life of the Army of Northern Virginia in his book, *Lee's Miserables.* This work offers a dismal tale of an army gradually disintegrating in the face of trench warfare and the collapse of the Confederate home front. Desertion within Confederate ranks increased dramatically over the course of the Petersburg siege, as "many members of Lee's army began to question the wisdom, or even the necessity, of continuing to oppose the vast Federal army facing them."[34] Power offers a tale of a Confederate force breaking down in the last year of the war, at least partly because of the combat conditions to which they were exposed. Yet Power sees a solid core of Confederates enduring, which allowed the Army of Northern Virginia to weather the casualties and desertions while fending off Union forces until the end of March 1865.[35] Unfortunately, that is only half the story, and leaves the question of how "the vast Federal army" was able to suffer through the same combat conditions in opposition to the Confederates only yards away across no man's land.

The answer is a complicated one, made even more so when one examines the issue of desertion in the Army of the Potomac over the course of the Overland and Petersburg campaigns. Unlike the American conflicts of the twentieth century fought overseas, combatants north and south often fought in the same region, state, or town where they lived, allowing them to walk away from the war whenever they saw fit. Tens of thousands on both sides deserted over the course of the war, despite stiff penalties including execution for those caught away from their unit. In April 1864, on the eve of the spring campaigns, 7,072 Union soldiers were reported by their regimental commanders as having deserted, with 3,653 being arrested during that same month.[36] As will be demonstrated later in this study, desertion rates in all Union armies increased significantly as the violence of the summer continued. While the sight of men being hung for desertion did have a deterrent effect on those Union soldiers who were often forced to witness it, this alone does not explain why the bulk of the Army of the Potomac remained in the trenches. As Power demonstrates, the Confederate army nearly fell apart under similar conditions, despite Confederate authorities' use of the death penalty just as often as their Northern counterparts.[37] A major goal of this study will be to explain what kept Union soldiers from succumbing to the same pessimism and anxiety engendered by life in the trenches that obviously had such a profound negative effect on the Army of Northern Virginia.

The sources for an assessment of the peaks and valleys of morale in the Army of the Potomac are not to be found in the correspondence and remembrances of the famed figures of the conflict. The generals, politicians, and military bureaucrats may offer insight into the details of campaigns and operations, but only reveal in a limited fashion how an ordinary soldier living in the trenches would have reacted to his environment. The true focus belongs to enlisted men and regimental officers, those who were stationed on the front line and either had to endure the assaults, sharpshooting, and artillery fire that characterized warfare from 1864 to 1865 or had direct contact with those who did.[38] Their numbers were substantial; it has been estimated that 93.2 percent of all uniformed personnel in the Civil War held combat-related tasks, compared with only 28.8 percent of personnel in American forces almost a hundred years later.[39] Infantrymen were far and away the largest combat arm, though members of the cavalry and artillery branches of the Army of the Potomac also found themselves as exposed to the rigors of campaigning and life in the trenches as their infantry counterparts. By 1864, most of these men were veterans of at least a year's worth of campaigning, though influxes of new volunteers and draftees would increase throughout 1864–1865 to replace the casualties of Overland and Petersburg.

Whether three-year veterans or reluctant draftees, participants frequently endeavored to document their wartime lives by keeping diaries and relating stories of life at the front in letters sent to friends and family back home. It is in these sources that one may piece together the soldiers' story, since it is the letters and diaries that provide an immediate, honest response to what the men were facing on a daily basis. "Honesty" is a difficult issue when looking at the personal correspondence of soldiers on the front lines. While journals are perhaps the most accurate source for reactions to the combat experience, it is possible that some soldiers may have censored themselves and their tales of the battlefield when writing to loved ones. However, as will be seen throughout this study, most Union soldiers did not shy away from including the graphic and dismal depictions of the wartime environment in letters sent home. The literature of the war yields a flurry of postwar memoirs written by participants in a vast array of publications at the end of the nineteenth century. Written years and decades after Appomattox, these narratives were frequently, and unconsciously, affected by such factors as memory loss, a feeling of self-glorification, and a desire for self-justification. Consequently, while some memoirs will be utilized to gain a reflective element, primary attention will be given to the immediate wartime letters and journals of the soldiers. These sources, coupled with official correspondence, media reports, court-martial transcripts, soldier service records, and documentation from the numerous voluntary organizations that swarmed around the Union armies in the field, allow for the detailed account of soldier life that follows.

At its heart, this tale revolves around sources from approximately 170 Union participants in the Overland and Petersburg campaigns. Since all of the fighting in these campaigns occurred in the East, most of the soldiers in this sample were from northeastern and mid-Atlantic states. Pennsylvania, New York, and Massachusetts provide the lion's share of the soldiers referenced here, just as they did for the Union's wartime legions. Despite the eastern predominance, a few soldiers in the sample, just as in the Army of the Potomac, were drawn from western states. Due to casualties, the expiration of enlistments, and the transfer of units to other areas (the bulk of the 6th corps was sent to the Shenandoah Valley from July to December 1864), only about half of the men in the sample served the duration of both campaigns, and it was necessary to include those who were absent for parts of one or both of the 1864–1865 campaigns, a factor taken into account when performing any comparative assessments between the campaigns. While a large majority of the sample are enlisted men, officers ranking colonel and below are overrepresented in the sample, accounting for roughly a third of those researched, an outcome due primarily to their higher literacy rate and higher pay, which allowed for the purchase of letter-writing and journal implements. Little bonded these men together apart from their shared experience on the battlefield and perhaps their common notions of God and country. The reactions of these men to such issues as the combat environment, the decisions of their commanders, the actions of the enemy, and the war as a whole are demonstrated here as generalizations drawn from a limited sample. Yet, as one author suggests, "generalizing about the combat experiences of the Civil War infantryman is a useful tool for understanding some aspects of the battles he fought, the campaigns in which he served, the community and culture from which he came, and the war itself."[40] The conclusions reached in this study reflect the recurrent themes and ideas found within the sample described above, not the stray comments of one or two "outliers." By identifying sentiments expressed repeatedly throughout the sources in the sample, the peculiar nature of the fighting of 1864–1865, as well as the complex methods that originated from the men in the ranks to carry on, become readily apparent.

The combat experience of the last year of the American Civil War had a dual effect on Union soldiers in the East; the harsh conditions engendered by a lengthy period of frequent high-intensity field combat followed by an even longer period of low-intensity trench conflict degraded their will to fight while simultaneously serving to maintain it by giving the men increased control over their environment. As will be demonstrated in the following chapters, the Overland campaign had a crippling effect on the fighting power of the Army of the Potomac, reducing morale to the point of despair among most soldiers, with an open refusal of orders occurring in some units along with a general prevalence of lower-level insubordinate behavior. Petersburg, though a destructive environment that contained parallels to the apocalyptic battle plains of the First World War, was welcomed by those in the ranks for the escape that it offered from the frontal assaults and charges that characterized the fighting of May and June 1864. Safely ensconced behind some of the most sophisticated earthworks of the war, soldiers used their protected environment to reestablish control over their individual lives on the battlefield. As operations around the city persisted, their desire to continue fighting was reinforced by efforts taken on their behalf by their commanders, who provided a steady system of supply and frequent relief from the tedium of the trenches. As the men regained control over their surroundings they also observed that the North was regaining control over the war with victories across the country, a fact they could read about in the papers and see with their own eyes on the fields surrounding Petersburg. When the time came to emerge from their entrenchments in spring 1865 and once again meet their Confederate foes on the open battlefield, the men of the Army of the Potomac did so with little trepidation in a manner reminiscent of their confidence prior to the commencement of campaign season a year earlier.

There is much that one can learn from the story of how these soldiers kept the faith on the evolving field of battle. First, the fall and rise of morale among the men of the Army of the Potomac reveals how these soldiers were able to outlast their Confederate opponents and avoid the same erosive effects of desertion as those that distinguished the Petersburg experience of the Army of Northern Virginia. This ability to maintain unit cohesion and confidence in the face of the enemy gave Northern soldiers a decisive numerical and psychological advantage in the race to Appomattox Court House, and goes a long way toward explaining the brevity and decisiveness of that final campaign. Second, the story of these American soldiers on American battlefields offers insight into how the citizen soldiers of the United States have responded to warfare and been affected by it. Finally, the existence of Union soldiers during the last year of the war in the East reveals a picture of combat soldiers who were seeing warfare change before their eyes. While the debate continues on whether the Civil War was a "modern" conflict, strategic and tactical emphases were shifting in different, if not necessarily new, directions as the war reached its zenith.[41] The soldiers' ability to retain their morale in the face of a growing threat to their lives, while using the battlefield itself as a source for inspiration, offers important lessons for those historians who would investigate the effect of and response to static warfare in any time period. These men did not shirk from the increasingly foreign battlefield that greeted them day after day; they achieved victory at Petersburg and Appomattox in 1865 by silencing the demons of the Overland campaign and putting aside the terrors of trench life, at least until the war was over and they were safe at home. Then the nightmares would return, as they often do.

1

"Some One Will Have to Suffer"

THE OVERLAND CAMPAIGN, MAY 5–JUNE 15, 1864

We go on the Morrow where Cannon are booming.
—Sergeant Samuel Gilpin, 3rd Indiana Cavalry

The spring campaign in Virginia would kick off during the first week of May 1864, and the agents of the United States Sanitary Commission thought they were ready. Founded in 1861 as a private relief agency to support the Union war effort, the commission had almost three full years of war to develop and refine their methods for providing aid and comfort to the men at the front lines who most needed it. Each year, millions of dollars were raised and thousands of volunteers organized for this effort. Spring 1864 was no different; for the upcoming Virginia campaign, the commission had estimated ten thousand wounded would require their services, and they sought to mobilize the appropriate resources in support of that number above and beyond the services provided by the army itself. A "Field Relief Corps" was established to shadow the Army of the Potomac on its move south with seventy wagons filled with food and medicine; two hundred tons of additional supplies were to follow by steamship and railroad, hundreds of "Relief Agents" would be on hand to distribute these resources, and three "Feeding Stations" were to be located behind the army to provide warm coffee and food for the injured fleeing the battlefield. All told, the commission would spend $515,000 on supporting the Army of the Potomac alone in May and June. It wasn't nearly enough. Charles Stille was a member of the Sanitary Commission and one of the first historians of the organization immediately following the war; his conclusion about the commission's efforts reveals how the fighting in Virginia would unfold in 1864:

Vast as was the work performed by the Government, and its volunteer, auxil-
iary helpers on this occasion, and laborious and self-denying as was the zeal of
all who were engaged in the service of succoring the wounded, the mournful
impression still remains when all was done, of the utter inadequacy of the best
appointed means of mitigating, as the heart would fain desire, the horrors of
scenes like these.[1]

The casualties of the spring campaign would dwarf early estimates, and well-
meaning commissioners like Charles Stille found it impossible to keep up with
the demand for their resources.

There was arguably no bloodier time in American history than the months
of May and June 1864. During this period, the vast, combined armies of the
Union and Confederacy succeeded in slaughtering each other at rates never
seen before or after in the long military saga of North America. This was the
time of General Ulysses S. Grant's great offensive, intended to finally choke
off the Confederate cause by sending no less than five Union columns against
strategic points in the South, ranging from the rebel capital at Richmond to
the Red River valley in Louisiana. Every advancing Union column soon faced
obstructions, however; General Nathaniel Banks was quickly sent into headlong retreat by Confederate forces along the Red River, while the second largest
contingent, under the command of William Tecumseh Sherman, found itself
repeatedly obstructed and delayed in its drive on Atlanta by the skillful maneuvering of Confederate general Joseph Johnston. Nowhere did the fighting rage
more fiercely and with greater bloodshed than in the embattled Washington/
Richmond corridor, where the Army of the Potomac and the Army of Northern
Virginia once again found themselves locked in bitter struggle. It was here that
close to 200,000 American soldiers engaged in constant combat and maneuver
for nearly six weeks, before the exhausted and bloodied mass of men finally
reached the city of Petersburg and gained a period of "rest." For the men of the
Army of the Potomac, who had begun the 1864 Overland campaign in early
May with such high hopes of a quick Union victory, the spring days of May
and June proved to be a nightmare from which there was seemingly no escape.

Most of these Union men had been there before. The majority of those
enlisted men and officers in the Army of the Potomac by May 1864 were the
patriotic volunteers of '61 and '62 who had been in the service for years and
witnessed multiple engagements. Many were the men who had served under

General George McClellan in 1862, a man who failed to wield his force of men effectively in combat but went to great lengths to restore order and discipline to the ranks, which in turn established a sense of pride and common identity among the soldiers of the Army of the Potomac. That pride and discipline served the men well in the following years, as a series of general officers led the army through defeats and inconclusive encounters with Confederate forces under the command of General Robert E. Lee. Thus, these were men who had not only seen combat, but experienced almost continual frustration. They were veterans; they had seen the elephant and kept coming back for more, willingly or not. Many probably thought they had seen everything battle had to offer by 1864. If so, then they would be stunned as Grant's campaign unfolded, when a new level of violence was achieved that created feelings of confusion and frustration in almost every soldier. As historian Carol Reardon has argued, the experience of combat in the Overland campaign "forced even the toughest veteran to discard many old notions as romantic and outdated."[2]

It was not surprising that veteran soldiers would react in such a way, given that the Overland campaign was unlike anything that they had encountered before in their military service for the Union. The forty days spanning Grant's first contact with Lee in the Wilderness on May 5 until the arrival of the first segments of the Army of the Potomac outside Petersburg on June 15 witnessed unprecedented levels of violence and movement by the opposing forces.[3] Prior to this time, most campaigns in the eastern theater had been relatively short affairs, involving operational maneuvers punctuated by one large tactical engagement typically ending in a Union defeat. Large lulls usually separated each of these engagements, such as those that followed the battles at Antietam, Fredericksburg, and Gettysburg. While the fighting during these campaigns was some of the most ferocious seen during the whole war, the violence proved brief, and lengthy periods separated each battle, during which the opposing forces were allowed the opportunity to rest, refit, and rebuild their forces in the safety of camp. The most significant exception to this was the Seven Days campaign of 1862, wherein General Lee, newly appointed as commander of the Army of Northern Virginia, engaged General George McClellan in a series of fierce conflicts that drove the Army of the Potomac from just outside Richmond back to its supply base on the James River. Yet, as can be inferred from the title accorded to this campaign, operations lasted approximately one week and resulted in 35,000 combined casualties, and the battles that occurred did not approach the level of ferocity or casualty figures witnessed two years later.[4] Much of the explanation for the lower rate of casualties during the Seven Days campaign can be found in the willingness of the opposing commanders to engage in pitched battle. While General Lee proved more than willing to hammer away at the Union forces in 1862, General McClellan's primary goal during the campaign was to withdraw his army from the field until he could relocate his base of supply to the James River. In spring 1864, however, both Lee and Grant would prove willing to engage each other whenever and wherever possible.

In the predawn hours of May 4, 1864, more than 100,000 Union soldiers set forth from the region surrounding Brandy Station, Virginia on what many hoped would be the concluding, and triumphant, campaign of the war. Unlike in previous years, the target of this mighty host was not the Confederate capital at Richmond, but instead the Army of Northern Virginia itself. As Grant explained years later in his memoirs, "To get possession of Lee's army was the first great object. With the capture of his army Richmond would necessarily follow."[5] His strategy certainly appeared capable of annihilating the Confederate army. The goal was to interpose the Army of the Potomac between the Confederates and their capital; Grant knew that Lee would then be forced to attack at a time and place not of his choosing in order to prevent the Union force from moving on Richmond. Grant's plan was set in motion on May 4, as the five corps of the Army of the Potomac moved south in two massive lines of infantry, zigzagging through the scattered and complex system of country roads which made up the transportation network of northeastern Virginia. By nightfall on the fourth, lead elements of the Union army reached the area around the Wilderness Tavern, near the Chancellorsville battlefield where the Army of the Potomac met one of its greatest defeats exactly one year earlier. Progress had been slow due to the supply trains being delayed by the country roads, but confidence remained high, and all expected to continue the movement southward the following morning.[6] As Theodore Lyman, a member of General Meade's staff, had put it several weeks earlier, "I suppose we may call this the lull before the hurricane, which little short of a miracle can avert."[7]

As the Army of the Potomac stepped off on the great campaign of 1864, the numbers contained within it had rarely been greater. Returns from the army at this time indicate that 120,000 officers and men headed into the Wilderness on May 5, divided into four corps of infantry containing three to four divisions each, one cavalry corps with three divisions, and an artillery train with more than two dozen batteries of various size.[8] Though Grant was general-in-chief of all Union forces and would escort the Army of the Potomac as it moved south, the real commander of the Army of the Potomac since immediately prior to the battle of Gettysburg was Major General George Gordon Meade. A prickly Pennsylvanian who had demonstrated talent for the defensive and an efficient handling of his subordinates in the Gettysburg victory, Meade now found himself in the awkward position of being eclipsed and overseen by the hero of the West. The Union corps commanders were of varying backgrounds, but most had a fair collection of experience and had risen to their positions through talent, intellect, or something distinguished. In particular, Major General Winfield Scott Hancock in command of 2nd Corps and Major General John Sedgwick in command of 6th Corps had demonstrated bravery and command aptitude, and were respected if not loved by their men. Major General Gouverneur Warren, the "odd duck" and former chief engineer of the Army of the Potomac, was the new commander of 5th Corps, and while he had played a pivotal role in saving the Union left flank at Gettysburg, Warren had yet to be truly tested as a high-level field commander. The commander of the Cavalry Corps, Major General Philip Sheridan, was a transplant from the western armies who, though an unknown quantity to many in the East, would soon prove his bravery and skill in the field.[9] The 9th Corps, commanded by Major General Ambrose Burnside, had seen service across the country, most recently coming from the successful capture and subsequent defense of Knoxville, Tennessee. Due to Burnside's seniority in rank to Meade, Grant took the politically astute but operationally awkward step of making the 9th Corps independent of the Army of the Potomac for the Overland campaign. The 9th Corps would theoretically answer directly to Grant and work in tandem with Meade's army as it moved south until it was formally integrated into the Army of the Potomac on May 25.[10]

For the thousands of uniformed officers and men who found themselves marching through the scrub brush and irregular woodlands of central Virginia those first few days of May, anticipation grew with every step. While there was in no way a sense of doom in the air, it was clear to all that they were in enemy territory and contact was imminent. A familiar refrain was that of Sergeant Samuel Gilpin on May 3: "The boys are tired of Camp and will welcome the order—'Forward.'"[11] While the desire to end the monotony of the past few months was a strong motivation forward, higher-level officers like Lieutenant Colonel Horace Porter, a member of Grant's staff, perhaps overstated the issue by noting, "The quick, elastic step and easy swinging gait of the men, the cheery look upon their faces, and the lusty shouts with which they greeted their new commander as he passed, gave proof of the temper of their metal, and the superb spirit which animated their hearts."[12] More commonly, soldiers made their peace with God or held hope in a quick victory as comfort on the eve of inevitable battle. "But let come what will," noted Sergeant Samuel Cormany of the 16th Pennsylvania Cavalry on May 4, "as I know that my Redeemer liveth, and if He has nothing more for me to do on earth, I fain would die my countrys cause defending."[13] While anxiety was clearly evident, many sensed that they were moving forward as one of the most potent fighting forces the North would produce over the course of the war, and this facilitated what one author described as "the strong sense of collective identity necessary to the health of any organization."[14]

Though many guessed what lay ahead, few suspected that only miles away Robert E. Lee was already preparing his counterstroke. Seeing an opportunity to strike the much larger Union force at a point where it was spread out and mired in unfavorable terrain, Lee's army attacked on the morning of May 5 in the wooded region surrounding Wilderness Tavern, beginning the "epic confrontation" that would stretch on for weeks.[15] The battle that followed was a confused, shifting encounter with units on both sides entering the struggle in piecemeal fashion. Consequently, the battle was actually a collection of several small engagements as individual brigades and divisions stumbled across each other in the thick brush. Early success in withstanding and then counterattacking the Confederates on May 5 along the Orange Turnpike and Orange Plank Road encouraged Grant and Meade to continue the battle the following day. On the morning of May 6, General Winfield Hancock pushed his Second Corps against the right flank of Lee's line, only to discover that General James Longstreet had moved his Confederate corps into that position the night before. A back-and-forth struggle took place until around 11:00 a.m., when several of Longstreet's brigades slammed into Hancock's left flank with devastating results. One member of the Second Corps described the Confederate assault as overwhelming, with the result that "the Regt on our right flank gave way exposing us to a murderous fire . . . we tried to stand it but it was more than human power could do."[16] Thanks to the personal leadership of General Hancock ("I never saw a cooler man in a fight," noted one officer) and the hasty placement of reinforcements, a rout was avoided, and by late afternoon the Second Corps had reestablished their lines, thus securing Meade's left flank.[17] A disorganized Confederate assault against Meade's right flank took place late in the day on the 6th, but growing darkness and irregular terrain prohibited success. With both sides considerably weakened and in secure positions, the battle closed by nightfall on the sixth with the Army of the Potomac having suffered 17,666 casualties, of which more than 5,000 had come from the Second Corps (see Table 1).[18]

TABLE 1. Casualties Sustained by the Army of the Potomac during the Overland Campaign, May 5–June 15, 1864

Location and Date	Killed in Action	Wounded in Action	Missing in Action	Total
The Wilderness, May 5–7	2,246	12,037	3,383	17,666
Spotsylvania Court House, May 8–21	2,725	13,416	2,258	18,399
North Anna River, May 22–June 1	591	2,734	661	3,986
Cold Harbor, June 1–June 15	1,845	9,077	1,816	12,738
Cavalry Actions, May and June	214	1,075	848	2,137
TOTAL	7,621	38,339	8,966	54,926

Source: United States War Department, *The War of the Rebellion: A Compilation of the Official Records of the Union and Confederate Armies*, Volume 36, Part 1, 119–188.

Reactions to the Battle of the Wilderness, described by one as "a tragedy, grandly, awfully sublime," were numerous.[19] The Army of the Potomac would advance quickly after the battle, leaving little time to write or think about what had occurred, but those who did offer comment almost spoke in awe of the experience. The sights, sounds, and smells of May 5–6 assaulted the senses in unfamiliar ways. What distinguished the Wilderness from previous battles was not necessarily the body count (as many men had fallen on both sides at Chancellorsville a year earlier), but the terrain in which the fighting occurred. The Wilderness was exactly that: a thick tangle of underbrush that inhibited the movement of the masses of men on both sides and prevented the opposing forces from engaging each other in an orderly fashion. As reporter Sylvanus Cadwallader noted in his memoirs, "the face of the country, and character of the growing timber, was found to be the most unfavorable imaginable for offensive operations."[20] Sergeant Henry Keiser of the 96th Pennsylvania offered a similar analysis, commenting that the area around the Wilderness Tavern was covered with "the awfullest brush, briars, grapevines, etc. I ever was in."[21] The result was what Private John Haley referred to as "a dreadfully mixed-up mess," with Northern units getting lost and sometimes even firing on friendly forces.[22] An unexpected consequence of fighting in such overgrown terrain was the frequent occurrence of brush fires caused by the black-powder weapons being employed. Sergeant Clear of the 116th Pennsylvania described how his unit's part of the Union line seemed to be "one vast logheap on fire," which spread so quickly that it drove his unit from their position.[23] Unfortunately, some of those who lay wounded were unable to escape the flames before being consumed by them.

Beyond the woods and flames, the actual sounds of the battlefield elicited the most comment from the soldiers. Perhaps it was being deprived of a clear view of the battlefield that left the men dwelling upon the cacophony of warfare that surrounded them. Unsurprisingly, they sought something familiar with which to understand the unfamiliar. To Lieutenant George Bowen of the 12th New Jersey, the sound of the artillery booming through the woods resembled "the roll of marching in a million . . . times more intense."[24] Corporal John Pillings, a native of Lancashire, England and recently reenlisted member of the 70th New York, used similar imagery in a letter describing the exchange of fire on May 6: "of all the sounds of musketry ever know in history, there never was or could be any thing produced to equal the firing that continued for about one hour; it was just like a million drums beating one continual roll."[25] Writing his memoirs years later, artilleryman Frank Wilkeson remained fixated by the sounds of the Wilderness, describing enemy fire as "a steady roll," "deafening," and "thunderous," before concluding that it most closely resembled "the fury of hell in intensity."[26]

For some Union soldiers, including Wilkeson, this "fury" was their first trip to the battlefield, and their thoughts turned to how they stood up in the face of it. "I did better than I ever thought I could," was Corporal Samuel Clear's report of his performance, while another member of Clear's 116th Pennsylvania felt that the unit had "stood up and done their duty" in its first battle.[27] Veterans also measured up their performance in the wake of the Wilderness, and those like Corporal Cyrille Fountain of the 77th New York could not contain their disappointment in reporting that their unit had retreated in the face of an enemy attack.[28] Yet the fortunes of battle had been uneven; while drives against both flanks of the Army of the Potomac were at times successful, Union lines generally held in the face of repeated Confederate attacks. Thus, it was with no small sense of glee that Sergeant Jacob Lyons of the 120th New York wrote in his diary on May 6, "the enemy came up to the first line when we gave them the hottest fire that they ever got . . . we kept it up for about three quarters of an hour when the Rebels broke and run like the devil."[29] The back-and-forth nature of the fighting and the typical worm's-eye view of the soldier on the battlefield left many wondering on the evening of the 6th and in the days following who exactly had won. Few felt it was a defeat, but opinions ranged from how the army had "whiped the enemy by hard fighting at every point" to "Victory reported ours. Am too old soldier to believe it."[30] It was Sergeant Charles Wood of the 11th New Hampshire who caught the prevailing mood on May 7: "The generals feel good, a good sign."[31]

As the fires burned out on the Wilderness battlefield on May 7, Grant put the Army of the Potomac in motion. In point of fact, the battle had been a marginal defeat for the Army of the Potomac; the Union advance had been surprised and stopped dead by Lee, and Union casualties outweighed those of the Confederates.[32] In seasons past, this normally would have been the time when the Union commander would retreat back toward Washington to rest and refit his force. Grant did not follow this pattern, deciding to continue his original movement, altered slightly so that the Army of the Potomac would move past Lee's right flank and once again attempt to interpose itself between the Confederates and Richmond (see Map 1). Believing that "the enemy are

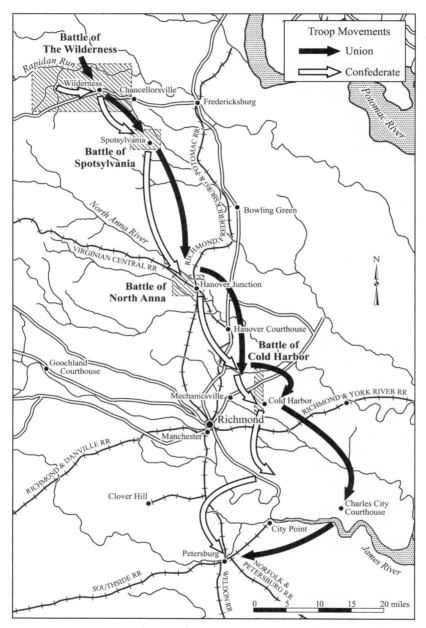

Troop Movements

➤ Union

▷ Confederate

Battle of The Wilderness

Rapidan Run

Wilderness

Chancellorsville

Fredericksburg

Potomac River

Spotsylvania

Battle of Spotsylvania

North Anna River

RICHMOND, FREDERICKSBURG & POTOMAC RR

Bowling Green

VIRGINIAN CENTRAL RR

Battle of North Anna

Hanover Junction

N

Hanover Courthouse

Battle of Cold Harbor

Goochland Courthouse

Mechanicsville

Cold Harbor

RICHMOND & YORK RIVER RR

Richmond

Manchester

RICHMOND & DANVILLE RR

Clover Hill

Charles City Courthouse

City Point

Petersburg

NORFOLK & PETERSBURG RR

James River

SOUTHSIDE RR

WELDON RR

0   5   10   15   20 miles

Map 1. Major Engagements of the Overland Campaign, May–June 1864

very shaky, and are only kept up to the mark by the greatest exertions on the part of their officers," Grant wanted to keep up the pressure on Lee's army.[33] This decision reflected a sea change in the conduct of war in the east. From this point forward, "the search for glory battles . . . was replaced by extended campaigns in which battles were the means to a strategic end, not an end in themselves."[34] Of course, this shift meant that an increased burden was now being placed on the men, who would be expected to "keep moving on" until the enemy was defeated. "The armies now clung in a death grip," was how one author noted this shift, an appropriate choice of words given how the body count would skyrocket over the next few weeks as Grant sidled his way closer to Richmond.[35]

The change was not lost on the soldiers, who were now being ordered to continue moving forward after two days of exhausting and ferocious conflict in the blinding conditions of the Wilderness. Despite their fatigue, the men were initially enthusiastic about sustaining the campaign against the Army of Northern Virginia. Joining Grant and the army on its move southward was Charles Dana, an assistant secretary of war, who noted in his memoirs how after the Wilderness "as the army began to realize that we were really moving south . . . the spirits of the men and officers rose to the highest pitch of animation. On every hand I heard the cry, 'On to Richmond!'"[36] Reflecting back years later, many veterans noted in their memoirs that the response to the advance had been uproarious and positive. "Our spirits rose. We marched free. The men began to sing," was how Private Frank Wilkeson recalled the moment when his unit realized they were heading south, while Major Abner Small of the 16th Maine noted that "Grant was seen, and a great burst of cheering greeted him as he rode swiftly and silently by."[37] As compelling as these reflections are, at the time few soldiers noted an outpouring of cheering and enthusiasm as they turned southward on May 7 for a renewed confrontation with Lee's army. There were no doubt some expressions of zeal as they moved on, but most men looked ahead with a grim determination that elicited few smiles and cheers.

By May 20, Captain Charles Davis on the Army of the Potomac headquarters staff had it all figured out. Writing to his mother, he detailed the experiences of the army to that point in the campaign, including the battle of Spotsylvania and how "the ground was covered for acres with the rebel & union dead." With no system of censorship during the war, he liberally described how they had been constantly on the move and listed some of the places they had been and where they were going. He also speculated on the enemy; "Lee will employ strategy that will detain us & we may not get to Richmond for months," he wrote, noting that while Lee had relatively few men "the choice of position & all is in his favor."[38] Davis was looking back with the luxury of two weeks of campaigning, but few in the ranks on May 7 knew that Lee was already moving once more to position his force between the Army of the Potomac and the rebel capital, and any cheering of Union men died away even before they reached the region centering on Spotsylvania Court House. The Union army pushed hard to reach that critical road juncture before the Confederates, and the result was a long day and night march immediately after one of the largest battles of the eastern theater. "It was a awful march, the mud over shoes all of the way, in some low plaices the mud was knee deep," Sergeant George Fowle reported to his girlfriend soon after his 39th Massachusetts regiment reached Spotsylvania.[39] Despite the rapid movement by Grant's men, when the first Northern units approached Spotsylvania Court House on the morning of May 8, they found elements of the Army of Northern Virginia waiting for them. Thanks to a "badly botched" march by Union forces and a little luck, Lee's 1st Corps had beaten Grant to Spotsylvania, albeit barely, and was rapidly entrenching its position.[40] Union soldiers now faced the prospect of attacking a well-fortified Confederate position. As artilleryman Frank Wilkeson noted of his regiment's arrival at Spotsylvania, it seemed that "wherever we went there were heavy earthworks, behind which the veteran Confederate infantry lurked."[41]

The subsequent fighting around Spotsylvania Court House lasted nearly two weeks, roughly May 8–20. After a long march on a day that topped out at 95-degree heat, the first to make contact was Warren's 5th Corps, which found Confederates dug in on Laurel Hill overlooking Old Court House Road. One of the first units to arrive was Sergeant Austin Stearns's 13th Massachusetts: "Gen'l Warren ordered us forward and on we went towards a pine woods. Just as we reached its edge came a volley, and then another, and our lines sadly thinned by the heat and our long run, gave way before the breastworks of the enemy."[42] The fighting on May 8 was inconclusive, and both sides spent the 9th shifting their available manpower in the direction of the lines that were extending across the Brock Road eastward toward the courthouse. The 10th witnessed attacks and counterattacks by both sides, with a particularly inventive one conducted by a young colonel in the 6th Corps, Emory Upton. His attacking column of twelve regiments briefly broke the Confederate lines on the western side of what was soon to be known as the "Mule Shoe" salient. Observing from nearby, Captain Oliver Wendell Holmes, Jr. labeled it "a brilliant magnificent charge," while Private Wilbur Fisk, who participated in the charge with the 2nd Vermont, fairly crowed in a letter home that "the advancing line was not checked. We drove the enemy out of his first line of works, and captured over 2000 prisoners."[43] Both Holmes and Fisk accurately noted in their commentary that it was only the failure of supporting units to come up in a timely manner that prevented Upton's attack from being more successful, in fact capturing less than a thousand Confederates.[44] Ultimately, the fighting on the 10th fizzled out and the 11th was spent with more skirmishing as Grant hatched a grand plan for breaking the strong Confederate lines that had grown up northwest of the courthouse.

The fiercest, and in many ways most horrific, fighting occurred on May 12, when Grant ordered an assault against the "Mule Shoe" salient, a protrusion in the Confederate line that appeared exposed and poorly defended, but also contained what one Union officer labeled "as well built and as scientifically laid out as any extemporized earthworks I ever saw."[45] Once again, the burden of the attack fell to General Hancock's 2nd Corps, which had already suffered five thousand casualties, more than 17 percent of its starting strength, days earlier in the fighting at the Wilderness.[46] Regardless, the 2nd Corps attacked the salient head-on at first light on the 12th and began what one historian considered "the longest sustained hand-to-hand combat of the Civil War."[47] The fighting at the "Mule Shoe" lasted for almost a full twenty-four hours as rain fell on the battlefield, adding to the "gloom and distress" of the fight while both sides poured more and more regiments into an increasingly confused heap of men, mud, and weaponry.[48] Private Haley, who participated in the assault with the 17th Maine, described the scene as "a seething, bubbling, roaring hell of hate and murder. In that baleful glare men didn't look like men. . . . Some were gashed and cut, and looked like tigers hunted to cover."[49] Captain James Latta of the 119th Pennsylvania reported his men firing over two hundred rounds each that day as more ammunition kept getting fed into the front lines.[50] The fighting went back and forth all day, but eventually Lee managed to withdraw his forces from the "Mule Shoe" and establish a new defensive line. This act frustrated Grant's efforts to exploit the small breakthrough that had been made along the salient, but his men were too spent to renew the endeavor regardless. Union forces sustained 9,000 casualties that day alone, with more than 2,500 of them suffered by 2nd Corps.[51] For hours after the Mule Shoe attack, the wounded bled and the dead sank into the mud on the field, leaving what one regimental chaplain called "abundant occupation for the priests."[52]

"The devil had broke loose" on the 12th, and the men struggled to put into words some of the horrors that they had seen.[53] In his memoirs of the war, Captain Mason Tyler remarked that the sight at Spotsylvania that day "is beyond the power of pen to describe," but still filled pages with graphic descriptions of bodies "chopped into hash" and a battlefield "soaked with blood."[54] The men found many ways to express to loved ones and themselves what they had seen, but it ultimately came down to two concepts: desperation and slaughter. Captain Charles Morey labeled it "the most desperate fighting I ever knew of" in his diary for that day, while others could not help but dwell on the way men had died and what had happened to their corpses after their death.[55] A particularly brutal letter written by Second Lieutenant Charles Brewster to his mother days after the attack on the salient vividly captures what the aftermath of such an action entailed:

> The most terrible sight I ever saw was the Rebel side of the breast work we fought over the other day. there was one point on a ridge where the storm of bullets never ceased for 24 hours and the dead were piled in heaps upon heaps and the wounded men were intermixed with them, held fast by thier dead companions who fell upon them continually adding to the ghastly pile. . . . when I looked over in the morning there was one Rebel sat up praying at the top of his voice and others were gibbering in insanity others were groaning and whining at the greatest rate . . . it is a terrible terrible business to make the best of it.[56]

It was, according to one officer, "the beastly nature of man in its glory."[57] The 2nd Vermont arrived late to the assault, but Private Wilbur Fisk still lost many of his comrades in Company E. Sickened by the piles of muddy corpses containing both friend and foe, Private Fisk mournfully concluded: "Any death but that."[58]

There was little to see as victorious about the fighting of May 12–13; the Confederate line had bent but not broken and the Army of the Potomac was little closer to Richmond. The position had been too strong, the weather too uncooperative, and the attack too uncoordinated. Private Robert McBride summarized it well: "men can not accomplish impossibilities."[59] The Army of the Potomac remained near Spotsylvania for another week after the Mule Shoe assault, continuing to put pressure on the Confederate position while Grant sought out some weakness in Lee's lines. By the time Grant decided it was time for another flanking movement on May 20, the Union army had suffered 18,399 casualties in all (see Table 1).[60] Prior to the next movement, the men did their best to rest as they dug into the muddy earth while the rain fell for much of the week following the Mule Shoe. Unfortunately, that meant maintaining close proximity with the outcomes of the previous assaults. "We lay in the pits on Friday the 13th, under a constant fire, expecting death momentarily," wrote one soldier from the 22nd Massachusetts in a letter home, "the putrid corpses, black and festering, lay all about us, repulsive and sickening, but from which we could not escape."[61] Despite the horrors, the men tried to get some rest following more than a week of marching and fighting. Captain Latta welcomed the comparative quiet along the line on May 15–16, but still felt that "it would take at least two weeks to thoroughly rest & recuperate the exhausted troops."[62] On May 16, a little over a month before he would be mortally wounded at Petersburg, Lieutenant Curtis Pollock of the 48th Pennsylvania wrote his mother that his unit was strongly dug in near Spotsylvania, but the Confederates were just as entrenched, and thus "when a break is made some one will have to suffer."[63]

The week that followed the fighting around the Mule Shoe could almost be labeled a lull in the Overland campaign if it were not for the fact that both armies remained in near constant contact with each other and fought several significant, albeit small, battles in the area near the courthouse. Rain fell for much of the week, and Grant ordered another attack on the now reduced salient for May 18. Unfortunately, a rushed assault plan led to another unorganized assault that washed up against Lee's fortified position with little effect.[64] Sergeant Charles Wood's 11th New Hampshire was part of the 9th Corps that went in with the assault, which resulted in his unit being "in a perilous position for 12 hours, being unsupported and our flank engaged, but got out all right."[65] Beyond the actual attacks, the two armies being in such constant proximity to one another day after day engendered a continual low-intensity struggle between artillerists, snipers, and pickets. "The same old story as usual," began the May 15 diary entry of Private Charles Edgerly, also of the 11th New Hampshire, "The Rebels opened a Battery on us and drove our skirmishers back a little. But they soon stopped and we put our pickets out as usual."[66] Recalling his time around Spotsylvania, artilleryman Frank Wilkeson noted the death of a fellow New Yorker visiting his battery from a neighboring unit as they engaged in an animated exchange of storytelling:

> As we laughed the handsome lad fell face down into the blanket and began to vomit blood. We grabbed him, turned him over, tore up his shirt, and saw where a ball had entered his side, cutting a gash instead of a hole. The wounded soldier did not speak. The blood rushed out of his mouth, his eyes glazed, his jaw dropped—he was dead. A chance ball had struck the tire of one of the wheels of the No. 1 gun and glanced forward and killed this delightful comrade. His death ended the game.[67]

As the soldiers of the Army of the Potomac were learning, the combat zone around Spotsylvania could turn a soldier into a casualty anytime day or night.

Beginning the evening of May 20, Grant launched the Army of the Potomac on another flanking movement around Lee's right, and Lee moved to counter at Hanover Junction (See Map 1). The period that followed primarily involved the two armies attempting to outmaneuver each other, with the sole exceptions being a few small, fierce battles at places such as Jericho Mills and Chesterfield Bridge along the North Anna River on May 23 and then Bethesda Church on May 30.[68] The 23rd saw the sharpest fighting, as several divisions crossed the North Anna River and exposed Lee's left to potential destruction. Confederate counterattacks followed, stopping the Union advance but doing little to retrieve the ground lost. Upon first arrival at the North Anna, Second Lieutenant Charles Brewster did not feel optimistic about what lay ahead, expecting "desparate fighting . . . by the time we get them out of thier strongholds there and on the South Anna we shall have very few men to take the works around Richmond."[69] The fighting was rough indeed, and Private William Greene of the 2nd U.S. Sharpshooters expressed surprise that they had been so successful on the 23rd: "On we went & charged the works on the north side of the river & after a pretty hard fight we compelled them to skedadle. We found the works very strong & had ought to have been held by the number of troops in them."[70] Much like the Union army, the Confederates were also straining under the constant campaigning; Lee himself was sickened with dysentery during this engagement, which perhaps prevented him from fully responding to the Union movements.[71]

While the fighting on the 23rd would rack up another thousand combined casualties for the armies, epic assaults on the level of the Wilderness and the Mule Shoe were absent for an almost two-week period at the end of May.[72] The violence did not cease, however; soldiers on both sides were almost continually exposed to sharpshooters, artillery fire, and minor skirmishes as the forces under Grant and Lee slid along the Virginia roads toward the North Anna River and beyond. Northern troops continued to march many miles almost every day, with some being called upon to lay waste to Southern rail lines along the way.[73] On May 17 at Spotsylvania, Private John Haley captured the growing sense of exhaustion among the men, noting, "Nearly two weeks in the immediate presence of death and the enemy, and in that time have scarcely had our clothes or equipment loosened, or our guns out of our hands. We haven't had the shoes off our feet, and a little *ablution* would be worth more than all the *absolution* of all the priests in Christendom."[74] That same day, as he lay in water-filled trenches near Spotsylvania not far from Private Haley, Sergeant George Fowle wrote his girlfriend a summary of what had occurred in the campaign, noting, "We need the rest as we have worked night and day sence we started."[75] The end of May provided the closest thing to rest that many men had had since the campaign kicked off, and soldiers took advantage to pause and reflect. On May 20, Captain George Whitman wrote his mother assuring her that his unit, the 51st New York, had been removed to a rear area and that they were "resting ourselves and having good times."[76] That same day, the lull became apparent for Lieutenant George Bowen when he noted in his diary that May 20 was the first day since the start of the campaign when there had not been anyone killed or wounded in his unit.[77] By the last days of May, Grant decided on a move further south once recognizing that Lee's forces were well entrenched along the North Anna. The Army of the Potomac continued its movement south and east, crossing the Pamunkey River on May 28 and reaching the crossroads near Cold Harbor on June 1 (see Map 1).[78] By that point, the previous week and a half had added almost another four thousand casualties to the rapidly growing number of killed and wounded Union soldiers (see Table 1).[79]

Fortunately for the dwindling numbers of Northern soldiers, help was on the way, but not exactly the help that had been planned. While the Army of the Potomac moved south, the Army of the James under the command of Major General Benjamin Butler moved north as it drove on Richmond along the James River in the area known as the Bermuda Hundred. On May 5, as the first engagements occurred near the Wilderness, Butler began to land troops at City Point, Virginia, eventually placing ashore at various points roughly 36,000 men in two corps, the 10th and 18th.[80] "All these transports are crowded with troops and the bay presents a grand appearance," noted Lieutenant Joseph Scroggs of the 5th United States Colored Troops as his all–African American brigade of the 18th Corps arrived on the scene.[81] As troops advanced inland, little resistance was met and expectations ran high; the Massachusetts native Private Francis Woods assured his mother and sister in a letter on May 7 that "we have not seen a single rebel yet and we suppose we have taken the rebs. by surprise and we are sure Richmond will fall this time."[82] Despite massively out-numbering the Confederate defenders upon first arriving at Bermuda Hundred, Butler hesitated when faced with opposition along the Petersburg Railroad, and, in the words of one historian, "worried more about his difficulties than his opportunities."[83] Caution took hold, and Butler slowed his advance until encountering a strong defensive line along Proctor's Creek; while he debated his next move with subordinates, the reinforced Confederate force under the command of General Pierre Beauregard took the opportunity to attack on May 16 in the same rain that was drenching the lines near Spotsylvania fifty miles to the north.

The battle at Proctor's Creek caught much of the Union force by surprise, quickly turning the army's right flank and endangering the entire force. Unfortunately, many units had not dug in to their positions, making it easier for the Confederate attack to drive off Northern defenders. "We had no breast works to fall behind giving us a very poor show for a fight, but we did the best we could," reported Private John Foote of the 117th New York in a letter to his mother, summarizing much of the outcome of the day.[84] Sergeant Daniel Sawtelle of the 8th Maine wrote his sister that his unit had just awoke and were preparing their coffee when the rebel attack commenced: "We left our breakfast for our guns and after fixing bayonets, we awaited for them to come up."[85] His unit managed to fight back several attacks before being forced to retreat, as was the case with Private John Bassett's 25th Massachusetts, which broke after it had repelled several attacks, resulting in Confederate forces "mowing our brave boys down by the score."[86] Thanks to the stand made by units like Sawtelle's and Bassett's, the Union forces managed to form a more consolidated position later in the morning, which withstood what was left of the Confederate assault. On the evening of the 16th, Butler decided to end what Private Foote called "these days of human slaughter & bloodshed" by withdrawing to a safer position in the Bermuda Hundred with his flanks protected by the James and Appomattox Rivers.[87] His advance against Richmond had failed.

From that point until the end of the month, the daily schedules for the men of the Army of the James involved mostly digging. Describing their defensive lines as "so strong that it is doubtful whether anything less than the whole of Lee's army will ever again venture to move against them," Private Edward Wightman of the 3rd New York noted that such power came from how for "twelve hours a day, when not detailed for picket, each regiment works with pick and shovel."[88] Butler, believing he had accomplished his mission by drawing Confederate forces to him from Richmond, reinforced his already strong position and awaited news of further developments from Grant.[89] While the Army of the James was secure, victory had proven elusive and the men knew it. "We aint got fort darling yet and that aint the worst of it I dont think we shall," Corporal Joseph Barlow wrote his wife, while Lieutenant Joseph Scroggs felt that "there has been a fine opportunity for decided advantages lost here by inexcusable tardiness" in not taking Petersburg and Richmond at the start of the campaign.[90] Contempt for Butler, not the most likable or inspiring figure to begin with, grew rampantly among the men. "There is no confidence felt in the *beast* at all," wrote Private James Horrocks of the 5th New Jersey Light Artillery, referring to the nickname that Butler earned during his time as occupation commander in New Orleans, "he would be more likely to get *hooted* than *cheered* by any regiment or Battery that I am acquainted with."[91] The men were not the only ones losing faith in Butler; recognizing an approaching manpower crisis as his men shifted to the Virginia crossroads of Cold Harbor, and seeing that Butler's army was effectively sealed off as a threat to Confederate forces, Grant arranged for General William Smith's Eighteenth Corps to be transferred from the Bermuda Hundred to the Army of the Potomac operating near the Chickahominy River.[92] The 18th embarked on May 29 with 17,000 men, bringing relatively fresh manpower to the bloodied Army of the Potomac as it struggled its way south.[93]

Lee had also obtained reinforcements, pulling forces from both the Shenandoah Valley and the Petersburg defenses in order to bolster his depleted Army of Northern Virginia.[94] Newly strengthened, both armies began to arrive in large numbers in the area around Cold Harbor, where a small cavalry fight occurred on May 31 followed by a larger engagement on June 1 between General Smith's just arrived Eighteenth Corps and the lead elements of the Confederate force. Fatigue and confusion were paramount in this opening fight; Smith's men had initially been ordered in the wrong direction after disembarking from their transports, arriving to the battlefield late and in little condition for a pitched fight.[95] As they joined the already much fatigued and diminished Army of the Potomac, the prospects for an immediate renewal of the battle were low.[96] On June 2, Grant resolved to attack the Confederate positions in the area, but the noticeable exhaustion among his men prompted a delay in the assault until June 3. As Grant explained in a communication with Meade, "In view of the want of preparation for an attack this evening, and the heat and want of energy among the men from moving during the night last night, I think it advisable to postpone assault until early to-morrow morning."[97] When the assault went in, the old reliable Second Corps once again took the lead in assaulting the enemy earthworks. Hancock's men would be supported by elements from the Sixth and Eighteenth Corps in the dawn assault, and smaller attacks would be made by the Fifth and Ninth Corps later in the day.[98]

Enthusiasm for the June 3 assault was nonexistent within the ranks; the exhaustion and repetitive nature of unsuccessful assaults against strong Confederate positions for the past month had left their mark. "We knew that a bloody battle was close at hand, but instead of being elated the enlisted men were depressed in spirits," recollected Private Frank Wilkeson of the night before the attack.[99] The only hope for these men in the lead-up to the battle that would soon become synonymous with Civil War slaughter was that the rebels across the trench lines were more spent than they. On May 24, Lieutenant Charles Brewster of the 10th Massachusetts noted that several Confederate prisoners "acknowledged themselves whipped," and took comfort in telling his mother "they are even more tired and hungry than we are."[100] Private Wightman with the just arrived 18th Corps wrote to his brother on June 1 that rebel prisoners "appear as tough and wiery as ever but rather bewildered and by no means so confident."[101] The shabby and hungry look of captured Confederates allowed most men to recognize the poor state of their enemy, but few thought it signaled an imminent victory. Second Lieutenant Charles Veil of the 1st U.S. Cavalry declared it a "desperate and saucy" force dug in near Cold Harbor, while Colonel George Barnard of the 18th Massachusetts wrote a week before the battle that "The rebs are about played out, at least so the prisoners say, but they will give us hard fighting yet as they are desperate."[102]

Desperate or defeated, Lee's men were ready when the first Union soldiers advanced at 4:30 a.m. on June 3. The Confederates had utilized the delay in Grant's attack to strengthen their position, and they eagerly delivered heavy musketry and artillery fire toward the advancing waves of Northern soldiers. The attacking forces were devastated, with the assault faltering within minutes. Private John Bassett's 25th Massachusetts had just arrived from the Bermuda Hundred, and it went into the attack only to face a "raking fire" that left close to three hundred men as casualties. "The bullets of the enemy did not stop for Officers or Privates, but took things as they came, white and black, high and low, rich and poor," Private Bassett wrote that day in his diary before sadly listing his comrades who had been killed and wounded.[103] Corporal Samuel Clear's 116th Pennsylvania went in with the 2nd Corps attack only to get stalled between the lines, exposed to "solid shot, shell, grape and canister and small arms." "Both armies were like hornets," he wrote in his diary, "we dug holes with our bayonets to protect ourselves and more than one poor fellow was shot before his little dugout would protect him."[104] One soldier in the Army of the Potomac expressed surprise that he managed to walk off the field with the survivors of his 22nd Massachusetts, noting how "amid such an iron hail of grape, canister, and bullets, I cannot conceive how any one escaped."[105] After surviving the assault on the Confederate position, Sergeant Daniel Sawtelle of the 8th Maine could only marvel: "It is a mystery how a man ever lived one moment in front of those woods."[106]

Many did not survive; Union forces suffered at least 5,000 casualties that morning alone, with 12,738 casualties cited for the operations occurring in the area around Cold Harbor the first two weeks of June (see Table 1).[107] Grant, who stood by his actions during the Overland campaign despite the high casualties, acknowledged in his memoirs that the June 3 assault had been unnecessary, since "no advantage whatever was gained to compensate for the heavy loss we sustained."[108] Though often ignorant of the bigger picture, the survivors of June 3 understood quite clearly what had been accomplished. "Nothing seems to have been gained by the attack today," Lieutenant Elisha Hunt Rhodes wrote in his diary, while Sergeant Daniel Chisholm of the 116th Pennsylvania summed up the battle to his father as "it didn't amount to anything, only getting hundreds of men killed and wounded."[109] The men would transmit these feelings back home, and within days media outlets would begin to spread the news. On June 6, the *New York Times* updated its readers on the campaign by noting that the assault at Cold Harbor had "gained no decisive advantage," and that "the fighting in these various affairs must have been more severe than might appear to some readers of the dispatches."[110] Many soldiers and civilians were reaching the conclusion that Grant's grand campaign was accomplishing nothing but casualties.

The Army of the Potomac would remain in its position near Cold Harbor for several days, waiting for Grant and Lee to conclude their haggling over the terms of a truce for clearing the dead and wounded off the battlefield. Rumors of another assault swirled through the Union ranks even before June 3 was over, arousing even less enthusiasm than before. Captain James Latta captured the pessimism of the men in his diary the day after the battle when he noted the rumors of another attack and wrote, "we are of the opinion that one attempted in our immediate front would be attended with fearful loss & result disastrously."[111] As rumors spread, the pause for more than a week following the battle gave the men plenty of time to reap the whirlwind of corpses that lay strewn across the landscape. The stench was overwhelming as the Virginia sun cooked the flesh of the recently deceased. As late as June 7, Lieutenant George Bowen of the 12th New Jersey wrote in his diary that "the stench had become almost unbearable, the bodies have been there since the early morning of the 3rd," while Captain Mason Tyler of the 37th Massachusetts recalled years later, "I well remember the sickening odors that greeted my nostrils on the second or third day after the battle."[112] Once a truce was agreed to, the bodies were placed in the earth by the comrades and enemies of those who had fallen. It was grim business; Sergeant Sawtelle explained that "it was almost impossible for burial parties to handle the dead on account of the smell. They had to make a big trench to put them in."[113]

As the men ventured between the lines to inter the dead, they obtained abundant opportunities to interact with their enemy. It was a peculiar moment for men of both sides; after more than thirty days of relentless violence and campaigning, here they were burying the bodies of their friends while looking into the faces of those who had killed them. While many commented on meeting the enemy, few expressed animosity toward them. "Done Sharp Shooting until about four o'clock when the Johnnys (some N. Carolina troops) came out & said if we would stop shooting they would & so we agreed to it & both sides laid down their guns & went out into the road & had quite a talk together," was the description of one such encounter on June 5 by Private William Greene of the 2nd United States Sharpshooters, adding "we exchanged some coffee for tobacco, etc. & then we went back to our post."[114] Sergeant Sawtelle found such interaction surreal: "While they are picking up the dead some of their men sent and exchanged papers with the rebs as friendly as though they had not been trying to take each other's lives an hour before. In a little while, the time is up, the men jump behind the works and again the ball opens and everyone is as bloodthirsty as ever."[115] Though not at Cold Harbor, Sergeant James Horrocks also noted the strangeness of such meetings and tried to convey to his father the mentality that would allow the two sides to interact in such a way: "although at war, there is no personal feeling of malice between the men. It is only a political difference between two sections of the country."[116] While truces were common in the Civil War before and after Cold Harbor (an issue to be addressed in more detail later on), the interaction of these men as they tried to cope with the aftermath of June 3 proved to be an awkward moment before the struggle was renewed and a new phase of Grant's effort to end the war began.

———

On the evening of June 12, the Union army began to disengage from its Cold Harbor lines and move toward the James River with the intent of crossing and driving on Petersburg. Fifth Corps took the lead, soon to be followed by the

Ninth, Second, and Sixth Corps as Smith's 18th Corps marched back to their transports to float their way to City Point. The march was a rough one, with the heat on the 13th being particularly tough on the soldiers as they tramped southward. Describing the march as "very severe, very dusty hot, and no resting, and the stench from the dead horses along the route was fearful," Private John Bassett of the 25th Massachusetts declared that "those that were on that march have reasons to remember to day as long as they live."[117] Captain James Latta of the 119th Pennsylvania also noted the difficulty of the march, but found solace in pointing out that it was the first time in almost two weeks that his men had not heard the booming of guns and rifle fire.[118] Upon reaching the James River, the men witnessed the full power of Union military might as they crossed a pontoon bridge 2,100 feet long while flanked by dozens of transports and gunboats.[119] "A grand sight," declared Sergeant Clear of the 116th Pennsylvania in his diary, before turning the next day to how tired his men were and how much they were suffering from hunger.[120]

By June 15, the lead elements of Grant's force reached the Confederate defenses surrounding Petersburg and began the preliminary assaults that would soon inaugurate the siege of that city. This effectively ended the Overland campaign, the longest and most intense period of sustained combat ever endured by the Army of the Potomac. While the emotional toll on the soldiers remained to be determined, the numerical effect on the army was visible to all involved. Over roughly forty days, the Army of the Potomac had marched more than one hundred miles, fought in at least four significant battles along with countless other minor engagements, and suffered almost 55,000 casualties (see Table 1).[121] Grant had driven his army night and day, and in the process almost half of his men had been killed, wounded, or captured on the route southward. Confederate losses had been proportionally equal, with the Army of Northern Virginia losing an estimated 33,000 men.[122] Colonel George Barnard of the 18th Massachusetts captured the outcome in a letter to his father at the end of May: "This campaign is a crusher."[123]

The Army of the Potomac that set off on the Overland campaign in May 1864 never experienced a sizable period of time out of contact with the enemy until it reached the Petersburg lines in mid-June, and even then Union forces would be forced to endure night and day within rifle shot of Lee's army. Forced marches, brutal combat, irregular supplies, and blistering heat characterized these forty days. The soldiers were constantly on their guard, with sniper and artillery casualties dominating the hours between major battles. The campaign also included a dozen smaller engagements, significant in their own right but dwarfed by the casualty numbers from Spotsylvania and Cold Harbor. For example, one of the "minor" engagements of the Overland campaign, the battle around Bethesda Church, Virginia, from May 28 to 31, 1864, resulted in a total of 2,322 Union and Confederate casualties.[124] As a point of comparison, the battle near Wilson's Creek, Missouri on Aug. 10, 1861, labeled "one of the most fiercely-contested of the war," cost both sides 2,419 casualties.[125] The Gettysburg campaign, rightly judged as the climactic engagement of the war, resulted in 48,514 combined casualties in only a few days of fighting.[126] The Overland campaign resulted in more than 85,000 men killed, wounded, or missing on both sides, a figure much greater than casualty figures from previous campaigns even if stretched out over a longer span of time. The most frustrating element of this butcher's bill was the indecision of the campaign; unlike Chancellorsville or Gettysburg, there was no clear winner by mid-June. While Lee's army had been cornered at Petersburg, it was still a potent combat force that avoided destruction by Union forces or the loss of the Confederate capital while bleeding out a healthy portion of the Army of the Potomac. What had been achieved for the cost was a question on everyone's lips well before the army settled into its trenches around the Cockade City.

2

"Perfectly Brutalizing"

SOLDIER RESPONSES TO THE OVERLAND CAMPAIGN

I had had enough of marching and fighting—enough of seeing good men's lives
squandered in assaults against earthworks. The continuous strain was greater
than the soldiers, poorly fed and exposed to the weather . . . could bear.
—Private Frank Wilkeson, 11th New York Battery

David Coon was not an average Union soldier. Born in New York state in 1822,
his age of 42 years in 1864 was well above the average enlisted man's age for
either side, though apparently nobody noticed at his enlistment when he
declared his age to be 31, possibly to avoid being disallowed from the service.
While his stated occupation as a farmer put him among the most commonly
identified career grouping, being a married enlisted man with seven children
placed him in a select minority. He joined the newly formed 36th Wisconsin
in Madison on February 24, 1864, possibly to get his hands on the $300 en-
listment bounty, $60 of which he received up front. Leaving his wife Isabel
to take care of the children and farm, Private Coon and the 36th were immediately sent to Virginia, joining the 2nd Corps in the middle of the Overland
campaign despite most of the men never having loaded or fired their weapons.[1]
By June 5, his unit was in the thick of the action, pinned down in hastily dug
entrenchments following the failed assaults near Cold Harbor. After a brutal
initiation to army life, Private Coon could not help but express his fears of
death in a letter to his young daughter Emma written on her birthday:

I tell you that I have suffered a great deal, which, if you have read the letters I
sent home since I come to this country, you know something of, but I can tell
you no words that I can write can give you an idea of it. How would you feel to

see your father lying in a ditch behind a bank of earth all day, with rebel bullets flying over his head, so that his life was in danger if he should raise on his feet, without a chance to get anything to eat, and about four o'clock P. M., starting with several hundred others and running across an open field towards a rebel battery with rebel bullets, grape and canister, flying like hail, and men falling killed and wounded all about him. . . . Oh, my dear daughter, your father may be lying dead on the field of battle and you may not know it. Even now, while I write, sitting in a ditch with the deadly bullets flying over my head, they are striking the bank behind me. . . . I am sorry I can't write with ink, as I perhaps may never write to you again.[2]

Fourteen-year-old Emma must have been shocked at this brutally honest missive from her father, but even more shocked when his fears came true: Coon was wounded and captured in August, fatally succumbing to pneumonia in a Confederate prison shortly thereafter.[3]

While the leaders of the two great eastern armies engaged in a seemingly endless spectacle of slaughter in spring 1864, the men on the ground did their best to survive the carnage, which for those like Private Coon meant accepting the strong possibility (inevitability, for some) of their own death. At the beginning of the Overland campaign, the men of the Army of the Potomac carried with them certain expectations of what lay ahead on the road toward the rebel capital. Unfortunately, in the days and weeks that followed, these expectations would be entirely shattered by the level of violence reached on battlefields such as Wilderness and Spotsylvania. Even veterans found themselves reduced to the level of fresh recruits as they struggled to cope with the new and unfamiliar dangers that faced them in the combat environment. No other campaign had tested them in such a way, but more than just combat was involved in this shattering of expectations. The Overland experience as a whole was one that granted its participants little rest and seemingly little hope for survival. Lack of sleep, exhausting marches day and night, and an inadequate system of supply combined with the frequent exposure to combat conditions in breaking down the ability of some soldiers to continue onward. As historian Carol Reardon has argued, the campaign illustrated how "soldiers in both armies needed to develop a hardiness of spirit and endurance to persevere for their respective causes. Nothing in their training or experience readied them for this."[4] There has been great debate in the historical community as to whether the intensity of the Overland campaign ushered in more "modern" methods of making war. Whether or not the actual strategy and tactics employed in May and June 1864 were "new" in the history of warfare is open to question, but Union soldiers who actually participated in this campaign quickly came to the conclusion that something unexpected and unfamiliar was unfolding before them. This feeling appeared evident from the very beginning, as the Army of the Potomac faced its first clash with the Confederates at the Wilderness, and it would express itself more forcefully as the campaign wore on.

It began with the Wilderness, where many veteran soldiers reported that the combat environment of this engagement was unlike others, characterizing it as more intense and violent than anything previous. A frequent comment was one made by Corporal Henry Keiser of the 96th Pennsylvania, which was engaged with the 6th Corps along the Orange Turnpike, who claimed in his diary entry for May 6 that "The musketry on the right was the heaviest I heard during the war."[5] Superlative declarations such as these were not uncommon in reference to combat; every battle was in a way different, new, and excessive to the soldiers who endured it. Nonetheless, the recurrent commentary on the increased level of ferocity at Wilderness suggests that men like Keiser, a "veteran volunteer" of 1861 who had recently reenlisted for three more years of service, were already having difficulty placing their new experiences in the mental framework of their previous encounters on the battlefield.[6] "We have experienced one of the hardest fights the last two days we have ever had," Surgeon William Watson wrote to his father on May 7, while Corporal Anson Shuey of the 93rd Pennsylvania would use similar language in a letter to his mother that same day, writing, "Yesterday we had one of the hardest fights that we had yet."[7] Another three-year veteran, Second Lieutenant Charles DeMott of the 1st New York Artillery, who would be killed in action within the month, described the intensity of the battle at Wilderness as "the most awful carnage the world has ever known."[8] Yet while this early in the campaign most men were able to process the sights and sounds of the Wilderness within their past experiences, some recognized that trouble lay ahead. "Human nerves were not made to stand the strain of such a warfare as this," reflected Captain Mason

Tyler of the 37th Massachusetts in his memoirs as he described the "savage" violence of the Wilderness.[9] Unfortunately, the warfare of which Tyler spoke was only beginning.

Soldiers would face far worse in the coming weeks as Grant's army "kept moving on" from the Wilderness, and nothing provoked more commentary than the protracted fighting along the trench lines at Spotsylvania. Whereas most men had been able to place the Wilderness within their earlier combat experiences, soldiers were shocked by the savagery and extended nature of the fighting around the "Mule Shoe" salient at Spotsylvania. Some comments mirrored those expressed following the Wilderness: Captain Albert Rogall of the 27th United States Colored Troops described "musketry without parallel" in his diary.[10] Others employed more extreme rhetoric, such as Lieutenant George Bowen, whose 12th New Jersey was part of the Second Corps, which spearheaded the major assault on May 12. He could only marvel at what had occurred as he described the event in his diary:

> Now commenced the most stubborn fight of my experience, it was almost a hand to hand fight in fact it was at times, the enemy made charge after charge right up to the muzzle of our guns only to be repulsed again and again this continued without interruption all day long and until 2 or 3 oclock of the morning before there was a lull in the fighting, the attacks were impetuous the resistance was stubborn. . . . it has been the worst day I have as yet seen.[11]

Private Wilbur Fisk of the 2nd Vermont echoed Bowen's comments, declaring in a letter to a hometown newspaper that Hancock's attack was "the most singular and obstinate fighting that I have seen during the war, or ever heard or dreamed of in my life."[12] Once again, these men were not fresh draftees new to the horrors of war; each of them had been in the army for at least a year and had joined in repeated campaigns against Lee's forces.[13] One sees in their comments a despairing acknowledgment that soldiers were increasingly finding themselves in a foreign environment.

Men fixated on particular details of the Mule Shoe attack, with some expressing disbelief that the Union assault had seen any success given the obstacles in its path. "We have stormed no such formidable earthworks ever before," wrote Private John Haley of the 17th Maine, and Private Henry Howell noted with some pride that "they had the strongest position I ever seen carried by assault since I have known anything about military."[14] To some the attack was "one of the most brilliant, successful charges of the war," but Lieutenant Thomas Galwey summed it up best as "one of the most sanguinary, as well as the most glorious I have seen."[15] The "sanguinary" aspects captivated many; the fighting at close quarters left many in awe of its consequences. Captain James Latta of the 119th Pennsylvania noted that many of his men fired over two hundred rounds in the Mule Shoe fighting, describing how "the Enemy's dead are heap in masses at one point & ours are strewn thickly over the field. Every ball that struck seemed to kill."[16] Spotsylvania would be the peak of men documenting their fascination with the violence of the battlefield. As the unfamiliar became familiar, and the horrors of the battlefield became more of an everyday experience rather than an occasional trauma, the men registered a growing sense of desensitization by reducing their commentary on what surrounded them.

Such lack of commentary was evident by the time of the attack on the Confederate lines at Cold Harbor. Spotsylvania in some ways represented the worst fighting during the Overland campaign; indeed, nowhere did the fighting occur with such ferocity for such an extended period at such close quarters. While the assault at Cold Harbor was horrific in its failure and body count, it was over quickly and few units made it near enough to the rebel lines to engage in the type of sustained hand-to-hand melee as was seen at the "Mule Shoe" salient. It is partly because of this that few soldiers bothered to comment on Cold Harbor as being something new and unfamiliar to them. There were a few such comments, such as that of Corporal Alex Chisholm, whose 116th Pennsylvania participated in the main assault on June 3. Writing to his father, Chisholm echoed Henry Keiser's reaction to the Wilderness by stating, "I never had balls to whistle so thick apast me no[r] never want them to whistle half so thick again."[17] Of course, it should be noted that Corporal Chisholm was in a new unit, only organized four months earlier, and was thus undergoing some of his first exposure to combat. Regardless, such statements were rare, as most men merely commented on how the attack had failed while tallying those who had been lost. Typical were the comments of George Prescott of the 32nd Massachusetts, who wrote of Cold Harbor, "An awful day yesterday. Charged breastworks, or rather across an open field. Lost 9 killed, 40 wounded, 2 missing."[18] While Cold Harbor offered another bloody battle to soldiers, sadly there was nothing new and exceptional about the carnage of June 3 to elicit the kind of spectacular commentary associated with Spotsylvania. These men were reaching a point where the shock of such appalling engagements no longer affected them as it had only weeks earlier.

As May turned to June and the fighting continued, the soldiers began to doubt whether they would ever gain a rest from the bloodshed. The only respite for some, such as Corporal Frederick Pettit of the 100th Pennsylvania, involved becoming one of the vast numbers of killed or wounded. Wounded at Cold Harbor, Pettit wrote to his mother from a Washington, D.C. hospital, reflecting on the campaign up to that point: "The hardships endured by the Army of the Potomac for the 30 days commencing May 4th were such as I supposed it impossible for any set of men to endure . . . For 25 days I did not sleep but a single night and this was the average of the whole army."[19] Having a relatively minor wound, Pettit spent his time "very pleasantly" in the hospital after a long campaign; for William Ray of the 7th Wisconsin, his campaign would end barely after it began when he took buckshot to his right calf on the first day at Wilderness and was evacuated to a hospital in Belle Plain, Virginia soon after.[20] Casualties like Ray and Pettit would be counted in the official reports as some of the 38,000 Union wounded of the campaign, but many others fought through their injuries to stay with their unit. Lieutenant Colonel Charles Cummings was struck in the head by a minié ball the first day at Wilderness; despite a wound that "bled with such profuseness from the breaking of a branch of the temporal artery," Cummings only stayed at the hospital long enough to get stitched up and was back with his unit the next day.[21] Corporal Samuel Clear of the 119th Pennsylvania was struck in the belt plate during the May 18 attack at Spotsylvania, knocking him senseless and leaving him badly bruised and vomiting for most of the day. Despite the regimental surgeon ordering him to the hospital, Clear refused, writing in his diary, "I had made up my mind to never be taken prisoner or go to the hospital if I could possibly avoid it."[22]

Given the plight of the wounded in the campaign, it is not surprising that some men refused to get sent back to the hospital. Close to 40,000 men would be wounded in six weeks, straining the medical apparatus of the Army of the Potomac to provide for them. The descriptions left by some soldiers vividly display why men like Corporal Clear and Lieutenant Colonel Cummings did their best to avoid a lengthy stay in the field hospital. New volunteer Private John Arnold of the 49th Pennsylvania could not reach his unit in time for the Wilderness and instead was sent to tend to the division's wounded. What he found was a powerful display of the battle's bloodletting: "it was a auful site to see the wonded come in by loads some had thare legs shot off some thare armes some ware shot in thare heads."[23] Down on the Bermuda Hundred following the Battle of Proctor's Creek, Sergeant Daniel Sawtelle went behind the lines to visit some comrades from the 8th Maine and was overwhelmed by the rows of wounded waiting to be treated: "Poor boys, so young, and there they were on the ground and some of them had nothing but the sky to cover them."[24] Looking back years later, Private Robert McBride still was affected by the suffering of the wounded as his unit camped near a hospital at Spotsylvania: "the tents were not sufficient to contain the wounded, and they lay on the ground on the outside by thousands. Those long rows of suffering forms, gashed and mangled in every conceivable manner, told a dreadful tale of human wrath."[25] Driven by sympathy, McBride would do his best to help the wounded; when he discovered a schoolmate among the injured, he managed to obtain an ambulance for him, only to learn later that this "royal soul" of a friend had gone on to die of his wounds.[26] Unfortunately, the stacks of wounded continued to grow and the army would play catch-up, evacuating the critical cases until the lines stabilized around Petersburg in mid-June.

The hardships of the Overland campaign proved to be a great deal more than merely facing death and debilitation on a twenty-four-hour basis. As Grant did his best to outflank, and thus outmarch, Lee's Confederates, the men of the Army of the Potomac were repeatedly forced to march for miles on end both day and night. The route southward for Union forces was not a direct one; due to the zigzagging nature of Virginia's country roads, it would not be unusual for units to move more than a dozen miles in order to cover a linear distance of only a couple miles. Or worse, as in the case of Lieutenant Lewis Luckenbill's 96th Pennsylvania, a unit could be "manuevered round back and forward all day from one position to another. Then marched back to the same place where we left the night before."[27] The frequent movements took their toll on the men, as the exhaustion suffered on these long marches only added to the physical and emotional toll of the near continual combat environment. In particular, the experience of Corporal Cyrille Fountain and his comrades in the 77th New York demonstrated the nonstop life of those in the Army of the Potomac that spring. His 6th Corps regiment participated in every battle of the Overland campaign and consequently found itself repeatedly moving back and forth along the line of advance. By mid-May, Fountain was detailing in his diary the long marches undertaken by the 77th New York and documenting how the movements were affecting his comrades. On May 22, Fountain described the nonstop marching of the previous twenty-four hours and noted how "the boys ware mad enough to kill." Less than a week later, a march of more than thirty miles prompted Fountain to comment how the men around him "were as good natured as a wasp," and, despite waking up "feeling awful Sore," the 77th found itself on another long march the following day.[28] The rapid flanking maneuvers of the Army of the Potomac called for men of the 77th New York to conduct frequent movements, and often fight pitched battles at the end of them.

This marching, coupled with the stress and exertion associated with being in or near constant contact with the enemy, wore down the men to the point of collapse. The poor weather conditions that developed midway through the campaign only exacerbated the issue. In a letter to his father, Colonel George Barnard detailed the effects of a particularly devastating march on the night of May 13:

> At seven o'clk last night, pitch dark, raining like fury and the mud knee deep we had to march about ten miles to Spotsylvania. The suffering of the men is almost indescribable, this lasted till this morning, the men falling over at every step as our road took us by woods filled with uncared for wounded, howling for help as they heard us groping along while I saw men the ranks so utterly wretched that they threw themselves in the middle of the road wallowing in the mud under the horses' feet, howling and crying like mad men. I never knew such a horrible night, all mud, rain, darkness and misery. As soon as we arrived here we took up our line of battle and attacked the enemy . . . [29]

Given the crippling impact of such sustained movements, it is no surprise that many men began to use the same excessive commentary on their movements as they did on the battles during the campaign. Corporal Samuel Clear of the 116th Pennsylvania declared the May 11 night march into position for the Mule Shoe attack "the worst march we had to endure up to this time," while Captain Oliver Wendell Holmes, Jr. viewed the marching throughout the day on May 14 as "one of the most fatiguing we have had."[30] Unlike the declining commentary as to the level of ferocity of the battlefield, men continued to speak in exceptional terms of the marching even later on in the campaign. For Corporal Pettit, the "day and night" movement of his unit from May 27 to May 29 ranked as "the most wearisome march we ever had."[31] A similar day-and-night march on June 1 for Corporal Timothy Bateman of the 12th New Jersey left him noting in his diary, "Never had such sore feet in my life."[32]

These long marches were only aggravated by the extreme weather conditions that characterized the Overland campaign. The temperature continued to rise during the months of May and June to meet the normal levels of a Virginia summer, with 90-degree heat becoming common, and the result was painful exposure to heat and sun for men on the move and in battle.[33] The escalating temperature and dry conditions turned the Virginia roads into beds of dust, which added to the misery of advancing northern troops. As his New York regiment progressed toward Petersburg with the Army of the James in mid-May, Private Edward Wightman wrote to his brother that his unit was "almost smothered in a cloud of dry dust and steaming with perspiration from the heat of the sun. Men suffering from sunstroke were lying in the ditch."[34] As early as the Wilderness, men were making comments similar to those of Sergeant George Fowle, who tried to explain to his girlfriend why his 39th Massachusetts regiment retreated from the battle: "I then went to the rear and found the Regt pretty well demoralized. A good many were sun struck as it was very hot and we had a running fight of about three miles and marched all night before."[35]

As Fowle's comments indicate, the heat had such a debilitating effect on the men that it left them vulnerable to sunstroke and diminished their combat ability. As noted in the previous chapter, Sergeant Austin Stearns of the 13th Massachusetts believed that the heat had contributed to the failure of the 5th Corps attacks the first day at Spotsylvania.[36] In his diary on May 23, Lieutenant Thomas Galwey of the 8th Ohio noted, "Day became intensely hot, so much so, that between the heat and the rapid marching, I nearly gave out."[37] Another officer, Lieutenant Elisha Hunt Rhodes of the 2nd Rhode Island, had a similar story, declaring once his unit reached the James River, "the men are used up by the intense heat and fatigue of the past week."[38] Sergeant Daniel Sawtelle was certainly "used up" as his 8th Maine maneuvered against a Confederate position near Swift Creek on May 9; Sawtelle reported, "The sun was pouring down, not a breath of air stirring, and it seemed as if we could not get our breath. . . . everything seemed to turn black to me and I began to get dizzy."[39] The moment passed and Sawtelle went in with his unit, but not before stepping over other Maine men who had collapsed from the heat. Reflecting back on the campaign years later, Chaplain William Corby of the 88th New York still remembered the "untold hardships from heat, dust, hunger, and thirst. Many of our horses died from thirst or were overcome by the heat. Men, too, dropped in the road and expired."[40] While no one else reported deaths from sunstroke, clearly the heat added one more challenge to Union soldiers trying to endure the campaign.

Perhaps the extreme heat and long marches would have been easier to bear had there been a steady and reliable supply of water along the routes taken by the Army of the Potomac. The heat worked to shrink standing bodies of water such as rivers and ponds along the march, and rainwater that collected on the ground was often deemed unfit for human consumption. Men such as Henry Keiser often followed their comments on the extreme heat and humidity with complaints regarding the lack of an available water supply.[41] Sergeant Stearns's unit, which suffered considerably in the rain at Spotsylvania, fought the opposite problem by mid-June, when Stearns noted how "no water could be found, and the boys suffered with thirst."[42] Availability was not always the problem; sometimes soldiers were forced to make do with water supplies contaminated by mud, and human and animal waste, along with other pollutants. After being turned away from a fresh spring that was reserved for officers (a policy he described as "official selfishness"), Private Frank Wilkeson and his comrades were forced to cope with "water in the sluggish runs [which] had been roiled by artillery horses drinking, and been additionally befouled by hundreds of vermin-infested men bathing in it."[43] The cumulative effect of poor weather conditions and lack of water certainly told on the men, contributing significantly to the demoralizing effect of the campaign as a whole.

Not only the heat, but rain contributed to the growing discontent within the ranks. Spring rains saturated the weary army for several days during the campaign and turned the ground to a thick muck, which impeded movement and made for very uncomfortable conditions when the men had the rare moment to settle down and rest. Perhaps the worst rains fell during the fighting around

Spotsylvania, where everyone mentioned how the wet conditions contributed to that engagement. Men marching to Spotsylvania reported that the mud was "knee deep" thanks to the rain, and Lieutenant Rhodes would observe that the downpour during the Mule Shoe attack only served "to add to the horrors of the day."[44] Sergeant Stearns noted in his diary on May 13 how "last night was a most miserable night for some of the boys. It rained, we lay in line of battle: there was not much sleep or rest."[45] Stearns's comments also demonstrate a tendency among the men to allow the weather to affect their use of metaphor when describing the battlefield. Following his entries about the Mule Shoe assault and sleeping in the rain, Stearns thanked God for allowing him to pass "through the storm of battle safely."[46] Lieutenant Thomas Galwey also found metaphorical inspiration in the rainy conditions, describing how at Cold Harbor it "rained all night. Along with this, a perfect shower of bullets would pass over us about every half hour, so that our sleep was rather poor."[47] Poetic license aside, the rain and mud were not welcomed by the men as their increasingly exhausted and depleted regiments faced seemingly fresh Confederate defenders in every battle.

In addition to the constant exposure to the elements and the lack of fresh water, many Union soldiers were forced to subsist without rations for extended periods of time as the logistical network of the Army of the Potomac proved inadequate for the pace and conditions of the Overland campaign. It was not that there was not enough food to go around; by this point in the war the Union supply system was in full swing. Instead, the near continual movements by the Army had supply wagons scrambling to keep up with the soldiers while still remaining far enough behind the lines to be secure from enemy forces.[48] The result was that men frequently contended with a case of moderate to severe empty stomach, and their complaints about the problem just as frequently ended up in their letters and diaries. By mid-May, Samuel Cormany of the 16th Pennsylvania Cavalry was already claiming that his unit was short of food, writing how "men have turned their haversacks inside out and licked up the crumbs in the lower corners" out of desperation for some sort of sustenance.[49] A month later, Sergeant Samuel Clear noted a more desperate condition of hunger in his own regiment of Pennsylvanians. As the army marched day and night to beat Lee's Confederates to Petersburg, Clear's men found themselves out of rations by June 15 and suffering severely. By nightfall that evening, "hunger began to tell on us . . . we became very weak, and staggered along like drunken men. We were too hungry to sleep."[50] Yet even comments such as those of Sergeant Clear and Samuel Cormany do not compare with those of Surgeon William Watson, who served with the 105th Pennsylvania throughout the campaign. On May 19, Watson sent a desperate letter to his superior in the hospital of the Third Division of the Second Corps: "I have in charge 275 wounded, including 50 amputations and resections and have neither food, clothing, nor supplies of any kind, the men have been living on hard bread and water for three days, the Coffee was expended on Sunday 12th, the sugar on the 13th, and I feel satisfied that many have already died from want of proper sustenance."[51] While the overall condition of the army never quite reached the state reported by Watson, hunger among northern soldiers was a common occurrence as the Army of the Potomac continually outmarched its supply lines.

The worst supply breakdowns occurred at the end of May and in mid-June, when the army was undertaking more rapid marching to get ahead of Lee's men at Cold Harbor and Petersburg, respectively. Sergeant Henry Keiser noted on May 29 that the rations for the 96th Pennsylvania had run out with no word on when more would arrive.[52] One of the officers in that unit, First Lieutenant Lewis Luckenbill, confirmed Keiser's account, writing in his diary: "Men nearly all out of rations. Teams could not come up."[53] That same day a Massachusetts officer noted that his regiment had "difficulty in getting supplies" and how all the men had eaten the last of their hardtack, while on May 30 another Massachusetts soldier commented on the food situation by simply stating, "the men have nothing."[54] Two weeks later, as the army crossed the James River for its move on Petersburg, the hunger issue returned with a vengeance. Sergeant Clear's 116th Pennsylvania had descended into hunger by this point, joined by Private Robert McBride's 190th Pennsylvania. As the 190th spent three days and nights marching toward Petersburg, McBride recollected feeling the "pangs of extreme hunger" to the point that "it seemed as if I was all stomach, and each several cubic inch of that stomach clamoring incessantly for 'grub.'"[55] The supply lines would be much improved upon the army's arrival at Petersburg, but only after the men fought a pitched battle for that city with mostly empty stomachs and the strained nerves and sore feet of six weeks of campaigning.

While there were many components to the escalating physical breakdown of the Army of the Potomac, the long campaign also posed several challenges to the state of mind of the men, who were facing death on a daily basis. One issue that always seems to arise when discussing the morale of fighting men is mail. The frequent interruptions in the supply of food would have contributed to corresponding interruptions in the supply of mail, had mail delivery to the Army of the Potomac been allowed in the first place. Immediately prior to the start of the spring campaign, General Grant ordered a temporary halt to the delivery of mail to the Army of the Potomac, most likely to free up roads and horses for support of the southern movement. The men noticed immediately, and often commented on the decline in mail calls. In mid-May, Corporal Frederick Pettit acknowledged in a letter to his parents that his unit had stopped receiving mail, but still encouraged them to keep writing him as they usually would.[56] Later that month, First Lieutenant Thomas Jane Owen of the 50th New York Engineers noted with regret that regular mail service had been cut off, but acknowledged, "we have scarcely any time to write."[57] The men may not have had the time to write, but they still longed for a word from those at home.

It was this lack of contact with the home front that greatly added to the corrosive elements of the campaign. The interruption in the army's mail service would last anywhere from a week to a month, depending on the unit and its location, and the effects would eventually have an effect on the men. At the exact moment that these men sought reassurances from those they loved in order to remind them of what they were fighting for, that tenuous link was severed. As Massachusetts captain Mason Tyler would note in a letter that June, "if ever a man would appreciate letters, it is at such a time as this, in the midst of a severe campaign with all its fatigues and anxieties upon you."[58] At roughly the same time, another Union soldier wrote to a friend of how "it is very consoling for a soldier so far from home to receive letters from those that they left at home."[59] "No mail since we marched on the 3rd," remarked Lieutenant Colonel William Tilton of the 22nd Massachusetts in mid-May, declaring that "it is hard to be so long without a word of love and sympathy from home."[60] Union soldiers were out of contact with the home front for the bulk of May and June, and while the effect may not have been a destructive one, the benefits afforded by mail to men in war were noticeably absent.

Taken with the intermittent pitched battles and the near constant exposure to enemy attack, the forced marches, excessive heat, and unreliable supplies of food, water, and mail only served to further degrade the fighting ability and morale of Union soldiers. A good night's rest would have helped to alleviate these challenges, but after days of marching and fighting in the elements men often spent their evenings in hard labor. By this point in the war, construction of field entrenchments was an automatic response to movements on campaign, and night offered the safest time in which to construct field fortifications within range of the enemy.[61] "This has been the hardest campaign this army has ever seen," reported Lieutenant George Bowen of the 12th New Jersey on May 29, "we have been force to fight all day and then work on entrenchment or march all night."[62] Sergeant George Fowle concurred, writing to his girlfriend in early June, "we have been under fire of shells every day which makes us hug Mother earth a good deal day times and we have to dig earthworks a good deal at night."[63] "Work, work, fight, fight, takes all our time. We sleep but from two to four hours per day," wrote Colonel Robert McAllister as his 11th New Jersey lay dug in along the North Anna, "it is the hardest campaigning I have ever seen."[64]

Construction of field fortifications took a great deal of effort, which was normally expended immediately following a lengthy march and/or preceding an engagement. Yet, as the campaign continued, the men began to realize the power that such entrenchments granted them on the battlefield. Despite Sergeant Fowle's comments on danger by day and work by night, by June 15 he recognized the value of such labor in keeping his men alive, noting in a letter that earthworks had helped to reduce the number of casualties in his unit.[65] Sergeant Austin Stearns was more blunt on the matter, noting in his diary mid-June that "every time we stopped we began to dig, deeming it much better to let a bank of earth stop the minniés than our bodies."[66] Private John Haley of the 17th Maine, who had a tendency to calculate the odds for/against his survival, had this maxim to justify the digging: "It is well known that *one* man behind works is as good as *three* outside the works."[67] While beneficial to survival, trenches and breastworks did not create themselves, and the constant labor on their construction provided yet one more physical challenge to the men of the Army of the Potomac as it crept its way southward. In a chapter of his memoirs entitled "Shoot, Shovel, and March," Major Abner Small of the 16th Maine described his unit's arrival at Spotsylvania where his "weary men" spent much of the day engaged and then digging fortifications into the night. "When at last the work was done we got some rest," Small recalled, "but the dawn of another day was near; we slept only two hours."[68]

As the campaign wore on, the physical exhaustion became more pervasive, and its relief became the only mission of some soldiers. Captain Charles Mills expressed such a sentiment when he began his May 29 letter to his mother: "I am afraid my letters have been very dull lately, but the life we lead is perfectly brutalizing, and one ceases to care much for anything but food, sleep, and a wash."[69] The reaction of Private David Coon to the stresses of campaigning was slightly more extreme. Shortly before he would compose his heartbreaking soliloquy to his daughter on her birthday, he sent his family an equally alarming letter on May 26 declaring, "when I have been on the march in the hot sun and so weak and sick, and have seen wounded men being carried off on stretchers, I have wished that I could change places with them, for then I thought I could at least get a chance to rest."[70] Other men repeatedly peppered their correspondence and journals with attempts to describe their exhaustion, using expressions such as "played out," "terribly tiresome," and "completely worn out."[71] Private Charles Edgerly's diary entry for June 16 was perhaps the simplest and most appropriate: "No sleep at all are tierd out nearly."[72] Officers reported seeing their troops collapsing from exhaustion at various points in the campaign, and by the end of May men like Captain Mason Tyler found that they "could hardly put one foot before the other."[73]

As the men struggled to survive the ordeals of the campaign, veterans recalled past operations with the Army of the Potomac and correctly came to the conclusion that they were experiencing something new and unfamiliar. Not surprisingly, Gettysburg, the bloodiest single battle of the war, elicited the most commentary, but few could find reason to place that confrontation above the fighting in 1864. Frank Morse, a chaplain with the 37th Massachusetts, reviewed the condition of his unit in May and remarked, "we never had such rough experience. At Gettysburg we had hard marching, but otherwise the campaign was much more agreeable than at the present time."[74] Looking over the human wreckage left after the Mule Shoe attack, Elisha Hunt Rhodes counted more dead bodies than he had seen the previous July in Pennsylvania, while another soldier in mid-June declared that "the Gettysburg campaign does not *even compare* to this in point of hardships and fighting."[75] Most men, however, did not mention specifics, but spoke generally about the excessive nature of the current campaign. "All previous campaigns are love spats compared to this," declared Colonel George Barnard, who was echoed by Colonel Robert McAllister writing to his wife, "this is a hard campaign, putting in the shade all others."[76] Sergeant George Fowle correctly put his finger on the difference from past campaigns on May 17: "In all other fights it has not lasted but two or three days but we have been in [this one] about two weeks."[77] The veterans of '61 and '62 had learned to endure the isolated battle now and again, but the near continual engagement with the enemy allowed the men no respite between the particularly ferocious battles of Overland.

Fifty years later, the British physician Lord Moran would observe the morale and motivations of Allied soldiers as they struggled to survive in the trenches of the Western Front in France. Writing after the Great War in his book *The Anatomy of Courage,* Moran reached the conclusion that something different had occurred in the First World War: "The real difference between the war of 1914 and the wars of history lay in the absence of a close period, when men safe for the moment could rest and build up a reserve."[78] Moran perhaps overlooked the American Civil War, since from May 5 to June 15, 1864, the Army of the Potomac underwent six weeks of campaigning without letup. As Union soldiers faced their physical limit, they correctly diagnosed their exhaustion as a consequence of the continuous nature of the campaign. On May 11, after telling his father of the seven days of constant fighting experienced by his 18th Massachusetts, Colonel George Barnard declared that the campaign "exceeds anything we have been through yet."[79] By May 17, Captain Charles Mills was already reporting to his mother that "I feel as if I had been out in this horrible bloody wilderness for months, instead of a fortnight."[80] "We are fighting pretty nigh every day," wrote Private William Oberlin of the 148th Pennsylvania in a letter on June 5, "it is a common sight for me to see men killed and wounded every day."[81] What the men most needed was rest, or a "close period," and that was something denied to them by the frenetic drive of the campaign. As Second Lieutenant Charles Brewster lamented on May 15, "I wish it might end soon for it is dreadful to be kept in a constant state of excitement like this."[82]

As stated earlier, mail call was often a welcome sound for men in the field, but the arrival of mail did not always provide benefits as the campaign wore on. On May 23 the 10th Massachusetts finally received its first mail delivery of the campaign, and Lieutenant Brewster noticed how "there was terrible sorrow connected with it which was the many letters for our dead and wounded comrades."[83] Such professions of grief indicate another effect of the Overland campaign, one that was both physical and emotional in its impact. As the campaign continued, the men found their ranks thinned to an extreme degree as increasing numbers of their longtime comrades fell to the bullets and shrapnel of their Confederate foe. As previously demonstrated, almost half of those who set out with the Army of the Potomac on May 4 were killed or wounded over the following six weeks. This high loss elicited much commentary from the survivors, especially when those lost were popular commanding officers. The death of General John Sedgwick, the commander of the Sixth Corps, on May 9 during the opening hours of the Spotsylvania engagement elicited the most commentary within the ranks. "I'm sorry and with pity do I pen these few lines in my memorandum," wrote Private Mortiz (Maurus) Oestreich of the 96th Pennsylvania in his diary near the beginning of the fight around Spotsylvania, "this day about noon our brave and noble Corps commander, General Sedgwick, was shot thru the head by a rebel sharpshooter. . . . He is mourned by all who knew him."[84] "His Corps weeps," was Lieutenant Brewster's simple valediction for "Uncle John" Sedgwick.[85] Roughly a dozen general officers, not to mention hundreds of company and regimental commanders, fell over the course of the campaign, and the loss of those leaders who stood at the head of their unit only added to the emotional burden carried by growing numbers of Union men.

While the loss of commanding officers certainly imposed a symbolic and inspirational toll on many soldiers, the far more devastating losses occurred within the ranks. The significance of comrades and "primary group cohesion" for men in battle is well documented, and the Civil War was no different.[86] With regiments formed out of preexisting communities, and many units having been together for as long as three years by mid-1864, tight-knit groups had formed within the larger company, regimental, and divisional structures. When these groups began to suffer high losses throughout the battles of the Overland campaign, attachments were broken and men found themselves isolated in a combat environment, a condition that only sped the deterioration of their morale. Men noticed the rise in losses almost immediately; Private Wilbur Fisk noted in a letter soon after the Wilderness that his 2nd Vermont regiment had already lost more than four hundred men, and that "all of our former battles put together have not reduced our ranks like this one, and the end is not yet."[87] Such tallies of the fallen were common: Surgeon Nathan Hayward of the 20th Massachusetts counted only 250 men left in the regiment by May 22; Private John Arnold found only 42 of 106 men left in Company I of the 49th Pennsylvania by June 5; and Corporal William Ray could only find 20 survivors left in his company by late June.[88] Others tried to ignore the losses during the campaign, only to have the full weight of the missing hit them as the Army of the Potomac approached Petersburg in mid-June. On June 8, one member of the 22nd Massachusetts recorded with some amazement that "as I look over the regiment, I can only count twenty familiar *friendly* faces. . . . It is so sad."[89] Shortly after the commencement of the Petersburg campaign in late June, Private John Steward reflected on the costs of the previous weeks for his 1st Maine Heavy Artillery. Noting that his unit had lost well over two-thirds of its starting strength (including the highest single-day loss of any unit of the war on June 18), Steward mourned the "butchery of hummen beings" and concluded, "it makes me sick of the war."[90]

Among other things, the continual nature of the campaign left little time for grieving, but the mounting losses could not be ignored and the men did their best to express their pain whenever they could find the time. The total numbers lost were in ways insignificant to the enormity of a personal loss, and these struck deepest at the men's hearts. In the same diary entry where he noted General Sedgwick's death, Private Moritz (Maurus) Oestreich related how his company B had lost twenty-three men killed and wounded that day, "among them my best comrade, Jacob Kifer. I feel sorry for him. He was a good soldier, a good fellow and always in good humor."[91] After his unit's participation in the Spotsylvania assaults, Captain Mason Tyler of the 36th Massachusetts noticed one less friend among the survivors, and the effect was immediate: "I had a deep sense of depression as if I were being deserted and left alone. My weariness added much to the force of this impression."[92] For Private Austin Kendall of the 117th New York, it was the interment of a complete stranger that brought it all home for him:

> A man was shot in the thigh and did not have proper care and he bled to death. we could not find out what his name was, nor what Regiment or anything about him and some boys from our Regiment went and brought him up to where our

Regt. was and dug a grave and laid him in it and I think that was a little the hardest thing I ever saw. but that was better than thousands of others are cared for who are killed on the field of battle.[93]

By June, bloodshed and death had become a pervasive part of the lives of every soldier in the army, and, as with the long list of other challenges brought on by the campaign, the men struggled with how to handle their grief.

An increasing number could not face this grief and the continued rigors of the campaign, succumbing to the most dangerous element of the combat environment: demoralization. Taken individually, the various factors at work in the Overland campaign may not have broken the men who journeyed southward toward Richmond, but together they contributed to an alarming decline in morale as the fighting continued. Simply put, the men increasingly doubted their ability and desire to go on. Colonel George Barnard of the 18th Massachusetts began to see this phenomenon immediately after Cold Harbor, noting how "men who have been through everything in the whole war heretofore, are now beginning to cave."[94] Corporal James Beard of the 142nd New York, Irish-born and two-year veteran of the war, wrote to his brother in late May of the bodies lying in the sun following the fighting around Bermuda Hundred and concluded, "well Isaac i have seen all the soldiering that i wish to."[95] Surgeon Horatio Soule of the 56th Massachusetts repeatedly confided to his diary the exhaustion that he faced tending to the unit's wounded day and night, finally declaring on May 24, "O dear how I want to go home. I am tired of this. Have been running around all day down in Front, hospital, etc."[96] Many did go home, often without orders, an issue to be addressed in the next chapter. But most stayed; whether they desired to stay or felt obligated to, the army kept together and the men carried on. Yet by staying, the men needed to find a way to carry on and allow themselves to emotionally process the ordeal before them.

The solution, one often turned to by men in war, was to stop feeling; accept the deadliness and horrors of the battlefield without letting them affect you. This condition, known as desensitization, is one of the most common themes expressed by Union soldiers in their writings toward the end of the Overland campaign. It began with men becoming inured to the conditions around them, a necessary condition for continued functionality in an environment where instant death was a real possibility. Men at all levels throughout the campaign wrote, sometimes with a bit of pride, how the violence around them was no longer having the same grip on their souls as it had before. Putting aside one's fear of the bullet was usually cited as a significant achievement. "Our boys are not now to be intimidated by a few minie balls," wrote Corporal John Pillings about the men of his 70th New York regiment on June 10, "it seems as though, to a man, they are unmindful of personal danger."[97] Captain James Latta of the 119th Pennsylvania concurred, noting around the same time as Pillings that the men in regiment "are getting so accustomed to the continuous whiz of the bullet that we do not mind it half as much as when it began."[98] Others focused more on overcoming the fear of artillery, which became a more prominent element of the campaign as the fighting moved out of the Wilderness and the lines became more static. After describing to his daughter how men in his unit had bathed in a nearby pond despite enemy shells landing around them in the water, Colonel Robert McAllister of the 11th New Jersey explained, "you would be surprised to learn how little these tried veterans care about shells. If they are making coffee and one bursts close by, they will continue to make their coffee and have their meal."[99] In another letter to his wife describing the same incident, McAllister concluded, "Such is war. So accustomed do we becom to such scenes that we can brave danger to an extent almost incredable."[100]

Of course, the ultimate goal was to get "accustomed" to it; the idea was that a true warrior does not allow his fears to overcome his duty. As the numbing process continued, the men were at first happy to be given some sort of protection against fear. By the 1st of June, Corporal Frederick Pettit of the 100th Pennsylvania marveled at the miles marched and battles fought to that point in the campaign, writing to his sister that "the campaign is not over yet but is going on as vigorously as ever only we are becoming more accustomed to it."[101] Pettit realized that while the campaign may not be changing, the men were, and that seemed to be allowing them to continue through the trials ahead. "Calm" was a favorite word to describe this phenomenon: shortly after his first battle at Cold Harbor, Private John Steward wrote with a hint of pride that "I feel as calm on the battlefield as any where else."[102] The more experienced but far younger Massachusetts officer Charles Mills wrote to his mother from the North Anna, "I find that the practice of three fights in this campaign has made me take things quite calmly."[103] For these men, being "accustomed to it" and achieving "calm" gave them what they needed to keep it together on the battlefield, but it would not save their lives. Corporal Pettit would be killed by rifle fire only weeks into the operations around Petersburg. Steward and Mills would be killed on the same day, March 31, 1865, in the waning hours of the Petersburg campaign and the final days of the war itself.

Death was everywhere during the campaign; from the heaps of bodies at the Mule Shoe to the loss of a single man to a sniper at Cold Harbor. Despite, or perhaps because of, the numbing process, the men increasingly fixated on their own death as an inevitable consequence of the ceaseless campaign that stretched before them. By the end of May, one soldier was already hoping for a small wound to get him out of the fight, and by mid-June expressed his concern over the decimation of his unit as he took stock of his own chances in what promised to be more fighting around Petersburg: "All of us see the frail threads that our lives hang upon more vividly day by day, as our little band dwindles away."[104] The growth of a fatalistic attitude among the men was dangerous; fighting for family, friends, and country all fade to irrelevance once a soldier begins to believe that he is doomed to die, and men were certainly beginning to question their ability to survive from a very early point during the Overland campaign. Some managed to look upon the prospect of death with a positive attitude, such as Private John Foote of the 117th New York, who wrote to his father at the end of May, "the terrible realities of war are now before us and many of us no doubt will be under the sod before this campaign shall end. Whatever may be my lot, if success shall only crown our arms, it is all I ask."[105] Private Daniel Sawtelle expressed similar optimism to his sister shortly after reaching Petersburg, declaring that "they cannot keep us from it now. . . . But we must not suppose that we are going unscathed. Many of our brave boys must fall."[106] After the casualties of the previous weeks, Sawtelle knew that more fatalities would be forthcoming, but he did not appear to include himself on that list.

Other Union men were not as sanguine about their chances, expressing thoughts in their letters and diaries that indicated a creeping sense of fatalism as the campaign continued. Few soldiers stated outright that they expected to die (although the legendary account of Union soldiers sewing their names on their jackets prior to Cold Harbor seems to suggest such an expectation); most men were more subtle, with their increasing fixation on death demonstrating a growing fear of their own mortality.[107] Spotsylvania was the wake-up call for most; the extended intensity of the battle, coming so soon after the pitched battle at the Wilderness, elicited some of the first doubts that survival was a reasonable expectation. Lieutenant Charles Brewster of the 10th Massachusetts noted with satisfaction the arrival of reinforcements in a letter to his mother, but still felt it was useless, seeing as "we should not have any army left by the time we should get to Richmond at the present rate."[108] Others began the inevitable task of calculating their odds for survival, which Private John Haley calculated as "a ten-to-one chance that I will expire before my term does," while counting out how many months were left in his enlistment.[109] In a tale that would become familiar in the lore of twentieth-century conflicts, a chaplain in the Irish brigade related the story of a soldier who handed him a letter with the request that he "send it to his wife in case he got killed, as he expected." The soldier was killed days later, and the chaplain was left with the unhappy task of mailing his final correspondence.[110]

The numbing process went beyond being calm on the battlefield and accepting (possibly embracing) the possibility of death; often it included the growth of a callousness to life and authority that had a detrimental effect on the discipline and psyche of the men in the ranks. With men often doubting their ability to live out the war, it seemed foolish for them to follow the rules of military life and even common decency. As Lieutenant Brewster wrote to his mother soon after the Wilderness, "I cannot give you an idea of half the horrors I have witnessed and yet so common have they become that they do not excite a feeling of horror."[111] Horror was now the norm, and no longer elicited comment or a feeling of shame for making light of it. Moving on from the Spotsylvania battlefields, Private John Haley's unit passed by the spot where the green soldiers of the 1st Maine Heavy Artillery had been engaged and the men took morbid advantage of the bodies and debris strewn across the field. "We found an excellent chance to replenish our wardrobes," Haley wrote in his journal, "they had just come from the defenses of Washington and had several changes of clothing and diverse other extras."[112] Beyond benefiting from the deaths of fellow soldiers, some even found humor in the fear and suffering of their comrades. Even years later in his memoirs, Major Abner Small of the 16th Maine seemed to crack a smile recalling this story from the May campaign:

> Tuesday some raw recruits came up, and just as they arrived a huge shell exploded over their heads with a shattering crash and a spatter of iron. It was like

the splash of a great stone in a frog pond. The startled recruits jumped and dove in all directions. One man went head first, like a solid shot, into the midriff of Colonel Farnham, who fell in a heap, convulsed with laughter. Some went shooting among the old settees in the churchyard, where General Warren and his staff were sitting. One man was hit; a fragment of iron took his right thumb off. He started running aimlessly around, holding up the bleeding stump and howling; but a veteran corporal stopped him with a scolding. "What ye makin' such a hell of a fuss about a thumb fer?" he asked. "There's a man over there with his head shot off, and he don't say a damn word. I'm ashamed of ye."[113]

With disfigurement and death all around them and the prospects of a continued campaign across Virginia in the scorching summer heat, it seemed ludicrous to these men to feel bad about responding in such ways to the violence. As we shall see in the next chapter, to others it seemed just as ludicrous to continue their voluntary submission to daily life in the Army of the Potomac.

———

As the Army of the Potomac shifted south across the James to move on the rail hub at Petersburg, many of the men in its ranks took stock of the previous six weeks and thanked the Almighty for allowing them to be among the survivors. Throughout the campaign men had praised God for continuing to grant them the gift of life, believing that only His protection could explain their survival in the face of such combat. "I am thankful to Almighty God for permiting me to live see an other Sabbath Day," wrote Corporal Timothy Bateman of the 2nd Corps only days after surviving the fighting around the Mule Shoe, while the former gardener from England John Pillings wrote on May 29, "through the whole God has been ever near and precious to me, and I can unfeignedly thank Him for His great goodness to one so unworthy of even His notice."[114] It is hard to determine whether the experience of the Overland campaign shook the faith of the men; while plenty looked to charge someone for their misery and the frustrations of May and June, no one shouted to the heavens when playing the blame game. The religious rhetoric noticeably dropped off in some diaries and correspondence, but the campaign seemed to reinforce belief rather than crushing it.

One man whose beliefs were never shaken was Private Frederick Pettit, who was unaware that he was living the final weeks of his life. Yet, reading his letters, it seems hard to believe that knowing his death was imminent would have altered his convictions. Despite losing more than a dozen men from his company in the Wilderness and at Spotsylvania, the tall, blue-eyed Pettit could still write to his parents back in western Pennsylvania, "A kind hand guides us and watches over us. Our trust is in God."[115] On June 1st, Pettit reiterated his faith to his sister: "Through the watchful care of Him who never sleepeth my life and health has been preserved. My trust is still in Him. I never knew the comfort there is in religion so well as during the past month. Nothing sustains me so much in danger as to know that there is one who ever watches over us."[116] The next day, Pettit became one of the 55,000 Union casualties during the campaign when he received a major wound in his left arm at Cold Harbor. After spending much of June in the hospital, Pettit would return to his unit on July 7 and receive word that he had been promoted to corporal. Two days later, at seven in the evening, a sharpshooter's bullet would strike him in the neck, ending his life.[117] His commanding officer wrote a letter of condolence to Pettit's parents the following day, giving special notice to the man's faith, describing him as "a devoted and exemplary Christian and I trust and believe your loss is his eternal gain."[118]

Faith in God was one way that the men dealt with the recurrence of death's hand around them; the attempts to benumb themselves to the violence around them was another. However, the men could not stop feeling any more than they could stop thinking, and the swirl of combat continually closed in on them. Perhaps the men would have been fine if the Army of the Potomac had taken Petersburg and Richmond in mid-June; then they could have sealed up the horrors in a package of victory and moved on with their lives. But Petersburg would not fall; when Northern forces began to appear outside the city's defenses on June 15, they faced defenders who would stubbornly beat back their assaults just as they had at the Mule Shoe and Cold Harbor. There would be no pause to the campaigning, no return to the safety of Northern Virginia and the comfort of winter quarters. The churning grist mill of violence would continue as the men descended into some of the most taxing and revolutionary warfare of the American Civil War. At first, it did not appear that they were ready for the challenge ahead of them after the travails of May and June. The facade of unity and discipline in the Army of the Potomac was crumbling, and the opening weeks of what would soon be known as the Petersburg campaign revealed the dysfunction that had been building among the men throughout the suffering and slaughter of the Overland campaign.

3

"The Men Were Becoming Dangerous"

TRANSITIONING TO PETERSBURG AND
THE PROBLEM OF MORALE

It seems as though men in the time of war lose their civilization.
—Unknown Union Soldier

On June 14, immediately prior to the Army of the Potomac's arrival at Petersburg, Virginia, Sylvanus Cadwallader of the *New York Herald* came across the men of the 36th Wisconsin, a new unit that had joined the campaign only a few weeks earlier. Cadwallader had been following the campaign's progress for several weeks, having been attached to General Grant's headquarters for years and following the general to the east when Grant took control of Union forces. Having been with Grant through most of his campaigns out west, Cadwallader was quite familiar with war and its terrors, but the reporter was obviously shaken by the Overland campaign's impact on the men who continued to endure its traumas. His description of the men of the 36th Wisconsin was almost horrific: "They were literally incrusted in mud, dirt, dust, perspiration and blood—unwashed, unkempt, unfed, for rations had not always reached them as needed. Col. [John A.] Savage [the regiment's commanding officer] was lying on the ground, a picture of suffering, emaciation and exhaustion, never to be forgotten." Only days later, Cadwallader noted that Savage had been wounded while leading the 36th Wisconsin in one of the early attacks against the Petersburg lines. Colonel Savage died of his wounds soon after, since, as Cadwallader explained, "he had succumbed because of his debilitated and exhausted physical condition, born of his thirty days' hardships and exposures, since entering the ranks in front of Spotsylvania."[1]

Stories such as Cadwallader's illustrate how the physical capability of the men to both continue the struggle and survive the fighting was declining rapidly by the end of the Overland campaign. The physical condition of the Union army had deteriorated to a severe degree by mid-June; the men were exhausted, hungry, and filthy. They reached a physical breaking point and sought only some relief from the nonstop warfare that they were facing. As one soldier noted upon reaching the Petersburg lines on June 17, "I have been deprived so much of sleep that it is with the utmost difficulty that I march at all nights; the whole campaign has been a series of night marches and bloody fights."[2] Long marches, short rations, and frequent assaults were common during the campaign, and the men were clearly reaching their physical limit after six weeks of campaigning. Beyond that, they were quite simply traumatized by the horrors they had experienced but were given no time to cope with such horror as the campaign continued.[3] As General Grant maneuvered his dwindling force south of the James River to strike against the rail center at Petersburg, there would be no relief for the men of the Army of the Potomac. Instead, the fighting continued and the men increasingly displayed an inability and unwillingness to continue the struggle as the rapid movements and assaults of the Overland campaign gave way to the static nature of siege warfare surrounding Petersburg.

———

Despite the excitement of the previous weeks, as the Overland campaign wore on most men were in the dark as to the larger operational picture. They only understood that they were heading south, and many convinced themselves that they were somehow winning the campaign despite the casualties. As early as May 15, Private Henry Carr of the 8th New York Cavalry wrote in his diary with mixed confidence, "We are whipping the Rebs all over every place that we attack them. That is, the papers say so. And I hope that it is so."[4] Yet it was men like Private Charles Smith who captured the prevailing thoughts in the weeks leading up to Petersburg: "there is no news here for we do not know what is going on except right where we are."[5] Private Edward Wightman agreed, writing from Cold Harbor, "I don't know whether we are on the extreme right or not, neither do any of our officers. Our knowledge of affairs is very limited."[6] With such a paucity of information available, the men in the ranks often turned to their officers to provide greater meaning to their struggles in the Overland campaign. Unfortunately, most men discovered that the regimental officers they turned to were just as ignorant of the bigger picture as those beneath them. "Our officers know but little better than we," wrote Private Wilbur Fisk of the 2nd Vermont on May 25, exposing how the lack of information extended well above the enlisted men.[7] On June 11, First Lieutenant Theodore Vaill of the 2nd Connecticut Heavy Artillery wrote a plea to his brother: "As to the general situation & lookout, *we* know nothing beyond our immediate scope of vision, whereas *you* are posted every morning by the papers . . . I wish you would *write* me & send me *daily papers*."[8]

As the men in the ranks flailed about for information in the waning days of the Overland campaign, they turned to whatever sources were immediately available. For most, it was the ever-present soldier rumor mill. "There is so many rumors agoing that we dont know what to believe," noted one Maine artilleryman, while Curtis Pollock of the 48th Pennsylvania optimistically wrote to his mother in May, "we have heard the rumor of the capture of Richmond but do not know whether to believe it."[9] Obviously the rumor mill could not be trusted, and frequently led the men astray with overly optimistic or cynical interpretations of whatever slim information filtered its way down to enlisted ranks. One soldier, Private Frank Wilkeson of the 11th New York Light Artillery, notably put far more faith in the soldier rumor mill than others might have. In his memoirs of the Overland campaign, Wilkeson wrote:

> In all our armies in the civil war there was among the enlisted men, the volunteers, a system of gathering and distributing news that beat the information we received from division and corps head-quarters both in time and accuracy. . . . There was a burning desire among these men to know how other commands fared, and to gather accurate information, so as to correctly judge the battle's tide, the progress of the campaign, and the morale of the army. The enlisted men knew of defeats and successes long before they were published in general orders. The truth is that the privates of the army—the volunteers without bounty I mean—never believed a report that was published from head-quarters, unless it corresponded with the information the "camp-walkers" had gathered.[10]

Despite claims as to the accuracy of this underground system of "camp-walkers," it is clear that most soldiers, including many line officers, remained ignorant of the bigger picture of the campaign as the Army of the Potomac transitioned to new operations around Petersburg in the middle of June.

Following a respite of several days after the failed assaults at Cold Harbor, Grant settled upon a bold, new turning movement. He would direct his army to cross the James River and seize the city of Petersburg, a rail hub twenty miles south of the rebel capital. Upon capturing that city, he could isolate Richmond from much of the rest of the Confederacy and, more importantly, force Lee's army to move and fight from an unfavorable position. From June 12 to June 16, the five corps of his army pulled out of their trenches near Cold Harbor and marched to the James River. At this point, Grant's force had dwindled to under 70,000 men, though 12,000 reinforcements in the form of William "Baldy" Smith's 18th Corps had arrived to raise that number prior to Cold Harbor.[11] Beginning on June 14, Union troops either boarded transports for relocation to the south side of the river or crossed the 2,100-foot-long pontoon bridge that Grant's engineers had constructed. By June 17, the Army of the Potomac had successfully pulled out from along a ten-mile front and marched fifty miles to engage in another series of desperate battles in front of Petersburg.[12]

At first, the situation appeared quite favorable for the Union operation. Lee was slow in anticipating Grant's movement, so the 2,200 men under General P. G. T. Beauregard in the "Dimmock line" protecting Petersburg were quickly outnumbered by the arrival of Smith's 18th Corps on the morning of June 15. The initial assaults by Smith's men went quite favorably for the Union, with attacks throughout the day seizing most of the outer line of Confederate defenses with limited casualties. That evening, Smith rested his troops and waited for Hancock's 2nd Corps to come up and extend his lines so that they could together take the city the following day. On the 16th, more Union troops came up but few substantial assaults were made. Lee and Beauregard used the time to its fullest, forwarding reinforcements to the Petersburg lines at an increasing pace. A coordinated attack by Union forces on June 17 seized more of the Petersburg defenses, but Confederate commanders merely moved their men to a final defensive line that was being continually reinforced and extended. With most of the Army of the Potomac now at Petersburg on June 18, another Union assault was made but met with failure in front of the now strongly fortified Confederate positions.[13] As First Lieutenant Thomas Galwey of the 8th Ohio noted that same day, "Our lines have advanced at all fronts, but the enemy contests every inch of ground with desperate resistance, so our loss has been very heavy."[14] The opportunity to seize Petersburg in one swift movement had passed.

It was at this point that General Grant settled in for the long haul outside Petersburg. Writing in his memoirs, Grant would declare that, following the assaults on the 18th, "I now ordered the troops to be put under cover and allowed some of the rest which they had so long needed." He would spend the next few days positioning his troops, so that "the Army of the Potomac was given the investment of Petersburg, while the Army of the James held Bermuda Hundred and all the ground we possessed north of the James River. . . . Thus began the siege of Petersburg."[15] His goal was to drive Lee's army out of its defenses so that it could be destroyed; cutting off the supply lines into Petersburg would accomplish this objective and possibly gain him the rebel capital in the process. The operation was not technically a siege since the city had not been completely surrounded by Grant's forces, which would spend the next nine months endeavoring to do just that. One officer remained optimistic, believing that Petersburg would be taken within months, but admitted that it would be "a very bloody affair at best."[16] Captain Charles Mills was more pessimistic in a June letter to his mother: "The Army had made little or no progress here, and we are feeling somewhat blue about the campaign. We may be able to isolate Richmond tho' I am doubtful of that, but we shall never take it any other way."[17] Despite their numerical superiority, Union forces had been stalemated in early June and forced to trade the destruction of Lee's army for an investment of the city of Petersburg.

As the Army of the Potomac began arriving at Petersburg around mid-June, it was obvious to those in both the higher and lower ranks that the martial enthusiasm of April had all but disappeared and that the force was exceedingly diminished in size, strength, and morale. Lieutenant Colonel Horace Porter was perhaps in the best position to observe the status of the Union army and offer an explanation as to how it had reached such a low point. Being a member of Grant's staff, Porter's responsibilities included relaying information on unit strength and morale from subordinates to the commanding general. Thus, the dire image displayed in his memoirs presents an informed view of an army in trouble:

It was apparent in the recent engagements [near Petersburg] that the men had not attacked with the same vigor that they had displayed in the Wilderness campaign; but this was owing more to the change in their physical than in their moral condition. They had moved incessantly both day and night, and had been engaged in skirmishing or in giving battle from the 4th of May to the 18th of June. They had seen their veteran comrades fall on every side, and their places filled by inexperienced recruits, and many of the officers in whom they had unshaken confidence had been killed or wounded.[18]

Speaking from his position, Porter recognized that the previous six weeks of campaigning had a very destructive effect on the soldiers, if not on their will to fight then most definitely on their capability of continuing the struggle. Theodore Lyman, a member of General Meade's staff, concurred with Porter's assessment of the Army of the Potomac following the Overland campaign. Writing in a letter about the initial assaults on Petersburg, Lyman commented, "forty-five days of constant marching, assaulting and trenching are a poor preparation for a rush! The men went in, but not with spirit."[19] Among the enlisted men, Private Wilkeson also recognized a distinct negative change in the fighting power of the Union soldiers. Looking back on the end of the Overland campaign, Wilkeson's recollections almost mirrored those of Porter: "in the latter part of June, 1864, it was freely charged by the generals employed in the Army of the Potomac that the army was not fighting as stanchly at Petersburg as it had fought in the Wilderness or at Spottsylvania. The charge was true."[20] It was readily apparent to all those involved that the Overland campaign had severely deteriorated the combat effectiveness of the Army of the Potomac, but was this merely a problem of physical exhaustion, as suggested by Lieutenant Colonel Porter, or were there more serious morale issues facing the army as it began operations around Petersburg?

For the survivors of the Overland campaign, the combat conditions that they faced would continue well into the operations around the city of Petersburg, as Union efforts to surround that city met with repeated failure and more casualties in the thousands. Soldier discontent and plummeting morale continued into the opening weeks and months of the Petersburg operations as the men struggled to adapt to the loss of comrades, particularly commanding officers. As historian Bell Wiley has argued, it was company commanders in particular who exerted a powerful role in military discipline throughout the war, and "a regiment was well disciplined if it had good lieutenants and captains and poorly disciplined if it did not."[21] What would happen to unit discipline when a large proportion of these line officers fell as casualties during the Overland campaign? Assistant Secretary of War Charles Dana observed the consequences for the Army of the Potomac around this time, explaining how "members of Grant's staff told me that our operations were unsatisfactory, owing to our previous heavy loss in superior officers. The men fought as well as ever . . . but they were not directed with the same skill and enthusiasm."[22] In letters to his father throughout the Overland campaign, Fifth Corps staff officer Colonel George Barnard repeatedly noted the high loss of officers, writing with dismay in early June, "It seems to be the chance that our *best* officers high & low are the ones to be killed."[23] From the perspective of the surviving commanders within the Army of the Potomac, it appeared that the extreme loss of officers and comrades inhibited the ability of Union soldiers to operate effectively in the Overland campaign and opening phases of the Petersburg campaign.

Aside from the obvious physical deterioration of the men at the conclusion of the Overland campaign, it is clear that the will of Northern soldiers to continue fighting was also suffering by the middle of June. One of the more significant results of soldiers losing their will to fight is when individuals or units begin to disobey orders from their commanding officers and, although rare, this was the case in the Army of the Potomac toward the end of the Overland campaign and into the early stages of the operations around Petersburg. Incidents of soldiers disobeying orders and refusing to participate in assaults are well documented and have been utilized by other authors to demonstrate the intensity of the fighting during this point in the war. Except for the first battle at the Wilderness, examples of units or men refusing to initiate or follow up assaults can be found for all the major battles of the campaign.[24] One historian labeled this growing indiscipline a "Cold Harbor syndrome," evidenced by situations where "if the ranks determined that an attack was fruitless, then no order or frantic waving of the colors would drive them forward more than a hundred feet."[25] This was the case for Lieutenant George Bowen's men in the 12th New Jersey at Cold Harbor. After the first attack on June 3 failed, Bowen wrote in his diary that "The order was again given to charge but the men positively refused to attempt another assault."[26] Perhaps the most famous example of combat refusals at Cold Harbor occurred at a more elevated command level, when brigade commander Emory Upton deliberately prevented his men from participating in the disastrous assaults on June 3.[27]

The "Cold Harbor syndrome" persisted into the opening days of the Petersburg campaign, when once again Lieutenant Bowen found his men unwilling to move forward. On June 18, his unit was ordered to make an assault on the Confederate defenses around Petersburg, but the men would have none of it. As explained by Lieutenant Bowen, "the position was of unusual strength . . . our men positively refused to attempt it and no urging to get them to make even a show of going."[28] It is important to recognize that although such incidents were sporadic, they represented a clear and present morale problem facing the Army of the Potomac. In fact, Bowen's comment suggests that the early failed assaults at Petersburg may not have stemmed as much from the physical condition of the men, as Horace Porter believed, but instead resulted more from soldiers no longer willing to follow orders. Grant clearly agreed in his memoirs that there had been a missed opportunity when Union forces first arrived at Petersburg: "I believed then, and still believe, that Petersburg could have been easily captured at that time."[29] While he found the fault in the slow movements of Smith's and Hancock's corps against the city, the implication remains that, despite the advantageous position in which Union forces found themselves near Petersburg on June 15–18, failure may have had more to do with the strength and morale of the men rather than the planning and speed of general officers.

Evidence of soldier refusals continued for weeks into the Petersburg campaign. On June 24, the 11th Pennsylvania Infantry Regiment found itself maneuvering into position near a strongly fortified portion of the Confederate line south of the city. The 11th had spent the previous six weeks participating in some of the bloodiest fighting of the Overland campaign, which had taken a horrific physical and psychological toll on the men of the regiment. Years later, Private Robert Ekin McBride of the 11th Pennsylvania would relate what happened that day in front of Petersburg when the exhausted men of his unit finally had enough of the bloodshed:

> The column was led by Colonel Carle through open ground, less than eighteen hundred yards from rebel batteries. These, of course, opened on them with shell, causing considerable loss. . . . The men, without waiting for orders, but without disorder, moved obliquely to the right, to reach the protection of lower ground,

which there led up to the works. This called forth such violent protest and condemnation from Colonel Carle, that the result was a serious mutiny . . . Both
officers and men felt that it was a blunder and an outrage to be thus needlessly
exposed; and when Carle cursed them as cowards, they resented it. Confusion
followed. The officers, almost to a man, refused to obey orders, or do any thing,
until the insult should be retracted. The men were becoming dangerous. . . .
Carle laid his hand on his pistol. Instantly a score of rifles were leveled on him.
Yells and curses resounded on every side. He withdrew his hand, apologized
to both officers and men, and they moved on to the rifle-pits without further
trouble.[30]

In this situation, when their commanding officer committed a perceived act of
incompetence, the men in the unit took it upon themselves to countermand
his orders. When the officer registered his strong objection to their behavior,
the men (and apparently even some of the other officers) proved willing to
use violence to enforce their judgment. In so doing, the officers and men of
the 11th Pennsylvania demonstrated the often cited and praised independence
of the American citizen soldier, a concept that would significantly impact the
perceptions of the soldiers and officers of the Army of the Potomac throughout
some of the most traumatic and transitory fighting of the war.[31]

The explanation for such challenges to authority ultimately can be found in
the poor conditions that the men faced throughout May and June, but much
of it can also be seen in the steady decline in the level of faith the enlisted
men had in their commanding officers. Company and regimental officers were
common targets for accusations of cowardice or incompetence. At an action
along the Po River in mid-May, Private John Haley's 17th Maine regiment found
its flanks exposed to enemy fire, an occurrence he attributed to the "stupid,
drunken cuss" Major Briscoe. Later in the engagement, as the 17th Maine
struggled to hang on in the firefight, Briscoe jumped on his horse and made a
run for the rear, prompting Haley to record in his diary that it was "no thanks
to him that we were not shot or gobbled and sent to Richmond to enjoy a spell
at Libby Prison or Belle Island."[32] As suggested by Haley, alcohol was often cited
by the men as an explanation for the questionable and/or disastrous behavior
of superior officers. As Samuel Cormany noted in his diary near the middle of
May, it seemed that for much of the campaign "most of our officers have been
drinking freely—some are pretty drunk."[33] Comments such as these only grew

in number as the campaign dragged on and the enlisted men frequently found ways to blame the poor conditions and heavy losses on those above them in rank.

As the fighting grew more severe, the label of cowardice was often bandied about in reference to officers. Private Edward Wightman of the 3rd New York claimed that many of his unit's officers were seen hiding behind trees in a mid-May engagement, and wrote to his brother of "the incapacity of our officers. In the present state of affairs they were merely an incumbrance." Two weeks later he would once again identify the cowardice of his officers, claiming that "The men despise their officers thoroughly and purposely insult them almost daily." After relating the story of some of the early attacks on Petersburg in a letter home, Wightman noted once again how "our officers, as usual, were nowhere and the men commanded themselves. The majority of the officers, pale as ghosts, came after the fight was done."[34] Some men looked above their regimental officers to affix blame and responsibility on those with stars on their shoulders. In his memoirs, Abner Small of the 16th Maine criticized his division commander, Brigadier General Lockwood, for commanding his unit in a "feeble way" during the Overland campaign, while Colonel George Barnard routinely criticized the conduct of his superior officers throughout the campaign, declaring simply, "I am glad I am not a General."[35] Private Wilkeson would recall a conversation with a Pennsylvania soldier around the time of Cold Harbor who claimed, "in no other campaign have I seen so many general officers shirk as they have in this one."[36] The soldier suggested that the unwillingness of most generals to actually come to the front and reconnoiter the ground was contributing to the repeated failed efforts at breaking the Confederate defenses. With the extensive losses being suffered by the officer corps during the Overland campaign, it is hard to sustain a label of cowardice for the entirety of the command staff of the Army of the Potomac. However, for some men, the very fact that some officers survived was enough to question their bravery and command ability. While the men mourned the senseless loss of the brave officers, they perhaps unjustly criticized those who had not displayed such conspicuous and sometimes reckless valor.

While comments indicting officers for incompetence were many, perhaps no single individual received as many negative comments as the general-in-chief himself, Ulysses S. Grant, or "Old Useless" as one soldier labeled him.[37]

The significance of the soldiers' comments is fully appreciated when weighed against the optimism and enthusiasm that greeted General Grant upon taking command of the Army of the Potomac in the spring. The experience of the Overland campaign had changed the opinions of some soldiers by mid-June, as by then many had found fault with Grant's motives and ability as a commander. One of the most vociferous critics of Grant throughout the campaign (and there were many) was Private Haley of the 17th Maine; his diary is peppered with disparaging comments about both his immediate commanders and Grant himself. Indicative of Haley's opinion of Grant was his assessment of the early battle of the Wilderness; the Confederates won the battle because they "have unlimited confidence in their commander while we have little or none in ours. We can see that whatever success attends Grant must be by sheer brute force. No strategy, just hammer, hammer, hammer, until the enemy is flattened."[38] The word "butcher" was increasingly tossed around by soldiers over the course of the campaign, as many thought their lives were being wasted by Grant in futile frontal attacks. A soldier in the 22nd Massachusetts appeared to feel this way by early June. Although this private expressed his faith in much of the higher command structure, his faith in "old Grant" was wavering because "he is almost too much of a butcher, and has too little regard for human life."[39] Surprisingly, few soldiers targeted Grant's famous (and, in many cases, alleged) drinking binges as a source of his failures as a commander. Instead, a feeling prevailed that his tactics were unoriginal, achieving nothing except upping the body count.

Shortly after his unit's arrival at Petersburg, the future Supreme Court justice Captain Oliver Wendell Holmes, Jr. of the 20th Massachusetts wrote to his parents to update them on the status of the army. His comments were bleak as he recounted the sacrifices paid by the men in his unit. "I tell you many a man has gone crazy since this campaign begun," he reported after a description of recent army movements. He recounted the morale issues facing the Army of the Potomac, noting that "feeling for McClellan has grown this campaign."[40] It is perhaps not surprising that George McClellan, former general-in-chief of the Union armies and soon to be the Democratic nominee for president, reappeared in the minds of soldiers like Holmes at a time when they were increasingly questioning the ability of their current leadership. Although there had been little mention of him prior to the start of the Overland campaign,

George McClellan soon became the most frequently cited individual who could step in and provide victory as Grant's efforts against Richmond faltered. The reasoning behind this belief in McClellan's attributes as a commander was twofold. First, by the time the Army of the Potomac reached the James River in early June, many Union soldiers had come to the obvious conclusion that thousands of lives had been lost reaching a point in enemy territory that had already been obtained two years earlier during the Peninsula campaign of 1862. As the 16th Maine marched past Yorktown in late May, the veterans in the unit "couldn't help thinking how McClellan had got the army almost to Richmond with hardly the loss of a man, while Grant had lost already more thousands than we cared to guess."[41] Surgeon Nathan Hayward of the 20th Massachusetts expressed a similar sentiment in mid-June when he wrote to his father, "I suppose that the country is at last satisfied that McClellan's projected approach by the S. Side of the James was good generalship after all. But at what a fearful sacrifice has the experience been bought."[42] Colonel Barnard reached a similar grim conclusion: "It seems funny that we are now in our old ground of two years ago. Only it has cost us about 70,000 men to get here this time instead of coming here without the loss of any, under McClellan."[43] He would write again two weeks later noting that they had reached a similar point as they had in 1862: "McClellan however would never have sacrificed his men in this way."[44] For veterans such as these, crossing the familiar grounds of 1862, particularly at Cold Harbor, which was fought nearly on top of the Gaines Mill battlefield, brought forth obvious doubts as to the value of the sacrifices paid by the Army of the Potomac in the 1864 campaign.

The second reason for the sudden upswing of support for McClellan's return grew out of the lingering pride many veterans of the Army of the Potomac felt from having him as their commander. As the horrors of the Overland campaign began, First Lieutenant John Rumsey Brincklé of the 5th United States Artillery turned to his memories of McClellan's leadership to get him through. Noting the beginning of the campaign, he wrote to his sister that "McClellan once said, 'You will yet be proud to say that you belonged to the Army of the Potomac.' I did feel proud."[45] One night during the campaign, Private Wilkeson found himself chatting over the campfire with a veteran from a New Hampshire regiment who told him that McClellan "taught us to fight, and all that is good in this many-tongued crew of Grant's . . . is the remnant of McClellan's army Grant has not moulded one man in this vast mob."[46] Comments such as these were intended more to degrade Grant than to elevate McClellan, but their appearance raises an interesting question. With McClellan only weeks away from being declared the official Democratic presidential candidate to oppose Lincoln in the 1864 election, such calls for McClellan's return suggest a corresponding growth of support for the oppositional Democratic Party in the presidential race. This issue, particularly why such feelings did not last until the voting began in November, will be addressed in a later chapter, but for now it is important to recognize that the frequent discussion of McClellan represented an implicit condemnation of Grant as a commander and a potential threat to Lincoln's reelection in November.

While there were specific condemnations of line officers, generals, and Grant, by the end of the Overland campaign the attitude of Union soldiers was more of a vague distrust of those in command—a feeling that no one was looking out for them and their needs. This attitude is best displayed by the comments of Captain Albert Rogall of the 27th United States Colored Troops. An officer himself, Rogall frequently found reason to tirade against both those in charge of military affairs as well as those directing the more bureaucratic and organizational affairs of the army. The Union army, with its mixed character and lax discipline, must have been quite a shock for Rogall, who had served as an officer in the Prussian Army in the 1840s before emigrating to the United States in 1851. After getting severely ill in early June and being confined to an ambulance, Rogall offered his assessment of those above him in rank:

> I wish I was out of the Army of the Potomac. . . . The unnecessary loss of human life in this army beats all records in the history, a man's life is not more considered than a dog's, yet no justice for it, a man offering his service to defend the government is treated worse than a criminal, but in every respect. Stealing is going on wholesale, but the punishment for little things. All the Eastern army is one set of money speculators from private to the highest general. . . . More dirty, contemptible spirit in social view between men and officers in this army is exceeding anything.[47]

As Rogall's comments suggest, the already deep divide between officers and men grew significantly during the Overland campaign, as the soldiers in the ranks grew distrustful of the motives and actions of those above them. This distrust, coupled with the declining morale and physical condition of the men, began to manifest itself in ways beyond writing unfavorable comments in their letters and diaries.

Shortly after Cold Harbor, Private Wilkeson found himself unexpectedly called to army headquarters. Wilkeson panicked; he recalled that over the previous weeks he had committed many misdeeds, including "stealing haversacks" and being "exceedingly impudent to some officers." As he rode to headquarters, his fear grew as "I knew that I ought to be court-martialed and that I deserved to be shot," yet his regrets seemed to stem not from the fact that he had committed such actions but more that he had been caught. Wilkeson had nothing to fear, though; he had only been called from his unit to be notified that his father had secured him a commission as a second lieutenant with the 4th United States Artillery. He was soon removed from the ranks and joined his new unit near Washington, where he would spend the remainder of the war on relatively quiet duty behind the lines.[48] While the war was essentially over for Wilkeson, his fear that day in June when he was nearly held accountable for his insubordinate and criminal actions reflected a growing, dangerous issue for the Army of the Potomac.

A corollary to the decline of faith in army commanders was an increase in the independence expressed by those in the ranks, one witnessed in the insubordinate and criminal actions of Private Wilkeson. As historian Bruce Catton once observed, "even after 2 years of war, [soldiers] would insist on remaining more citizen than soldier," and this dictated much of how men on both sides perceived their role as a member of a large military organization.[49] The citizen soldier's sense of equality with superior officers continued throughout the conflict and put a great deal of pressure upon officers at all levels to live up to such expectations in order to obtain the respect and consent of their subordinates. Catton argued that the key to the system was leadership from the officer corps; discipline "was not something that he [the officer] could very easily enforce; it had to come out of his own qualities of leadership. If he lacked those qualities, he had no discipline."[50] Historian Reid Mitchell agreed with this concept in his work *The Vacant Chair*, arguing that many Union soldiers accepted the military lifestyle as a voluntary subjugation of their rights to the army only so long as "officers . . . recognize[d] that their authority, while necessary to military discipline, must operate in accordance to law."[51] The successful officers understood this, and rather than trying to beat the independence out of their subordinates, they accommodated their men whenever possible, leading by example and demonstrating the shared burden that the war placed upon the officer corps and those in the enlisted ranks. The result, as demonstrated by Stephen Ramold in his work on notions of discipline and justice in the Union army, was that officers had to be "flexible" in their relationship with the enlisted men and their treatment of indiscipline.[52] From the early days of the war, this sense of mutual accommodation permeated (perhaps unevenly) the Union army, and became a defining element of the conduct of the citizen soldier during the conflict.

From a military standpoint, however, accommodation, equality, and in-dependence do not go hand in hand with the necessity of discipline on the battlefield, especially a nineteenth-century battlefield involving complex, methodical maneuvers performed under fire. Article I, Section 1 of the *Revised United States Army Regulations of 1861* stated unequivocally: "All inferiors are required to obey strictly, and to execute with alacrity and good faith, the lawful orders of superiors appointed over them."[53] This form of obedience, although not a blind one, was required for the system to function. Thus, some historians have argued that the prevalence of an independent streak within the American soldier was perhaps destructive to military discipline throughout the war. Frederic Klein noted in his work on wartime military trials that "Civil War armies have the reputation of having been decidedly weak in discipline."[54] Bruce Catton agreed, declaring that "the Civil War army tended to be loose-jointed, informal, almost slap-dash. Yet somehow it got results."[55] Clearly a significant acceptance of discipline occurred among the armies of both com-batants in order for them to function, and most historians claim that while Union forces suffered a "tardy evolution" in this area, they grew in discipline and subordination to command authority as the war went on.[56]

The primary means that the army had for enforcing such discipline and subordination was the court-martial, a process dictated by the Articles of War dating back to 1806 and outlined in Article 38 of the *Revised Regulations for the Army of the United States.* A general court-martial could consist of five to thirteen members with a president appointed and minutes kept, the precise format of which was spelled out in the *Regulations.* The process was specified whereby the defendant could ask for a delay or postponement, submit pleas, and call witnesses. No appeals system was set in place, although superior officers could mitigate sentences and the president technically had the final say in any and all judgments. Although no specific crimes were specified, it was assumed that any offenses would be those considered violations of the *Regulations*. Sentences allowable for imposition ranged from formal reprimands to the death penalty, and herein lay the difficulty with the system.[57] Each court had their own discretion to render a penalty that they felt appropriate for a specified offense, and this created a wide variety of sentencing patterns based on local conditions in particular military units throughout the Civil War. As the Overland campaign wound down and the forces settled into trench lines surrounding Petersburg, this system would be put to the test by a fresh wave of soldier independence and insubordination.

As previously demonstrated, soldiers often expressed their independence by griping about their officers in their correspondence and even refusing to engage in combat operations, but the open defiance of some men became a significant problem for the Army of the Potomac in the summer of 1864. Many soldiers resisted their officers outright, with violence sometimes being the result. Private Charles Abbott of the 2nd New York Mounted Rifles was brought up on charges of "conduct prejudicial to good order and military discipline" after a confrontation with his lieutenant at Petersburg in late June. Coming in from a long night of fatigue duty in the field, Private Abbott was denied his whiskey ration and responded by directing abusive language toward Lieutenant August Budd, decrying him as "a G-d d-d white livered son of a Bitch."[58] It was no surprise that the denial of alcohol was a factor in pushing the weary Private Abbott over the line of disobedience; alcohol was often cited as a contributing factor to incidents of violence that summer. Private George Black of the 63rd New York regiment found himself in a condition later described as "saucy and impudent" while working on his unit's fortifications near Petersburg on July 15. Lieutenant Benjamin of that unit had ordered Black back to work, but he refused and took a swing at the lieutenant with a shovel. Black had to be forcefully restrained by the captain in charge before he was placed under arrest. Several witnesses testified that alcohol had been a factor in Black's state, but also that Private Black had served for the duration of the war with no prior misbehavior.[59] Privates Abbott and Black, both veterans with no previous record of insubordination, had clearly, if only momentarily, lost their respect for their commanding officers and had acted in a manner far outside the boundaries of military discipline.

The decline in respect for military discipline did not just manifest itself in a changing attitude toward superior officers, but also in the way that soldiers related to one another within the ranks. Incidents of violence and thievery among the enlisted men abound in the court-martial records for the summer of 1864, with officers struggling to keep order and impose appropriate punishments. The rising number of court-martial cases over the course of the war, with the peak occurring in 1864, demonstrates either an increase in soldier insubordination or an enlarged effort by the officer corps to crack down on soldier indiscipline.[60] Either way, the court-martial records for the Army of the Potomac that summer reveal the nature of such insubordination along with the efforts to quash it. The case of Private Joseph Hagen of the 63rd New York regiment, who was tried and convicted of assaulting and attempting to kill fellow private Hugh Mills on July 17, is indicative of the nature of soldier indiscipline in 1864. Additional charges indicated that he was intoxicated at the time and assaulted his commanding sergeant, who tried to arrest Hagen. Hagen's unsuccessful defense is particularly telling. He pled with the court that "I was drunk. At the first charge at Petersburg I was hit in the head, this was the first time I ever drank any liquor. Since I was wounded very little liquor knocks me over."[61] While this may not have been a truthful argument (the court certainly thought it did not mitigate his actions, since Hagen was sentenced to loss of pay and additional duty), it reveals at least the perception that the 1864 campaigns had negatively affected the men and was contributing to their current misbehavior.

Perhaps the worst example of declining morale and discipline was the case of Private Henry Hobbs of the 19th Indiana, part of the vaunted Iron Brigade. In a hearing held on July 22, 1864, in the field near Petersburg, officers of the 4th Division, 5th Corps questioned witnesses as to the involvement of Private G. W. H. Hough of the 7th Indiana in the death of Private Hobbs the day before. Witnesses testified to the good character of both the victim and defendant, but it was clear that Private Hobbs had been drunk and lunged at Hough with a knife, calling him "a son of a bitch." Private Hough defended himself with a stick and the result was the death of Private Hobbs. After deliberating, the officers concluded that there was no need to convene a full court-martial since Hough was "innocent of any crime" and that his actions were "unpremeditated." It is clear that Hough was only defending himself, but the actions of Private Hobbs merit notice here. That a "good fellow" such as Private Hobbs could become intoxicated on duty should be no surprise in the Army of the Potomac at any phase of the war, but that he would lunge at someone who was apparently a friend with the intent to kill indicates a change had occurred in his demeanor.[62] The combat environment in which he and Private Hough were submerged could have only worsened their state of mind and their commitment to the accepted rules of conduct, deteriorating to the point where a drink between friends could turn into a deadly encounter.

While the relationships between enlisted men were placed under additional stress during the summer campaigns of 1864, the actions of several line officers demonstrated that the stresses of constant campaigning were affecting their ability to endure as well. Only days after the commencement of siege operations near Petersburg, two officers in the 118th Pennsylvania regiment, First Lieutenant George Moore and Second Lieutenant Henry McManus, openly brawled in front of their superiors and subordinates in the regiment while only yards from the enemy position, with alcohol apparently being a contributing factor. Although some testimony suggested that McManus forced the fight on Moore, both officers were convicted and sentenced to be cashiered.[63] No alcohol was cited in the case of First Lieutenant George Lacey of the 2nd New York Heavy Artillery, who was charged with "conduct unbecoming an officer and a gentleman" for his lambasting of two of the regiments' superior officers.[64] According to the court transcript, on June 27 Lacey had a confrontation with Major Hogg of the regiment and referred to Hogg "sucking the arse of Major Thomas Maguire, and did say that 'he,' Lacy [sic], 'was a God-damned sight better man than either Major Maguire or Major Hogg,'" before going on to challenge both of them to a fight. Lacey pled guilty to all charges, but brought in multiple witnesses, including the Major Hogg in question, to testify to his good conduct and character over his three years of service. Major Hogg testified that Lacey was "an excellent officer, attentive to your command, obedient and respectful until this." Lacey's defense failed, however, and he was dismissed from the service.[65] A case like this demonstrates that line officers, even "obedient and respectful" ones like Lacey, were not immune to the stresses of the marching and the bloodshed of that summer. Many of them, like their men, were driven away from that which bound them to the larger military family. However, the harmful actions of the officer corps were multiplied in the ways they contributed to the poor perspective of them held by the men following the Overland campaign, and only reinforced the perceptions of the independent-minded among the enlisted ranks.

Perhaps the most extreme form of indiscipline involved those soldiers who sought one of the most desperate escapes from the battlefield and the reestablishment of their independence through the application of a self-inflicted wound. Court-martial records indicate that there were multiple cases of apparent self-inflicted wounding in the opening weeks of the Petersburg siege. Two men, Privates Wilford Tucker and Lorin Johnston of the 31st Maine, were tried by courts-martial for "maiming himself for the purpose of avoiding military duty." Both men had served on picket duty in the trenches near Petersburg on June 22, 1864, when they returned from the front line with similar wounds to each of their hands. Multiple surgeons were brought in to testify against the defendants, and Surgeon J. D. Mitchell of the 31st Maine described how "not only the wound, but the skin for some distance around was filled with powder," indicating that the injury could only have been sustained at close range. Both men were convicted and sentenced to three years of hard labor at the federal prison in Dry Tortugas.[66] While such instances of self-inflicted wounds were rare in the Civil War, the nature of combat in the East in 1864 fostered a mentality among some men that seemed to justify such desperate attempts to escape the bloodletting. At its most basic level, the self-inflicted wound demonstrated restoration of control over one's future; Tucker and Johnston apparently decided that they would decide when and how they would leave the war.

While some of the more violent forms of rebellion and indiscipline can be viewed as typical behavior emerging from the diverse elements (and access to alcohol) found within the Army of the Potomac, the primary form of soldier independence was far more frequent and difficult to control. By all accounts, desertion was an ever increasing problem for the Army of the Potomac throughout 1864 due to the escalating ferocity of combat conditions and the growing number of conscripts and bounty men in the Union forces.[67] While there are no specific desertion figures available for the Army of the Potomac itself for the time period in question, an examination of the Union-wide figures for desertion indicates some interesting conclusions. One set of numbers, the totals of desertion reported by regimental commanders in all of the Union forces, indicates that beginning in May 1864 desertion continued to rise until that October (see Table 2).[68] Another set of numbers, those deserters actually arrested each month across the North, indicates a similar trend, only with the numbers peaking in December 1864 rather than October.[69] While some might look to gross examples of insubordination as proof of soldier rebellion, such indiscipline can also be found in the large numbers of soldiers who simply chose to exercise the voluntary nature of their service by walking away from the war.

TABLE 2. Desertions from Union Forces, April 1864–April 1865

	Desertions Reported by Regimental Commanders	Arrests for Desertion
April 1864	7,072	3,653
May 1864	5,371	3,106
June 1864	6,827	2,667
July 1864	6,422	2,850
August 1864	8,776	3,055
September 1864	8,780	2,927
October 1864	10,692	3,191
November 1864	10,673	3,353
December 1864	8,162	3,824
January 1865	6,753	2,979
February 1865	6,404	2,394
March 1865	5,621	2,075
April 1865	7,019	1,173

Source: Ella Lonn, *Desertion during the Civil War* (Lincoln: University of Nebraska Press, 1998), 233, 236.

An examination of courts-martial pertaining to desertions during the summer of 1864 demonstrates the motivations of those who were caught away from their unit and sought to offer a defense of their actions. Even here, few soldiers were brave enough to state openly that they sought to desert, especially with the threat of capital punishment hanging over their heads. Instead, the court-martial transcripts reveal soldiers who found multiple ways to flee the battlefield and took the opportunity to do so. The case of Private Joseph Reed of the 90th Pennsylvania regiment is particularly telling. The charges indicated that at the Wilderness, Reed "did in the most shameful manner abandon his arm and equipments and desert his Company and Regiment." Reed claimed that he had helped the wounded off the field at Wilderness and eventually found himself posted in Fredericksburg serving on detached guard duty, though he could bring no witnesses to support these claims. Instead, he brought out his company officers who testified to him being a veteran and a man of "good character." Perhaps this was what saved him from the gallows, since the court reduced the charge to being absent without leave and sentenced Reed to hard labor for ninety days.[70] In September 1864, Private George Seibert, a recent addition to the 48th Pennsylvania regiment, was more candid about his motives. During his court-martial, Seibert pled guilty to deserting his unit on July 27 and again on August 20, claiming that he was trying to head north to see his family.[71] Such accounts are plentiful and reveal large numbers of green and veteran soldiers exercising their perceived right to cease their voluntary service to the Union army whenever they saw fit.

What is surprising about cases such as those of Reed and Seibert is that theirs, along with many others, demonstrate an apparent unconscious campaign by Union officers to limit the punishments of those convicted of major violations of military discipline in the Army of the Potomac following the Overland campaign. Reed's sentence was reduced, and although Private Seibert was convicted of three counts of desertion (having only pled guilty to two of them), the court cited Seibert's "evident youth and weak mental faculties" as justification for dropping his sentence to the loss of eight dollars of pay per month for four months and an obligation to make up the time he had missed.[72] In some cases, the court seemed to go out of its way to provide leniency for the survivors of the Overland campaign. Private James Young of the 40th New York was charged with desertion and cowardice for disappearing for three days in the action near North Anna River. Although he offered no defense other than a plea of not guilty and the prosecution brought in numerous witnesses against him, the court found Young innocent of all charges.[73] Private Darby Flaherty of the 4th New York Artillery seemed to be one of the largest beneficiaries of the new leniency. Flaherty disappeared while the unit was engaged near Spotsylvania on May 13 and did not return until brought back under guard on August 18. At his court-martial, Flaherty pled not guilty to the charge of desertion, testifying that he had been sick at the 5th Corps hospital, while declaring flatly, "I had no intention of deserting." Flaherty offered no corroborating evidence, and Major S. F. Gould of the 4th New York Artillery submitted to the court his opinion of Flaherty by stating, "As a soldier he was never counted on, he has never been in any action." Despite the lack of evidence from the defense and the damning critique from Major Gould, Private Flaherty was acquitted of all charges without explanation.[74]

Other soldiers were punished, but perhaps not to the extreme that the law may have dictated. Instead, a wide variety of "shaming" punishments were utilized to publicly humiliate perpetrators but not remove them from duty. Such punishments were common throughout the war, but in the summer and fall of 1864 they were facilitated by the relatively stable nature of the trench lines surrounding Petersburg, which allowed officers to make an example of some men that could be witnessed by whole units. One instance was the case of Sergeant Thomas Butters of the 116th Pennsylvania, who was found guilty of being drunk on duty in September. His punishment was precisely dictated by the court: Butters would be "marched under guard, carrying a log of wood on his shoulder weighing twenty five (25) pounds, eight hours each day for twenty days."[75] Most such cases involved issues of desertion or cowardice, with the desired effect being that other men would think twice before seeking escape from the confines of the army. Yet these punishments, while public, demeaning, and occasionally designed to cause physical harm, could often be seen as lenient when viewed in the context of the circumstances and charges of a particular case. Private George Sawter of the 7th New Jersey regiment was charged with desertion, a capital crime, after disappearing from his regiment in front of Petersburg for more than a week in mid-July. Sawter was returned to his regiment under guard and offered no defense other than a not-guilty plea at his trial. After he was found guilty, the sentence imposed involved a loss of pay for four months and the orders that he "carry a log of wood weighing not less than twenty pounds for *four* hours each day for *ten* days, then be returned to duty."[76] Sawter may not have considered this a positive outcome to his case, but given the possibility of a death sentence associated with the charge in question, the Jersey private got off lightly. The court obviously saw more value in Sawter's continued service as an infantryman than in his incarceration or execution.

Much of the evidence cited above regarding sentence leniency varies from the accounts of other historians who point to the increasing use of capital punishment by Union forces as evidence that military justice increased in its harshness over the course of the war.[77] So what explains this trend toward leniency in the Army of the Potomac in 1864 even as the number of desertions and courts-martial increased? The clearest explanation is seen in the records of the aforementioned Private George Black of the 63rd New York regiment. Convicted of the charges of being drunk on duty and attempting to strike a superior officer in July, Black was sentenced to forfeit all pay, be dishonorably discharged, and submit to hard labor for the duration of his enlistment. However, Black's division commander, General Nelson Miles, reviewed the sentence and declared that "in view of the interests of the service which requires the service of every man in the ranks," all but Black's forfeiture of pay would be commuted.[78] Months later, General Miles was still in a generous mood, reducing the sentences of three men convicted of desertion and sentenced to imprisonment and hard labor. In each of these cases, Miles "suggested" to the court that "most cases of desertion may be punished within the Army with greater benefit to the service than by confining them."[79] After the stresses of the summer campaigns, it appears that officers like Miles did not have the stomach for imposing harsh sentences on the survivors of battles like Spotsylvania and Cold Harbor, especially when the Army of the Potomac was in short supply of veteran soldiers. The words of General Miles and the merciful pattern among the sentences imposed by military courts throughout the summer and fall of 1864 indicate an understanding by many of those in command that soldier independence and indiscipline during this period was an understandable, though still unacceptable, response to the recent campaigns in the East. It also indicates a recognition that harsh responses to such attitudes could prove counterproductive. Successful officers understood the independence of their men and, rather than aggressively stamping it out, sought to accommodate and contain it whenever possible to maintain the numbers of the Army of the Potomac as operations in front of Petersburg stretched out before them.

By early June, Private Abram Feistwhite of the 93rd Pennsylvania had had enough of the Overland campaign. Shortly after Cold Harbor, he disappeared from his unit and was not located again until his arrest for drunkenness in Washington, D.C. on November 26. Returned to his unit, he would face a court-martial before officers of the 2nd division of the 6th Corps on January 13, 1865. Faced with the charge of desertion in the face of the enemy, Feistwhite pled not guilty and offered a defense for his prolonged absence. Before the court, he claimed (and apparently provided some evidence) that he had been detailed as a teamster in the ammunition train for the 2nd Division until mid-September, when he was transferred to the artillery. In this capacity he ultimately ended up in Washington, where he eventually received orders to return to his unit. It was at that point when, according to his testimony, misfortune stepped in: "when we got on board the cars to go to our Regiments we were all pretty drunk; and I left the cars, went up town, and was arrested for drunkenness, and being in the city without a pass." The court rejected Feistwhite's defense, sentencing him to a forfeiture of all pay, dishonorable discharge, and three years of hard labor at a military penitentiary in Albany, New York. General Meade would approve this sentence, and Feistwhite would find himself incarcerated in a military prison immediately prior to the Confederate surrender at Appomattox.[80]

While Feistwhite may have had legitimate reasons for being absent from his unit for such an excessive period of time, his initial disappearance at the height of the Overland campaign suggests that he was one of the many Union soldiers who were negatively affected by its high-intensity combat. The extreme violence of the Overland campaign, the physical deterioration of the men, and the hostility toward officers all led to a serious morale crisis in the Army of the Potomac in mid-June 1864. In his study of the combat motivation of soldiers, sociologist Anthony Kellett concluded that "fatigue, difficult climatic and terrain conditions, inadequate food and drink, casualties, and defeat can all significantly strain motivation."[81] All of these factors preyed upon the men of the Army of the Potomac by the end of the Overland campaign, and the result was growing demoralization within the ranks. The zeal and energy with which the men had begun the Overland campaign in April and May had been entirely drained away. While Grant's soldiers increasingly transformed into fatalistic automatons who kept moving on out of habit and the faint hope that tomorrow would bring some sort of finish to the endless marches and horrific combat, they began to turn on those above them whom they held responsible for their suffering. Both the ability and desire of Union soldiers to continue the fight was waning rapidly, as evidenced by the lackluster assaults in the opening days of the Petersburg operations and the growing talk of units and men refusing orders from their commanders. Together with the examples of individual insubordination and the growing desertion problem within the army, these developments revealed the Army of the Potomac itself to be a truly damaged organization by the summer of 1864.

All that these men were looking for was an escape, a break in the fighting during which they could recover from what they had seen and done. Unfortunately, in the early days of the Petersburg campaign they would only find more charging and casualties, culminating in further frustration. By the end of June, however, Grant had temporarily accepted the stalemate at Petersburg and begun operations designed to surround and isolate that city. The men now had time to lick their wounds, but the experience at Petersburg would pose its own challenges to the fragile morale of the survivors of the Overland campaign. Months of trench warfare loomed before them, and with it came many of the horrors associated with modern warfare. Surprisingly, the men would not falter in the face of these horrors, but rather would use the Petersburg environment as a regenerative experience. In fact, while ensconced in the trenches surrounding Petersburg, the men of the Army of the Potomac would once again find their will to fight.

4

"A Cut-Up Country"

UNION SOLDIERS EXPERIENCE TRENCH
WARFARE AT PETERSBURG

We are now having war in earnest with all its attendant hardships.
—Sergeant George Tate, 120th New York

For Captain John Hackhiser of the 28th United States Colored Troops, his Petersburg experience began with a close call and ended in tragedy. A 29-year-old native of Dearborn County, Indiana, prior to the war Hackhiser worked as a clerk in a general store to provide for his widowed father, who had been debilitated by a bout of typhoid that left him nearly blind. Once he joined the Union army, Hackhiser continued to send $10 of his monthly pay home to care for his father. Hackhiser was a multi-year veteran of the war, and in May 1864 he accepted a commission with the 28th USCT. His unit, as part of the 9th Corps, saw action in the Overland campaign and soon found itself posted along the lines at Petersburg. By the end of July, as his men were preparing for the assault at the Crater, Hackhiser found time to compose a letter to "Miss Sarah." First, he described the nature of fighting in the Petersburg trenches: "we are very clost to the Enemies and there is fighting to be done evers day, our lines, and the Rebbs lines are very clost to gether not more than a 100 yards a part, there is a constant firing from morning till night." After relating how dangerous it was for any men to expose themselves above their earthworks, he described how he had been nearly killed a few days previous. "A shell came near senting me to my long home of rest, it covered me with dirt," Hackhiser reported. "I thank god for his guiding hands and protection and hope that will thou always protect and guard me so that I may come home and enjoy the pleasures of Peace." After giving his regards to Sarah's family and discussing a few financial matters, Hackhiser closed his letter, "I shall remain your Friend as in former days." Around the time "Miss Sarah" received this letter, her friend was dead; Captain Hackhiser was killed in the assault on the Crater on July 30.[1]

As John Hackhiser's tragic experience demonstrates, the Army of the Potomac would face a new series of challenges once the summer of 1864 commenced. By the middle of June, the men of this army were in a tenuous state. The previous six weeks had witnessed levels of violence rarely seen in the Civil War, and the result was a severely reduced and demoralized Army of the Potomac. After enduring the loss of tens of thousands of comrades, the survivors of battles such as the Wilderness and Spotsylvania arrived in the vicinity of Petersburg, Virginia in a greatly depleted condition, and early attempts to break through the Confederate lines surrounding that city were slowly organized and less than energetic. Morale was at low ebb, with many soldiers within the Union ranks openly questioning the orders of their commanders along with their own personal capabilities to continue fighting. Little did these men know in the opening days of what became known as the siege of Petersburg that in some respects the worst part of the war was over; the months that followed would offer them a break from the unrelenting violence of the Overland campaign. From the middle of June 1864 until almost the conclusion of hostilities, the Army of the Potomac entered into a period of combat operations radically different in size and duration from any of its prior experience. The war went on and the near constant threat of death continued, but living conditions improved for the average Union soldier, and there was at least the perception within the ranks that their chances for survival had improved as well. It was the transition to the fighting around Petersburg, and the gradual acceptance of siege life, that began the process of empowering the Army of the Potomac to survive and ultimately to attain victory in one of the longest campaigns of the war. But first the men would have to learn to live in the trenches.

———

The experience around Petersburg could not have been more different from the Overland campaign, as both the Union and Confederate armies shifted from a campaign of near continuous high-intensity combat to one involving near continuous low-intensity combat. What distinguished the Petersburg campaign from what came before it was the extensive use of field fortifications on the battlefield. The utilization of trench warfare by both sides resulted in a slow and methodical form of conflict where men were generally protected from battlefield projectiles and "battles" (in the context of previous engagements of the war) increasingly gave way to the sporadic sniper and artillery firing that characterized the campaign. As historian Earl Hess noted in his detailed study on the evolution of fortifications in the campaign, "Petersburg saw the longest period of close contact of any campaign in the Civil War and produced the longest, most sophisticated system of field defense as well."[2] Labeled "the culmination of engineering in the Civil War," elaborate fortification networks including forts, breastworks, and rifle pits spread quickly across the landscape as the opposing forces spent months strengthening and lengthening their lines.[3] Consequently, daily casualties would increasingly be counted by the dozens instead of by the thousands as during the Overland campaign. While attacks on enemy positions did occur, some nearly to the level of Overland battles, the vast majority of the nine months spent besieging Petersburg involved Union soldiers holding their positions and doing their best to avoid being targeted by enemy sharpshooters or artillery. The result was more digging than fighting. As one Union man noted as his unit moved toward Petersburg, "I think there will be considerable shoveling for some time to come."[4]

While the employment of trench warfare during the Petersburg campaign involved the most extensive and systematic use of such battlefield fortifications during the war, it is important to recognize that the use of trenches on the field of battle was hardly innovative, either during the war itself or within the American military in the years prior to the conflict. Historian Paddy Griffith has demonstrated that West Point had been producing military engineers for decades before the war who were fully prepared to utilize constructed fortifications on the battlefield.[5] Despite the prevailing images of long lines of men moving in an orderly manner across Civil War battlefields, both sides often resorted to entrenchments when seeking to hold and defend tactical positions. As the war continued, both North and South increasingly adopted field fortifications as a perceived solution to the problems associated with the linear warfare tactics being employed on the battlefield.[6] By the time of the Overland campaign in the spring of 1864, "digging in" was no longer an option for either side; "the two armies now instantly entrenched whenever they stopped."[7] Yet most of these battlefield fortifications involved individual soldiers hurriedly digging shelter from enemy assaults the day or night immediately before a battle. The extended nature of the Petersburg campaign offered men far more time to construct massive and elaborate defensive networks that some might have considered impregnable. This, along with the length of the campaign, distinguishes the Petersburg experience from all previous experiments with trench warfare on the American battlefield.[8]

Looking forward from the Civil War, the question becomes whether the trench experience at Petersburg bears similarity to the later horrors of more modern battlefields. One twentieth-century author once noted that "spending *months* of *continuous* exposure to the stresses of combat is a phenomenon found only on the battlefields of this century."[9] While the length and nature of the Petersburg campaign appears to challenge this notion, the real test is a comparison with the First World War. Judging from the experience of those soldiers who served in World War I, it is clear that prolonged exposure to trench warfare can have destructive effects on a soldier's morale. The experience of the French in 1917 is especially telling. In May and June of that year the increasing epidemic of desertion in the French Army developed into widespread mutinies within more than half of the units stationed along the front lines. Many factors contributed to the mutiny, including the actions of French soldiers (reminiscent of those by Union personnel at the end of the Overland campaign) after the disastrous Nivelle offensive who "adamantly refused to take part in any more futile assaults."[10] An important component of the mutiny, however, can be found "in the stinking filth of the trenches, where life was expected to be miserable," which provided a constant reminder of the discomfort and nearness of death associated with trench life.[11]

While the French mutinies were quickly put down, in the case of the German Army a year later, the effects of trench life had far greater significance. By October and November, the German Army was on the verge of disintegration, with units in open rebellion against their commanding officers. Once again, though many factors were at work, life in the trenches contributed to "the gradual deterioration of morale which hastened the final collapse" on the Western Front and forced the Germans to sign an armistice ending the war.[12] Thus, it appears that trench warfare, when coupled with the general stresses associated with a nation at war, can have a fatal effect on soldiers exposed to such conditions for an extended period of time. While this is hardly a remarkable conclusion for a twentieth-century audience, it is important to recognize that Union soldiers, when first introduced to the Petersburg experience, were more accustomed to the linear, Napoleonic methods of warmaking. Long lines of men marching across open fields on the assault in battles such as Fredericksburg or Gettysburg would have been the idea that most soldiers on both sides had of the combat experience, and Petersburg posed a continual challenge to that notion.

While there were at least superficial similarities to the First World War, the Petersburg campaign was still a remarkably primitive trench experience when compared with the later conflict. By the early twentieth century, the technology of firepower and the sophistication of defensive obstructions on the battlefield (such as the use of barbed wire, not employed in the Civil War) had made the combat zone much larger and deadlier than what was witnessed by those at Petersburg.[13] As Paddy Griffith has argued, during the Civil War "staff work was of an altogether lower order of sophistication, the battlefields were tiny by comparison, and the duration of combat far less" than what was witnessed from 1914 to 1918.[14] Beyond the physical differences of the battlefield, the fundamental shape and employment of Civil War armies differed from what followed in the twentieth century. A study conducted on the utilization of manpower during the war indicated that "during the Civil War 93.2 percent of soldiers had combat-related tasks while only 0.6 percent had mechanical or maintenance tasks, 0.7 percent had administrative and clerical tasks, and 0.2 percent had technical and scientific tasks."[15] Almost every soldier was employed in a combat capacity, and thus found himself frequently exposed to the deadly environment of the battlefield such as at Petersburg. This was different from the experience of those who served in World War I, where a significantly smaller percentage of manpower was devoted to manning the lines and undertaking assaults due to the increasing requirements of the logistical network needed to supply a twentieth-century fighting force. Thus, while the battlefields of the First World War were in ways deadlier than those of the Civil War, a Union soldier's chances of actually ending up in combat at Petersburg were far greater than those of a French, German, or British soldier in 1917.

Regardless of how far the similarities and differences of the two conflicts may be stretched, there is little dispute over how the experience of trench warfare places a particularly heavy burden on those who participate in it. One historian concluded his study of trench warfare in the First World War by stating that "the Western Front became a self-contained nightmare whose rules and traditions became ends in themselves, the only thing a man could cling on to in the midst of chaos."[16] Extended exposure to such conditions could eventually wear down a soldier's ability to endure the combat environment, the results of which can be seen in the French and German armies in 1917 and 1918, respectively. As Lord Moran noted in his study of soldiers at war, "a man's courage is his capital and he is always spending"; it is only a matter of time before a soldier finds himself drained of that "capital" and succumbs to the terrors of the battlefield.[17] Given these pessimistic assessments of men exposed to trench warfare, one would expect both Union and Confederate soldiers to respond negatively to the circumstances surrounding the Petersburg siege and eventually break down from the effects of such battlefield conditions.

Yet while there were noted increases in desertion and evidence of soldiers rejecting the traditional authority of their officers at the conclusion of the Overland campaign, the Army of the Potomac did not collapse and managed to retain its cohesion in the face of the lengthy trench experience spreading before it. To understand how the Army of the Potomac kept itself together, one must look at the beginning: how the men first reacted to and coped with the conditions that they faced upon their initial arrival at Petersburg in mid-June 1864. While the siege of Petersburg never acquired the length or sophistication of the trench stalemates of the First World War, from the beginning of the campaign the conditions faced by Union soldiers were some of the most brutal of the American Civil War. Most Union soldiers (especially those in the western theater) had employed some form of defensive protection by the middle of 1864, ranging from a hastily dug hole in the ground for protection from enemy fire to scientifically engineered forts for housing artillery and men. When Union forces arrived in Petersburg in mid-June 1864, they found that "the line that Lee would have to hold to defend Petersburg and Richmond was twenty-six miles in length, well located on the best possible ground."[18] The Confederates worked tirelessly, expanding and improving their defensive positions while Union forces replied in kind, with both sides making the most of nearly every contemporary form of defensive technology in the creation of two parallel lines bristling with men, dirt, and firepower. The nine-month campaign soon became a continual experiment in the architecture of death, with siege lines expanding and casualties mounting on a daily basis. The images of trench lines that would become common to twentieth-century onlookers in the years and decades following the disasters of 1914–1918 grew to surreal proportions for Union soldiers, who had never seen fortifications taken to such an extreme scale before. As one officer noted as he surveyed the Union lines in early September 1864, "Our entire Army very nearly is enclosed in one vast entrenchment."[19]

Union soldiers wasted no time commenting on the nature of the trench life before them; in fact, the tedium associated with service in the trenches gave them ample time to do just that. "It is close work now," wrote Sergeant Charles Wood from Petersburg a month before he would be mortally wounded at the battle of the Crater, explaining on a different day that "the enemy is very strongly fortified in front—too strongly for us to drive out."[20] As the physical landscape around them was transformed, the men could not help but comment on the violence that surrounded them. While writing a letter to his sister in July, Corporal Henry Heisler unexpectedly interrupted his correspondence with, "Whiz! this word was written by mistake for I was writing in such a hurry and a ball just struck my tent and I was just thinking of the sound it made."[21] "The stillness is occasionally broken by the booming of cannon and the sharp crack of the sharp shooters rifle," noted Captain Steve Clark of an Ohio cavalry unit stationed at Petersburg. "There are some killed along the line every day but usually not more than two or three."[22] As demonstrated by Captain Clark, the apparent security of the trenches and fortifications often proved to be of limited value to those operating within them day after day. Artilleryman John Brinckle's assignment in a large fort proved to be no blessing: "My Battery is in *Fort Hell*, & it well deserves its name. I expend about 100 rounds of Ammunition every day, and the pickets and Sharpshooters pour in such a continuous stream of bullets that the said fort is anything but an agreeable place."[23] After describing the deadliness of the trenches in a letter to his wife, Private John Steward claimed that he would not recommend joining the army to any friends at home, "if he can stay at home he may consider him self a lucky boy."[24] Captain Charles Mills of the 56th Massachusetts summed it up simply in a letter to his mother; the fighting around Petersburg was a "most useless and senseless mode of warfare."[25]

While the trench lines often blended together for the soldier observers on the ground, there were essentially three different levels to the Union fortifications that faced the Confederates' defensive lines: the rear area, the main line, and the front area containing rifle pits from both sides.[26] While the Union army's fortification levels grew in depth and sophistication over the course of the siege and at times overlapped, the basic division between the three remained more or less intact throughout the Petersburg experience. Arguably the safest position in the lines was in the reserve and supply camps to the rear, which also included the thousands of civilians who were involved with maintaining the Union side of the siege. Combat units were typically rotated from the front lines to the rear for a "rest" ranging from a few hours to a few weeks, but they were always within a quick march of the front in case the enemy made an assault on the main line. Thus, their constant proximity to the front lines offered little in the way of protection for those in the rear, as evidenced by Corporal Frederick Pettit of the 100th Pennsylvania in the last letter written before his death, when he noted how "there is not much advantage in being in the rear line as both lines are equally exposed to the enemy's fire and it is necessary to keep under cover."[27] Corporal Edwin Bearse agreed, arguing that more men were hurt in the rear areas since there was less protection available.[28] Others, such as Private James Horrocks of the 5th New Jersey Light Artillery, viewed the issue from a comparative perspective, explaining how "it is very interesting to see the rear of a fighting army, perhaps more interesting and certainly more safe than to witness the operations right in front."[29] Soldiers were generally mixed in their reactions to the safety of rear areas, but many correctly recognized that, while trips to the rear did not necessarily provide immunity from enemy shot and shell, they did provide an escape into a relatively safer environment than the front lines.

Beyond the rear areas were the main lines, where most of the action and casualties occurred. The main lines had no typical appearance to them; factors such as proximity to the enemy, individual unit preferences, and landscape features prompted the trench lines to vary widely from one point of the line to another. Most trench lines would have been familiar to a modern-day observer, however, with multiple, zigzagging rows of trenches dug deep and wide enough to accommodate men either sitting or standing. These trenches would usually be adorned with slightly elevated logs on the top facing the enemy to provide head and shoulder protection for Union soldiers firing at the Confederate position. At periodic intervals along the line would be forts or batteries composed of logs and dirt for housing artillery and siege mortars. Huddled within these earthen constructs, soldiers would frequently fill the time by offering lengthy descriptions of their positions to family members, such as Lieutenant Colonel George Hopper of the 10th New York in a letter to his siblings near the opening of the campaign:

> You would be astonished to see what formidable work men will erect during a night. If in a woods we cut down trees place three or four on top of each other after trimming of all branches then dig a ditch outside & through the Earth against the logs making the Earth work about six feet at bottom four on top and five feet high. this will stop a cannon Ball, at the same time allow the men to fire on any attacking party.[30]

Continuous labor, under the supervision of Northern engineers, was employed by the men in the ranks to make their defenses as secure as possible against any conceivable enemy movement.

Many positions, particularly the forts and batteries, contained "bomb-proofs," which were deep holes fortified with logs to provide protection during an enemy artillery bombardment. At first, these underground enclosures were a novelty to those along the line, with one soldier describing "these bomb proofs, dug deep in the ground, logged up, covered over with timber, and the whole coop covered with earth and banked up."[31] Enlisted men typically had to sleep out in the trenches or rifle pits, but officers frequently made "bomb-proofs" their permanent home. When the firing started, however, all men sought out shelter of these "gopherholes," a term explained by Lieutenant Joseph Scroggs of the 5th United States Colored Troops when he wrote in his diary, "the reason of these Subteranean abodes being called gopherholes is that when a shell comes over, officers and men without distinction . . . incontinently '*go for*' them. See the *pud?*"[32] The trenches at the front were hardly a comfortable experience, but the time and effort spent creating various forms of protection from enemy fire helped to blunt some of the more dangerous aspects of a soldier's position on the main line.

No such accommodations were made for those men who were at the actual "tip of the sword" of the Union line: those who manned the rifle pits serving picket duty. Companies and regiments would typically rotate through this assignment, and those placed on picket were obliged to position themselves well in advance of the main Union line and serve as sentries who could warn of and possibly inhibit a Confederate assault. The only protection for those who served on this detail was a hastily dug hole in the ground, a rifle pit (or what modern observers would label a "foxhole"), which offered scant protection from artillery and sniper fire. There was near universal disdain for picket duty, as all soldiers who spent any time in the rifle pits realized that they were far more exposed (and expendable) than those on the main line. M. T. Haderman of the 3rd U.S. Infantry tried to offer a balanced look at life in the rifle pits in a letter back home, but still expressed the prevalent fear when he wrote, "we have a good share of picket duty to do also which I like very much though it is a dangerous business the pickets are apt to be picked off by the enemies sharp-shooters and they are pretty plenty in places."[33] The consequences for those on picket were not just death or injury by enemy fire, but also the possibility that they would be overwhelmed by an enemy attack before they had time to escape. The description of Sergeant Francis Waller of the 6th Wisconsin of one of his experiences on picket was typical: "Was on the picket line and the rebs attacked us and we have to run to keep out of Libby [Prison]. Came out three men behind."[34] Death or capture was a very real prospect for those at the extreme front of the Union position, and consequently those assigned to picket duty quickly realized that they were at much greater risk than their comrades only yards to the rear.

Beyond, and in most cases surrounding, the rifle pits was the desolate landscape between the Union and Confederate lines filled with debris and devastation that those familiar with the First World War would call "no man's land," though no Civil War–era sources referred to it as such. This was the battle space only entered by those intent on assaulting the opposing position, and as such both sides filled the terrain with anything that could impede or break up an enemy assault. Obstructions of this sort varied in abundance and sophistication, with some units merely throwing brush and unused logs be-tween the lines. Others constructed elaborate *chevaux-de-frise*, which consisted of logs with sharpened spikes hammered into them in the hope of impaling or at least delaying the attacking forces. The June 30 diary entry of Private Julius Ramsdell of the 39th Massachusetts offers a description of his unit's position while revealing some of the efforts made at obstructing no man's land:

> Work upon our breastworks which are about twelve feet thick. In front of them we cut down trees and make an abattis by ranging them in rows in front of the works, and sharpening all the stout limbs with a hatchet, so that it would be almost impossible to get through them. In front of this we felled large trees over the ground for two or three rods, so as to offer every possible impediment to the enemy if they should attempt to advance.[35]

Such obstacles presented a disturbing sight to those staring across the open space at one another, a sight made all the more troublesome by the frequent presence of the uncollected dead of both sides left between the lines. These could be either those left behind from a failed assault or pickets who had been caught by sharpshooter or artillery fire. The presence of such corpses was unnerving to those who were forced to stare at them for days on end. In writing to a friend at the end of June, Harrison Montague of the 10th New York Heavy Artillery could not help but note that the ground to his front was littered with the dead from a recent attack. "I can count 8 or 10 on a few rods square from where I sit," Montague wrote, adding that the rebels had not allowed a flag of truce to collect the dead, and as a result, "they have lain there about a week and are getting very offensive."[36] The ripped-up ground, the torn-down trees, and the frequent presence of enemy and friendly dead were the sights that welcomed Union soldiers day after day as they manned the Petersburg line.

As if this tortured landscape was not enough to wear down the psyche of those in the Union lines, the constant threat of death was enough to tax the endurance of even the most veteran soldier. The exchange of artillery fire was one of the most persistent and deadly threats to men of both sides, as solid shots of cannon fire came bounding in their direction coupled with the more dangerous shells, which would explode either in the air or on the ground and threaten the lives of all within range with searing hot pieces of shrapnel. While the Union artillerymen tended to be more cavalier in their expenditure of ammunition (especially when celebrating a Union victory in other theaters of war, such as a hundred gun salute to the capture of Savannah), Confederate fire was a pervasive component of the Petersburg experience. Soldiers frequently found reason to comment on artillery fire, especially Union artillerymen who were often directly targeted by Confederate batteries in an effort to silence their guns. "Heavy fireing to night," wrote Private Alexander Rose of the 11th New York Independent Battery of Light Artillery in his diary, "the air is full of bursting shell and three or four have come pretty close to our Camp and we do not sleep much."[37] Artillery fire was such a common element for most other soldiers that they rarely commented on it unless incoming rounds directly affected them or their comrades. Such was the case with Sergeant Samuel Clear of the 116th Pennsylvania, who noted in his diary on September 3 how "while we was eating a shell came over (a very common thing) and took a mans arm off. I got back to quarters safely."[38] The threat of enemy artillery fire was a particularly traumatic one; one historian has stressed the effect that this had on Civil War soldiers, noting "that soldiers in a passive position of helplessness—such as those subjected to artillery bombardment—feel intense terror and anxiety, and may be at greater risk for psychological breakdown."[39]

The men reacted to the artillery threat in a variety of ways, perhaps all designed to take the menace out of the amount of metal thrown in their direction on a daily basis. Some tried to find enjoyment in the artillery spectacle. After noting the tedium of trench life in his diary, Sergeant Charles Wood of the 11th New Hampshire remarked that "the only fun is to watch our mortar shells, they look like foot-balls."[40] Private John Bassett evoked more pleasant imagery in his account of an artillery barrage: "the shells and cannon balls come all round us, in front and rear, on left and right flank, in trenches and on parapet, they would spin like a top, and sing like a good fellow till they did not stop for friend or foe."[41] Others tried to see the beauty in the artillery displays, but could not always separate the threat of death before them. Captain Thomas Bennett of the 29th Connecticut marveled at how "a shell thrown from a mortar is a very pretty piece of firework, when one stands at the right distance in the proper direction; otherwise they are unpleasant in their effects."[42] For Private Henry Heisler, simple counting was his reaction to the artillery fire in the vicinity of "Fort Hell." "On Tuesday of last week the Rebs' threw 132 mortar shells in our camp but they did not hurt any one," was his account in one letter to his sister, "on last Friday they threw 129 into camp, wounding three of our men, one of them since died."[43]

These coping mechanisms aside, most men took their minds off of the possibility of becoming an artillery casualty by focusing on the power of their defenses, which did offer them at least some protection against the incoming projectiles. Captain Bennett gave the impression of confidence when he stated in a letter, "They [Confederates] throw a great many shells at us but we don't mind them much as we have bomb-proofs to get into. The men on guard sing out 'shot,' or 'shell,' and if it is shell we all dodge into our holes like so many rats. They have not hit any of our men with shell."[44] However, even the elaborate defensive network could not always defend against the threat of death from above, as bombproofs often could not withstand a direct hit from artillery, especially the large mortar projectiles. This particular hazard was stressed by Colonel Edward Hastings Ripley of the 9th Vermont when he wrote in a letter to his mother how *"we have been almost constantly under mortar shelling, the most villainous kind, as they come straight down from the sky and* its no use trying to get behind anything for protection as you do for other shells."[45] Major Charles Chipman, serving in the Headquarters of the 14th New York Artillery, attempted to evaluate the chances of being hit by mortar fire in a July 25 letter home, writing that, despite the wounding of eight men by a shell the day before, "they don't do very much damage usually." Chipman went on to explain that, while mortar shells were not normally a threat, "breastworks are not much protection if they happen to strike just right." Breastworks were obviously not much protection for Major Chipman; two weeks later he was killed by a shell fragment along the Petersburg lines.[46]

Equally as random and ubiquitous as artillery projectiles was enemy rifle fire, which made exposing any part of one's body a dangerous if not lethal risk. This fire could be from any Confederate soldiers along the opposing lines or in the enemy rifle pits, often never more than a "pistol shot" away. The most accurate fire came from sharpshooters armed with rifles who would position themselves in a protected location and patiently wait for a target. "The enemies sharp-shooters claim everybody that exposes himself," was Sergeant Wood's succinct description in his diary.[47] The consequences of such gunfire could be more brutal than those of artillery, since, unlike with the loud report of incoming shells, death or wounding from a sharpshooter came without warning. "Sometimes they put balls through our loop holes and no doubt we do the same to them," wrote Sergeant A. H. Sanger of the 24th Massachusetts in a letter to his parents, "altogether our men keep pretty well covered and wary of Reb shots. Yet once in a while a man gets hit. One of co. A was shot through the bowels. He died in a few minutes. And yesterday a copl. of co. D was shot through the head."[48] Upper torso and head wounds such as that of the Company D corporal were the most common, since these were the most exposed parts of a soldier's body when he was standing or sitting in a trench or rifle pit. The threat from this accurate rifle fire kept nerves on edge, as the constant threat of unexpected death to anyone at any point of the line wore down the ability of men to cope. Soon, many were expressing the fears of Private John Haley of the 17th Maine when he confided his "indefinable dread" to his diary on June 20, "nothing for excitement except that a few men were picked off by sharpshooters. A feeling prevails that sooner or later this experience will befall us all."[49] This fatalistic view of the sharpshooter threat bore heavily on the men in the line as they struggled to survive.

Perhaps most telling of the threat posed by rifle fire is the story of a Union sharpshooter, Private Daniel Sawtelle of the 8th Maine. In early July, Sawtelle voluntarily transferred from his regiment and joined a unit of sharpshooters with the 1st Division of the 18th Corps. Sawtelle joined the sharpshooters to escape the everyday drudgery of life in the trenches, and his new position did indeed allow an escape from the typical experience of most Union soldiers. "Our duty was to go into the trenches every other day and pick off all we could of the enemy," Sawtelle recalled in his memoirs nearly fifty years later; "we had no guard duty nor fatigue duty. As long as we behaved and did our duty, we had a pleasant job in some ways though dangerous."[50] Sawtelle achieved this independence by becoming one of the most despised figures on the Petersburg battlefield; soldiers on both sides decried the actions of the sharpshooters, with one expressing his "disgust" with them.[51] His daily life involved primarily waiting; patiently looking for an enemy to expose himself where he could be targeted by Sawtelle and his comrades: "We never fired without a mark, and we could always find one. We often fired a hundred rounds in one day and seldom less than forty."[52] His willingness to serve in this capacity grew out of the Petersburg experience and the Overland campaign, which preceded it. Sawtelle's compunction about shooting men in one of the closest examples to cold blood on the battlefield had been eradicated through long weeks of campaigning: "As to sharpshooting the Rebs, we had been shot at so much and had had comrades shot down at our sides so often that we had come to have no more feeling or sentiment in regard to the matter than as if they had been wild animals."[53] For every Private Sawtelle, there was a Confederate sharpshooter only yards away perfectly willing to target the "animals" in the Union lines, and their continual fire kept Northern men in a state of permanent aggravation.

Despite the static nature of the trench lines surrounding Petersburg, assaults on the scale of the Overland campaign occasionally punctuated the daily sniper and artillery exchanges that characterized the fighting around the city. These battles, although infrequent, were another threat to the lives of Union soldiers and a reminder of how much worse Civil War combat could be. As the summer of 1864 unfolded, the Army of the Potomac, with the support of General Benjamin Butler's Army of the James, continued their investment of Petersburg with the aim of pinching off the city from its supply lines. Four rail lines linking into the rail network of the Confederacy merged at Petersburg to form the Richmond & Petersburg line, which ran twenty miles north into the capital. Two of the four rail lines, the City Point and the Norfolk & Petersburg, fell into Union hands in the June assaults east of the city. To capture the city and force the Army of Northern Virginia out into the open, Grant needed to either break their defensive lines or seize the remaining railroads to fully isolate Petersburg from its supply lines. The repeated movements and assaults of the Overland campaign had demonstrated the folly of the former, so Grant turned to the latter as the most promising alternative. For nine months, Grant would utilize various movements to either sweep his forces toward the western railroads, the Weldon and Southside lines, or strike at Confederate defenses north of the James protecting the Richmond & Petersburg line (see Map 2). Unfortunately, these movements would be repeatedly and bloodily stymied and Grant's progress would remain minimal until the fall.

While there were many such engagements over the course of the Petersburg campaign as Grant continued extending his lines around Lee's left flank in the Deep Bottom region and the Confederate right flank near the Weldon Railroad line, one of the earliest and most well known involved the assault on the "Crater" on the morning of July 30, 1864. Throughout July, Pennsylvania soldiers from Ambrose Burnside's 9th Corps dug a five-hundred-foot mine beneath a salient in the Confederate trench lines in front of Petersburg. After stuffing the chamber beneath the Confederate position with kegs containing thousands of pounds of black powder, they lit the fuse on the morning of July 30. The

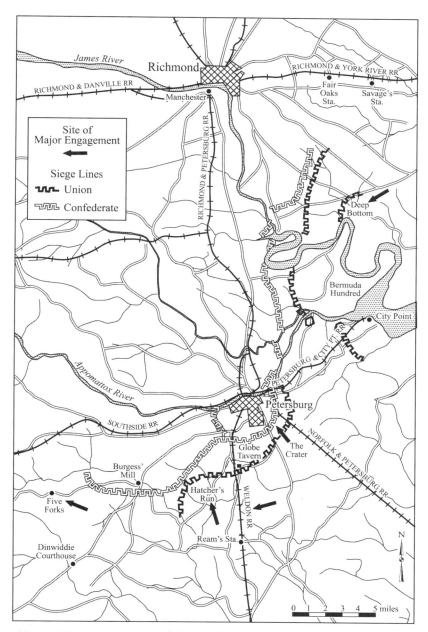

James River

Richmond

RICHMOND & YORK RIVER RR

RICHMOND & DANVILLE RR

Manchester

Fair
Oaks
Sta.

Savage's
Sta.

Site of
Major Engagement

Siege Lines

Union

Confederate

RICHMOND & PETERSBURG RR

Deep
Bottom

Bermuda
Hundred

City Point

Appomattox River

PETERSBURG & CITY PT. RR

Petersburg

SOUTHSIDE RR

Globe
Tavern

The
Crater

NORFOLK & PETERSBURG RR

Burgess'
Mill

Hatcher's
Run

WELDON RR

Five
Forks

Dinwiddie
Courthouse

Ream's Sta.

N

0 1 2 3 4 5 miles

Map 2. Major Engagements of the Petersburg Campaign, June 1864–April 1865

resulting explosion breached the Confederate lines and inaugurated a morning of combat that was plagued by poor command and organization on the Union side. The Union assaults failed, and the resulting bloodshed inflicted approximately four thousand additional casualties on the Army of the Potomac.[54] The battle's outcome quickly became infamous, as accusations of incompetence and intoxication within the Federal officer corps would carry on long after the battle through a court of inquiry that was tasked with investigating the actions (and inactions) of Burnside and his subordinates on July 30.[55] While a failure, the Crater did reveal that the Union command had achieved a healthy level of respect for the power of Confederate entrenchments and was seeking alternative ways of achieving a breakthrough at Petersburg. Unfortunately, for those in the ranks the attack provided yet another demoralizing setback in the conduct of the war.

TABLE 3. Casualties Sustained by the Army of the Potomac during the Petersburg Campaign, June 15, 1864–April 2, 1865

Location and Date	Killed in Action	Wounded in Action	Missing in Action	Total
Initial Assaults, June 15–19, 1864	1,298	7,474	1,814	10,586
Petersburg Trenches, June 20–30, 1864	112	506	800	1,418
Weldon Railroad Assaults, June 22–23, 1864	694	2,494	2,217	5,405
Petersburg Trenches, July 1–31, 1864 (excluding Crater)	419	2,076	1,200	3,695
The Crater, July 30, 1864	419	1,679	1,910	4,008
Petersburg Trenches, August 1–31, 1864 (excluding Deep Bottom and Weldon)	87	484	n/a	571
Deep Bottom, Weldon Railroad, and Ream's Station, August 14–25, 1864	739	3,456	6,345	10,540
Petersburg Trenches, September 1–October 30, 1864	170	822	812	1,804
New Market Heights and Preble's Farm, September 30–October 1, 1864	541	2,817	1,756	5,114

TABLE 3 (*continued*)

Location and Date	Killed in Action	Wounded in Action	Missing in Action	Total
Hatcher's Run and Fair Oaks, October 27–28, 1864	276	1,830	1,099	3,205
Hatcher's Run, February 5–7, 1865	232	1,062	186	1,480
Fort Steadman and Petersburg Trenches, March 25, 1865	171	1,201	715	2,087
Fall of Petersburg, April 2, 1865	296	2,565	500	3,361
TOTAL	5,454	28,466	19,354	53,274

Source: Frederick Phisterer, *Statistical Record of the Armies of the United States* (New York: Charles Scribner's Sons, 1883), 217–218.

The failed Crater assault prompted comments from both participants and observers similar to those heard during the Overland campaign. Private Austin Kendall, serving in the 117th New York, expressed amazement at the sounds that greeted him on the day of the battle, reporting in a letter to friends that "the cannonading Saturday [the 30th] in front of Petersburg was the heaviest I ever heard."[56] The resulting defeat for Union forces only reinforced the lingering resentment of the high command expressed by the enlisted men during the Overland campaign. After his unit participated in one of the assaults near Deep Bottom that accompanied the Crater attack, Corporal James Beard of the 142nd New York remarked, "I dont think much of the General ship I see. . . . i don't wish to be any longer in the army of the Potomac for the[y] have don a great deal of hard fighten and it has never amounted to much."[57] Whenever the daily possibility of death in the trenches threatened to overwhelm them, Union soldiers could imagine the Overland campaign or battles like the Crater and remember that the protection of the trenches was a lesser evil to what had come before.

While few aspects of the Petersburg campaign compared to the sustained bloodletting of the Overland experience, the occasional battle, combined with the near constant rifle and artillery fire between the trench lines, continued to inflict significant casualties on the Army of the Potomac. As Table 3 demonstrates, the Federal forces surrounding Petersburg suffered more than fifty thousand casualties over the course of the campaign, primarily due to operations such as the Crater and the attacks in the Deep Bottom and Weldon Railroad sectors. This total almost equals the number of casualties sustained in the Overland campaign, but it is important to highlight the distinctions. First, the battles of May and June were fought in such close succession that the casualties piled up much more rapidly than the slow hemorrhage of the nine months of operations around Petersburg. Second, fifty thousand casualties for the Petersburg campaign is a deceptive figure, since it does not take into account the daily loss of men along the line. After October 1864, there is no army record for the loss of men to sniper and artillery fire in the trenches, an attritional factor that would have steadily increased the casualty figures. If the last recorded number of daily trench losses for September and October is taken as representative for the remainder of the campaign, then it is likely that the Army of the Potomac was losing as many as nine hundred men a month to enemy action over the winter of 1864–1865. This would add another 4,500 casualties for the last five months of the siege, and would put the final cost of the campaign closer to 58,000 men killed, wounded, and missing. Such numbers demonstrate that, while rarely reaching the intensity of such battles as Spotsylvania and Cold Harbor, the Petersburg trenches and the operations associated with them were still a very hazardous environment.

Along with the ubiquitous threat of immediate death or wounding within the Union lines, soldiers in the trenches had to face the slightly lesser threat of living in a setting inhospitable to men at war. The Virginia weather that greeted Union soldiers upon their arrival at Petersburg created an additional burden on those in the trenches. An oppressive summertime heat quickly descended upon the Virginia countryside, and Union soldiers, many of whom were from northern, milder climates, found it difficult to cope. As Boston native Horatio Soule wrote in his diary in June, "hot all day, it seems I never knew it so hot."[58] Late June and early July, just when Union men were settling in for the new campaign, appeared to be the worst heat wave, as nearly every soldier, with little else to report, noted in their diaries and letters the effects of the sun. "*Hot, Hoter, Hottest.* Today has been the hottest day of the season, uncomfortably warm," was the opening notation of Sergeant Austin Stearns of the 13th Massachusetts in his postwar recollections of June 23.[59] Captain Elisha Hunt Rhodes of the 2nd Rhode Island managed to find a shady spot on

July 2 to record with some amazement that "the thermometer stands today at 124, and the men are suffering severely."[60] The heat was a difficult burden for these men, who spent nearly their entire day out in the sun working hard labor to improve their defensives while wearing heavy uniforms designed with little thought given to summertime comfort.

The effects of the sun were threatening, if not deadly, to those forced to expose themselves to the heat. With the sun came drought, and men found supplies of freshwater increasingly difficult to obtain; thirst became the order of the day for those at work or on guard along the line. "The weather is hot—a great drought, water scarce, and vegetation burnt up," reported Colonel Robert McAllister, temporarily in command of a brigade in the Second Corps, in a letter to his wife on June 24, continuing with some dismay, "we are all worn down with our fighting and hard work. The like of it was never known."[61] Coupled with the heat and thirst, the dry weather brought dust, which when kicked up by soldiers on the march could prove especially troublesome to anyone nearby. The same day that Colonel McAllister noted the deteriorating conditions caused by the heat, the 22nd Massachusetts moved into position near Petersburg after a long march through the dust. At the conclusion of the march, a soldier in that unit could not help but comment, "the suffering which we endured from our dry, dusty, parched throats was inconceivable agony. . . . I never witnessed such suffering on the march; no water then, nor now; we need rain dreadfully."[62] Unfortunately, the heat would last through July and well into August, although periodic rain showers would provide a temporary relief from the harsh temperatures. "The weather is intensely hot & dry. A sprinkle last night which lasted five minutes is the only rain we have had for over three weeks," reported Veteran Volunteer George Tate of the 120th New York in late June, "we breath dust & the smoke of gunpowder. Water is very scarce in this section."[63] Perhaps Sharpshooter Sawtelle was the most astute at calculating the effects of the heat on the men when he noted in a letter on July 10, "this laying in the sun and dirt uses up as many of our men as the enemy's bullets."[64] While rarely fatal, sunstroke and heat exhaustion were considerable factors affecting the morale and physical strength of those in the trenches. In the early stages of the Petersburg campaign, when the men were already weakened from their exertions in the battles and marches of the Overland campaign, they were particularly vulnerable to being overwhelmed by the heat.

As the campaign progressed, relief from the heat arrived in the form of milder temperatures, but was soon replaced by the bitter cold and wind of a Virginia winter. While soldiers took steps to protect themselves from the elements by establishing permanent quarters behind the lines in the winter months, these shelters were rather roughly constructed and could not entirely protect the men from falling temperatures. With the cold came wet weather that only added to a soldier's discomfort. Even with access to comfortable quarters, the call of duty frequently pulled men away from the warm glow of the campfire to man the trench line or serve on picket. This latter duty was held liable by Private John Foote of the 117th New York when he woke up on the morning of November 26 with a strong fever and concluded, "it was brought on by standing on picket 24 hours through a cold rain storm & with wet feet."[65] Daily life along the Petersburg line could be cold and uncomfortable during the winter months, but it was often made worse for some units when they were called away from their quarters to play a part in one of Grant's operations to flank and cut off Lee from his railroad supply lines. One such movement was the Hatcher's Run (also known as Dabney's Mills) operation of February 5–7, 1865, where elements of the Second and Fifth Corps attempted to move around Lee's right flank and seize Confederate supply wagons in that area but were met by Confederate defenders along with hostile weather. Newly promoted Lieutenant Colonel Elisha Hunt Rhodes endured this campaign with the rest of the 2nd Rhode Island and found the conditions nearly unbearable. In the middle of the operation, he noted in his diary that "this morning when I awoke I found as did all the troops that I was covered with snow and ice. It had snowed during the night and then turned to rain which froze as it fell. I never felt more uncomfortable in my life."[66] With such exposure to the elements, the winter months proved to be just as large an obstacle to Union soldiers as the burning sun of the summertime.

While the winter months generally were a time of increased precipitation, excessive rain and the mud that it created could be a nuisance at any time of the year. The long drought of June and early July was broken by August, and the result, as noted by Sergeant Samuel Clear of the 116th Pennsylvania, was that "the rain falls increasingly and mud, Oh! Geminee."[67] Water and mud were particular problems in the trenches and rifle pits, which collected the moisture and made life difficult if not unbearable for those forced to remain inside to prevent being targeted by enemy fire. As early as July, downpours were proving to be a nuisance for those in the trenches, with Private Charles Edgerly of the 11th New Hampshire waking up in a puddle on July 24 and Major Chipman noting the next day that "it rained hard all night Our trenches were filled with water our men were obliged to stand in water nearly up to their knees all night."[68] As any veteran of the First World War would confirm, mud and moisture are prevalent aspects of the trench experience, and the effects can be more than just discomfort. Physical symptoms can manifest once the flesh is exposed to such damp conditions for an extended period of time. Private John Haley of the 17th Maine exposed the full range of harmful effects prompted by life in a muddy trench when he noted in his diary on September 6, "rainy and cool. . . . In rainy weather the water in the saps lies three to twelve inches deep, and mud is everywhere. These narrow trenches act as sewers and receive all the surface water, turning our hardtack into sodden dough and assisting the onset of rheumatism. Our coffee is diluted, our sugar and salt dissolved, and our pork flabby from the drenching."[69] Regardless of the weather, dampness and mud were as troublesome to those on the front lines as the heat during the summer and cold of winter. Yet while cool shade could often be found in July and a warm campfire found in January, there was little that the men could to do to escape the mire of a wet trench.

The trenches often were an inhospitable environment for man, but all sorts of small pests found the moist, dirty conditions appealing for setting up residence. Union soldiers were no strangers to fleas, mosquitoes, rats, and other pests, but the confined spaces and close proximity between men made the trenches a perfect breeding ground for all sorts of creatures that would feed off of the waste and flesh of any nearby human. Pests such as these were primarily a summer and fall irritation, but during these times they could make a soldier's stay along the line nearly unbearable. "I understand that you collect bugs," wrote Captain Bennett of the 29th Connecticut to a friend in mid-September, "if you were only to search our bomb-proof you would find it hard to get pins enough to stick them all on."[70] The pests most frequently cited by soldiers were flies, which would swarm toward a battlefield to feed on the human waste and decay that could be found in abundance in or near the trenches. Union soldiers could only marvel at their new neighbors and try to cope with them as well as they were able. Private Henry Metzger of the 184th

Pennsylvania expressed his exasperation with the situation when he wrote to his sister, "I wish you was here to see the number of flys we have, you know nothing about them at home . . . they are a great pester, one can hardly do anything for them."[71] Lieutenant John Brincklé of the 5th United States Artillery noted the great menagerie of pests one day in July: "The fly plague has commenced. Preparatory to pitching a tent, we killed a Copperhead & a lizzard immediately took possession of my bed. I always find a half dozen huge beetles sleeping with me in the morning, & have to empty the same number out of my boots." Brincklé would try to look on the bright side of things, explaining to his brother, "As long as they do not evince any carniverous propensities, I can stand it."[72]

Unfortunately, apart from a healthy fear of snakes, soldiers never made the connection that their very health was threatened by the presence of so many of these creatures, which could transfer lethal diseases by their bite. Living in the company of these pests, coupled with an unsanitary lifestyle in a climate that was foreign to most Northern soldiers, contributed to the spread of various maladies within the ranks. One of the most prevalent contagions, and unfortunately among the deadliest for Civil War soldiers, was diarrhea. The climate of the Virginia tidewater, along with the unsanitary conditions in which food was prepared, contributed to the spread of various intestinal problems within the Army of the Potomac. For some, diarrhea was merely a discomfort, but for many it could prove incapacitating. "I am not feeling real well," noted Lieutenant Samuel Cormany of the 16th Pennsylvania Cavalry in September, "this diarhea attacking me so often and so severely keeps me too weak for the satisfactory performance of my many duties."[73] Unbeknownst to soldiers like Cormany, diarrhea was a symptom of dysentery, a much more dangerous disease that took many lives throughout the war.[74] Almost as common in the testimony of soldiers was the "fever," which was the catch-all term to describe most of the ailments afflicting soldiers on the line. As with diarrhea, a high fever was a symptom of the more lethal illnesses malaria and typhoid, which were another frequent cause of non-battle mortality during the siege.[75] Life in the trenches contributed to all of these disorders, and the physical discomfort created by trench conditions even had a name: the "ground itch." As one Massachusetts soldier reported, "I am covered with the 'ground itch'. . . . It is very troublesome night times, and irritates my flesh almost beyond endurance."[76]

While not always a threat to the life of Union soldiers, the "itch" made their existence all the more difficult.

———

Shortly after his arrival with the 57th Massachusetts at Petersburg, First Lieutenant John Cook composed his own depiction of life in the trench lines of the Army of the Potomac. While there is no date on the letter composed by this 22-year-old Boston native, it likely was written prior to July 15; on that date, Cook would receive a bullet wound to the abdomen that would put him in the hospital for months and leave him to "recover slowly and imperfectly, if at all," according to one surgeon's report.[77] In his letter from the Petersburg lines, Cook recounted the futile nature of fighting along his point of the line: "There is scarcely 15 minutes during 24 hours but that shell are dropping in the fort on the enemy's right. Our artillery will tear the works to pieces in the daytime, and at night they (the rebels) will build it up again." He marveled at some aspects of the warfare around him, explaining that "At night picket duty is pleasant, as out there one can see the shells from both mortars and artillery that are constantly passing between our lines." While he tried to focus on the positive elements of the brutal environment around him, he could not help commenting on how the fighting was affecting him and his comrades. "You cannot realize the soldier's life, because you cannot believe that human nature can endure what soldiers do," Cook concluded in his review of Petersburg life. "You do not realize the horrors of war, because you do not believe that men can become so hardened as regards these dreadful scenes as are every-day business."[78]

Every day and night in the trenches Union troops faced a variety of dangers, ranging from the lice crawling on their flesh to the enemy only yards away intent on killing them. The trench environment was one that could be equally dull and life-threatening. The static nature of the campaign theoretically allowed for an improvement in the lifestyle of those surrounding Petersburg; being in one position would allow for a more secure line of supply that could make life more bearable for those at the front. However, it would take time for the Union logistical apparatus to be established, and the close proximity of the enemy lines made notions of "comfort" dubious at best. The conditions before them were horrific, and while they may not have equaled or surpassed those in evidence fifty years later on the fields of France and Belgium, they were enough to tax the ability of the American citizen soldiers who experienced them. Coming off of the perils and physical hardships of the Overland campaign, these men were particularly vulnerable to the continued threats to their well-being and morale. With such factors at work within the Army of the Potomac threatening to destroy those who composed its fighting force, it becomes necessary to understand what counterbalances were utilized by soldiers to maintain their morale and their lives in the face of trench warfare.

FIGURE 1. Union breastworks in the Wilderness, 1864.
Courtesy of the Library of Congress.

FIGURE 2. Dead Union soldiers being buried at Fredericksburg following the Wilderness, May 1864. Courtesy of the National Archives.

FIGURE 3. Union troops occupying breastworks on the north bank of the
North Anna River, May 1864. Courtesy of the Library of Congress.

FIGURE 4. Union soldiers making coffee along the Petersburg lines, 1864.
Courtesy of the Library of Congress.

FIGURE 5. Union soldiers constructing a bombproof shelter at Petersburg, August 1864. Courtesy of the Library of Congress.

FIGURE 6. Union *chevaux-de-frise* and breastworks at Fort Sedgwick along the Petersburg lines, 1865. Courtesy of the Library of Congress.

FIGURE 7. Union soldiers in front of their wooden winter quarters.
Courtesy of the National Archives.

FIGURE 8. Supplies being landed at City Point, Virginia.
Courtesy of the National Archives.

FIGURE 9. Nurses and officers of the U.S. Sanitary Commission at
Fredericksburg, 1864. Courtesy of the Library of Congress.

FIGURE 10. Union soldiers at rest after drill, Petersburg, Virginia.
Courtesy of the National Archives.

FIGURE 11. Soldiers boxing in camp at Petersburg.
Courtesy of the Library of Congress.

FIGURE 12. Dead Confederates in the trenches of Fort Mahone at Petersburg, April 3, 1865. Courtesy of the Library of Congress.

5

"Great Is the Shovel and Spade"

ADAPTATION TO TRENCH LIFE

I would as soon dig the rebels out as to fight them.
—Lieutenant Elisha Hunt Rhodes, 2nd Rhode Island Infantry

The recollections of Private Robert Ekin McBride, who served with the 11th Pennsylvania throughout the Petersburg campaign, are but one example of a soldier looking back on his time in the Army of the Potomac and trying to make sense of how he was transformed by the war. McBride was a farmer from Butler County, Pennsylvania, whose first experiences with combat were the Overland and Petersburg campaigns; he had only enlisted the previous December at the age of seventeen. After several close escapes in the battles of May and June (including one where he wandered behind Confederate lines for three days before making it back to his unit), McBride's introduction to life at Petersburg provoked much commentary even seventeen years later as he wrote his memoirs. Looking back, he seemed shocked at the change that had occurred within him and his comrades that summer in the Petersburg trenches:

> It is remarkable how indifferent men become to danger under such circumstances. While myself and another soldier were engaged in washing some clothes one day, at a little stream to the right of this place, a bullet passed within a foot of our heads. The only effect was to turn our conversation to the subject of the range of rifles. It would naturally be supposed that, under such constant danger of death or wounds, men would be in continual dread of what *might* happen. As a rule, it is quite otherwise. Feelings of dread and uneasiness gradually give way to a sense of comparative security. Coming under fire for the first time, a man usually feels as if he were about as large as a good-sized barn, and consequently

very likely to take in all the balls, shells, grape, and canister, and such odds and ends, coming in his direction. After a while he begins to realize that he is not so large, after all, and frequent and continued experience confirms him in the view.[1]

Whether they realized it at the time or understood it years later like Private McBride, the horrors of everyday life at Petersburg gradually lost their hold over those Union soldiers who lived day after day in the trenches amidst the filth, vermin, and carnage. While such hardening to the terrible conditions could prove an asset to functioning in a combat environment, it could also prove as detrimental to a soldier's morale as the violence surrounding him and the inexplicable decisions of his general officers.

Despite these ongoing challenges to the Union combat soldier, the Army of the Potomac did not disintegrate during the Petersburg campaign. While desertion increased and the men faced new threats in the trenches, the army kept its cohesion and soldier morale actually began to improve relatively quickly. To understand how the Army of the Potomac kept itself together in the weeks and months following the Overland campaign, one must look to how the men first reacted to and coped with the conditions that they faced upon their arrival at Petersburg in mid-June 1864. It is here that one sees how Union soldiers originally welcomed life in the trenches for the break that it offered them from the relentless, high-intensity battles of the previous six weeks. The men recognized the protection that the elaborate breastworks around Petersburg offered them, and their near constant labor on these entrenchments provided ever-increasing benefits to their personal security. The end of active campaigning combined with the men's ability to construct their own defensive positions to create an increased feeling of independence on the battlefield. No longer did these men consider themselves pawns of their commanders as they had at the end of the Overland campaign; rather, they were once again active participants in a war against the rebellion. These emerging feelings would ultimately prove useful as their experience in the deadly, unrelenting environment of the Petersburg trenches continued into the fall and winter months.

———

"This war is a very uncertain kind of work," noted Private Allen Landis of the 116th Pennsylvania midway through the Overland campaign, "but we have become accustomed to it and take it cooly."[2] Despite the physically troubling conditions in which they lived, the ever-present enemy fire, the extremes of hot and cold, and the various pests that joined them in their trenches, soldiers gradually grew accustomed to the deadly, uncomfortable environment that surrounded them. This desensitization process has been recorded in nearly every war, where men become relatively immune to the fear and anxiety that first greeted them when exposed to combat conditions.[3] This was certainly the case along the Union side of the Petersburg line, as the sound of gunfire and the imminent threat of death gradually lost its hold over the nerves of the soldiers in the trenches. This deadening of fear and emotion had much to do with the transformation that occurred during the Overland campaign. While there were certainly major battles at Petersburg, they were scattered across the nine months of the campaign, and few could compare with the savagery of the Bloody Angle at Spotsylvania. Thus, they added little shock value for Union soldiers and usually allowed them ample time to recover between engagements. Of greater threat was the consistency of low-level violence in the trenches.

Yet even the trenches soon came to lose their effect on the men as they dwelt in them day after day. Desensitization grew as the Petersburg campaign commenced, when many soldiers noticed the growing apathy to the terrors around them and frequently commented on how the daily threats to their life no longer concerned them. As early as June 11, 1864, as his 10th Massachusetts regiment approached Petersburg, Second Lieutenant Charles Brewster reached the grim conclusion in a letter how "these are miserable long dreary days for even the bullets now fail to furnish cause for attention or a remark as they go singing by our ears."[4] The violence around them became just another part of the background, as shown by First Lieutenant Harrison Montague of the 10th New York Heavy Artillery, who commented to a friend, "would you believe that we get so used to the picket firing that is constantly going on that we don't hear it no more than you hear your clock tick?"[5] Private Charles White, a veteran volunteer with the 21st Massachusetts, somehow found music in the continual sound of weapon discharges: "There is a not a minute, day or night, but what we hear the cannon's roar or the rifle's crack. But we don't mind it much. We have gotten used to it. It is our trade, 'tis music to us. We go to sleep to it, we wake to it; but I cannot say we like it."[6]

In other cases, soldier indifference toward risk went in a different direction, with some able to find humor in the violence that surrounded them. The experience of Private Edward Wightman and his comrades in the 3rd New York as they fled from a sharpshooter did not create terror, but instead prompted the comment, "we are so used to that kind of fun now . . . that the closest shots only provoke a laugh."[7] Major Howard Malcolm Smith and the men of the 19th New York Cavalry may not have found humor in their surroundings, but Smith still claimed that they were all very positive in July: "We are a happy set generally, notwithstanding our hardships and scenes of death and horror. We become hardened to such things and have learned to laugh and joke when Death is standing at our elbow."[8] As Smith notes, all of this contributed to loosening the fear of death; so much so that the men could almost disregard the loss of those around them. As Corporal James Beard of the 142nd New York noted in July, "a shell from the rebel Mortar by chance may drop nere us but that is a common thing here and would give no alarm should it kill half a dozen."[9] Such hardening may have been necessary for the men to function in a deadly environment, but one sees in such comments the elements of a dangerous callousness toward the loss of human life.

The opening of the Petersburg campaign brought dangerous new challenges for the men in the ranks that in some cases furthered their growing desensitization, but it also brought a period of inactivity that allowed the men to pause and reflect on things. Not only were they exposed to imminent death twenty-four hours a day, but now they had almost all of that time to dwell on their situation and their role in the campaign along with the war itself. Writing to his wife in July, Theodore Lyman, a member of Meade's staff, sorrowfully proclaimed, "it seems sometimes sort of lonely and hopeless, sitting here in the dust by Petersburg, and hearing nothing except now and then a cannon in the distance."[10] Others who felt this loneliness longed for home, filling their letters not with details of their daily life, but with questions for their loved ones regarding the situation in their hometowns. One soldier speculated that these feelings manifested themselves in a physical sense. Commenting on the hospitalization of his tent mate in the 39th New Jersey in a letter to his uncle, Private George Chandler remarked that his comrade "contracted the worst possible disease that a person can get in the army that is homesickness. It may sound strange to you folks at home to hear of such a disease but hundreds die of it."[11] While it is unlikely that homesickness actually killed many within the

Army of the Potomac, the dreariness of life for those surrounding Petersburg was a real threat to the already beleaguered men.

Apart from homesickness, an additional outgrowth of the hardening process was a growing sense of tedium. The lack of an emotional charge brought by the threat of death joined with the monotony of daily life in an army at a standstill to create a strong sense of boredom among the men on the line. Besides watching for enemy movements or assaults and the periodic work on their entrenchments, soldiers had little with which to occupy their time in the trenches, a factor that few commented on directly. Yet even a superficial examination of the diaries and letters of Union soldiers reveals that they were suffering from the effects of tediousness. "Same old story. Nothing going on," was the only entry in the diary of Sergeant Francis Waller of the 6th Wisconsin for October 21, reflecting how little he had to entertain himself if he could not find anything around him to report in his journal.[12] Waller's story was typical, as the diary entries of soldiers grew shorter once they found themselves writing the same barren descriptions of trench life over and over again. During the Overland campaign, the journal entries of Sergeant Samuel Clear of the 116th Pennsylvania included lengthy descriptions of the battles and maneuvers involved. By the end of the summer, after more than two months in the trenches, the typical entry from Sergeant Clear was usually one sentence or a fragment, along the lines of his September 1 comment: "To day no change from usual routine of camp life."[13]

Paradoxically, the diary entries of some soldiers grew longer over the course of the siege, as men filled their journals with the minutiae of life along the line. With nothing but time on their hands, men like Corporal William Ray of the 7th Wisconsin filled their diaries with camp rumors, news from home, descriptions of their work on fortifications, and even lengthy treatments on what they ate each day, but after doing so ended their entries with comments like "things around here are about the same."[14] Others inserted into their diaries and letters pleas for some sort of activity to occur in order to relieve the boredom around them. As Captain Thomas Bennett of the 29th Connecticut noted toward the end of the summer, "I begin to get very tired of this monotony and hope something may occur to break it very soon. I don't much care what it may be."[15] Major Smith of the 19th New York Cavalry agreed, writing, "we are all getting tired of this kind of life and anxious to be back at work again. You cannot imagine how irksome it is lying in camp with nothing to do."[16] Some men attempted to alleviate their boredom by becoming more verbose in their diaries and correspondence, while others prayed for something to happen, but most did not bother to comment on their continuing struggle against ennui.

Those who did comment in detail on the dreariness of their daily lives offer a glimpse into the consequences of boredom for the average Union soldier on the front line. Some attempted to resist becoming inured to the violence around them by focusing on its prevalence as a means of passing the time, but often they failed. "The same tiresome monotony which even the bursting of our 8 in. shell cannot relieve," was the only entry for July 9 in the diary of Lieutenant Joseph Scroggs of the 5th United States Colored Troops as he dwelt upon his boredom amidst an exchange of artillery fire.[17] Others commented on how the tedium contributed to the delinquency of some soldiers, as noted by Private John Haley in his diary on August 1 when he wrote how "with nothing to do the hours drag wearily. Time is divided into small portions devoted to eating and sleeping; some prefer gambling."[18] Obviously, vice proved quite a temptation for those men with nothing else to engage their time. Drinking was a popular escape for some such as Captain Albert Rogall of the 29th United States Colored Troops, who frequently commented on his drinking habits in his journal. Rogall rather conspicuously noted on the day that his unit participated in the attack on the Crater that the "day was the hottest in whole summer, curious that I could stand it, drank great deal whiskey with quinine."[19] The most telling comment on the effects of boredom comes from Sharpshooter Sawtelle, who, despite his change of vocation from infantry to the sharpshooters, still found himself succumbing to the tedium that pervaded trench life. Toward the end of the campaign, Sawtelle noticed how lazy he had become living the day-to-day existence along the line, and concluded that his boredom was the cause of his laziness: "The less I have to do the less I want to do."[20] Sawtelle realized that the languor among the men could be a vicious cycle that seriously deteriorated their ability to continue the siege, let alone renew active operations.

While desensitization and boredom created a corrosive effect for men in the Army of the Potomac during the summer of 1864, they also contributed to a surprising reawakening of the independence of the American citizen soldier and a rehabilitation of the morale that had plummeted during the

Overland campaign. As one historian has demonstrated, prior to the Civil War the American soldier firmly believed "in his right to exercise some form of independence or individualism as a free citizen of the Republic," a belief that reached back to the revolutionary ancestors who were still a fresh memory among those serving in the years leading up to the Civil War.[21] They resisted military discipline, not because they were uneducated or unruly by nature, but because they felt that their "service was not a total surrender of the right of self-governance, but was, instead, a voluntary, negotiated, and temporary abjuration of that right."[22] Through such means as the use of officer elections, unit constitutions, and petitions to their commanders, "the vast majority of volunteers celebrated their democratic traditions."[23] Such a feeling of equality with their officers was clearly present at Petersburg, as evidenced by Sergeant Samuel Cormany of the 16th Pennsylvania Cavalry, who noted in his diary after a social function attended by some general officers, "it was a truly pleasant hour to be thus associated with the men away above us in rank and yet in many ways simply our equals! Our Comrades! and to find we had so many things in common, while all the while we were ever ready to lift our hats and receive orders from them and obey."[24]

The tight discipline exerted over the Army of the Potomac during the McClellan period, coupled with the stresses of combat, had succeeded in reducing feelings of citizen soldier independence by the summer of 1864.[25] However, this latent feeling reemerged as the men struggled with the trench experience beginning in June of that year. The Overland campaign had convinced these men that their commanding officers did not have all the answers, and signs of rebellious behavior at the end of the campaign lingered into the beginning of the Petersburg operations while affecting how those in the ranks responded to the trench environment. While members of the Army of the Potomac may have been willing to passively obey orders like good republican volunteers throughout the Overland campaign, the violence of that experience reawakened within them an active desire to have a say in the way their lives were utilized on the battlefield. For the most part, military discipline continued to hold them to their service obligations, but their ability to sacrifice autonomy for their military service appears to have diminished by the start of the Petersburg campaign as the men proved more willing to question their superiors, both in private correspondence and in overt mutiny. Desensitization was a contributing factor as well, since as men grew disconnected with the terrors of the battlefield environment they commonly grew disconnected with the rest of the world around them. While this higher expression of independence could have been dangerous for the cohesion of the Army of the Potomac, conditions existed which allowed this passion for self-governance to be redirected into the productive labor that filled the daily lives of Union soldiers.

It is easy to point to the horrors of siege life and its effects on those in the trenches, but such analysis does little to explain how Northern soldiers survived such conditions and continued in their service to the Union. The key to understanding how soldiers initially adapted to, and in some cases welcomed, the siege environment lies in understanding how one of the most basic motivations of the combat soldier worked within the Army of the Potomac. As Anthony Kellett has demonstrated, there are heroes and cowards on the battlefield, but most soldiers fall within a middle paradigm: those who are "guided by a highly personal and pragmatic objective—self-preservation."[26] The ability to safeguard their own lives had been one denied to Union soldiers during the Overland campaign, and by mid-June they recognized that charging headlong in a frontal assault against enemy positions would greatly hinder their chances of surviving the campaign, let alone the war. Petersburg brought an end to the charging, if only temporarily, and the men welcomed the control that they once again exerted over their own survival. In a letter to his girlfriend back home in Woburn, Massachusetts, Sergeant George Fowle best expressed this notion when he wrote in early July, "if we can lay here during the hot weather and cut their railroads and siege them out rather than to charge and lose thousands of men, I for one shall be better satisfied."[27] Survival was the order of the day for those within the ranks of the Army of the Potomac, and rather than be horrified at the lifestyle in the trenches, Union soldiers hailed the power that trench life gave them over their own lives.

As previously demonstrated, there was no shortage of condemnation toward those in command by the end of the Overland campaign. This censure from those in the ranks did not carry over long into the Petersburg campaign, as most soldiers rapidly came to the conclusion that use of a siege strategy to reduce Petersburg and its Confederate defenders would prove much preferable to the strategy employed in May and early June, and would eventually be successful. Even after the horrors of Overland, the preponderance of evidence appears to support the assertion by historian Paddy Griffith that by 1864, "the Northern fighting man now knew in his heart that he was on the winning side."[28] Union soldiers understood that a siege would place the Confederates in a difficult position, one that would make a Northern victory all but inevitable. In an early July letter to his brother and sister, Lieutenant Colonel George Hopper spent a great deal of time discussing the casualties within his regiment over the previous weeks, but found himself asserting, "still I think grant will get the best of Lee-the north is as sure to win in the long run as the sun rises & sets & there is not much dont [doubt] about that."[29] This confidence in Union victory did not dissipate quickly, as the men continued to believe that time was a Northern ally. As late as October, four months into the campaign, men like Colonel Robert McAllister, at this point in command of a brigade in the Second Corps, seemed convinced that the small movements on Lee's flanks would bring victory. In a letter to his wife, McAllister proclaimed, "when persons talk of Grant doing nothing, it shows how little they know. Richmond will be ours. All is right."[30] Rather than be angered or horrified by a new trench environment that stretched out interminably before them during the summer of 1864, soldiers boldly predicted that trench warfare would bring about a long-awaited Union victory.

Recent battles had involved large numbers of Union soldiers being thrown against well-entrenched Confederate positions and being repulsed with heavy losses nearly every time. The men in the ranks had long ago recognized that such methods would not win the war. As demonstrated by historian Noah Andre Trudeau, the lesson was clear to those both in the higher and lower ranks that "the defensive works of the Wilderness, Spotsylvania, North Anna, and Cold Harbor had made impossible the kind of rapid marching and open-field fighting that Grant had managed so successfully at Vicksburg in 1863."[31] The Army of Northern Virginia had not stymied each and every one of Grant's turning movements due to more men, better supplies, or better morale; Lee's men had nearly always managed to utilize interior lines of movement in order to get to the right place at the right time and erect a solid system of field entrenchments capable of withstanding the inevitable Union assaults. By mid-June, Northern soldiers had seen this scenario played out roughly half a dozen times, and they could not understand why their leaders were not seeking another, hopefully more successful, way of breaking through the Confederate lines. Unfortunately, their leaders were slow learners. According to one author, Grant's actions in 1864 demonstrated that "the tactical thought of the Union general in chief frequently lagged not only behind the reality of the changed character of warfare, but also behind his own actions."[32] The men on the line, those who actually had to storm what many considered "impregnable" enemy positions, would have agreed with this analysis. They believed that a change had come on the battlefield and that their commanding officers were slow to recognize what had occurred.

This is not to suggest that all Union soldiers rejected the idea of open-field, linear combat outright. In fact, many felt quite the opposite: meeting the enemy face-to-face on the field of battle was the only way to win the war. The problem was that the Confederates refused to play along. As Private Frank Wilkeson recalled soon after the fighting around Spotsylvania ended, he and his fellow enlisted men had reached the conclusion that "the Second Corps, which we judged to number 30,000 men, could whip an equal number of Confederates in the open. At least we could try it, and a fight of that character would have been an agreeable change from assaulting earthworks."[33] What men like Wilkeson failed to recognize, however, was that this was precisely the goal of those in command: to find the enemy in an exposed position and strike them in force. Unfortunately, the Confederates had the uncanny ability of getting into position before the Union forces could, and as a result Grant and other Union commanders felt compelled to utilize massed forces in a frontal assault designed to break a hole in the enemy line that could be exploited. The consequence of this was the soldiers' perception that the frontal assault was the primary method being employed; hence the vociferous calls for a change in tactics to something more in keeping with the experience of previous battles.

While the idea of facing the Confederates out in the open proved attractive to Union soldiers, during the campaign it dawned on an increasing number of men that what was needed was a reversal of role, a situation that would place Northern soldiers safely behind entrenchments with the Confederates exposed and compelled to assume the role of the assaulting force. One sees this growing realization in its infancy as early as the Wilderness, where the back-and-forth nature of the battle allowed for several situations where Union forces defended entrenched positions. "We done the first fighting we ever done in breastworks day before yesterday," Private Henry Howell of the 124th

New York wrote in a May 8 letter to his mother, explaining to her how "the Johnnys tried to charge us out. We could not see the point though so we just let them come up close and then give it to them. Some fell some run and the rest surrendered."[34] This subtle appreciation for the power of constructed defenses only grew over time, convincing some men that open assaults were a thing of the past. Shocked by the bloody repulse at Cold Harbor, Private Haley of the 17th Maine came to the conclusion in his diary that "We were tired of charging earthworks . . . It is well known that *one* man behind works is as good as *three* outside the works."[35] Perhaps no soldier was as perceptive on this issue as Lieutenant Theodore Vaill, whose 2nd Connecticut Heavy Artillery regiment had lost its "green" status in early June when it was badly cut up during the assault at Cold Harbor. "Lee could be whipped to death in open fight, or if the positions of the two armies were exchanged," Vaill stated in a letter to his siblings on June 21, adding somberly, "but modern warfare is largely made up of *intrenching, fortifying.* 100 men behind intrenchments are a match for a thousand in front."[36] Soldiers were well aware of the power of earthworks on the battlefield, and many proved envious of the Confederates, who always seemed to be the ones with the most protection from enemy fire.

By the time the survivors reached Petersburg, they were firmly convinced that the Confederates needed to be coaxed into adopting the role of attacker. Shortly after his unit was badly mauled at Chaffin's Farm, Corporal Theodore Skinner of the 112th New York declared "chargin on forts is fool business," explaining in a letter that "if they would just charge on us and let us be in fortifications as they are, there would not be enough of them left to tell the story."[37] As the Petersburg campaign unfolded, there would be moments when Confederate counterattacks would occur in attempts to drive out Union forces from key portions of the trench lines. Union soldiers looked upon these moments with glee as the conditions of the two armies were finally, if only rarely, reversed. In an August letter to his mother written shortly after his return to the 40th Massachusetts following a wound at Cold Harbor, Corporal Edwin Bearse noted that "I would like to see the Johnies come on they tried our Regt one day and out of 800 picked men about 5 got back I guess they won't try it again."[38] Second Lieutenant Henry Jacobs of the 51st Pennsylvania seemed overjoyed when he reported the consequences of a failed Confederate assault in early July: "The Rebels attempted yesterday to push back our lines but they didn't have enough pushers, our Batteries knocked them higher than a kite in less than no time."[39]

While Northern men praised the strategy being employed to oust the Confederates from Petersburg and longed for a role reversal in the tempo of assaults, their ultimate acceptance of the static trench warfare on the battlefield was more complex. By the start of the Petersburg campaign, soldiers of the Army of the Potomac had come to the seemingly obvious conclusion that the defender would always be at the advantage on a Civil War battlefield. The empirical evidence certainly seemed to confirm this; men only had to recollect the bloody charges against Confederate breastworks at Spotsylvania and Cold Harbor to agree with this supposition. However, as Paddy Griffith has shown in *Battle Tactics of the Civil War*, the power of entrenchments was in some ways illusory. Field fortifications provided little in the way of actual physical benefit to the defender, but instead created an overwhelming psychological advantage. Fortifications *looked* intimidating, and thus "by 1864 the mere existence of a fortification, however technically weak it might be, would usually be enough to forestall a serious attack."[40] While such a claim appears dubious for the Overland campaign, where assaults were frequently made against well-entrenched defenders, this was the case within the Army of the Potomac by the start of the Petersburg campaign, as soldiers continually reported the strength of enemy positions and expressed hesitation at assaulting them. Private Wilbur Fisk of the 2nd Vermont best demonstrated this hesitancy when he wrote:

> Petersburg remains impregnable. The prospect of its falling into our hands eventually is as sure as anything of the kind can be, but not so immediate as we would wish to have it. We have tried to carry their works and have failed. The bare facts are the rebels are too strong in their position to be beaten in a direct assault. . . . So long as they act on the defensive they have the advantage. One man behind a good breastwork is worth three outside, and unless we can oblige them to fight us in open field, or, what would be better, make them attack us in our breastwork, they have us to a serious disadvantage.[41]

Those in the ranks were not the only ones to be intimidated by fortifications, as those in the high command obviously sought to end the stalemate without throwing rows of men against well-entrenched positions. Union commanders instead targeted the unprotected flanks of Lee's line and attempted more

unorthodox methods such as the use of mining at the Crater. Their subordinates recognized the change and were pleased that those in the higher ranks
finally understood something that those beneath them had known for a long
time. They knew that seizing Petersburg, at least at first, would not involve
as much fighting as waiting, with the intention of starving or maneuvering
the Confederates out of the city. Captain Steve Clark, in command of the 13th
Ohio Cavalry which found itself dismounted and serving in the trenches in
mid-July, stated in a letter with no little satisfaction that "there will be but
little danger unless we have to charge which is not likely at this stage of the
sieg."[42] Soldiers accepted the monotony and danger of trench life since it was a
far cry from the constancy of danger and terror that they had witnessed in the
Overland campaign. As one Massachusetts soldier noted that July, "I guess I
can stand two months of siege work; no more charging to be required of your
humble sergeant-major."[43] Perfectly willing to sit in the trenches for at least
the immediate future, these men dreaded a return to the nightmarish frontal
assaults of May and June.

Nearly every man was willing to allow the Confederates to attack their
fortifications; many were even eager for them to do so, but the primary emphasis for the soldiers investing Petersburg was the construction of formidable
defenses to match those being erected by their opponents. In the trenches,
perhaps the most ubiquitous element of a soldier's existence, besides the
constant threat of death, was the ever-present need to expand and modify the
earthworks, forts, and obstacles that made up the Union line. A position could
always be improved, a trench could always be dug a little deeper and thus
rendered a little safer, and a bombproof could always be made more secure or
more comfortable. Such work was difficult; manual labor performed all day
in the summer sun made for some grumbling in the ranks as they now had
to deal with exhaustion in addition to the continual threat of sudden death.
"We have hard and constant duty. We are on fatigue duty through the day
and guard and picket at night," reported Private Bayard Cooper of the 203rd
Pennsylvania in a letter to his brother.[44] Work was such a fundamental part
of their life around Petersburg that, as with the boredom that characterized
their daily lives, some soldiers stopped commenting on it in their letters and
diaries other than in brief notations. The journal entry of Corporal William
Ray of the 7th Wisconsin for July 26 offers one example of this; it concluded an

assessment of the general war situation with, "Dig, dig, & keep digging."[45] Ray and his fellow Wisconsin soldiers evidently took such work in stride, as seen when he noted a day earlier, "digging road today again. We don't get much rest now. Well we would rather do that than fight."[46] The constant work on their fortifications was a substantial burden on those within the Union lines, but the soldiers who bore the brunt of the labor quickly realized that such work was significantly better than the alternative.

"Fatigue duty" was the most frequent requirement for Union soldiers in the trenches. Put simply, this was the physical improvement of their positions; soldier labor would be allocated to officers and engineers for the general construction requirements of a 100,000-person entrenched army. While an individual unit was usually given responsibility for the erection of breastworks along its own portion of the line, such work could be completed quickly. Portions of the unit could then be moved nearby for the erection of forts and rear trenches, which would provide support for the main line. "The duty is very hard here now," wrote Private Julius Ramsdell of the 39th Massachusetts in a July letter to his aunt, "we are building a line of forts around Petersburg. They are all in sight of each other and are to be connected by a strong line of breastworks."[47] "Fatigue duty" could be far more rigorous than normal work on the trench line, since construction of forts involved the use of massive amounts of earth and lumber in addition to the labor associated with bringing pieces of artillery to the fort and placing them properly. Around the same time that Private Ramsdell assisted in the creation of a line of forts, Colonel Robert McAllister's Third Brigade found itself participating in a related effort. In a letter to his wife, McAllister reported that his brigade had been ordered on fatigue for July 19, and "at 5 a.m. we started towards the front . . . The object was to dig a covered way 4 feet deep and 12 feet wide, to convey artillery, ammunition, and troops to the front in safety from shells. This covered way is more than a mile long."[48] Work such as this continued throughout the campaign, as the Union line became more sophisticated and achieved greater depth, with the use of multiple lines of fortifications to guard against a breakthrough on the front. Thus, there was always some sort of labor for soldiers to perform that, while exhausting, occasionally allowed an escape from the front line to the more secure rear areas.

While a good many men complained about their "fatigue" obligations, over time soldiers began to look upon their work as a significant accomplishment. The labor they performed was tangible and was something in which they could take pride; they could see what they had achieved and this feeling, coupled with the understanding that the work they performed benefited the Union cause, gave them a physical sign of the Union war effort and their contribution to it. Some men became attached to their accomplishments, perhaps because they had constructed them with the intention of using the fortifications for their own protection and not for the benefit of some stranger. After having spent more than a month working on a fort along the Petersburg line, Private Ramsdell's 39th Massachusetts was transferred to another portion of the trenches. His unit's response to the move is evident from his diary, where he noted on August 15, "we marched out of our fort upon which we have spent so much time and labor, with a feeling of as much sorrow as if we were parting from some tried friend."[49] Others stressed the success of their efforts, commenting on how they had manufactured a powerful, fearsome feat of military engineering that would soon test itself in combat as if it were an actual soldier along the line. After spending weeks perfecting the breastworks of his unit's position near Chaffin's Farm, Private Bayard Cooper of the 203rd Pennsylvania could not contain his pride at what had been created: "They are the strongest works I ever saw I dont think the Jonnies will have any call here without they want a good deal whipping for in my opinion the whole southern Army can't drive us out of our position here."[50]

This notion of Union soldiers taking pride in their physical accomplishments on the battlefield is one that is confirmed by historian Earl Hess in his book *The Union Soldier in Battle*. While not referring directly to Petersburg, Hess stressed the working-class nature of Union forces and argued that they used their agrarian and industrial backgrounds as a means of adapting to the combat experience. Hess noted that "on an open, conscious level many Northern soldiers used work as a model to shape the battle experience and make it familiar."[51] Whether it was the actual physical work involved in firing their weapons on the battlefield or the "job" of overcoming the rebellion, Union men framed their role in the war in a context that they could understand. Focusing on the "work" before them "gave them something to think about other than the danger of getting hit."[52] For men like Private Cooper, who was a carpenter before the war, and Private Ramsdell, who worked in the leather trade, the construction of the Petersburg line gave them another opportunity to place the war within a familiar context. Rather than being overwhelmed by the tortured and brutal landscape that surrounded them, their work at creating that landscape helped to make trench life more manageable and under their personal control. For those thousands of farm and industrial laborers serving within the Army of the Potomac, the supreme physical effort demanded of them proved taxing, but ultimately provided the benefit of a recognizable experience even as they enclosed themselves within an increasingly unfamiliar environment.

The benefit to the men in the trenches is obvious when one notes that, despite their complaints over having to perform such work, soldiers expressed satisfaction at the labor before them and what they were accomplishing. For those who understood that the static warfare around Petersburg offered them an escape from the open field assaults of the Overland campaign, it was not long before they realized that the work on their entrenchments only added further advantage to their situation. The advantage was noticeable almost immediately, as soldiers identified a dramatic drop in the number of casualties in their units. "It is a month ago yesterday since we have had a man wounded in our Co but we have been under fire a good deal but have been protected by earthworks etc.," noted Sergeant George Fowle of the 39th Massachusetts near the beginning of the Petersburg campaign.[53] From the perspective of a Union soldier, the utilization of entrenchments not only appeared to lower the body count, but it also took some of the fear out of the constant threat of enemy fire. As Private Clarence Bell of the 13th Massachusetts wrote in a letter to his sister, instead of incoming projectiles inspiring terror in his comrades, the men "all shelter themselves in, and laugh at the Rebs for trying to get them out of their works by shelling, for they don't hurt a man."[54] Others, such as Colonel Robert McAllister, could only gaze in wonder at the spectacle that greeted them on daily basis. After witnessing a particularly violent artillery exchange, McAllister wrote to his wife how "it is one of the strangest scenes I have witnessed in campaigning. There is an immense amount of firing; but as both parties are so well protected, there is but little destruction of life on either side."[55] Whether Northern troops were responding to the protection of breastworks with amazement, humor, or simple satisfaction, the early weeks of the Petersburg siege were physically demanding yet rewarding ones. They understood that instead of being marched out into the open field for assaults, they now had direct control over their survival by playing a greater part in the creation of their own protection on the battlefield.

With this understanding came an increased willingness to participate once again in active, high-intensity combat with their Confederate foe. This was not a change that occurred overnight, however, and many soldiers throughout the campaign would continue to decry the use of open assaults against enemy positions. Yet while Union soldiers seemed unwilling to engage in almost any form of active combat upon their arrival at Petersburg in mid-June, once they settled into the protection of their earthworks the men expressed a desire to once again face the Confederates, but this time from the safety of their fortified positions. "We have a very strong position and are having pretty good eaysy times," wrote Captain George Whitman of the 51st New York in mid-September, "if he [General Lee] thinks he can drive us away I wish he would pitch in, as we are all prepared for him, and I would about as soon as fight it out on this line as any other, and if they will only attack us here it will suit us first rate."[56] The constant labor by Union soldiers at fortifying and improving their earthworks was a continual reminder of their defensive power, and while few said they wished to take the attack to the Confederate defenses, men like Whitman were almost eager to have enemy soldiers strike at their own position. As First Lieutenant Harrison Montague of the 10th New York Heavy Artillery explained when relating a normal day "in the rifle pits before Petersburg Va." to a friend back home, "I fairly ached to have them charge us for we would have swept them like grass before the scythe."[57]

The more these men worked on the environment around them, the more they felt that it was the key to their survival and ultimate ability to defeat the enemy. Thus, it was no surprise that they often went on and on in their correspondence about the strength of their fortifications and how badly the Confederates would fare if they dared to attack. Private Henry Heisler, a student from Hazelton, Pennsylvania, had originally enlisted as a musician in the summer of 1861. By the summer of 1864, he was a veteran volunteer with the 48th Pennsylvania and had three years of service under his belt. Heisler wrote to his sister in early September, explaining how the power of his unit's defensive positions would prove key:

> We are expecting the Rebels to attack us every day and our boys are all anxious
> for them to come for we are certain of whipping them. They will have half a

mile of clear field to cross in front of our Regiment and over there we will never allow them to come. They will never be able to drive us from here even if they charge in five or six lines for we can mow them down like grass and our works are too strong for them to batter down with either shot or shell. They are built of heavy logs and about eight feet of dirt against them so that a shell will take but very little effect on them. Never were our boys more anxious for the enemy to attack us or ever more certain of whipping them.[58]

Not only could Heisler take pride in the defenses that his men had constructed, he could use them as a means to once again face the enemy on the field of battle.

The confidence that had been sorely lacking at the end of the Overland campaign first found its expression in comments such as these, as soldiers boldly predicted how the Confederates would be defeated if they brought the fight to the Union lines. Few expressed concern over a possible enemy breakthrough at their portion of the line. The usually pessimistic Private John Haley of the 17th Maine expressed uncharacteristic self-assurance in his journal on November 1, commenting that "it is quite certain that the Rebs will not attack us openly, the forts being so arranged that such a move would be courting annihilation. We can fire cross-ways and every other way, and should the Rebs get in they couldn't stay five minutes. We often wish they would be thoughtless enough to try it, though."[59] Other soldiers did not need to hypothesize on how quick a Confederate attack could be destroyed; some were able to witness firsthand the strength of their defenses when Lee's forces would occasionally strike at the Union line in an effort to blunt a movement by Grant. These engagements, as with the assaults of the Overland campaign, demonstrated to soldiers on both sides the power of a well-fortified position. Reporting in his diary on an engagement with the Confederates early on in the campaign, Sergeant Samuel Clear of the 116th Pennsylvania fairly crowed with delight: "On came the rebels flushed with victory, but we were now in our works. . . . And when they cam[e] close up we let them have a warm reception. It was fun to see them fall like gross, and the rest run like the devil was after them."[60] This opportunity to strike at the Confederates while at the advantage was an obvious first step in the Union forces' rehabilitation following the Overland campaign. Whether their elaborate breastworks really put them at the advantage or not, these soldiers felt safe and powerful within them, and it allowed them to begin the long process of rebuilding their faith in their commanders and faith in their own ability to continue the war effort.

However willing Union soldiers were to be attacked in the opening weeks and months at Petersburg, there was near universal consensus within the ranks that the Army of the Potomac was not yet ready to take the offensive. Much of this stemmed from the understanding that if the Confederates were fools to charge the Union lines, then the opposite must also be true. "The rebs are now well entrenched, and so are we. Neither could carry the other's works without vastly superior numbers," was the assessment of Private Edward Wightman of the 3rd New York as summer gave way to fall and the campaign showed no signs of diminishing.[61] Northern men protected in their trenches fully recognized that the daily life of a Confederate trench-dweller mirrored their own, with countless hours spent improving and expanding the defenses intended to inhibit and destroy an assault by the Union army. Soldiers could see the obstacles before them, and few were enthusiastic about the prospect of being sent charging across no man's land. Much of what contributed to this feeling was the lingering effect of demoralization suffered during the Overland campaign, as some soldiers and units had difficultly overcoming the exhaustion and losses suffered in May and June. "It is almost impossible, owing to our many and disastrous defeats, to get our men to charge the rebel works. They have been charged till they themselves say it is 'played out,'" wrote Major William Watson, a surgeon serving with the 105th Pennsylvania, in a letter to his family after seeing the effects of an attempted assault by his regiment near Deep Bottom in mid-August.[62] The Overland campaign and its legacy were not something that could be overcome by a few weeks of trench warfare around Petersburg, but the mode of fighting and the methods used by soldiers to react and adapt to it allowed them to overcome their fears and regain their willingness to become active participants on the battlefield.

———

Such factors as desensitization, labor on fortifications, and a reawakened sense of independence all worked together in helping to create a relatively smooth transition from the intense combat of the Overland campaign to the reduced violence of trench warfare around Petersburg. Looking back from the twentieth century, one may expect the experience of trench warfare to be severely degrading for the human condition, and, based on the experience of the French and German armies during the First World War, it would only be a matter of time before an army in such a situation would collapse or at the very least rebel against their living circumstances. Yet while signs of discontent and turmoil did appear within the ranks, this was not the case for the Army of the Potomac in the summer of 1864 as the Petersburg campaign began. Instead of destroying the Army of the Potomac as a fighting force, trench life, coming on the heels of the horror and casualties of the Overland campaign, proved regenerative to the men who had survived May and June. The exhaustion and demoralization of Union soldiers in the middle of June soon gave way to hope and even enthusiasm for the future. As Private Clarence Bell of the 13th Massachusetts reported to his sister in mid-July, "the boys are all getting rested and in good spirits again. They had all got some down and tired of fighting all the time, but now they are ready again."[63] That men like Bell could view the hostile landscape around Petersburg as a place to get "rested" is a testament to the positive effect that trench life could have on Union soldiers. Once they could get past the violence around them, which was not as difficult following what they had seen during the Overland campaign, the men were better able to cope with the deadliness encircling them and find ways to make it work to their advantage.

Regardless of how effectively Union soldiers adapted to the opening phases of the Petersburg campaign, there was no guarantee that they could maintain such optimism and steadiness as the siege dragged on month after month. None of them could know that the campaign would last until April 1865, and even had they known, they may have doubted their ability to survive in the trenches to that point. The longer they were exposed to the deteriorating conditions of trench warfare, the more difficult it would be to persevere; two or three months of trench life coming on the heels of the terrible battles of Overland were a far cry from three full seasons living in the ground under constant enemy fire. Most realized that at some point they would be called upon to leave their trenches and attack the Confederate defenses, and even after their recuperation over the summer of 1864, some still had their doubts as to whether they could fight in such a manner again. Corporal Alexander Adams of the 100th Pennsylvania, a veteran volunteer of the Army of the Potomac, certainly had his doubts as to the future when he wrote to his sister in the middle of the campaign, "I am afraid if they have another campaign like they had last summer I will get very much demoralized. I would like to see it over without having to do any more fighting but I suppose there will have to be two or three more fights yet before it is over."[64] Men like Corporal Adams were right; the Army of the Potomac would be expected to fight again. Understanding how soldiers in that army survived to April 1865 with a willingness, even enthusiasm, to meet the Confederates in open battle entails looking not just at how the men reacted to and shaped their environment, but also how those at all levels of the Union army sought to aid Northern troops as they spent nine months digging their way toward Petersburg.

6

"Very Good Fare Nowadays"

UNION SOLDIERS RESPOND TO LOGISTICS AND CHARITABLE ORGANIZATIONS

A soldier is happy as long as his food is good and sure.
—Private Carter, 22nd Massachusetts Volunteer Infantry

"I am well and enjoying good health," wrote Private Frederick Ployer of the 187th Pennsylvania in the opening paragraph of a letter addressed to "Friend Daelhouser" dated July 5, 1864. Ployer, a 19-year-old schoolteacher from Chambersburg, Pennsylvania, had no doubt been considered "green" by most Union soldiers, having only joined the Army of the Potomac that February, but his experiences in the Overland campaign had earned him veteran status by July. In his letter, Ployer described the Virginia heat, the "dust, dust, dust," and the ever present threat of enemy fire. He also noted how disease was affecting his unit, leaving only about half of his regiment fit for duty, though he acknowledged "the old troops do not suffer so much from sickness as they have become used to it." Despite these challenges, Ployer expressed his continued faith in General Grant and the Petersburg campaign while relating an account of some recent holiday cheer for the 4th of July in the form of vegetables from the United States Sanitary Commission. In fact, the supply situation had so improved since the Overland campaign that Ployer could report, "we have plenty to eat, and once in awhile we get rations of whiskey." While he added, "it is in such small rations that you do not get enough to wet your eye," Private Ployer certainly considered the advent of a whiskey ration as a plus for his daily diet.[1]

For the nine months of the Petersburg campaign, more than 100,000 Union soldiers found themselves immersed in the most intricate system of entrenchments devised during the war. General Grant's repeated efforts at seizing the city provided the occasional escape from the trenches onto the field of battle, which continued to provide the men with some disturbing memories of the Overland campaign. However, the vast majority of time was spent by soldiers in camp to the rear or in the trenches on the front lines, a situation that quite a few soldiers found barely tolerable. One soldier compared this state of affairs to "the punishment of criminals," while another professed, "never was there such a beastly life as this."[2] Sergeant James Rush Holmes of the 61st Pennsylvania looked around at his life in the trenches in June and declared that "human nature cannot stand to[o] much."[3] Those within the Army of the Potomac were clearly facing a rough and dangerous environment that provided a constant threat to the preservation of their morale. Yet despite an increase in desertion in the Union army, the mass collapse that would have indicated a serious slippage of soldier morale never occurred within the Army of the Potomac. As demonstrated in the previous chapter, Union soldiers were able to use the opening months of the Petersburg experience to rebuild their morale by focusing on the changes in battlefield tactics and the strength of their constructed fortifications. The question still remains as to how the men within the Army of the Potomac were able to withstand the horrors of trench life and sustain their morale over the long term as the campaign stretched on interminably before them. Part of the answer can be found in the fact that Union troops were not without assistance in their efforts to stay alive and sane; a great deal of money and effort was spent keeping those in the trenches well fed, connected to home, and emotionally prepared to sustain the siege lines for as long as necessary.

———

Soldiers of the Army of the Potomac, who had taken the lion's share of casualties during the bloodletting of the Overland campaign that spring, had come a long way from the demoralized state in which they had entered the Petersburg campaign in mid-June, expressing increased faith in the army to hold its own against the Army of Northern Virginia. The Federal efforts to capture the city had also made notable progress. The creation of a vast network of forts and trench lines served as a clear indication that Union forces were prepared for an extended stay in the heart of Virginia. The summer months had seen a resurrection of morale from the depths of near mutiny to confidence that Northern forces could once again meet and defeat their Confederate opponents on the field of battle. But for how long could these men find solace in a hole in the ground? While many understood that a significant period of time would be needed to complete the investment of Petersburg, few realized that the campaign would last well into 1865 and that many more battles would be fought and lives lost before final victory was achieved. Most soldiers, though willing to carry on, merely wanted the campaign and the war to be over so that they could return to their homes and carry on with their lives. "I am in hopes the War will be settled some way or other by Spring for all are getting sick and tired of it," noted Sergeant William Coffee of the 3rd New Hampshire at the end of the summer, a lament that echoed the comments of many of his comrades who sought an escape from the stalemated situation in the trenches as one season bled into another.[4]

Union general Ulysses S. Grant sought to provide his men with that escape, but found his efforts thwarted at nearly every step by Confederate resistance and Union limitations. Grant was operating under basic siege principles: if you wish to capture a city, you must first sever its communications and supply lines. Of the five rail lines extending outward from Petersburg, and thus connecting the city with the rest of the Confederacy, the Army of the Potomac had seized two, the City Point and Norfolk & Petersburg lines, when it began the campaign. Now Grant's attention turned to capturing or destroying the remaining three rail lines with the aim of choking off Petersburg and forcing the surrender or flight of General Robert E. Lee's Army of Northern Virginia. From the first days of their arrival, Union soldiers had been at work extending the left flank of the Federal line ever westward in order to cross first the Petersburg & Weldon and then the South Side Railroad lines. Recognizing the danger, Confederate forces contested every inch of this advance, and the result was a series of sharp engagements near the Weldon Railroad, particularly during the months of August and December 1864. Once a significant portion of the Weldon was captured, Grant's attention turned to the South Side Railroad, near which fierce fighting occurred in early February 1865. However, Grant did not neglect his right flank, and, in an effort to keep the pressure on the Confederates and maybe capture Richmond in the process, he initiated a series of assaults in the Deep Bottom area, with a particularly savage battle occurring there in late September 1864. As evidenced by the Crater operation in July, Grant never abandoned the option of seizing Petersburg by direct assault, but he recognized the impossibility of repeating the methods employed during the Overland campaign. Despite his efforts to seize the railroads, threaten Richmond, and blow holes in the Confederate line, Grant was unable to break through the Confederate defenses and seize Petersburg until early April 1865, more than nine months after the campaign had begun.[5]

As summer shifted to fall and the presidential election approached, Grant's operations around Petersburg picked up tempo and he increasingly sought breakthroughs along the western railroad lines or north of the James River. Operations at Petersburg became increasingly dependent on larger strategic considerations, with a resurgence of Confederate operations in the Shenandoah Valley that included an invasion of Maryland in July. In mid-August, Grant sought to overwhelm the Confederate defenses by driving in both directions simultaneously. North of the James, portions of Hancock's 2nd Corps would join the 10th Corps from the Army of the James in a concerted attack in the Deep Bottom region, hopefully to turn Lee's left flank. Though there was a promising breakthrough on the 16th, Lee's forces successfully contained the break and drove off the Union movement. Thinking that Lee had weakened his lines to drive off the Deep Bottom assault, Grant authorized Warren's 5th Corps to attack the Weldon Railroad. On August 18, Warren's men succeeded in securing a lodgment on the rail line. Despite repeated Confederate counterattacks over the next few days, and an operation involving Hancock's 2nd Corps that was turned back near Ream's Station, Union forces retained their foothold on the railroad and connected the new position with their trench lines east and south of the city. At the cost of more than seven thousand casualties in a week's worth of fighting, Grant's army had taken one more step toward completing its encirclement of Petersburg.[6]

Operations continued into the fall as Grant's probes against the Confederate left and right flanks brought further fighting. The end of September witnessed another effort to simultaneously pressure Lee's army north and south of the James River. A substantial movement by the Army of the James up the New Market Road north of the river succeeded in securing Fort Harrison and a portion of the Confederate line, but Southern forces sealed the breach and prevented a larger breakthrough. Meanwhile, on the left flank of the Union line men from Warren's Fifth Corps managed to extend their positions farther west.[7] After another few weeks of consolidating their positions, Union forces struck again on the right and left at the end of October. A flank attack along the Williamsburg road to the north made only minimal progress, and an attack by the 2nd Corps near Hatcher's Run to the south nearly resulted in Hancock's men being surrounded and destroyed.[8] By the time of the November election and with winter closing in, Union forces had made only modest gains, but presented an increasingly difficult challenge to the Confederates by forcing them to stretch their numerically inferior force to meet the Union flank movements.

As these engagements continued into the fall, what concerned many Union soldiers was not their own ability to survive or bring the campaign to a successful conclusion, but rather the willingness of those on the home front to continue the struggle to its proper completion. Many coupled proclamations of imminent victory with stern warnings for their relatives back home that they should not flag in their support of the war effort. In response to those who condemned Grant's inability to capture Richmond, Private Edward Wightman of the 3rd New York angrily wrote to his brother that he and the men in his unit "do not think Grant's campaign a failure. We care nothing for Richmond except as a stronghold which shields Lee's army. We seek to destroy the army, not the city, and . . . we will do it if properly backed by the people at home."[9] Men in war have long had a complex association with those on the home front, but the commentary aimed toward civilians indicates the belief that Petersburg was a critical component of a fast-approaching Union victory, and the assistance of the population was deemed more necessary than ever before. "Rest assured that things will come all right side up in the end," noted Private Ployer in an early July letter after condemning those who challenged Grant and his strategy for taking Richmond. Ployer added that he was ready to keep fighting, and that the Army of the Potomac's only requirement was "for the people to stand steadfast and uphold the government and be of good cheer and in my estimations matters will soon come to a successful issue."[10]

While men like Ployer challenged those at home to keep up the fight, some displayed a growing feeling of anger toward some on the home front, particularly the "Copperhead" opposition to the Lincoln administration. This anger would grow over the summer, peaking in time for the November presidential election, but early on, Union soldiers stressed the danger posed by the "cowards" on the Northern home front. "We do not like to be cheated by cowards at home that never thought of going to the front," wrote Maine soldier Charles Smith to his wife in early September, "if ever we get a chance we will show them what we think of them." Smith concluded his rant by suggesting that these "cowards" be mobilized and sent to the front since Grant would need the soldiers for his fall campaign.[11] Lieutenant Martin Connally of the 57th New York also criticized the "cowards" up north, stating, "I also pity that class of beings," but reached the opposite conclusion from Smith's. Describing how their arrival did a disservice to "plenty of *brave* men" in the army, he declared, "if a man is coward, let him stay home and act right towards our cause, and I for one will defend him as long as I have an arm to do so."[12] These men, among others, took the opportunity to criticize those whom they felt were dropping the ball on the home front, but their comments indicate that they still felt that proper moral support from the Northern populace was a necessity for their continued struggle against the Confederate armies.

While moral support was key, the physical maintenance of a force of over 100,000 combat soldiers in the field was no easy task during the nineteenth century (nor is it any easier today). On a daily basis, such a large force required tons of food, ammunition, feed for horses, clothing, and the various other accoutrements utilized by men in war. While the increasing use of railroads during the war has been identified as a technological harbinger of more modern methods of supplying armies in the field, rail lines were not ubiquitous, particularly in the South with its limited transportation network.[13] Consequently, a Civil War army that expected to complete rapid and lengthy movements primarily relied on horse-drawn wagons to support its men and animals in the field. While the freight wagon was the key logistical tool for almost every campaign of the war, its slow speed and limited carrying capacity impeded the efforts of commanders to perform swift advances and surprise maneuvers.[14] Attempts to compensate for this limitation met with mixed success, as demonstrated by General Grant's policies during the Overland campaign of May and June 1864. Hoping to improve the speed and mobility of the Army of the Potomac and thus steal a march on their Confederate opponents, in early May Grant authorized the reduction of the number of wagons in the Union supply train and ordered soldiers to carry six days' worth of rations on their person.[15] The extended length of the campaign, coupled with the tendency of soldiers to eat whenever they desired rather than when they were ordered to, resulted in a frequent shortage of food and other supplies as the Army of the Potomac marched deeper into Virginia. By June, the situation had become critical, as evidenced by Lieutenant George Bowen of the 12th New Jersey, who noted in his diary on June 15 that his unit was "entirely out of Rations and [we] waited until near noon for them and then marched without them."[16] Marching with empty stomachs was a frequent complaint within the Army of the Potomac during the Overland campaign, and a problem that contributed to the rapid weakening of morale.

The difficulties caused by supplies and logistics during the Overland campaign disappeared almost overnight once the Army of the Potomac dug in around Petersburg. The swift movements over long distances in May and June had resulted in Union forces frequently outrunning their supply lines, a problem that was nonexistent for a force conducting a static battle of attrition. Northern quartermasters were now able to stockpile large quantities of matériel in order to ensure an uninterrupted supply for soldiers stationed along the front lines. Depots bulging with supplies were established, the most significant of which was the port at City Point, Virginia, located at the convergence of the Appomattox and James Rivers. This supply point, "the greatest advance army base of the war," rapidly swelled into a self-contained city with enough hospitals, barracks, bakeries, and warehouses to provide for tens of thousands of Union soldiers.[17] While such depots had been established for the Overland campaign, the advance of the Army of the Potomac into enemy territory had increased the distance between the Union force and its base of supply, thus lengthening the time needed to bring provisions to the men on the move. City Point, located less than ten miles from the front line of an army that was in a fixed position for the majority of the campaign, presented no such problems and proved ideal for connecting Union troops with the immense resources of the Northern war effort. As General Rufus Ingalls noted in his assessment of the supply depot, City Point represented "the most convenient, commodious, economical, and perfect ever provided for the supply of armies."[18]

The significance of City Point was not lost on those Union soldiers who frequently passed through the port on their way to and from the front line. Numerous soldiers noted the bustle of activity at City Point that was its most obvious aspect to any visitor. "It is quite a lively place," reported Private William

Oberlin of the 148th Pennsylvania in a letter home, who then went on to list some of the components of daily life at City Point: "Horses, mules, waggons, rail road trains, army supplies, ships, steam boats, gun boats, sutter shops, relief associations from different states, lots of contraband Negroes, wounded and sick soldiers. There is also a goodly number of women here, cooks, waiters and some doing nothing. If you were here you could see quite a sight."[19] Those who had the opportunity to gaze upon the loaded wharves and warehouses of City Point expressed amazement at the amount of food and equipment stored there to support those at the front. Upon arriving at City Point in October with the 11th New York Light Artillery, Private Alexander Rose appeared impressed when he noted in his diary the size of the port and wrote, "the place is one Grand Store house of supplies."[20] To men like Private Rose and others who passed through its docks, City Point was visual evidence that a tremendous effort was being expended to provide for the welfare of those who spent their days and nights in the trenches.

Most of those soldiers laying siege to Petersburg did not have a frequent opportunity to view the logistical hub that was City Point, but the railroad line connecting the supply depot with the front was something that nearly every soldier noticed. Beginning almost immediately after Union forces arrived near Petersburg in mid-June, engineers went to work reconstructing the City Point and Petersburg Railroad line that had been demolished during the Confederate retreat. Its east-west connection of those two cities proved ideal for supporting the Federal line, and, after the tireless work of civilian laborers, a seven-mile length of the railroad was in full service by July 7.[21] Not content with connecting by rail merely one portion of the Union position to City Point, engineers used the stable nature of the fortifications surrounding Petersburg to construct a series of branch rail lines and spurs that would eventually parallel the portion of the Federal line south of the James River. As Grant extended his lines to the west in order to turn Lee's right flank, the railroad line was likewise extended, eventually to a point beyond the Weldon Railroad, more than twenty miles away from City Point.[22] Construction was done rapidly and sometimes under fire from the Confederate lines, and, as one soldier noted, the result was a railroad that was "simply laid upon the ground without any grading, so that the trains go up hill and downhill just as the natural land lies," making for a slow and uncomfortable ride for passengers and cargo.[23] Lieutenant Colonel Horace Porter, a member of General Grant's staff, also noted the rough assembly of the rail line, observing that the lack of grading was so obvious that "a train moving along it looked in the distance like a fly crawling over a corrugated washboard."[24] Regardless, this railroad would become indispensable and possibly decisive. Historian Christopher Gabel has noted that "Grant's army, supplied by one jerry-built but professionally operated railroad, fared better logistically than did Lee's Confederates in Petersburg, who had several pre-existing rail lines at their disposal."[25]

Just such a conclusion was reached by those in the trenches, who witnessed the spread of rail lines across the Virginia landscape and eventually heard the daily whistles of trains bringing supplies to the front. Union soldiers realized that they stood to benefit from the utilization of this technology on the battlefield, and their initial curiosity at the poorly constructed railroad paralleling their lines soon turned to satisfaction and even pride at "Gen. Grants Great Military Rail Road."[26] Describing the continued expansion of the railroad lines in December, Private Wilbur Fisk of the 2nd Vermont suggested that "in a short time I expect they will issue rations to us on the picket line, from the cars. They run almost out there now."[27] Other men noted not only the advantage that the railroad gave soldiers on the front line, but also the overall advantage it provided for the Union efforts against Petersburg. In a letter to his mother, Private William Hamilton of the 191st Pennsylvania explained that the advantage of the railroad lay in the fact that "in case the Rebs should make a break upon us they would get neither clothing nor food for none is kept on hand the depot being at City Point and all brought out here is immediately issued to the troops."[28] Beyond the recognition of the tactical and strategic benefits brought about by the construction of the rail line was an understanding by Union soldiers that it directly contributed to an increase in the quality of life for those in the field. "This is getting to seem really like a civilized land," wrote First Lieutenant Charles Stinson of the 19th United States Colored Troops in a letter from the front, "and why? because I am today stand in my cabin door and see the iron horse winding his way around the curve on its way to Weldon. . . . You might say that almost nothing is impossible with the Yankees."[29] Much like the swelling wharves at City Point, Union men took notice of the expanding railroad network and understood the positive impact that it was having on their life in the trenches.

In addition to providing sustenance for those at the front, the railroad infrastructure also connected the trench lines with the medical support apparatus located in and around City Point. As with the distribution of rations, the rapid movements of the Overland campaign had seriously disrupted the ability of medical personnel to treat those suffering from wounds and illness.[30] With the Army of the Potomac in a stationary position, City Point became the central location for the treatment of the wounded and sick. It was there that the separate hospitals of each army corps were merged into a single facility that could house six thousand men on a normal day and ten thousand soldiers during a crisis.[31] Unlike during the Overland campaign, Union soldiers now had access to a sizable medical facility only a short distance from the front. However, fewer Union soldiers found the need to utilize such a facility as the siege carried over into 1865. Except for a slight rise in December 1864, the monthly number of men in the Army of the Potomac listed as sick by medical personnel descended steadily from more than 19,500 men in July to roughly 13,700 the following March.[32] The decreasing number of ill soldiers in the trenches can be explained not only by the better food that they received while in a fixed position around Petersburg, but also by the increasing ability of the medical apparatus to treat and prevent illness. Efforts at controlling sanitation improved over the course of the war, and charitable organizations such as the Sanitary and Christian Commissions devoted considerable resources to improving the living conditions and diet of Northern soldiers across the country.[33] The Army of the Potomac received all of these benefits, and consequently one historian concluded that "in the last autumn and winter of the war the Eastern troops were healthier than ever before."[34]

To those thousands of Union soldiers who fell ill during their stay in the trenches, such a conclusion might have sounded ludicrous. However, for every soldier who offered comments on the various maladies that afflicted the ranks, there were those similar to Lieutenant John Owen of the 36th United States Colored Troops who wrote to his mother in July, "I am very healthy & sound & think I can easily bear the hardships of the field."[35] Some soldiers even noticed the drop in sick calls that occurred as the campaign continued. After his unit settled into their position in late August, Lieutenant Thomas Owen of the 50th New York Engineers wrote to his family, "the health of the men is, I think, a little better as a general thing."[36] Those unfortunate soldiers who did fall ill, such as Private James Horrocks of the 5th New Jersey Light Artillery, often reported a positive experience when treated by army doctors. Writing to his family back in England, Horrocks informed them, "I have the Camp Fever and am now getting better. Every care has been taken of me and every kindness shown to me."[37] Sick soldiers who found themselves removed to the hospital at City Point echoed Horrocks's praise for the army's medical apparatus. Sergeant Joseph Young of the 184th Pennsylvania came down with a "bad cold" in November, but assured his wife and family that "I am in the hospittle and I am well taken care of."[38] While there was no such thing as universal good health within the Army of the Potomac, the perspective of these soldiers indicates that the general well-being of the ranks stayed at a modest level for much of the campaign and the men felt that they were being properly cared for by medical personnel.

Despite the satisfaction expressed by soldiers with City Point, the Military Railroad, and their medical support, most of the men and officers in the Union army did not think in grand terms of logistics; their criteria for determining the effectiveness of Federal supply efforts came down to one issue: food. Union soldiers, as with those in any army, did indeed march on their stomachs, and accordingly one of the most prevalent topics in their correspondence and diaries was how well they thought they were being fed. In fact, the drudgery of trench life left them little else on which to comment. Their statements regarding the abundance and variety of rations being distributed to the front lines suggest that the men were receiving a steady, though not lavish, supply of food on a daily basis. Almost immediately upon their arrival near Petersburg in mid-June, Union troops realized that a change had occurred from the irregular and limited meals of the Overland campaign. On June 26, only a week after his unit's arrival at Petersburg, Lieutenant Colonel William Tilton of the 22nd Massachusetts provided a lengthy description of the varieties of food available to his men (including ice, a rare commodity in the field), and concluded, "altogether we are more comfortable than at any time since we began the campaign fifty-three days ago."[39]

As time went on, and the Union position was consolidated and connected by rail to City Point, an increasing number of soldiers reported that their food situation was one of the positives of their daily existence. They also clearly understood whom they should thank for their improved standard of living.

"The Government furnishes us very good fare nowadays, considering that we are in the field," wrote Private John Foote in a summer letter back to his parents in New York.[40] Private David Coon, who had gone through hell with the 36th Wisconsin during the Overland campaign, wrote to his wife and children in July that he was having "easier times," describing his recent meals and concluding, "I have a plenty to eat & drink, and that it is very good."[41] After assessing a late August meal in his diary, Sergeant Samuel Clear of the 116th Pennsylvania noted, "We are living very fat for the first time since leaving home."[42] By mid-October, Captain Steve Clark summed up the supply situation of his 13th Ohio Cavalry by stating simply, "we have plenty to eat, and are doing as well as soldiers can expect to."[43] The feeling was almost universally held by the men in the ranks that their lives had been considerably improved by the Federal supply efforts since the army's arrival at Petersburg.

What impressed these men about the state of supply was not necessarily the stable nature of their rations but their variety. Soldiers on the march typically only had the benefit of salt pork, hardtack, and coffee to sate their appetite. When this bill of fare was expanded at Petersburg, men filled pages of correspondence with stories of foods that seemed like delicacies to those who had subsisted on bland meals for weeks on end. One soldier reported with pride how his unit had just received "flour, dried apples, pickels, and some fresh bread," while Sergeant Major Christian Abraham Fleetwood of the 4th United States Colored Troops proudly noted the "Cakes cheese & watermelons" received by his unit in August.[44] "I have just eaten my supper, which consisted of something I have not had since I left home," reported Private William Greene of the 2nd United States Sharpshooters in a letter to his mother in early August, describing the "Tea, Toast, Soft Bread & butter, Boiled cabbage & Pork, fried beef stake. Coffee with a little condensed *cow* in it. I can assure you that I made a supper of it & am now enjoying the pleasures of a Havana Cegar."[45] The same week that Private Greene informed his mother of his feast, Andrew Linscott of the 39th Massachusetts reported to his family the typical provisions that reached him each week: "I generally get up three good soups a week, have my beef steak four or five times a week, one or two loaves of bread, some potatoes and onions and any quantity of hard bread." Linscott concluded the description of his weekly allotments by assuring his parents that "we dont suffer for food by any means."[46]

The accounts of Greene and Linscott should not be taken to mean that Union soldiers surrounding Petersburg were receiving beefsteak and cigars with every meal, but only to indicate that such supplies were prevalent among those facing off against the Confederates. The static nature of the Union lines offered improved ability to service the frontlines, but those in more exposed positions, particularly on the far flanks, could still find themselves removed from the plenty of Union supply efforts. Occasionally, men were forced to return to the old standbys, as demonstrated in November by one of Linscott's comrades in the 39th Massachusetts, Private Caleb Beal, who remarked that "we got nothing but raw pork for rations to day." However, Beal followed this comment soon after by stating that "as a general thing we live bully soups, beef, fish, onions, sweet potatoes &c."[47] Many men did report subsisting off of hardtack and salted meat, but typically soldiers were offered a much larger diet once the Army of the Potomac settled into its entrenched position surrounding Petersburg.

While the daily fare of Federal troops increased at least moderately over the course of the campaign, the men occasionally received meals that greatly exceeded their daily allotments. These feasts usually coincided with a holiday occurrence, such as Thanksgiving or Christmas. Thanksgiving received the most attention from observers, if only because such a concerted effort was made by civilian, political, and military personnel to provide a meal commensurate with the holiday tradition. Despite the vast effort, their success was mixed, with men such as Captain Albert Rogall of the 27th United States Colored Troops complaining, "we were promised turkeys and apples from ladies of New York, but by some rascality of the commissary and quartermaster we didn't get anything."[48] Others noted the tremendous effort made for Thanksgiving, but also pointed out a noticeable imbalance. "The people of the North have sent 40,000 turkeys and chickens to the Army of the James and also apples and nuts, so the men are having quite a feast," wrote Lieutenant Joseph Scroggs of the 5th United States Colored Troops. "The officers are not counted in. What they get they have to pay for always. We did not attempt to get up anything sumptuous at Hd. Qrs."[49] While perhaps it was understandable that the better paid officers would be left on their own for Thanksgiving, one can detect a trace of disappointment in these words that Scroggs confided to his diary.

The vast majority of Union soldiers, however, received a sizable meal on or near the Thanksgiving holiday, which added greatly to their spirit as the grim winter months approached. Praise was abundant and effusive, with men describing their meals as "a bully one," "something huge," and "a very good supper."[50] Once again, it was Private Beal of the 39th Massachusetts who effectively articulated how soldiers responded to the culinary efforts made on their behalf:

> Last Thursday was Thanksgiving day, and I hereby take the opportunity to express my thanks to those liberal people at the North . . . who contributed to us so bountifuliy with luxuries on that day. I assure you such a donation as the one we received was highly appreciated and will long be remembered by the recipients. No one could he have been present and witnessed the pleasure and gratification of the soldiers as they received their share of the good things would ever regret that he contributed for the occasion . . . We had turkeys already cooked, mince-pie, apples, sausage pickles etc etc &c.[51]

While viewing the stocked wharves at City Point might have impressed upon soldiers the might of the Union war effort, nothing could better convince men such as Private Beal of the power and support of the home front than the arrival of such great meals designed for their direct benefit. Despite not getting his feast until the day after Thanksgiving, Private John Foote of the 117th New York praised the meal and wanted thanks directed where it was deserved: "The loyal people of York State have truly shown their good will, this time and may God bless them."[52]

The large quantity and quality of foods at the disposal of Union forces was augmented by the foraging efforts of individual men and units, which, although rare for the Petersburg campaign, were always a welcome means of expanding one's daily meal allowance. Such a luxury was only available to those units somewhat removed from the front lines, but foraging was still performed rather liberally by Union troops, particularly early on in the campaign before the immediate area became too "picked over" by foraging expeditions. Shortly after joining the 2nd United States Sharpshooters in early July, Private Daniel Sawtelle realized the benefits of being a member of a somewhat unorthodox unit when he joined his new comrades on a foraging expedition into the Virginia countryside. "Every planter has a large garden and we generally find poultry in abundance," Sawtelle explained in a letter to his sister, noting that "as there are no orders against foraging, the boys help themselves to everything they can find."[53] Over the course of the winter of 1864–1865, Federal troops continued to extend the Union left flank past the Weldon Railroad and in the process entered territory with fresh supplies for energetic foragers. This did not always mean procuring supplies from the (dis)loyal of the surrounding community, as evidenced by future Medal of Honor recipient Captain Samuel Rodman Smith of the 4th Delaware, who described his unit's activities near Weldon in early February 1865 as "shooting gray squirrels, rabbits, turkey, and deer, and pike out of the swamp to the rear of us." As a consequence of this expedition into the wilderness, Smith "committed the indescretion . . . of eating too much. I *was* hungry, and there was plenty in abundance, so I think I was excusable."[54] When the occasion presented itself, resourceful soldiers found ways to supplement their daily rations and thus greatly improve their life in the Union lines.

Resourcefulness also contributed to the proliferation of a substance that was as basic to some soldiers as hardtack: whiskey. Civilian sutlers and ambitious soldiers found ways to introduce large amounts of whiskey into the ranks of the Union armies. The result is best illustrated by Private Robert McBride of the 11th Pennsylvania, who noted that one day during the campaign several men from his unit held a party where "Commissary whisky was provided in abundance."[55] The effect that the whiskey had on the 11th Pennsylvania's festivities can be surmised from McBride's postscript to the affair: "It required about two days' diligent labor to clean up and repair, to say nothing about Dunn's head, stomach, and general constitution."[56] Most commentators condemned the use of whiskey in the Union lines, echoing the words of Assistant Surgeon Horatio Soule, whose evident frustration with the situation was revealed in his diary: "I wish Whiskey could be banished from the army. It would, I think be better for all concerned. What fools some men make of themselves."[57] Private Charles Field of the 108th New York agreed, writing to a friend that "there has been more Whiskey in the Army during this Campaign, than in any previous one," and expressing his desire that General Grant would forbid its distribution by the Commissary Department.[58]

While many objections to the abuse of alcohol among Northern soldiers were based on moral grounds, some comments suggested a more complex dynamic at work. The fact that officers had the financial means to acquire whiskey more easily than enlisted men might help to explain Sergeant Francis

Waller's description of one September night within the lines of the 6th Wisconsin: "All of the officers were drunk last night and had a lot of N.Y.'s in their tents and it made some of the boys mad so there was a fuss and one of the boys was wounded."[59] As seen previously, verbal attacks on officers by enlisted men often involved reference to liquor as having a deleterious effect on the capability of army commanders. For example, Private John Steward of the 1st Maine Heavy Artillery blamed alcohol as contributing to his unit's disastrous early assault on the Petersburg lines, declaring, "whiskey is accountable for the larger share of this . . . one glass of whiskey is worth more to our officers than a soldiers life."[60] The presence of abundant supplies of alcohol could prove damaging to the maintenance of military discipline in the face of the enemy. Such was the case of Sergeant Thomas Butters of the 116th Pennsylvania, who was convicted by a court-martial in September for being drunk while on fatigue duty and in charge of a group of prisoner laborers. His punishment: "to be marched under guard, carrying a log of wood on his shoulder weighing at least twenty five (25) pounds, eight hours each day for twenty days."[61] Alcohol appeared as an issue in many court-martial cases, and while the military authorities appeared to be somewhat lenient with cases of desertion due to the need for manpower, discipline violations involving whiskey were rarely forgiven. Nevertheless, while many objected to and attempted to curb alcohol's ill effects on the discipline and moral diligence of Union soldiers, the abundance of alcohol along the front lines appeared to make for some lively escapes from the grind of trench life.

Some of the organizations that targeted soldier drinking for destruction were also the ones that contributed to an expansion in their daily diet and general standard of living. Charitable organizations such as the United States Christian and Sanitary Commissions provided a key addition to the lives of Union soldiers since representatives of these organizations sought to alleviate the burden of war on the men at the front. While these two groups frequently found reason to diminish each other's activities, the Christian and Sanitary Commissions contributed millions of dollars and thousands of hours of labor toward providing for those fighting or affected by the war.[62] The Christian Commission typically focused on the spiritual well-being of soldiers while on campaign, providing chaplains, religious papers and sermons, and relief supplies for those in the hospitals. The Sanitary Commission, a secular organization that utilized paid workers more than volunteers, focused more on the everyday living conditions of Union soldiers, striving to improve the hygienic standards of Northern hospitals while working to provide fruits and vegetables to those at the front in order to prevent outbreaks of scurvy and other nutritional deficiencies. The activities of both groups were complementary, however, and during the Petersburg campaign members of these organizations provided much needed food, reading material, and a general sign of the home front's role in the war effort to those in the trenches.

The relief efforts of the United States Sanitary Commission had been growing over the course of the war, garnering millions of dollars of private donor funds for assisting the men in the army. Following a mixed effort at providing aid during the Overland campaign, the Sanitary Commission sprang into action once the Army of the Potomac came to a halt at Petersburg. As one wartime history of the commission noted, "The peculiar hardships of the campaign rendered it very apparent, that when the Army had fought its way through, and reached a permanent base, its vital force would be very much impaired, and a scorbutic taint would be found to prevail among the men."[63] During the month of June, the commission would forward more than one hundred tons of vegetables to the army in order to repair the health and stamina of the Overland campaign survivors. As the history noted, the men were "frantic" to receive such supplies.[64] The commission would carry out its activities throughout the Petersburg campaign, continuing the provision of aid to the men at the front. While their support often included practical forms of assistance such as vegetables, clothing, and hospital supplies, they also provided literature and stationery to those in the trenches. For example, *The Soldier's Friend*, a pamphlet published by the Sanitary Commission and distributed to the ranks, contained a variety of helpful information for the troops, such as a calendar, hymns and psalms, pay scales for enlisted personnel, the privileges available to discharged soldiers, and a detailed description of the commission's activities and depots. It also included "Warnings to Soldiers," which advised men to "Beware of persons offering to help you, unless you are sure they belong to some responsible relief association. The camps . . . are full of *pretended friends* of soldiers, and there are hundreds of soldiers robbed every week by these imposters."[65]

The United States Christian Commission clearly had a more spiritual focus, with Northern Protestant churches and religious organizations providing volunteers and resources to assist with the soldier's life. Over the course of its existence, Christian Commission volunteers "preached 58,308 sermons, held 77,744 prayer meetings, and wrote 92,321 letters for sick and wounded soldiers."[66] During the Petersburg campaign, the commission would set up a headquarters in City Point with approximately one hundred delegates on hand to assist in the hospitals and staff the commission's storehouse, chapel, and offices.[67] In the field, commission delegates served a variety of functions, as described by one delegate, Andrew Cross, in his wartime account of the organization:

> After every battle . . . our delegates have been on hand with stores to supply their immediate wants, and at every hospital of the wounded, whether brigade, division, corps, base or general, they have been present to render aid as nurses, surgeons, as christian ministers and laymen, ministering to the necessities of any and all who needed aid. Beside this, they have attended to aid friends in finding their wounded and doing for them those acts of kindness which at such times becomes duty, and relieve and comfort the hearts of fathers and mothers, sisters and brothers, who are at home.[68]

While the Christian Commission's efforts never reached the level of the Sanitary Commission's, their approach provided a more personal connection to the men in the field that established the link with home that so many felt was lacking in the trenches surrounding Petersburg.

Charles Bolton, a student from Amherst College who volunteered for the Christian Commission in the summer of 1864, not only represents the type of person involved in such endeavors, but also reveals what kind of assistance was being provided on the ground for Northern troops. Upon his arrival at City Point in late July, Bolton's initial duties involved providing care for the plentiful number of wounded soldiers held in the port's hospitals awaiting transport to Northern states. "Here I labored faithfully . . . cheering up the men, talking with some on Religion, writing letters for others, and furnishing little delicacies to the weak," Bolton noted in his diary after his first few days stationed in the hospitals.[69] Before long, Bolton found his responsibilities extended beyond City Point to the front lines, where he began making frequent forays to the trenches with reading material for those with nothing but time on their hands. On August 15, Bolton described the start of his day: "I loaded myself heavily with books and papers for the Front. Found many *many* boys just out of the [rifle] pits, who rejoiced to see me."[70] Most of his work, though, was confined to caring for the wounded, and it was at the hospitals that Bolton felt that he was doing the most good. One day, Bolton headed for a hospital filled with African American soldiers wounded during the fighting at the Crater and "distributed peaches in my hospital among the faithful negro boys. How their eyes sparkled! 'Thank you,' 'Thank you,' I heard everywhere from all. One said 'God will bless you, I know.'"[71] From Bolton's perspective, those at the front or in the hospitals were always eager to see him, whether he was bearing water, books, or fruit.

Despite the positive perspective provided by men like Bolton, some soldiers and officers leveled criticism against both the Christian and Sanitary organizations. Such complaints did not typically question the goals or ideals of these groups, but instead targeted the methods by which they pursued their activities. Usually, the problems stemmed from a perception of unfairness; certain units or groups were getting the lion's share of the commissions' resources at the expense of all others. Colonel Robert McAllister, in command of the 11th New Jersey, noted just such an issue when he described the distribution of vegetables to his unit and remarked, "the Sanitary Commission is doing a good deal in this way. But the army out here at the front don't get much. It is principaly used up at the Hospitals."[72] While such a disproportionate use of resources could be excused given the greater demands of the wounded, some soldiers hurled condemnations at a different kind of disparity that appeared to have its origins in the dishonesty of some within the ranks. Heaping blame on men like Colonel McAllister, one Massachusetts soldier noted in a July letter that the efforts of the Sanitary Commission were "all a humbug" thanks to the officers of the Army of the Potomac:

> You see by the papers the accounts of the distributions of canned meats, porter, tobacco, lemons, etc., by the Sanitary Commission, to the soldiers. . . . The commission sent these articles for distribution to the troops; headquarters take a share, and send it as a lot to the division for a second pick; then it goes to brigade, and after they deduct two dozen milk, a barrel of beer, canned stuff, etc., it is sent to regimental headquarters, who divide it up into company shares, and yesterday, such a distribution footed up *four cans of meat* for each of our com-

panies, of an average of twenty-two men each. . . . This is the way the 'Sanitary' get taken in, and the manner in which your large Northern sums of money, the result of patriotic fairs, goes to the *soldiers*. The stars, eagles and bars get all the cream of that part, sent to the privates proper of the army.[73]

What comments such as these reveal is that while the activities of the commissions were generally lauded and appreciated, some of those in the trenches felt that corruption and inefficiency were preventing commission assistance from reaching those who needed it the most.[74]

There may have been some legitimate criticisms raised by the men against the relief efforts, but most members of the Army of the Potomac expressed genuine appreciation for the actions of the commissions on their behalf. Union soldiers recognized that those involved with these organizations, whether volunteers or paid workers, did not have to be at the front spending their time, and in some cases risking their lives, for the welfare of Northern combatants. Some soldiers acknowledged receiving the greatest benefits from the Christian Commission, the religious activities of which were of great interest to the more devout among the rank and file. Private Solomon Rose stressed the religious benefits in a spring 1865 letter to his mother, commenting that "we have the privilege of going to church every sabbath at the Christian Commission where we can hear a good sermon and also get plenty of Christian papers."[75] Others noted more substantial contributions to their lives, such as Lieutenant Andrew Robeson, whose engineering unit received some boxes of peaches from the Christian Commission, leading Robeson to exclaim in a letter, "Bully for the U.S.C.C.!!!!!"[76]

As Robeson's comments suggest, most Union soldiers chose to comment on the positives of how the commissions contributed to their physical lives on the war front. From that perspective, the Sanitary Commission's activities far outweighed those of the Christian Commission. Many soldiers acknowledged the Sanitary's efforts in their correspondence, simply noting the "extra rations" and "good things" received from commission delegates.[77] Others were more effusive with their praise of the commission's activities. After receiving a load of apples and potatoes from the Sanitary Commission in mid-July, Private Julius Ramsdell of the 39th Massachusetts complimented the delivery by noting that "these things are just what we crave and need." Ramsdell added further praise by noting in a letter to his aunt that "every soldier has reason to bless the

Sanitary Commission."[78] Other soldiers were overwhelmed by what was provided for them, such as Private James Horrocks of the 5th New Jersey Light Artillery, who seemed pleasantly surprised when both the Sanitary and Christian Commissions provided men in his unit with lemons, tobacco, and newspapers "all *free, gratis,* and for *nothing.*"[79] The men clearly recognized the benefits of the volunteer organizations, and the cumulative effect of the various commissions soon began to pay dividends in the form of troop morale. As Private Clarence Bell of the 13th Massachusetts noted after describing the various vegetables provided to his unit in July, "the men have been dining better for the last two weeks than they did before, and the boys are all getting rested and in good spirits again. They had all got some down, and tired of fighting all the time, but now they are ready again."[80]

The soldiers of the Army of the Potomac clearly recognized and drew morale from the resources and logistical apparatus directed to support them, but this in no way meant that soldiers along the line were being universally supplied in a steady and luxurious fashion. Most men praised the logistical effort, but a sizable contingent of soldiers reported being short on food or other items for either a portion or the entirety of the siege. The comments of one of the most frequent critics of supply efforts, Private John Haley of the 17th Maine, exemplify the shortages that plagued some units at various portions of the line. Haley's regiment, like most others, had suffered short rations while on the march during the Overland campaign; but as other soldiers reported an improving situation upon the arrival of the Army of the Potomac around Petersburg, Haley continued to note in his journal the paucity of supplies for his unit. In mid-July, he reported an outbreak of scurvy and other maladies among Union soldiers, which was "the result of having little or no vegetable food. . . . We live mostly on *promises* of potatoes and 'desecrated' vegetables." As a consequence of this nutritional deficiency, Haley concluded: "Not only the morale of this army but its health is fast disappearing."[81] While these comments were still early in the siege and could be excused as the Union logistical network still getting off the ground, more than two months later Haley once again noted dire supply conditions within his regiment, suggesting in early

October, when he finally received a good meal, that he had "been on the verge of starvation for many moons."[82] As autumn turned to winter, Haley once again reported being short of food and speculated as to the source of the problem. Writing on December 17, he noted that "No government under the sun ever made such generous provisions for its soldiers, and yet we profit but little from it. We are continually robbed by the villains who handle our rations."[83] Much like the grievances with the charitable commissions, Haley's complaints did not suggest that there was an overall shortage of supplies (as was the case with his Confederate opponents), but rather that corruption and inefficiency were interfering with the distribution of rations to the front lines.

The largesse of the Union war effort clearly made great strides in providing for the men in the Petersburg trenches, but that is not meant to suggest that logistical support equally contributed to every single combatant within the Army of the Potomac. Some units were in more isolated segments of the line and thus could not be steadily supplied, while many complained that they did not receive one or more of the privileges granted to other units or men. Yet taken collectively, the efforts made by Union military personnel, politicians, and civilians at sustaining the men along the Petersburg line and alleviating their exposure to combat conditions proved enormously successful at reaching the vast majority of men within the Army of the Potomac.[84] Such efforts helped to ease some of the psychological burdens that trench warfare placed upon men in the field and continued the mental adaptation to siege life, which the soldiers themselves had begun almost immediately upon their arrival near Petersburg. As the months rolled by outside the city, the casualties mounted and the weather turned foul, but the men were able to live a relatively comfortable and secure lifestyle within one of the most dangerous landscapes on Earth. As Major Abner Small of the 16th Maine noted in his recollections of the war, it was only after being immersed in the Petersburg environment for an extended period of time that he and his men "enjoyed some extraordinary lapses into life."[85]

7

"The Warm, Loving Heart of Peace"

MAIL AND ESCAPES FROM THE FRONT

A soldier can do without hard bread but not without his letters from home.
—Major Elisha Hunt Rhodes, 2nd Rhode Island Volunteer Infantry

Private George Chandler arrived late to the war. A ship carpenter from Brooklyn, Chandler enlisted as a private in the 39th New Jersey on September 23, 1864, joining the camps of the 9th Corps at Petersburg soon after. The campaign was still active, however, and shortly after his arrival the 39th was involved in an action near Poplar Grove Church. Chandler survived the engagement physically unscathed, emerging with a newfound respect for African American soldiers who "fought well saving us the honor of being shot at by the Jonnies." Chandler was not discouraged by his first battle, writing to his uncle in November, "I am not at all tired of soldiering but like it first rate. I keep in fine health & spirits."[1] The following month, things were more sedentary for Chandler as he described the work that was going into their "permanent" quarters for the upcoming winter months. "It would do you good to see the architectural style of our Mansions," he reported in another letter to his uncle, "we build up logs about four feet high & put up four tents for a roof & log up one end completely." The result of these efforts "leaves us about six feet square clear to move around in, but that's plenty." Despite this pride in his wartime home and continued satisfaction with his service in the army, Chandler closed his letter with a lengthy description of a bunkmate who was in a hospital. He claimed with clear dismay that his friend had come down with a case of homesickness and appeared to be suffering greatly from it: "I never saw any one fail so fast before and that with no physical disease."[2] As he wrote these comments on

Christmas Day 1864, Chandler no doubt felt a tinge of homesickness himself as the Petersburg campaign stretched endlessly before him.

While a steady source of food and shelter could be a positive source of morale for the army, meeting the physical needs of the men in the trenches was only part of the picture. Union troops needed a distraction from the deadly environment that surrounded them, lest they succumb to the belief that there was no world outside of the trenches and return to the fatalistic perception of their role in the war that followed the Overland campaign. Distractions were few in the trenches, but escapes from the melancholy of life in the field did occur on a frequent basis. This was achieved through connection with the home front, either through a literal escape to the safety of home for the short duration offered by a furlough, or a psychological escape provided by correspondence with loved ones in the North. As demonstrated in the previous chapter, men expected the Northern populace to support them, and part of that expectation was for them to be reminded of what they were fighting for. News from home, either in a letter or a newspaper, allowed them to feel part of the "normal" world, far from the surreal landscape of the trenches. Furloughs offered a taste of freedom, a chance to reconnect with those at home and recharge their morale before a return to the front. As the challenge of trench life engulfed them, these connections with the home front provided a necessary safety net for those soldiers who spent month after month before Petersburg.

As almost every historian of the modern soldier has argued, mail from the home front provides a positive reinforcement for those exposed to combat conditions. Mail from home serves as a reminder of the people and cause for which a soldier is fighting, reassuring them that they are not alone in the world. Historian James McPherson has claimed that "letters from home have been of crucial importance in sustaining morale in all literate armies," and the high literacy rate of soldiers during the American Civil War, particularly those within Union forces, guaranteed that men would utilize the pen and paper to express their feelings to those back home.[3] In fact, Anthony Kellett has suggested that the first time mail created an effective link between a home population and soldiers in the field was during the Civil War.[4] Thus, it is no surprise to find mail playing a decisive role for those men mired in the trench systems surrounding Petersburg as the monotony and violence of the campaign dragged on before them.

As was the case with rations, mail delivery depended on a stable and effi-cient logistical network connecting the Federal base of supply with the front line. Consequently, the early days of operations against Petersburg continued the erratic mail delivery that characterized the hectic pace of the Overland campaign. After surviving the bloodshed of May and June, Private John Ar-nold of the 49th Pennsylvania finally received his overdue mail on June 24. "I hadent Received no letter from home For over a month and that was tu long," Arnold complained in a letter home that same day.[5] Once the siege lines were established, however, mail service attained regularity and speed that was widely praised by those men who were almost always eagerly awaiting news from the home front. Slightly over a week after his regiment's arrival along the Petersburg line, Lieutenant Colonel William Tilton of the 22nd Massachusetts implied a dramatic increase in the speed of the mail service when he wrote on June 26, "the mail carrier brought me a cheerful & cheering letter from my other and better half date June 23. The date is so recent that I begin to feel as if really near civilization again."[6] Regularity continued into the fall, with one Massachusetts soldier writing to his mother on November 6, "I got your letter of the 2nd last night, remarkably good time."[7] When men such as these could hear of news from family and friends only days after it occurred, the delivery of mail significantly contributed to the sense of connection that soldiers felt with the home front. The arrival of mail soon resumed its place as a regular and uninterrupted daily tradition. Only weeks after the beginning of the siege, men like Second Lieutenant John Brincklé of the 5th United States Artillery were able to report that "our mails are very regular now. Sometimes two a day, & always one."[8]

The benefits derived from steady correspondence with loved ones were many, but most important was the view that they offered of home: an idealized world to which every soldier yearned to return someday. Reading about the occurrences back on the farm or in the city could provide the citizen soldiers of the Army of the Potomac an escape from the dull and deadly reality of life in the trenches while presenting an image of what they had to look forward to upon the conclusion of hostilities. "Letters have been the bright spot of my existence," Captain Charles Mills wrote to his mother in mid-June, writing again two weeks later, "I feel pretty lonesome sometimes, I assure you, letters, letters, letters, are my only comfort."[9] First Lieutenant Joseph Scroggs of the 5th United States Colored Troops recognized the power of distraction that mail offered, pointing out in his diary that "Rebel shells and leaky bombproofs have a very demoralizing effect, letters from home, however, containing substantial testimonials of affection, work a countercharm."[10] While the bonds formed by men within the ranks could help to sustain them in the face of combat, enduring the day-to-day monotony of life at the front demanded a consistent ability to stay in contact with those back in the "real world."

Most soldiers along the Petersburg line expressed their gratitude for the letters that occasionally graced their existence, but no one explained the power of correspondence more clearly than Private Julius Ramsdell of the 39th Massachusetts. An eighteen-year-old from Lynn, Massachusetts, this young apprentice in the leather trade had only enlisted in December 1863, and the homesickness must have been particularly acute for him as he endured his first campaign that summer. Two weeks before he would be captured in the fighting around the Weldon Railroad, Ramsdell recorded in his diary on August 4:

> We receive our mail now, at about nine o'clock every evening, and if friends at home could see how anxiously we all gather around the Serg. to hear it read, and could see the happy countenances of those more fortunate than the rest, they would write oftener and take a pleasure in so doing. Tis not the letter itself we so much value but because it is a reminder of home, and confirms the thought which we prise more than any other, that we are not forgotten by those dear to us at home, that their thoughts and sympathies are with us and every letter, which we receive we look upon as proof of all this, and even if it is nothing but a piece of paper with some friends name written upon it, it does more to encourage us amid our sufferings and dangers here than almost any other earthly thing.[11]

Private Ramsdell's comments clearly and poignantly express the key role that the arrival of mail had for those in the trenches. Ramsdell no doubt would have agreed with one soldier who stated the matter more simply: letters were "the only pleasure the soldier can receive."[12]

The substance of a mail call for Union soldiers was usually more than letters or packages from loved ones; newspapers and magazines from points north were also received by those on the front lines. These types of periodicals were usually directed toward the officers, men who had the interest and the means by which to acquire them. Whoever the intended recipient, Northern newspapers and magazines were passed around for the men of whole units to enjoy. Andrew Linscott of the 39th Massachusetts stated as much in a letter written only days after his bunkmate, Private Ramsdell, documented the psychological advantages of a mail call. Noting the recent arrival of a *Harper's Weekly* sent by his parents, Linscott remarked, "that magazine was a treasure to me. I have read it through every word of it and it is now circulating through the company."[13] The response to the arrival of even one outside periodical in a company or regiment could be electrifying to those eagerly anticipating news from home or from other war fronts. Sylvanus Cadwallader, the special correspondent for the *New York Herald* working near Grant's headquarters during the campaign, followed *Herald* delivery boys to the front one day and observed the effect that a newspaper could have on those in the trenches: "Arriving at the outskirts of camp the boys would soon be surrounded by officers and privates, and hundreds of bronzed, weather-beaten veterans could be seen sitting on stumps and logs, studying *Herald* war maps, discussing the 'military situation,' and forgetting for the time, cold and hunger, home and friends, war and its realities."[14] For thousands of Union soldiers, the Northern press provided another connection with a world that seemed far removed from the war front.

Not only was the arrival of mail and papers from home a source of excitement and a distraction from the daily experience of the siege, but the act of writing a letter intended for those at home also proved helpful to those facing week after week of entrenched tedium. Apart from keeping watch for Confederate activity or performing physical improvements on their entrenchments, Union soldiers had little with which to occupy their time in the trenches and rifle pits. With so much time on their hands, they turned to writing. The number and length of letters sent to those at home dramatically increased once troops settled in for the campaign, as men at the front found one way to fill the minutes of the day and thus combat the effects of boredom. "I will endeavor to write you a few lines this Eve as I have nothing in particular to do," was how Private William Greene of the 2nd United States Sharpshooters began a July letter to his brother.[15] This sentiment was pervasive in the letters of Greene's comrades in the Army of the Potomac. With such little activity going on in the

Union army, many soldiers worried that their boredom would be reflected in a decrease of substance in their correspondence. Private Warren Goodale of the 11th Massachusetts Light Artillery was almost apologetic in a November letter to his children: "since writing you last Monday there has been nothing special to write about. The most important event for me has been the receipt of a box from New York and an overcoat from Quartermaster." Despite his claim of slow times in the army, Goodale went on to fill six pages with stories from the front and comments regarding affairs back home.[16] Such lengthy missives to friends and family members were common, and Private Daniel Sawtelle of the 8th Maine offered an explanation in his memoirs as to why this was the case at Petersburg: "I used to amuse myself with letter writing. I had quite a good many correspondents, some of them unknown to me. This served to take my mind from the things around me and kept me informed of the things up in God's Country, as we called the North."[17] A soldier could not always be guaranteed a letter from home everyday, but the mere act of writing a letter intended for someone away from the battlefield could help carry a man's mind far from the bloodshed that surrounded him.

While filling the time may have been the primary reason for writing numerous and prolonged letters to loved ones, the comments of Private Sawtelle also suggest that a subconscious motive may have been to encourage those at home to write just as many long letters in return. Another means of obtaining a larger amount of letters each week was demonstrated by the complaints that frequently found their way into soldiers' correspondence. Union men generally praised the postal effort, but the occasional complaint about missing or delayed letters found its way into communications sent northward, with blame evenly distributed between letter writers and carriers. When a long-awaited letter arrived from home more than two weeks after it had been sent, Thomas Owen, an assistant quartermaster with the 50th New York Engineers at Petersburg, could only speculate, writing, "why this delay and who is to blame for it is entirely out of our knowledge. There seems to be something wrong."[18] Some soldiers began to believe that lack of mail was a sign that there was a lack of letters being received by those at home, but not necessarily because they were not being sent. "I dont believe you get one half the letters I write," remarked Private Henry Metzger of the 184th Pennsylvania in a letter to his sister, adding, "I write one a month, and sometimes two."[19] The obvious implication in the comments of both Metzger and Owen was that the postal carriers were inefficient or incompetent, but the Federal government was not always the target for condemnation. Some suggested, usually in a subtle fashion, that those on the receiving end of letters were not pulling their fair share of the writing load. Private John Foote of the 117th New York appeared to be utilizing the time-honored tradition of the guilt-trip when he began a letter to his sister by commenting on the lack of mail received recently, asking, "What is the reason? It must be the fault of the post, for I cannot believe you neglect to answering my letters."[20] Foote was no doubt hoping that his sister would read between the lines and step up her correspondence to him.

While some like Foote exercised subtlety, most soldiers bluntly requested, demanded, or begged for more letters from the home front. "I think you orte to write as often as I do I would like to get a letter every male now do write often," was the polite request of Private John Arnold of the 49th Pennsylvania in a letter to his family.[21] Others sought to add to their share of the mail delivery by communicating to writers in the North the importance that letters carried for those at the front. A Union soldier named Howard writing from the Petersburg line tried to convince his "Dear Friend" of as much in a June letter, remarking, "it is very consoling for a soldier so far from home to receive letters from those that they have left at home. Your letters are very consoling and I assure you that they are acceptable at all times."[22] For some, however, a lack of letters from home for an extended period led to frustration and anger at the thought that they had been forgotten by those they held dear. First Lieutenant John O'Brien of the 1st Connecticut Heavy Artillery was only half-joking when he issued an ultimatum to his cousin: "if people will not write to me I take it for granted that they do not want to see me—so I am going to stay at the front all the time Providence permitting."[23] The desperation apparent in the words of Lieutenant O'Brien demonstrates the power that a letter carried for soldiers in the field, and the lengths to which some would go in order to create a steady and abundant stream of such letters.

From the standpoint of morale, mail from home, whether it was in the form of a letter from loved ones or a newspaper full of war news, proved as beneficial to those in the trenches as the food that was being forwarded to them through City Point. Both the supply of mail and rations were tied to the Union logistical effort, and thus the efficiency that characterized the delivery of food to the front lines was also reflected in the efficient mail delivery. Mail could be a positive psychological boost for men in the trenches, especially when it contained relatively mundane items reflecting matters far from the battlefield. Northern troops spent almost as much time writing letters intended for loved ones as they did desiring and reading letters from the home front. Union soldiers, perhaps more so than their Confederate counterparts, had exceptional access to writing materials.[24] If a soldier could not find enough money in his pockets to finance a letter, several voluntary organizations provided an abundance of stationery, envelopes, and postage, all free of charge. John Arnold, who often filled his letters with demands for more letters from his correspondents, wrote one of his letters on stationery stamped by the Christian Commission.[25] With such easy access to pen and paper and a reliable postal service providing a steady supply of correspondence from home, Union soldiers had little difficulty finding distractions from the severe conditions of trench life around Petersburg.

A reliable means of contacting home could prove wonders for the men on the front line, but nothing was more regenerative and advantageous for Union soldiers than an actual escape from the destructive environment of the trenches. The idea that there was a world outside of the front line, where life was more comfortable and people were not trying to kill them, was of vast importance to those men just attempting to hold on a little longer in their entrenched positions. As Anthony Kellett has argued, twentieth-century conflicts demonstrated the notion that "the prospect of rest and of an escape from stress provided the soldier with a short-term personal goal against which he could plan his survival."[26] While the Petersburg campaign may not have reflected the same intensity as later conflicts, the utilization of an entrenched position created a situation where soldiers on both sides were exposed to the stresses of combat for days and weeks on end. Fortunately for Northern troops investing Petersburg, opportunities were available for an escape from the filthy, deadly holes along the main line to rear areas that usually offered greater protection from enemy fire and the elements. There was even the possibility open to them of a blissful venture back home for a short period. In addition, the uneven character of the violence along the opposing lines of fieldworks ensured that some soldiers would feel secure and comfortable even though they were still in close proximity with the enemy. Taken collectively, such factors frequently removed men and units from the foulness and violence of the battlefield while mitigating the stresses of combat on the men of the Army of the Potomac.

Prolonged exposure to the forward line of trenches or the advanced positions of the rifle pits was never welcomed by those men who quickly recognized the negative conditions of such duty. Particularly during the early weeks of the campaign, there were numerous reports by Northern soldiers of spending an extended amount of time at the front and being worse off for the experience. Private Austin Kendall of the 117th New York expressed the exasperation of his entire unit when he wrote home in early July, "our Regiment has been there 7 days in the trenches and last night they was relieved and fell back to the last line of pits, they all are pretty well worn out as they could not get out to wash themselves or anything, but lay there in the hot scorching sun."[27] John Foote, also a member of the 117th New York, reported nearly the same story in a letter written only days after that of Private Kendall, commenting to his sister that "for 8 days we remained in the front line of Rifle pits without being relieved, one of the most uncomfortable places on earth Nothing to protect us from the burning sun but our shelter tents, it seemed as if we should surely melt."[28] Later that summer, Private Caleb Beal of the 35th Massachusetts stressed the discomfort of the rifle pits, but for different reasons. Writing at the end of August, Beal remarked that "Picket duty is rather hard here. they have to go out in front almost a mile and deploy there in thick wood and stay on past 24 hours without sleep or relief, and as it has rained a great deal lately and the ground is very swampy, it is anything but pleasant."[29] As Beal demonstrates, exposure to the elements and the enemy for even short periods of time could prove detrimental to the men stationed along the main Federal line.

Such comments suggest, however, that the stay of men and units in the forward line of trenches and rifle pits was neither a consistent nor continuous one. Beginning soon after the establishment of formal operations at Petersburg, many of those in the Union command structure, typically at the regimental and brigade levels, began to implement a system of rotation that ensured that no man would spend more than a few days at a time exposed to the conditions of the front line. Several regimental commanders diffused responsibility for the rifle pits along their portion of the line by rotating companies through them every one to three days. A similar policy was adopted by most brigade commanders, who also rotated regiments, usually two at a time, through the primary line of trenches, with units staying at the front anywhere from three days to a week. While the rotation of companies into the rifle pits did not necessarily guarantee an escape from potential death, wounding, or capture, the regular movement of regiments to the rear promised that men would spend lengthy stays in more protected areas frequently located out of the range of enemy fire. Since brigades typically contained four to eight regiments, the result was that some men may have spent as much as half of their time during the siege out of the trenches in a more traditional base camp environment. As one historian of the Civil War soldier noted, "Union policy varied widely" with regards to the implementation of rotation by low-level commanders, "but few Union soldiers were compelled to remain a week in the trenches without respite."[30] Such rotation of units was not official policy handed down by the high command of the Army of the Potomac, but was merely a pragmatic recognition by lower-level commanders that their men could stand only so much.

The soldiers who actually served in the front lines understood this more than anyone else, and thus they welcomed the breaks that rotation offered them from the dangers of the trenches. The relief that the men felt was exhibited in how they described the rotation system to their loved ones, as evidenced by Sergeant Augustus Sanger Jr. of the 24th Massachusetts. Writing to his parents in September, Sanger explained, "now as we do picket one regt. goes out on the skirmish line for 24 hours. There, is relieved by another and goes into the . . . trenches nearest the camp and stays 2 days. Then comes in and stays in camp 2 days. Then out again through the same performance. So you see we are in camp 2/5 of the time."[31] All soldiers recognized that intermittent trench life was a dramatic improvement over the fast-paced and violent conditions of the Overland campaign and even the early days of the Petersburg siege itself. After grumbling to his sister about spending more than a week exposed to the sun and enemy in the main trenches, John Foote noted with some relief that things had changed, stating that "we are there now only half the time being relieved every 48 hours."[32] Others were blunter with their praise for the rotation policy and singled out limiting the exposure of men and units on picket duty in the more exposed rifle pits. Looking back on the campaign years later, Private Robert McBride of the 11th Pennsylvania recalled that during the siege, "pickets were only changed every third day, 'three day picket,' we called it. We preferred this, as it gave us such a long time without any duty of this kind."[33]

As usual, it was the men in the field, often the savviest when it came to the maintenance of their own survival and morale, who recognized the value of being regularly removed from the immediate proximity of the enemy.

As the campaign progressed, soldiers began to realize that unit rotation was unnecessary along some portions of the Federal line. Not every segment of the trench lines involved opposing forces unleashing immense amounts of ammunition in a vast effort to destroy one another. Several soldiers reported positions that were entirely devoid of violence and enemy activity for days or weeks on end. This was the case for some units as early as July, when men welcomed the relative peace coming on the heels of the furious pace and violence of the Overland campaign. "We are having a quiet time here to what we have been having," noted Sergeant George Fowle of the 39th Massachusetts on the 1st of July, before going on to describe the advantage of the quiet in the "chance to stand up strait without running a risk of your life."[34] The benefits of being able to move around without being fired on were obvious, and conditions grew so peaceful along portions of the line that men almost forgot that there was a war on. Private Charles Smith of the 8th Maine appeared to have no complaints when he wrote to his wife in August that "it is moore like home than it is like war here we can relieve picket in the day time and not get fired at . . . we will think it quite easy to stay here and do the duty."[35] Violence was not a universal characteristic of trench life; some soldiers had the fortune of serving in parts of the Union line where the risk of death was dramatically reduced and conditions approached a level of relative comfort.

The ebb and flow of combat operations between the opposing armies during the campaign makes it difficult to determine which areas were more peaceful than others. An area that was quiet one day could explode into bloodshed the next if one side chose to advance upon or harass their enemy. The correspondence of soldiers, however, indicates that one area of the line that was perceived to be calmer than others encompassed the Deep Bottom and Bermuda Hundred regions, located along the James River. These portions of the front were manned by units from the Eighteenth Corps, and, while several engagements were fought in this area over the summer of 1864, members of this corps reported quiet duty for large segments of the campaign. Lieutenant John Owen, whose 36th United States Colored Troops regiment was working near the Bermuda Hundred constructing a canal, observed in an October letter that "its been very quiet here lately. The rebs only throw a shell or two day, just to let us know they have not evacuated the swamp on the other side."[36] As Owen's comments suggest, the marshy terrain in the Bermuda Hundred region inhibited operations and made for more relaxed, if not necessarily more comfortable, duty at the front. Across the James near Deep Bottom, First Lieutenant Joseph Scroggs of the 5th United States Colored Troops remarked at about the same time as Lieutenant Owen that "picket firing is not practiced here, a very sensible arrangement for I never yet knew of any advantage gained in this way by either side."[37]

While some portions of the Federal line were more peaceful than others at various times, almost the entirety of both the Union and Confederate positions fell silent over the winter months. Most Federal units (along with those of the Confederates) were withdrawn from the front lines during the winter, as severe weather inhibited the ability of both armies to conduct active military operations. With skeleton units occupying the trenches on both sides of the line, Union and Confederate pickets and artillerymen rarely bothered harassing their opponents unless explicitly ordered to do so. As a consequence, those who rotated through the main trenches and rifle pits faced duty that was safer, if still cold and uncomfortable. After participating in several violent engagements with the Second Corps over the summer and fall, Lieutenant Colonel George Hopper of the 10th New York was relieved when things quieted down over the winter. Writing to his siblings in December, Hopper remarked, "we have been along this part of the line Eighteen (18) days [and] during that time we have hardly heard as many guns fired . . . we have been here days & without any loss, quite a change."[38] Even as winter began to yield to spring, large portions of the line remained devoid of hostilities. "Very quiet in camp and nothing to do but drill and study tactics," noted Lieutenant Colonel Elisha Hunt Rhodes of the 2nd Rhode Island in his diary on March 3, adding, "we seldom have to dodge Rebel shell on our part of the line."[39] While combat operations never ceased entirely along any portion of the line, and a smart soldier was always better advised to remain concealed from the enemy, some segments of the front were calm and occasionally even relaxing for those soldiers fortunate enough to be stationed in a quiet sector.

As the tempo of operations slackened over the winter months, most units found their removal from the main trenches being extended once winter quarters were established. The number of men in the front line was dramatically reduced, with the expectation that those removed to the rear could return quickly in the unlikely event of a Confederate assault across a no man's land inundated with mud and snow. Theodore Lyman, a member of General Meade's staff, described this practice and explained how in a typical unit, the main body of troops constituted a "reserve" force of men "concealed and who are ready to come to the assistance of the posts, if they are attacked."[40] In the rear areas, men were authorized to construct winter quarters, semipermanent dwellings usually built out of logs and mud that offered many benefits compared to normal camp tents in the field. "I have a large and commodious stockade, and if left alone can live very comfortably here," reported Captain George Bowen in December.[41] While officers typically received quarters to themselves (often constructed by enlisted men), soldiers had to share with their comrades. Still, Northern troops took pride in the construction of these homes away from home, with great care given to the installation of every possible comfort and amenity. "This season is characterized chiefly by perpetual rain, and penetrating cold that pierces through one's clothing and makes one shiver," observed Private James Horrocks of the 5th New Jersey Light Artillery in late November, before adding, "thank goodness I have a nice warm log shanty to live in."[42]

Struggling to fill the hours of their days, soldiers filled their letters and diaries with extensive descriptions of their winter quarters, and in the process revealed that during some of the harshest weather of the siege, most Union troops were able to live removed from the front line in a state of relative comfort. Men such as Captain Mason Tyler of the 37th Massachusetts went into great detail, describing "a grand house, a real palace, so to speak. It is fifteen feet long and some six and half broad, five feet high at the sides, and seven in the centre. Two of us occupy it."[43] Private William Hamilton in the 191st Pennsylvania offered a description of his winter home that had proportions similar to Tyler's: "We have excellent quarters—Holden (the clerk) and myself have a log house, with door and two windows, each having two glass lights—five feet high to the square, sixteen feet long and eight feet wide, with a good floor and canvas for a roof."[44] Though writing decades later in his memoirs, Private McBride offered one of the more detailed descriptions of his winter quarters:

> The tents built by the soldiers for Winter-quarters were generally about nine feet
> by seven, built of logs, five feet high. A ridge pole was fastened up at the proper

height, over which four shelter tents, buttoned together, were stretched and brought down to the top log on either side, and securely fastened. This formed the roof. The gable ends were closed with pieces of shelter-tent, boards, or some substitute. A door about three feet high was left in the side next the company street. A chimney, with fire-place, was made at one end, carried up a foot above the roof. It was built of clay and sticks. Usually the tents were uniform in this respect, the chimney of each at the same side of the tent. Two beds or bunks, one above the other, were made of poles covered with a layer of leafy twigs, if possible. On these were laid wool blankets, rubber blankets, extra clothing, etc., making a very comfortable bed. Cracker boxes furnished material for door, seats, and table. The chinks between the logs were closed with clay mortar. The Winter-quarters of a regiment was simply a neat, cleanly village of small log houses, with this peculiarity, that only one row of houses faced on a street.[45]

While the Virginia winters were abundantly cold and damp, the soldiers of the Army of the Potomac had the means at their disposal to mitigate the environment around them and make their life in the army a bit more like home.

Unit rotation and reduced enemy activity were certainly advantageous to Northern troops in the trenches, but nothing could surpass the full escape from war that a furlough provided. With the substantial numerical superiority that Federal forces had over the Confederates defending Petersburg and military operations at a minimum over the winter months, Union commanders were able to adopt a liberal policy of granting leaves of absence to both officers and enlisted men. Despite the relaxed furlough policies, not every soldier in the Army of the Potomac was granted one; only those deemed "deserving" were allowed to visit their homes over the winter of 1864–1865. Recently promoted Brigadier General Robert McAllister offered some insight on this issue, writing in a December letter what was needed to obtain a furlough: "The fact is that there are no leaves granted except in cases of emergency, sickness, or important business requiring immediate attention."[46] Those recovering from wounds or illness in the hospitals and still able to travel usually received some manner of leave, and a soldier who could offer a valid reason for being absent from his unit (such as having a death in the family) was also granted a furlough.

Leave was not always granted out of necessity; some units offered various rewards for those soldiers who could demonstrate particularly praiseworthy behavior. Some were simple rewards, with Sergeant Timothy Bateman reporting in his diary in September that "The Cleanest Regiment of each Brigade to be exempt from Picket duty for twenty days," an attractive prize for those seeking a lengthy absence from the forward trench lines in the hot summer months.[47] Corporal Edwin Bearse and his Massachusetts unit were the beneficiaries of just such a policy. "We have inspections about every other day the best Regt in the Brigade get excused from one weeks picket and fateague," Bearse wrote to his mother in January, "the 40th took the prize last time . . . so we get clear of a fortnights duty."[48] Surgeon Henry Millard noted a similar carrot approach being applied to furlough distribution in January, describing it in detail as one "giving the man who has taken the best care of his gun & equipment a furlough, one being selected from each company & then one from that number making one out of each Regt."[49] The chaplain of the 2nd Connecticut Heavy Artillery, Winthrop Phelps, described a similar policy that month in his diary, writing how "the cleanest soldiers in the Brig. [are] to have a furlough of 20 days," with one lucky recipient being selected from each regiment.[50] Twenty days was the average length of leave granted to Union soldiers over the winter months, which, when travel time to and from is taken into account, gave men roughly two weeks at home with their family and friends.

Such temporary breaks from the trench lines could offer Union troops an escape to the blissful, idealized world of home, and this benefit made furloughs particularly desirable for the men at the front. In January, after seeing many comrades awarded furloughs in his 5th New Jersey Light Artillery regiment, Private James Horrocks pined for a leave of absence in a letter to his parents, stating how "I long for civilized life once more, and should very much like to go."[51] Fortunately, Horrocks was finally able to find "civilized life" in March, when he was awarded a furlough and traveled to New York. However, "longing" rarely got a soldier out of the trenches, and many men did whatever it took to obtain a furlough, even if it included the creation of exaggerated or false stories. By the end of February 1865, after spending nearly the entire winter without a break from the front, Private Henry Heisler of the 48th Pennsylvania demonstrated his growing desperation by proposing a scheme to his sister:

> I am going to try for a Furlough in a few days. I want you to get Walter to write a letter to me as soon as you get this, and I wish you would get up a good story between you for a reason for me to get home. When I got your letter to day I

told the Lieutenant that you was very sick with the Black Smallpox, and now I want Walter to write a letter to me asking me to come home as soon as possible, that you have the Blk Small Pox very bad and are not expected to recover. as soon as I get the letter I will show it to the Colonel and apply for a furlough to go home and see you. That is about the only way to get one so I think I may as well take advantage of it.[52]

The scheming with his sister appears to have failed Heisler, since the last letter preserved from him during the war was written in mid-March and offers no indication that he had received the furlough he was seeking. While few soldiers went to such lengths as manufacturing stories about diseased relatives in order to obtain leave, the prospect of a furlough was enough to brighten the day of many Northern men who sought a release from the confines of life along the front line.

Of far greater benefit than the prospect of furlough was the reality of one. While there are no numbers available for the Army of the Potomac as to how many furloughs were granted during the Petersburg campaign, enough were provided to be considered a realistic option for the vast numbers of men hoping for one. It certainly became realistic for men like Lieutenant Colonel George Hopper and Captain James Latta, each of whom received a fifteen days' furlough over the winter.[53] Officers probably received a disproportionate number of furloughs, if only because they had the means to afford a trip north to visit their families or travel to other destinations. Enlisted men like Private McBride did have such opportunities, however, and they spoke highly of what escape from the front offered them. Following an illness in August, McBride was transferred northward where he was given a furlough to convalesce in Philadelphia. His experience during that time on the home front was revelatory: "I had looked so long on the forbidding, bloody front of war, that it was a most pleasing revelation to discover that back here was the warm, loving heart of Peace."[54] While letters offered the men a vision of what the home front looked like, only an actual visit there could confirm for them whether their memories of home matched the reality of a place far from the "bloody front of war."

Despite the measures taken by some Union soldiers in search of a furlough, there were those within the ranks who observed that both the opportunity and reception of leave was not always of positive benefit. Registering hostility to the furlough system, the often pessimistic Private John Haley of the 17th Maine remarked in his diary that a furlough "furnishes as much pain as pleasure. If I were to go, every moment of the time would be harrowed by the thought that I must soon return to these scenes of destruction and bloodshed. What, then, is a respite of a month, especially as we are now enjoying quiet?"[55] While few men adopted such an extreme view, some who actually had the opportunity to travel away from the front returned feeling the same emotions as those described by Haley. Brigadier General Edward Ripley, in command of a brigade in the Eighteenth Corps, could not get enough time away in order to make it home, so he was forced to settle for a brief visit to Norfolk, Virginia. His furlough did not appear to be very helpful; as Ripley explained in a letter after his return, "my trip was just enough to work much evil and not long enough to do me the good I hoped from it, and I am back here with seven devils of discontent and restlessness worse than the first."[56] Even those who were able to make a trip back to their homes found a mixed blessing from their journey. First Lieutenant Samuel Cormany of the 16th Pennsylvania Cavalry at first rejoiced upon hearing he had received twelve days' leave to visit his wife in late November, but upon his return to Petersburg the homesickness kicked in worse than ever before. Only days after returning to the front, Lieutenant Cormany wrote in his diary that he "spent rather a dull day . . . Oh! that this cruel war were over so all could go home."[57] Most men yearned for a furlough and welcomed one if received, but while a visit home could be a positive morale boost to some soldiers, others noticed how the pleasures of home made life in the squalor of the trenches even worse upon their return.

As thousands of Federal troops found an escape from the Petersburg trenches through the granting of furloughs, thousands more found themselves free from the trenches but not free from the dangers of combat. With the Army of Northern Virginia effectively trapped around Petersburg, Grant took the opportunity of dispatching Union forces from the siege lines and sending them to other theaters of war where they might prove more useful. The most prominent example of this strategic shifting of manpower involved the detachment of the Sixth Corps from the Army of the Potomac in July 1864 to Washington, D.C., and subsequently the Shenandoah Valley, where it would operate for much of the remainder of the year before returning to the Petersburg lines. The thousands of men heading northward with the Sixth Corps in mid-July at first seemed pleased that they were leaving the drudgery of the trenches, a feeling conveyed by Corporal Cyrille Fountain of the 77th New York. After grumbling over a late-night march through thick dust to City Point to begin their trip up north, Fountain noted that his unit was full of "awful looking men but good Spirits for we ware going the right direction."[58]

Fountain might have held his tongue had he been aware of the hard-fought campaign that the Sixth Corps would find in the Valley under the command of General Philip Sheridan. Operations in the Valley were a far cry from life in the Petersburg trenches, as warfare began to resemble the intermittent engagements of the first three years of the war rather than the static battle of attrition along the James River.[59] Despite several large battles, the campaign was welcomed by the men who often spoke in glowing terms of their time in the Valley. Private Daniel Faust of the 96th Pennsylvania wrote in mid-September how "we have got very good times now days we are encamped in a rich country we can get plenty of forage and foods are very plenty . . . this is the greatest farming country in Virginia."[60] The soldiers of the Sixth Corps were still at war, as Faust himself would find out only days later when his unit participated in the battle of Winchester, but war in the Valley offered Union men greater comforts than war at Petersburg. The costs were still high, however. In July, Corporal Anson Shuey of the 93rd Pennsylvania had expressed an eagerness to leave Petersburg and head north. "I have seen in the paper that the rebels are making another invasion of Maryland," Shuey wrote to his wife. "I would like to go up there myself." He got his wish, as the 93rd joined the Sixth Corps when it headed north later that month. Unfortunately, Shuey would not return to Petersburg with the Sixth Corps later that year; he would be shot at the battle of Winchester and die of his wounds on September 27.[61]

After successfully crushing Confederate General Jubal Early's forces at Cedar Creek in October, Union forces were transferred back to Petersburg in December to bolster Federal strength against Lee's dwindling band of Confederate defenders. Sixth Corps soldiers returning triumphantly from the pleasant weather and beautiful countryside of the Shenandoah Valley found an Army of the Potomac locked away in its entrenchments and mired in the deepening mud of winter. "This was the least desirable place to which they could have sent us," protested Private Wilbur Fisk of the 2nd Vermont in a mid-December letter, explaining that life in the "dirty trenches" along the front was "all fighting and no fun. We neither whip nor get whipped here. It is regular cold blooded dueling, day after day, with no decisive result on either side."[62] After the startling victories in the Valley, it was no surprise that those coming back to Petersburg did not look kindly upon the static nature of the conflict there. Yet, most of the soldiers reentering the trenches realized that their work up north had gone a long way toward winning the war, and they would endure whatever was necessary to be there at its conclusion. After expressing his disappointment at being transferred from the Valley, Captain Elisha Hunt Rhodes of the 2nd Rhode Island reconciled his feelings in his diary with the thought that "if it will end the war I am satisfied to go to any point they choose to send me."[63] Even Private Fisk, after registering his discontent, was forced to concede, "somebody must do this work, and they probably thought it might as well be us as anybody. We know how it is done."[64] Their stay in the Valley had not exactly been a pleasure trip for Union soldiers of the Sixth Corps, but it had removed them from the trenches for an extended period of time and gave them the opportunity to strike a serious blow against the Confederacy. This helped to sustain the men as they returned to the dreariness of trench life.[65]

The fact that large portions of the Army of the Potomac served on detached duty for more than half of the siege reinforces the notion that soldiers did not spend every waking moment huddled deep in the cold earth desperately trying to avoid being killed or maimed by enemy projectiles. Next to an open field charge across no man's land, duty in the front-line rifle pits or trenches was certainly the most uncomfortable and dangerous position on the Petersburg battlefield. Nonetheless, it is clear that those within the Federal command structure took steps to prevent soldiers from being exposed to the extremes of combat for more than a few days at a time. While a rotation to the rear did not entirely remove soldiers from the threats of the battlefield, it gave them an opportunity to rest their physical and emotional states in a reasonably safe and comfortable environment among their comrades. This was especially true during the winter months, when quarters in the rear grew more comfortable and even life on the main line was somewhat more relaxed than before. It was also during the winter of 1864–1865 that Federal officers took advantage of the reduced tensions at the front to release thousands of soldiers on furloughs to their homes and various other points away from the Petersburg lines. As noted above, a visit home did not always yield positive benefits, but generally

Northern soldiers were comforted by the idea of an escape from the front even though they faced the prospect of an imminent return. The utilization of unit rotation and furloughs was a conscious effort by those in command to alleviate the effects of combat on Union soldiers, and was thus a tacit admission, long before any effort was made to study the psychological impact of combat on the front-line soldier, that prolonged exposure to trench life could have a degrading effect on morale.

Furloughs would spike in the Army of the Potomac over the winter of 1864–1865, but the increase first began toward the end of October, when thousands of men were granted leave to travel home to vote in the presidential election. Colonel Robert McAllister, who at this point was in command of a brigade in the Second Corps, was one officer who was authorized to grant such furloughs. Only days before the election in early November, McAllister observed, "We are getting all our soldiers home to vote that will not be fit for duty in fifteen days. This will help to swell the vote for Lincoln."[66] Voting for Lincoln is precisely what Lieutenant George Bowen did when he was given ten days' leave to go home for the election, though his vote was in vain as his home state of New Jersey was one of the few that cast its electoral votes against Lincoln in 1864.[67] While thousands of soldiers were able to journey northward to join in the electoral process, few reported being able to take full advantage of their escape from the front. Corporal Theodore Skinner's story is typical of the mixed blessing of Election Day furloughs. With New York being a critical state for Abraham Lincoln and the Republicans, it was hardly surprising that Skinner and his 112th New York regiment were sent up to New York City for two weeks in late October and early November. "When we found out where we were agoing we made calculations on having a good time," Skinner wrote soon after his return to the front lines, but conceded that the men "were sorely disappointed. We we[re] only on land three days out of the whole time we were gone and that was on Staten Island." After spending much of his furlough aboard a Union transport, Skinner was forced to report, "I was glad to get back to Chapins Farm again. If that is the way that they treat Soldiers North, I had rather be a soldier down here."[68] The election furloughs were designed for one purpose—getting men to the ballot box—and it appears that little enjoyment was derived by those "fortunate" enough to receive one.

Despite the mixed blessing of the election furloughs, they were but one part of a concerted effort by the Union command structure to care for those in the field and maintain the fighting power of the Army of the Potomac for as long as possible. Those soldiers actually immersed in the struggle on the front lines had their own techniques for enduring life in the trenches, whether it involved emphases on patriotism, religion, comradeship, mail, or innumerable other methods for confronting and adapting to the horrors of the battlefield. The labors by Federal bureaucrats, politicians, and military officials to sustain soldiers at the front did not replace these methods, but instead reinforced them, making it easier for soldiers to love their country, their God, and their friends without the distraction of a rumbling stomach or a loss of hope. Once the base needs of Union soldiers were met, it became much easier for them to win their personal battle for morale and sustain their optimism for the future. This created a situation where a Union soldier could look at the volatile trench landscape surrounding him and comment, "we are having a pretty good time now. Something like we used to have when we thought soldiering a hard buisness."[69] When Union forces advanced against Petersburg in April 1865, the effects of protracted exposure to the violence and decay of trench life were hardly apparent in the confidence and strength of those on the verge of the final victory at Appomattox. Such vitality grew in no small part from the extensive efforts made on their behalf, which made certain that they were prepared to renew the struggle and end the rebellion in the spring of 1865.

8

"The Goose Hangs High"

PERCEPTIONS OF VICTORY WITHIN THE ARMY OF
THE POTOMAC, JUNE 1864–MARCH 1865

I heartily wish this cruel war was over but I fear it will last
more than one year yet.
—M. T. Haderman, 3rd United States Infantry

Private Charles Smith felt that he and his fellow soldiers were being stabbed in the back. A sailor from Maine, this New Englander had already done two years of service in the Army of the Potomac by 1864 and retained confidence in the Union war effort despite having endured the Overland campaign and months in the Petersburg trenches. "I am not discouraged yet," Smith wrote to his wife in September, "my faith is good that we will whip the rebbs yet and the government is worth three years service." For Smith, the only thing holding back the Union cause was trouble on the home front. "We do not like being cheated by cowards at home that never thought of going to the front," he wrote in the same letter, expressing his hope that all such men would get drafted and provide much needed reinforcements.[1] In a later letter, Smith explained his feelings in more detail, making sure that his wife understood whom he blamed for recent troubles. Writing in October, Smith stated, "Every cry for peace at the north is encouraging to the rebbs and helps lengthen this war and them that think that they are in favor of the soldiers when they ask for peace on any terms are very wrong and doing the very thing that will keep us longer in the service." Looking ahead to the upcoming presidential election, Smith told his wife to "look at the soldiers vote and that will show you what we think of your peace men."[2] Unfortunately, Private Smith, quite clearly a

Lincoln supporter, did not have the chance to vote in the election. Captured in the vicinity of Fair Oaks, Virginia on October 27, Smith would spend the winter in a North Carolina prison camp before being exchanged on March 1, 1865. He would be at home in Wells, Maine recovering when the war came to an end that April.[3]

By the summer of 1864, the Union war effort had reached a turning point, though at the time it was hard for soldiers like Private Smith to see it. The bloodletting of the Overland campaign was coupled with stagnation or reversal on other war fronts. General Franz Sigel's Union forces were driven into retreat down the Shenandoah Valley following the battle of New Market in May. Despite having three armies under his command in the Western Theater, General William Sherman spent the summer in a slow, frustrating campaign of maneuver in his drive toward Atlanta. As the summer continued, however, developments elsewhere began to trend upward for Union forces. Soldiers of the Army of the Potomac and the Army of the James reading their mail each day in the Petersburg trenches learned of the joyous Union victories across the Confederate frontier at places such as Atlanta, Cedar Creek, and Mobile. Union forces under the command of men such as Generals Sherman and Sheridan appeared to be marching at will throughout the Confederacy and bringing success in their wake. These tremendous military victories made possible what many of those in the field considered the most important political success of the war: the reelection of President Abraham Lincoln in November 1864. For those sitting stagnant in the Federal lines before Petersburg, such signs of success both across the country and right before their eyes allowed Union soldiers to come to an almost unavoidable conclusion: they were on the winning side and ultimate victory was right around the corner.

———

Hope is a vital element to morale, or the will to fight, for without hope why would a soldier continue risking his life on the field of battle? There are different types of hope on the battlefield, such as the hope in the survival of oneself or one's immediate comrades, the hope for the triumph of one's cause, and the hope that the actions of one's leaders will produce that triumph. As has been demonstrated, each of these qualities were lacking in the soldiers of the Army of the Potomac by the close of the Overland campaign in the summer of 1864, and the survivors of that experience faced a difficult challenge in reestablishing their hopes for victory following the repeated defeats of the summer. Union soldiers at Petersburg, as with soldiers of any war, found hope in a multitude of locations, whether it was in the divine wisdom of a God above them or in the cold comfort provided by a deep hole in the ground. Hope became a virtual obsession for some soldiers, as evidenced in the popular battlefield pastime of calculating one's odds for survival in either the short or long term.[4] However, the one overarching vision of hope for those exposed to the rigors of combat, besides the desire for their personal survival, is the desire for victory. Victory, brought about by God or man, brings an end to the battles and campaigns and is the surest manner by which long-term survival is achieved. All soldiers on both sides of a conflict hope for victory over their enemies, and they look to signs of battlefield success as another step forward toward the conquest of their foes and an imminent end to hostilities. Such triumphs on the battlefield, however small in nature, can give inspiration to those tired of war and ready to succumb to defeatism. After having invested so much for so long in battle after battle, men are willing to go on for just a little longer if they are convinced that the payoff, victory, is just around the corner. Even if they have lost faith in their cause or country, they will continue to fight so that they can be there at the end and witness what is to be gained by all of the sacrifice.

Hope was certainly a powerful force in the trenches surrounding Petersburg from 1864–1865, as it would be in the trenches near the Somme in 1916 or the foxholes surrounding Bastogne in 1944. Evidence indicates that as Union soldiers settled in, they turned inward, focused more on preserving their individual lives on the battlefield rather than on the increasingly vain hopes for a defeat of the Confederates. These efforts at reasserting their independence and control over their role on the battlefield were a direct consequence of the horrors of the Overland campaign. While these actions would prove tremendously beneficial in rehabilitating the men after the stresses that they had undergone in May and June, the positive effects for the soldiers in the siege lines could not be sustained without a sense that there was some purpose to their continued presence in an environment that threatened their lives daily. After seeing thousands of lives seemingly thrown away in the assaults of the Overland campaign, the men more than ever before needed some justification to leave the protection of their entrenchments and risk their lives assaulting the enemy. Victory, or even just a sense of its potential, gave them a reason to hold on and once more take to the field of battle. In other words, hope in an overall Union victory began to reinforce and even supplant the more basic hope for their survival. Such a restoration of hope in the success of their cause and country was a necessary prerequisite for the men of the Army of the Potomac to operate once again in an organized and energetic fashion. Thus, as Union forces marched virtually unmolested across the Confederate landscape in other theaters, these soldiers took the signs of an impending Northern victory as inspiration to continue risking their lives on the battlefield.

Victory had been on the minds of few within the Army of the Potomac over much of the summer of 1864 as setback after setback greeted Union forces across the country. The Northern soldiers who commenced the investment of Petersburg in June 1864 found that hope for victory was an increasingly rare commodity. By mid-June, six weeks of marching and fighting across the Virginia countryside had virtually eradicated the belief in a looming victory over the Confederacy—and, specifically, General Robert E. Lee's Army of Northern Virginia. Grant's primary force, the Army of the Potomac, had at best stalemated the Confederates, who met the Union army with rifles and breastworks at nearly every point of its advance toward Richmond. The result was a focus on the transportation hub at Petersburg, and a temporary reduction of active combat operations in the East as Union soldiers rested and refitted in the wake of the staggering casualties of the Overland campaign. "We seem to have come to an anchor here near Petersburg," was the apt assessment of one member of the Army of the Potomac soon after the new campaign began.[5]

Men rapidly recognized that the campaign had turned into one of attrition, with the army methodically isolating Petersburg and Lee's army from the remainder of the Confederacy. Noting the "standstill" of the army in late June, First Lieutenant Theodore Vaill explained to a friend that the goal was one of "cutting off of Lee's feed."[6] As Corporal Edwin Bearse stated just as succinctly, "Grant is going to starve the Confederacy in submission."[7] However, "standstill" and "starvation" would take time, possibly a lot of it. In a letter to his wife back home in Newburyport, Sergeant Joseph Barlow of the 23rd Massachusetts demonstrated his understanding of the implications of a siege strategy when he wrote her in late June that "it is hard to tell how this campaign will end. I tell you it looks blue enough . . . Richmond will not be taken this summer."[8] After surviving the Overland campaign, soldiers within the Army of the Potomac now found themselves digging in around Petersburg, with no prospect of capturing either that city or the Confederate capital in the near future.

News from other fronts was even less cheering that summer, as Union forces across the country met with either obstinate resistance or outright reversal in the simultaneous campaigns choreographed by Grant for execution that May. General Sherman's operation against Atlanta was especially discouraging, particularly given the string of successes that had met Western armies over the previous year.[9] But it was General Sigel's defeat at New Market that was potentially the biggest blow, as a Confederate force under General Jubal Early took advantage of the Federal setback by marching down the Valley to strike at Washington, D.C. in July.[10] Many of those besieging Petersburg saw this invasion of Maryland, the third substantial strike into Northern territory by the Confederates, as a new low for the Union effort. After learning on July 13 of the Southern move into Maryland, First Lieutenant Joseph Scroggs of the 5th United States Colored Troops strove to maintain his optimism in the face of defeat, noting in his diary, "our national affairs are not in a prosperous condition. It is one of the dark periods. May the day of our triumph soon dawn."[11] Others sought to lay blame, such as Second Lieutenant John Brincklé of the 5th United States Artillery, who linked the invasion with the failure of the Army of the Potomac to reach Richmond, writing, "the Rebels have cleaned out Maryland pretty effectually this time & carried off their plunder without any trouble. In the meantime we are doing nothing at all. This is the magnificent campaign of *Grant*."[12] In short, the promise of spring had dissipated by the time operations commenced against Petersburg in June and July, and those within the ranks surrounding that city found despair to be a much more common sentiment than hope.

Despair manifested itself through anger, but perhaps surprisingly not anger at their Confederate foe. As Early's men traipsed through Maryland and came only a few miles from entering downtown Washington, D.C., some Union soldiers began to express hopes for further Confederate success. No less a figure than General Francis Barlow, commanding a division in the 2nd Corps, declared in a July letter to his wife, "I am utterly disgusted with the craven spirit of our people, I wish the enemy had burned Baltimore and Washington and hope they may yet."[13] Coincidentally, another Barlow, Corporal Joseph Barlow of the 23rd Massachusetts, wrote on the day previous, "it is a Pity they did not get to New york and Burn down the Place they ought to have a little of this war north to Bring them to a sense of duty."[14] Soldiers' cynicism in the course of the Union war effort did not merely manifest itself in condemnation of those in command, but also in an assault on those on the home front who may not be providing proper support for those at the front. The focus on Baltimore and New York City is particularly relevant; antiwar riots in Baltimore in 1861 had resulted in the deaths of several soldiers, and the New York draft riots during the summer of 1863 were still a fresh memory for the country. Union soldiers were clearly sensitive to the idea that those on the home front were not facing the same challenges as those on the front lines, and this developed into an almost sadistic desire for them to face the realities of war. As Captain Frederic Winthrop explained in a letter,

> It is most extraordinary that you people up North get so horribly scared when a small column of the enemy come near you. It seems to me that you ought to have been able to crush them yourselves without calling on the Army for assistance & even with that assistance I fear that enemy will escape alive & unharmed. It is too bard [bad] . . . I wish they had taken all the plunder from Pennsylvania [and] Maryland.[15]

If those at Petersburg had to face off against a determined, deadly enemy, then perhaps it was appropriate for those at home to get a taste of the war as well.

As the dismal and bloodily inconclusive summer at last came to a close, the situation appeared to be improving for the Northern cause. After the earlier defeats and stalemates, Union forces resumed their advance on the Confederacy and soon began to see large gains in territory and objectives. While those Northern soldiers laying siege to Petersburg were not direct participants in the victories that soon greeted Union arms, they were kept well informed of the success of their cause. This was due in no small part to the efficient mail delivery to the Army of the Potomac, which brought them letters and newspapers filled with good news from across the country as summer gave way to fall. For the North as a whole, these victories brought a renewed prospect of success in the struggle against the rebellious states. For those Federal soldiers stationed near Petersburg, Union success signaled not only the increasing likelihood of victory, but also the possibility that their time in the trenches would soon come to an end. These men thus seized upon these victories as an encouragement to fight on, if only to see a triumphant end to the hostilities.

The first glimmer of hope on the horizon for those trapped in the trenches was the dramatic success of naval forces under the command of Admiral David Farragut in their assault against the Confederate forts protecting Mobile Bay in early August 1864. On August 5, Farragut's wooden and ironclad vessels sailed past the heavy fire of the Mobile defenses, thus rendering the port useless for Confederate supply operations and making Farragut a national hero in the process.[16] After having suffered through the dark days of July, soldiers focused upon this modest victory as a long-awaited bright spot in the affairs of their country. A week following Farragut's success at Mobile, Private Francis Woods of the 139th New York discussed the reaction of his unit to the news, writing to his family, "we are very much encouraged by the news from Mobile and we hope the good news from that quarter will be still increased within a few days."[17] Others such as Corporal Barlow focused upon the victor rather than the victory, remarking, "I wish that we had forty Farrguts in the service, some such a man we ought to have in the place of old welles as Sect of the navy."[18] Obviously, men like Barlow felt that the recent setbacks for the Union war effort had to do with personnel, and they hoped that successful leaders like Farragut would be placed in positions where they could do the most good. Having had their first taste of victory in quite a long while, the men of the Army of the Potomac hoped that the "very brilliant thing" at Mobile Bay would act as a turning point that would erase the disasters of the previous months.[19]

These expressions of trust proved well-founded by September, when news of a much larger Northern success reached the siege lines. After having been stalled outside the city's defenses for weeks, Union forces under the command of General William Sherman finally succeeded in capturing Atlanta, a major transportation and industrial center of the Confederacy. The significance of this victory dwarfed Mobile, and upon hearing the news, soldiers of the Army of the Potomac immediately recognized that a substantial blow had been directed against the South. Many soldiers stood up and took notice of this event, with their reactions varying from muted joy to overt jubilation. In his diary entry for September 6, Second Lieutenant Samuel Cormany of the 16th Pennsylvania Cavalry merely noted, "news comes 'Atlanta has fallen'—great jollification," before moving on to other topics.[20] Almost all men noted Atlanta's capture in their journals or letters, even if it was just to comment on how the men in ranks responded to it. "The news from Atlanta produced great rejoicing here," noted Captain Thomas Bennett of the 29th Colored Connecticut Infantry, and Private Austin Kendall noted how his unit gave three cheers for Sherman upon receiving the news.[21]

Other men could barely contain their enthusiasm, putting down on paper their delight over the fall of a city that had been a Northern objective for so long. "Atlanta!!! is ours!! The bloody drama draws to the final scene. All Hail to the glorious Army of the West. Nerves of steel tempered in the fire of an hundred battles," exclaimed Lieutenant Scroggs of the 5th United States Colored Troops, words that suggest the common feeling among Union soldiers that Atlanta's downfall indicated the imminent defeat of the Confederacy itself.[22] Not all responded to the news of Sherman's success with the belief that the war would soon end, but many commented on the effect that such a victory had on men like themselves who spent much of their daily lives in trenches dug deep into the Virginia landscape. Private John Foote of the 117th New York at first expressed his awe at the massive artillery barrage that was fired into the Petersburg defenses to celebrate Sherman's victory, *"fire works up north are nothing in comparison."* Foote comprehended a change at least within himself following Atlanta, writing to his mother, "what a glorious victory is the taking of Atlanta. I tell you it puts new energy into ones soul."[23] News of Union success, even halfway across the country, proved immensely beneficial to those who may have been losing their faith in the prospect of their cause emerging triumphant over the Confederate adversary. Upon hearing the news, Lieutenant Colonel George Hopper could confidently report, "we are in the best of spirits."[24]

Such a restoration of faith and hope in the Union cause would be boosted further by the rapid succession of victories in the Shenandoah Valley following the fall of Atlanta. Under the command of General Philip Sheridan, Federal forces (including the 6th Corps, which had formerly been a part of the Army of the Potomac) engaged in a destructive march through "the breadbasket of the Confederacy." Sheridan's soldiers defeated Confederate forces under the command of General Jubal Early at the battles of Winchester and Fisher's Hill in September, followed by a more decisive victory at Cedar Creek in October.

In the latter battle, the opposing Southern army was virtually annihilated, leaving the Valley wide open to Union forces.[25] As with the fall of Atlanta, soldiers were quick to express their delight over such resounding victories. Sergeant Major Christian Abraham Fleetwood of the 4th United States Colored Troops noted his men cheering upon hearing news of the Cedar Creek victory in October, while Private Austin Kendall of the 117th New York declared that the news of such victories was "one of almost unparalleled splendor."[26] "Good news comes thick and fast now and encourages our fainting hearts," were the words offered by Private John Haley of the 17th Maine upon hearing of Fisher's Hill. Haley also took joy in suggesting that Jubal Early should be labeled "the most thoroughly thrashed general in the Confederacy."[27]

Others conveyed similar satisfaction over Sheridan's victories but also a hope that, like Atlanta, they would create an opportunity to really strike at the heart of the Confederacy. Writing in his diary at the end of September, Lieutenant Colonel William Tilton of the 22nd Massachusetts noted that "Genl. Sheridan whipped Early at Winchester Sep. 19 and 20th . . . a great victory, and one that will have a vast influence on our further movements. I think Lee must evacuate Petersburg to protect Richmond."[28] Private Charles Smith of the 8th Maine also saw the beginning of the end with Sheridan's victories, writing in September, "I think thing look very prosperous all around now and I think this thing will play before another year."[29] Regardless of the strategic outlook, Sheridan's success increased the morale and determination of those who faced off against Lee's Confederates at Petersburg. Surveying the men of his brigade one day in September, Colonel Robert McAllister declared as much when he wrote to his wife, "we have received the glorious news of Sheridan's two greate victories. It gives our boys more spirit."[30] For those who may not have heard the "glorious news," the whole army was alerted to the victories in the Valley when Grant and Meade ordered a one hundred gun salute fired into the Confederate lines after each victory.[31]

As autumn descended and the weather turned colder, the soldiers of the Army of the Potomac began to look for a different sort of victory than one brought about by force of arms. The approach of the presidential election that November caused considerable discussion within the ranks as most soldiers viewed the contest as a crucial test of the war's aims. The incumbent, Republican president Abraham Lincoln, faced a challenge from George B. McClellan, a former commander of the Army of the Potomac running on a Democratic ticket that condemned Lincoln's handling of the war while suggesting that a negotiated peace was the best option to end the bloodshed. Lincoln, buoyed by the recent successes at Atlanta and in the Valley, stood by the military campaigns against the South and maintained his strategy of denying the Confederacy legitimacy by refusing to negotiate. Lincoln understood that the battlefield may very well decide the election, and soldiers in his army recognized that fact as well. "Every victory we gain twixt now and Election, secures to make 'assurance doubly sure' that Abraham Lincoln will be elected to occupy the White House another term of four year," wrote Private Charles Field of the 108th New York in September.[32] Whether they supported the incumbent or his challenger, the men in the field recognized that the result of the election would determine the future course of the war, and consequently the approach of the presidential contest evoked passionate discussion, as documented by the attention given to the election in their letters home. Political discussion was a favorite pastime for these Northern men, and with such a crucial electoral event on the horizon, they spent many an idle hour in their entrenchments speculating on the outcome and its significance.

To those supporters of Abraham Lincoln, the members of the Democratic Party who opposed the president (some of whom were known as Copperheads) were seen as traitors to the country who merely gave aid and comfort to the enemies of the Union by challenging the prosecution of the war. After outlining his reasons for supporting Lincoln's conduct of the war, Lieutenant Thomas Owen of the 50th New York Engineers turned to the subject of those who suggested compromise with the South, asking, "What shall I call them? Traitors. No they are not as honorable as an outright traitor. Ah, I hav it. Copperheads."[33] Veteran Volunteer Private Alexander Adams of the 100th Pennsylvania went further, perhaps exaggerating when he declared shortly before the election, "soldiers in the field are far more afraid of the copperheads than they are of the rebble army."[34] Another veteran volunteer, Sergeant George Tate of the 120th New York, expressed a similar feeling while sick in the hospital. Labeling the Democratic nominating convention in Chicago "a nest of traitors," Tate reached the conclusion that "this Fall, we fight & vote in the same direction."[35] Despite those who understood that the Democratic Party at least had good intentions, some soldiers were convinced that McClellan was the candidate of the Confederacy, and a vote for him and his party would be a vote in support of the enemy. For Sergeant Samuel Clear of the 116th Pennsylvania, just such a notion was confirmed one day as he sat in the trenches. After voting for Lincoln in his regiment's election while under fire on the front lines, Clear noted in his diary that "I knew I was right [voting for Lincoln] for the Johnnies would take off their hats by the hundreds and shout for McClellan."[36] With such vociferous support for McClellan and the Democrats emanating from their opponents, it would have been hard for soldiers on the front line to escape the idea that a vote against Lincoln would be a vote against the Union cause.

Despite the rhetoric and a perception that the Copperheads were traitors to the Union, there was still a large Democratic following within the Army of the Potomac composed of those who did not hesitate to announce their support for George McClellan. As with any American electoral contest, there were many reasons behind their choice, but among those who put down on paper why they threw their lot in with McClellan, some major motives stand out. First, there were the soldiers who, for a variety of reasons, disagreed with Lincoln's handling of the war and held the view that McClellan as president could bring an honorable end to the hostilities. As the election approached, one McClellan supporter, Private William Greene of the 2nd United States Sharpshooters, wrote to his brother that Lincoln "cares nothing for peace unless he can gain his own object in freeing the niggers, an object I hope will never be accomplished. If McLennon [McClellan] is not elected you can look forward to four years of war."[37] Private Charles Field of the 108th New York, a Lincoln supporter, offered a different view of the motivations behind this group when he suggested that "every soldier in the Army who votes for McClellan, does so because they are demoralized . . . they are sick and tired of War and are deluded into the belief that the election of Mc will insure a settlement of the War."[38] Given the high casualties of the Overland campaign and the stagnation that followed at Petersburg, a significant number of Union soldiers fell into this "peace at any cost" category. A second, yet much smaller, group of McClellan advocates were those who legitimately thought that a Democratic victory in November would end the war not through compromise, but through victory over the Confederacy. Sergeant Barlow of the 23rd Massachusetts attempted to explain why this was the case when he wrote his wife in July, "I think that if george Mcclellan was President of the country that a million of men would

Rush to arms . . . I hope that he will be nominated and elected."[39] Soldiers like Barlow believed that having a true military man at the helm would finally bring the North together under a strong hand and crush the South's rebellion.

The much larger and more vocal segment of the Army of the Potomac was solidly behind the reelection of Abraham Lincoln. They expressed their support for the president through both condemnation of his opponents and praise for his management of the war effort. Just as some soldiers identified the opposition Democrats and their candidate McClellan as being agents of the Confederacy, so did they identify Lincoln and the Republicans as promoters of the Union. The same day that Sergeant Clear of the 116th Pennsylvania noted Confederates cheering for McClellan, he wrote in his diary that in his regiment's election, "I voted the way we was shooting for Old Abe and the Stars and Stripes."[40] Some of those in the Petersburg lines were voting for Lincoln in order to defeat the enemy, but they identified that enemy not in front of them but to the rear. In writing to his mother that October, Sergeant Joseph Griner of the 8th Pennsylvania Cavalry stressed the importance of the upcoming election and stated, "I must not lose my vote for Uncle Abe, for it stands in hand for every true man to come forward and show his colors this fall to defeat the enemies of our country, the Copperheads."[41] While many soldiers considered a vote for Lincoln a vote against the Confederates and Copperheads, most voted to reelect out of the simple belief that Lincoln was the best man for the job. "I am still for Old Abe," wrote Lieutenant Colonel George Hopper of the 10th New York in a letter to his siblings, "I think he has shown himself a mighty man no man ever had half his trials to contend with . . . I dont think during these trying times we can afford to try a change in the administration. The man that is their suits me very well as I go in for fighting it out."[42] Generals had come and gone over the years, but for men like Hopper, President Lincoln had always been there, standing strong in victory and defeat. Therefore, it is not surprising that they felt themselves attached to Lincoln in a manner that they could hardly understand, and the only way that they could express their feelings was to support him in one of the most critical elections in the nation's history.

Simply stated, the men of the Army of the Potomac believed that Lincoln would bring them the victory they so eagerly desired. George McClellan, whether he represented surrender, betrayal, or simply change, could not gain the victory that the prospect of Lincoln's continued leadership seemed to promise, particularly after the recent Union successes. "Though I prefer McClellan as a man, I should vote for Lincoln, as I think that his reelection would be a worse blow to the Rebs than two victories," was how Lieutenant Andrew Robeson of the 1st New York Engineers explained his position in a letter to his father.[43] Corporal James Beard expressed his desire to end the "human butchery" of the war, but then asked himself, "how ar we to do this is it by election little Mc or is it by replacen old Ab in the chair another four years." He concluded that he would "go republicken" and observed that, while new recruits seemed to be supporting McClellan, the "old standbys" among the soldiers were going for Lincoln.[44] Corporal Alexander Adams of the 100th Pennsylvania expressed complete confidence in Lincoln's ability to achieve victory, declaring, "I am certain the war will be over soon and we will have a permanent and honorable peace." When the election arrived, Adams would proudly declare that his company had voted unanimously in favor of President Lincoln.[45]

The support of the men in ranks would prove beneficial for Abraham Lincoln, as the soldier vote contributed to his resounding victory over George McClellan in the November elections. Despite running against a former general who had once been tremendously popular among the soldiers, Lincoln still managed to pull in approximately three-quarters of the soldier vote.[46] Men proudly recorded the tallies in their regiments as votes were gathered in late October and early November. Private Bayard Cooper served as the clerk for the election in the 203rd Pennsylvania and happily reported to his mother that his unit voted "Union strong."[47] Not yet eighteen years old by the time of the election, Private Charles Edgerly of the 11th New Hampshire recorded that Lincoln won his regiment with a "considerable majority."[48] "I had the pleasure of casting my first vote for the *honest Rail-splitter*," wrote Private John Foote of the 117th New York, "I think he got about 2/3 of the votes in this Regt."[49] Similar numbers came in for the 124th New York, with Corporal Benjamin Hull noting the exact tallies of 132 for Lincoln and 32 for McClellan, before concluding, "I guess the majority is good enough for Lincoln."[50] Writing "Old Abe is the man" in his diary shortly before the election, Sergeant Francis Waller of the 6th Wisconsin counted 121 votes for Lincoln and 37 for McClellan in his regiment, with his own Company I voting unanimously for Lincoln. Waller closed his summation of the election returns with the cheerful declaration: "I am going to have two canteens of whiskey tonight."[51] While some men, such as Private William Hamilton of the 191st Pennsylvania, reported his and other units voting overwhelmingly for McClellan, the vast majority of soldiers proclaimed wide support for Lincoln as the fall elections were held within the Army of the Potomac.[52]

For those tens of thousands of soldiers who lent their support for the incumbent, Lincoln's reelection signaled an end to a perceived time of crisis as critical as any other point in the war. Lieutenant Owen of the 50th New York Engineers expressed a deep sense of relief following the election, remarking, "we have the glorious news that Mr. Lincoln is again to steer the good old ship of State, thank God. I verily believe that the country is now comparatively safe."[53] Other soldiers speculated on the effects that the election would have on the war, with most suggesting that the validation of Lincoln's leadership was yet one more blow to the Southern cause. "It is a greate triumph and will have very much to do with puting down the Rebellion," explained recently promoted Brigadier General Robert McAllister as he assessed the impact of the election on his unit, "all here seem to be pleased with the results."[54] Lieutenant Colonel Hopper went even further, proudly declaring soon after the election, "honest & Patriotic Lincoln is reelected president for the next four years. this is indeed good news to all lovers of our country. better than taking Richmond."[55] When Lincoln was reelected, Union soldiers in the Army of the Potomac who had supported his campaign experienced tremendous elation, as it became clear to them that the single largest internal threat to Northern victory had been removed and nothing remained that could prevent the destruction of the foundering Confederacy.

With the crisis of the presidential election settled in a perceived victorious manner, Federal soldiers near Petersburg could once again turn their attention to military affairs as even more positive news swept through the Union encampment in the last weeks of 1864. Continuing the string of victories begun prior to the election, Union forces under the command of General George Thomas decisively defeated Confederate general John B. Hood's Army of Tennessee at the battles of Franklin and Nashville in December, destroying one of the few organized Confederate forces remaining in the West.[56] As with the earlier triumphs of the fall, Northern men heard the booming of another one hundred gun salute being fired into the Confederate lines and looked to these victories as a sign that the war was in its last days.[57] Upon hearing the news of Hood's army being crushed at Nashville, Corporal William Ray of the 7th Wisconsin reported with glee in his diary, "Thomas has captured 13,000 of Hoods men & 61 pieces of artillery . . . All is well all around & the goose hangs high."[58] Once again, soldiers looked to the big picture, using Thomas's success as support for their growing belief in a rapidly approaching victory over the Confederates. Perhaps the most eloquent response to Nashville was delivered by Private Wilbur Fisk of the 2nd Vermont, who took time out from grumbling over delinquent paymasters to comment:

> But better than pay-days, paymasters or greenbacks, is the glorious news that is continually coming in from the armies all around. One hundred guns were fired Sunday morning in honor of Thomas's victory over Hood. The war news from all points is good. Victory—complete, decisive and glorious victory greets our armies everywhere. The rebellion is toppling down. Slavery's champions, vanquished in the field of open discussion, are being vanquished in the field before the bayonet and the cannon's mouth. The day-star of Freedom, dimmed by the smoke of battle, seems about to shine brighter and more beautiful than ever before. We have reason to rejoice, thank God and take courage.[59]

Such commentary would have been difficult for men like Fisk to muster after the carnage of May and June, with a Confederate invasion of the North following immediately afterward. Victories such as those at Nashville, coming so soon after the presidential election, had restored some of the faith in the cause of ending secession and slavery to those who stood vigil around Petersburg.

George Thomas was not the only Union general making headlines in the West; the exploits of General Sherman and the forces under his command on their March to the Sea aroused increasing interest across the country as Northern forces journeyed deep into the heart of the Confederacy. As in much of the rest of the nation, Federal troops stationed near Petersburg found themselves captivated by the stories sent northward as Sherman's men made their way across the state of Georgia to Savannah in late 1864, and then on to Columbia, South Carolina in 1865.[60] Expectations ran high when Sherman and his men first set off in November on the march that would make them famous; those soldiers of the Army of the Potomac who remarked on this campaign immediately recognized the impact that Sherman could have if successful. "All eyes are directed toward Sherman," wrote Sergeant George Tate of the 120th New York in a December letter to a friend, "if he can destroy Augusta & safely make his way to Savannah & occupy it, which is not improbable, the blow will about deprive the rebels of their already forlorn hope."[61] In early December, Corporal Adams of the 100th Pennsylvania described the men in his unit as being very positive about Sherman's expedition, and stated that he personally was "very much elated with the prospect of Sherman's success and feel confident of soon ending the war in an honorable way."[62] For First Lieutenant Theodore Vaill of the 2nd Connecticut Heavy Artillery, Sherman's movements across Georgia brought the larger Union strategy into clearer focus. "Grant is of course cooperating with Sherman & Lee is probably in as great a quandary as he has ever been in yet," Vaill recorded as he pondered the dangers facing the Confederacy's future.[63]

The faith that these men had in General Sherman was validated at the end of December when his force made it to the coast and captured Savannah. Like the rest of the country, they concluded that the success of this campaign signaled the rapid approach of the Confederacy's downfall. Writing to his sister in late December, Private Daniel Sawtelle of the 8th Maine exclaimed, "is not the news glorious from Sherman and the southwest? There is some prospect of this war's being ended yet and that in our favor."[64] The prospect of victory was most certainly welcome to the weary, cold soldiers in the trenches, and they seized on Savannah as a sign of future relief. When the first reports came in of Savannah's fall, Private Samuel Brooks of the 37th Massachusetts declared, "I hope it is [true] for it will do a good deal towards ending the war and I hope it will end for I am about sick of it."[65] His feelings were echoed by Private John Steward of the 1st Maine Heavy Artillery, who greeted the news with "it looks now as though the war might close this winter I hope it may."[66] As 1865 dawned, Sherman's successes, coupled with Thomas's victories in Tennessee, came as welcome news and buoyed the army's hopes for an imminent victory over the rebel armies.

As the New Year passed and city after city began to fall in the Confederacy once Sherman's men turned northward toward South Carolina, soldiers of the Army of the Potomac reveled in how Union forces were traveling across the South virtually unmolested. January brought another significant victory, with a Union force seizing Fort Fisher on the North Carolina coast and another force gaining control of Wilmington a few weeks later. For Lieutenant Colonel Hopper of the 10th New York, the fall of Fisher was "the beginning of the end to this rebellion."[67] When news of Fisher reached his 34th Massachusetts regiment, Surgeon Henry Millard noted that it "caused general rejoicing which is evidence of another nail being driven into the coffin of the Rebellion."[68] Captain James Latta of the 119th Pennsylvania enjoyed chalking up Union successes in February, remarking in his diary that "the news of glorious victories elsewhere is frequently heard. Charleston, Wilmington & Columbia have all fallen."[69] Writing to his aunt in February 1865, Private Julius Ramsdell of the 39th Massachusetts agreed with Latta, noting how "the glorious news which come from Sherman now every day are read to the different corps, divisions, and regiments of the army by the officers, amid the deafening cheers" of the men.[70] Private William Hamilton of the 191st Pennsylvania expressed his enthusiasm in a letter to his mother, but also seemed a bit jealous when he wrote, "Sherman certainly appears from the newspaper accounts to be having a real good time, traversing the country at will and doing not much fighting. Here a fight can be had at any moment desired."[71]

The fall of Charleston, South Carolina in February, although not directly linked to Sherman's operations, received particular mention from soldiers as they tallied up the increasing number of Northern victories. The capture of the city where the war had begun almost four years earlier, in the state that had perhaps the most fervent pro-secession population, created a symbolic impact on the men around Petersburg that far exceeded any strategic value gained. Private Alexander Rose of the 11th New York Light Artillery declared it "glorious news," while Sergeant James Horrocks of the 5th New Jersey Light Artillery viewed it as the death knell of the Confederacy. Horrocks proclaimed in a letter to his parents, "what do you think of the Confederacy—caving in very rapidly, or I may say collapsing like red hot flues."[72] It was hard to find any negatives behind the Union cause as the war news continued to roll in, and by the time of Lincoln's second inauguration on March 4, 1865, it was clear to most that the war was winding down. For Private Jacob Seibert of the 93rd Pennsylvania, only recently returned to duty following his wounding at the Battle of Winchester, the situation merited a clear statement in a letter home: "Father: I think the war is nearly over."[73]

Over the winter of 1864–1865, Bugler J. Chapin Warner of the 34th Massachusetts transformed into one of William Tecumseh Sherman's biggest admirers. Originally from Granby, Massachusetts, Warner had enlisted in 1862 and served a year in the ranks as a private before being made chief bugler for the regiment in 1863. His unit had been with Sheridan for the Valley campaign, and upon the regiment's arrival at Petersburg in December, Warner kept up a steady correspondence with his parents relating his faith in Sherman's actions further south. To Warner, Sherman was the "smartest general we have," and it was becoming clear that "this rebellion looks like tumbling down . . . The best way is to whip them a few times more and then they will stay whiped."[74] By February, Warner continued to predict that Sherman's successes were bringing an end to the war. "We have good news from Sherman," he wrote on February 22. "Now I hope that our army will be filled up this spring full And we can just wipe them out, the next campaign."[75] By March, his confidence was at its peak as a new campaign seemed to be gearing up against the Petersburg lines. After relating more positive war news, Warner proclaimed, "Every thing seems to be in our favor. And thank the *Lord* for that. I think sometimes before our Regts.' time is out we shall see the backbone of this *rebellion*."[76] Warner was correct; as he wrote those words on March 17, the surrender at Appomattox was less than a month away.

Warner's comments further demonstrate the impact that Sherman's campaigns, coupled with other Federal operations in the South, had on those soldiers besieging Petersburg during the final months of the war. Even while enduring a Virginia winter and huddling half-exposed for extended periods of time in the Federal earthworks, soldiers derived great satisfaction from the catastrophes suffered by the Confederates in the winter and spring months of 1864–1865. With the fall of Atlanta and Union successes in the Shenandoah Valley, the tide was clearly turning against the Southerners, but it was the presidential election in November that really indicated a turning point in the war. Following Lincoln's reelection, the Confederacy suffered wave after wave of crushing defeat that rapidly eroded what little power remained of the Jefferson Davis government in Richmond. Thanks to the availability of mail and newspapers within the Northern lines, none of these developments escaped the attention of the soldiers of the Army of the Potomac. As the Confederacy crumbled, they learned of it blow by blow and rejoiced that the cause for which they had fought so hard and so long was nearing a final victory. The comments of Colonel Edward Ripley, a brigade commander in the 18th Corps, clearly demonstrate the effect that these victories had on the soldiers. Assessing the state of the men in his brigade in late September following the first round of Union victories, Ripley wrote: "The Army . . . is elated, buoyant with highest hopes, and is eager for the struggle. Six weeks ago the reverse was the case. Atlanta, Mobile and Winchester have stirred up the blood of the men, and their confidence now amounts to fanaticism."[77] As the victories piled up for the Union cause over the winter of 1864–1865, the hopes of Northern soldiers around Petersburg continued to rise as well. However, there were limits to the effects of victories in other areas of the war, since they did little to improve the situation of those sitting entrenched before Petersburg. It was not until the soldiers of the Army of the Potomac began to receive firsthand information regarding the impact that these victories had on the Confederate forces before them that the flame of hope grew brighter than ever before.

9

"Treason's Going Down"

PERCEPTIONS OF THE ENEMY DURING
THE PETERSBURG CAMPAIGN

The poor fellows will get completely exterminated ere long
if they don't come to terms.
—First Lieutenant Charles Stinson, 19th United States Colored Troops

For some Union soldiers, the Petersburg experience offered an opportunity to actually interact with their Confederate foe as never before. Private Edward Wightman, a newspaperman from New York City, had originally enrolled in a New York cavalry regiment in 1862 before transferring to the 3rd New York Infantry regiment the following year. Having endured the Overland campaign, Wightman, along with the other survivors of the Army of the Potomac, adjusted as best he could to a trench experience that left him "in little holes behind the barriers of logs and clay." After the fast-paced violence of the Overland battles, the reduced tempo of combat operations made for some unusual circumstances. "As [if] by mutual consent picket firing has ceased," Wightman wrote to his brother at the end of June, "we expose ourselves without fear of consequences, walking about in plain view of each other." He went on to note that "the greatest good feeling prevails between the men of the hostile pickets," and that Union soldiers were meeting with the Confederates between the lines to exchange coffee and tobacco.[1] Eventually taking advantage of these exchanges, Wightman conversed with members of the enemy and observed that "there is great dissatisfaction between the rank and file of Lee's army. They wrote to us that they were convinced that 'we privates could finish this war' and protested that they were heartily tired of it." Based on these comments,

Wightman confidently predicted that the Union army would seize Petersburg by the Fourth of July.[2]

Petersburg would not fall to the Army of the Potomac in July, but this did not prevent Union soldiers from concluding that they were getting the better of their Confederate opponents. Apart from the steady stream of positive news from across the war front, almost every day along the siege lines brought soldiers like Private Wightman into contact with the enemy in a steady stream of unofficial truces that characterized the fluidity of life in the no man's land between fortified positions. While such truces were not unusual during the Civil War, the static nature of the Petersburg campaign coupled with the proximity of the lines allowed for such communication to occur fairly easily when both sides were willing. These encounters provided valuable information to Union men who knew little of life in the Confederacy, but who now discovered that their opponents were facing shortages and hardships not equaled within the Northern lines. As the campaign dragged on, Federal men did not have to risk consorting with the enemy between the lines to acquire this information, as large numbers of Confederate deserters brought in more tales of woe on a daily basis. Newspaper reports of Confederate military failures across the country were reinforced by the starving, bedraggled enemy soldiers who removed themselves from the war by seeking sanctuary within the Union lines. Desertion led to a steady attrition of manpower levels within the Army of Northern Virginia, and the packs of rebel soldiers who crossed the lines to surrender presented quantitative proof that the Confederacy was on its last legs.

———

While the prosecution of the war in other regions progressed favorably for the Union cause throughout the fall and winter of 1864–1865, the situation in the trenches around Petersburg remained as stagnant as it had been since the final days of June. Fall would see some heavy fighting along the Petersburg line, particularly in late September and early October when Grant launched a sizable force north of the James River to bypass Petersburg and strike directly at Richmond, an effort that met with modest success.[3] Abraham Lincoln's reelection on November 6 breathed new life into the Northern war effort, but the realities of impending winter weather kept operations against Petersburg at a minimum for several months. Grant still authorized an infantry movement against Hatcher's Run in early December, which was done in conjunction with a cavalry strike down the Weldon Railroad. Fighting in this operation was limited, partly due to the arrival of foul weather, but Union forces succeeded in imposing further damage to Lee's already poor supply situation.[4] With the arrival of winter conditions, active Petersburg operations entered a two-month lull until Grant once again chose to strike west along Hatcher's Run in early February. Portions of the 2nd and 5th Corps advanced the Union lines westward to the vicinity of Armstrong's Mill before being hit by Confederate counterattacks that halted the movement after the Union forces suffered 1,500 casualties.[5] Through a patient application of force along his flanks, Grant once again succeeded in extending his lines to the west, forcing a similar response from Lee, but the winter months provided no substantial breakthroughs for the Union operations surrounding Petersburg.

Despite such active operations throughout the campaign, fighting along the Petersburg line was not uniform. When one or both sides were not actively seeking to extend their lines or assault those of their opponent, a low level of hostilities characterized most of the siege lines where sporadic sniper and artillery firing were the order of the day. In some areas, particularly during the winter months, firing came to a complete halt. It was in such sectors where the two sides were locked in close proximity to one another that soldiers would partake in an activity that would become quite popular among the enemy combatants of not only the Civil War, but also some twentieth-century conflicts. Informal truces occurred with great frequency for much of the Petersburg campaign, and they are significant for many reasons, not the least of which for how they demonstrated opponents coming together and conversing in a civil manner after having been engaged for so long in efforts at killing one another. The truces between Union and Confederate pickets and units throughout the siege gave soldiers of both sides the ability to see their enemy and understand that they were not facing a bloodthirsty foe bent on their annihilation, but merely another American who was performing a duty for his country. For Union soldiers in particular, the truces and exchanges along the front lines allowed them to meet their enemy and learn just how desperate the Confederate cause was becoming as Northern forces closed in from all sides. In the process, this information indicated the approaching downfall of the Confederacy and contributed to a restoration of hope that proved vital to those Federal troops spending weeks and months in the trench lines.

Truces were an unofficial effort undertaken by the rank and file of one side or the other, typically occurring out in the rifle pits of the pickets where the two lines were in the nearest proximity. The actual type of interaction between soldiers could take many forms, but the most basic was a mutual lack of gunfire along a particular portion of the line. This was very common during the campaign; there was no general order for units to keep up the rifle or artillery fire against the enemy (something that Confederate ammunition supplies would not allow for), and most soldiers agreed with Colonel Edward Ripley when he applauded the lack of fire and asked "why should they [the pickets] keep up this villainous shooting day and night."[6] With such disgust aimed at the continual exchange of fire, it became a common occurrence for both sides to quit firing of their own accord. Occasionally, a deal was reached in a manner similar to the one revealed by Surgeon William Watson of the 105th Pennsylvania, when he wrote in September, "the pickets in front of our Corps have ceased firing by mutual consent . . . although farther to the right in front of the 10th and 18th Corps firing is constant."[7] When a cessation of fire occurred, either naturally or otherwise, men of both sides would take increasing risks in exposing themselves in an effort to test their opponents and see how much exposure they could get away with. "There is less shooting evry day & the Boys are more and more venturesome on each side," was how Corporal William Ray of the 7th Wisconsin described this slow process of exposure and communication in his journal. "They will get friendly soon so that the pickets will not have to lay in the ditches all day."[8]

This "venturesome" nature of the soldiers eventually established varying forms of communication along the line as men took advantage of the unofficial cease-fires. If the lines were close enough, pickets or even those in the trenches would shout across no man's land and carry on conversations in a manner that demonstrated not only the lack of strong antipathy toward each other, but also the sense of competition that had developed after years of war. One day in September, Captain Thomas Bennett of the 29th Colored Connecticut Infantry related a typical exchange between pickets:

> Videts [pickets] seldom fight, and when ours go out at night you may often hear laconic conversations 'Good evening, Yank' 'How are you Johnny?' Sometimes

when they are coming too near each other you may hear them say 'You's getting too near, Yank' 'No I ain't John' 'You are, Yank' 'They told me to come out here, John' 'Well, don't go any further, Yank.' If you don't look out 'I'll let the little thing go, John, right at you.' 'Keep still now, Yank.' And so their conversation will end.[9]

Conversations like these, with both participants physically proximate to one another but still respecting each other's space, could continue for hours. Gunfire, which still occurred infrequently in even the quiet parts of the line, was a sure end to such convivial exchanges. However, when a unit received word that either they or others would be opening fire on those with whom they had had conversations or exchanges, soldiers would be kind to their opponents and not betray the trust engendered by that interaction. After describing some of the encounters between Confederates and his men in the 16th Maine, First Lieutenant Abner Small explained, "when a battery was about to open fire, some friendly skirmisher would shout 'Down, Yank!' or 'Down, Reb!' as the case might be, and down out of sight would go every man."[10] In a similar situation, Sergeant Austin Stearns of the 13th Massachusetts explained how things worked along his part of the line, where the agreement was that at the conclusion of an exchange with rebel pickets, "if we were ordered to fire, the first volley over their heads, so they could get in their works, and they were to do the same by us."[11] While both sides recognized that they were at war, the pride and honor of both Federals and Confederates created an unwritten code of conduct for what constituted a good-faith exchange across the lines. What is particularly noteworthy about this code is how closely it parallels the system that historian Tony Ashworth identified in the First World War, which formed one of the hallmarks of his presentation of how the "live and let live" concept became prevalent in the trenches of that conflict.[12]

The communication between the opposing forces at Petersburg frequently went beyond mere conversation, with soldiers openly revealing themselves in no man's land to venture out and interact with their opponents. The motives were typically selfish, with soldiers seeking to expand their diet or comfort by acquiring materials from their enemy that were in short supply within their own lines. Both sides had resources that their opponents coveted, particularly those containing caffeine and nicotine. As previously demonstrated, Northern men had many rations and resources in abundance, but they did not have steady access to the one material of which Southerners had plenty:

tobacco grown throughout the Tidewater region. While serving on picket duty one day in August, Sergeant Jacob Lyons of the 120th New York discovered hospitable relations on the front line and noted in his diary how "the Pickets were exchanging papers and coffee and sugar for Tobacco."[13] A similar situation existed in the portion of the Union line manned by Lieutenant Small's 16th Maine, where "occasionally a Yank and a Johnnie would meet between the lines and exchange coffee for tobacco, or a New York *Herald* for a Richmond *Enquirer.*"[14] As Small's comments demonstrate, an exchange of information also occurred at the front, with the literate and curious nature of the Union and Confederate soldiers driving them to learn how the war was being portrayed in the enemy heartland. It is difficult to know how much stock soldiers put in the newspaper articles of their opponents, but the war news presented in them probably would have been as encouraging to Northern men as it would have been demoralizing to Southerners.[15]

The process whereby men risked wounding or death by communicating with the enemy could often be a simple one. Sometimes all it took was for someone to shout across the lines and get a verbal agreement from their opposite to conduct an exchange. Others entailed a more complicated series of rituals to ensure that both parties would be protected. Corporal James Beard, a native of Ireland and member of the 142nd New York, explained to his sibling the exchange process along his part of the line: "The picket lines is not over ten rods a part . . . we talk to them [the Confederates], Trade papers . . . we can write on a pece of paper what we want to trade role it round a cartridge and toss it into their pits and the[y] will the same with us."[16] When men wanted to reach out, there was often a Confederate counterpart across the lines willing to communicate with them, even if it took some doing to make it happen. As the men figured out ways of conducting such communications, other soldiers noted how surreal it was to witness enemies meeting in such a peaceful manner. One Union man witnessed soldiers exchanging between the lines and observed, "These men who take one another by the hand this minute, may the next send one another to the spirit-land. These who are now trading tobacco for coffee and sugar, may, ere another hour rolls round, be trading lead for lead. It seems as though men in the time of war lose their civilization."[17]

While most gatherings between the lines involved an exchange of objects or information, occasionally soldiers would engage in extended social interaction with their opponents that went beyond the acquisitive impulses of the men. In some areas, Union soldiers and Confederates intermingled in ways that suggested recognition of a shared experience in the trench lines, which could be utilized as a foundation for the friendly, respectful relations across no man's land. Writing in his diary at the end of August, Private John Haley of the 17th Maine reported, "no firing today, and our men and the Johnnies have been playing cards and trading all day. There is a large tree midway between the lines, and thither the card players and traders ply their arts."[18] The prevalence of card playing and games of chance among the rank and file of both sides made such behavior an obvious choice once a level of trust was established. More revealing of the motives behind the truces at the front is a story from Private James Nugent of the 5th Wisconsin, who wrote to his father late in the campaign:

> A very amusing scene occurred on the Picket line, the other day, in front of the 5th Corps: A piece of wood lay between the Picket lines. Neither party could get the wood to burn, and both needed it very much. So one day one of our boys called to a Reb to come out and divide the wood. So out came the Johnnie and the two paced it off and equally divided the wood they wanted and nobody [was] hurt. If a tree falls across the line, each party owns the wood that comes on his side . . . Very frequently it happens that a Johnnie is chopping on the butt of the tree and a Yank on the top.[19]

Much like the exchange of coffee and tobacco, the splitting of wood illustrates an understanding of shared experience; both sides recognized the mutual need for firewood, and were willing to put their ideological differences aside in order to provide for the immediate physical benefit of themselves and their opponents. Incidents such as these reveal a great deal about the shared sense of experience and comradeship that existed during the Civil War and persisted on battlefields well into the twentieth century.[20]

Despite the frequency and variety of truces, there were relatively few reports of one side or another betraying the rules of a cease-fire once it was established. Betrayals did occur, however, and the reactions to this form of treachery reveal more about how soldiers viewed the exchanges between the lines. Once a cease-fire had been established by common consent, Union soldiers expected it to be honored, and any breach was viewed as a violation of the conventions of war. After a private in his regiment was shot during a mutual cease-fire along his part of the line, Colonel Henry Morrow of the 24th Michigan declared the shooting "an unprovoked & wonton *murder*. . . . His death has deeply affected the Regiment for he was much loved & respected, one and all feel that his death ought to be revenged."[21] The breach of a cease-fire could destroy relations along that part of the line, as the trust previously established disintegrated with a rifle shot. In another case, two months after he reported pickets pleasantly playing cards between the lines, Private Haley of the 17th Maine noted that a soldier in his regiment had been shot while meeting with Confederates, an occurrence that was growing in frequency. Writing from the trenches on October 16, Haley explained how "several times of late we have agreed on an armistice and had a right to consider ourselves secure, when the first thing we know, down goes a man. Something severe should be done to teach them the sacredness of a truce." Haley filled nearly this whole day's entry with condemnation directed at the Confederates for breaking truces, declaring, "no one *compels* them to attempt to scatter our brains around when we are reposing special confidence in them and trusting in their honor."[22] Even though they were at war, men like Morrow and Haley believed that both sides were composed of men of honor, and a dishonorable act committed in the course of a truce was a powerful reminder of the war and its impact on their lives.

Fortunately, the betrayal of truces did not occur often, but perhaps it was fear over Southerners taking advantage of such armistices that prompted the Union command structure to frown upon fraternization with the enemy. While few high-level commanders issued formal orders prohibiting such unofficial communication between the lines, soldiers reported several cases of lower-level officers breaking up exchanges and issuing orders against consorting with enemy pickets. However, these efforts at preventing truces and exchanges seemed less than energetic. The case of Private William Greene of the 2nd United States Sharpshooters reveals the mixed messages on this issue being sent to the rank and file by the officer corps. Stationed in the rifle pits near Petersburg, Private Greene wrote in his diary in late June that "we were ordered on the picquett line to stop correspondence between the enemy's picketts & our picketts."[23] Two months later, Greene related the following story in a letter to his brother:

> I went out a little while ago & met a Johnny half way between the lines & traded some coffee for tobacco & in coming in I discovered Brig. Gen. Deterobian

[deTrobriand], commander of our Brigade, standing in the fort & as it is strictly against orders to have any correspondence with the enemy, therefore I considered I had got myself into a scrape & was rather backward about leaving the pickett line. But when I stopped there he sent one of his Staff officers to tell me to come in. . . . He was looking through his glass & when he took it from his eyes I saluted him in a polite manner. He asked me what I was doing out side of the line. I spoke up promptly & told him. He then asked me if I did not know it was against orders. I told him I did. Said he, can you get me a Richmond paper of late date? I told him I thought I could. He told me to try it. I went & called out a Johnny & told him how I had got caught & told him I wanted a paper to get out sound & he went back & got me one. I took it to the General. He smiled, bowed & told me I could go.[24]

Private Greene's tale reveals that not only were soldiers disobeying orders against fraternization with the Confederates, but some officers were willing to look past such insubordination, especially when it could provide them with valuable intelligence concerning the enemy.

Other officers were not as forgiving as General deTrobriand; soldiers could be and were punished for communicating and exchanging with the Confederate foe. On July 7, 1864, a court-martial was held in the 2nd Corps for Private G. F. Baum of the 40th New York with the charge that he had disobeyed orders. The specifications alleged that he had been meeting with enemy pickets on June 20, but more importantly on June 26 he "did go into the enemy's lines and remained there until he discovered the Division Officer of the day approaching the picket line." Baum pled not guilty to the charges, but the record does not reflect his defense, only that two captains in his regiment testified against him. He was convicted and made to forfeit a month's pay for the infractions.[25] On the same day as Baum's court-martial, another trial was held for Private I. G. S. Crandal of the 98th New York, a regiment in the 18th Corps. The charge was also disobedience of orders; in this case, Crandal had been caught exchanging papers with the enemy despite being specifically ordered by a superior officer not to do so. Crandal's defense was at least somewhat convincing. He alleged that he had been making plans for an exchange when he received the order to stop, and then "I turned around and went back to the rebel soldier and told him I could not get another paper. I then took the paper I had taken out and his paper, the Petersburgh Express and bid him goodbye and came in." The court did not accept this defense; Crandal was convicted and received a much harsher sentence than Baum: two months hard labor in a government fortification.[26] While cases such as Baum and Crandal deserve attention, courts-martial for soldier truces and exchanges were relatively rare during Petersburg. However, Union officers were not the only ones who appeared to be cracking down on soldier exchanges. Private Julius Ramsdell of the 39th Massachusetts recorded one instance in his diary in July where "the rebels punished one of their men for trying to exchange newspapers" by forcing the man to run back and forth along the picket lines for two hours.[27]

Punishments were still a rare prospect, and such reprisals definitely did not end the informal communications across the lines. What is ultimately significant about these communications is that the more often Union soldiers interacted with their opponents, the more information they received about their enemy. These meetings soon became a valuable means by which to learn of the dwindling resources of the Confederacy and revealed the "suffering and destitution" that increasingly afflicted the Southern armies.[28] After conversing with Southern pickets between the lines one day in July, Private Fred Ployer of the 187th Pennsylvania reported to a friend that Confederate soldiers "say they are short of rations and that they can not stand it."[29] Food shortages within the Southern lines were made even more evident through the exchange of various materials across no man's land, as Union soldiers discovered that the Confederates were growing increasingly desperate for all manner of foodstuffs. Once again, Private Haley of the 17th Maine offers insight on this subject through a story he related to his diary one day in late August. While on picket, Haley met a Southern officer out in the rifle pits who practically begged him for something to eat. Private Haley handed over the only food he had, a rancid piece of meat, and noted how "with nervous haste, he clutched it as a starving dog would a bone. What could they be feeding on when a commissioned officer deems such stuff edible? Why men will stay in the Southern army and support such a tottering cause is almost incomprehensible."[30]

This astonishment expressed toward the state of the Confederate forces was one of several unexpected benefits gained by Union soldiers through their meetings and exchanges with the enemy between the lines. First, Northern men, along with their opponents, certainly gained materially from the truces that occurred, particularly in the form of foodstuffs and luxuries such as tobacco.

These items allowed men to supplement their dietary allotment and make life in the trenches slightly more comfortable. A second benefit available to both sides was an opportunity to amuse themselves and escape the boredom of trench life. This was particularly true for those on the picket line, who took advantage of being in such close contact with their enemy to chat, either from the protection of their rifle pits or face-to-face. These conversations were a way for a soldier to relieve stress and pass away the long hours on the line by communicating with someone who, although an enemy, was being subjected to an experience nearly identical to his own. It is this point that explains the prevalence of truces during campaigns utilizing tactics such as trench warfare, which place the opposing forces in close proximity. Exactly fifty years later, European soldiers positioned in the trench lines of France and Belgium would meet in a similar fashion on Christmas Eve 1914.[31] However, what distinguished the situation of Union soldiers in the Petersburg campaign from that of their Confederate opponents of 1864–1865 and the European soldiers of 1914 were the final benefits derived from the exchange of information across the lines. As they communicated and traded supplies with Southern soldiers, Federal troops learned of the increasingly precarious state of the Confederate army. Food shortages, military defeats, and the effects of siege life were sapping the will of the Southern fighting men, and Northern soldiers correctly recognized this as a sign of impending victory for the Union cause.

The men of the Army of the Potomac did not have to risk exposure between the lines in order to learn of the dwindling state of the Confederate cause. As the campaign continued into the fall and winter, large numbers of Southern deserters crossed the lines, bringing tales of desperation and confirming the weakening of Confederate morale. In his book on the final year in the life of the Army of Northern Virginia, historian J. Tracy Power discussed in some depth the problem of Confederate desertion at Petersburg. Noting that it grew in severity over the course of the campaign, Power argued that the causes for desertion were many; but a lack of adequate rations and the dramatic increase in Union successes in the field were both major contributing factors to the increasing demoralization within Lee's army (factors that were providing corollary benefits for the Northern forces). These problems became particularly acute over the winter months, when shortages led to much suffering within the Southern lines as many soldiers huddled together in the trenches without proper clothing or rations.[32] The effect was nearly catastrophic; Power demonstrated that at one point in the campaign more than 60 percent of the Army of Northern Virginia was absent without leave, and another author speculated that Lee was losing 8 percent of his force per month in "an attrition rate between battles that foreshadowed the slow hemorrhage that World War I armies commonly endured between offensives."[33] Power cited Confederate desertion as a major cause of the North's victory, since "by the winter of 1864–65, as scores of miserable men crept away from the lines almost daily, desertion had all but destroyed the Confederate armies and made their final defeat a matter of time."[34] While the problems facing the Army of Northern Virginia certainly contributed to its downfall, historians like Power have not discussed the effect that Southern desertion had on those members of the Army of the Potomac who witnessed the gradual disintegration of the Confederate army. The reaction of Federal troops to the growing numbers of enemy soldiers surrendering to them each day illuminates another manner by which Union men sustained themselves in the siege lines through the long winter months of 1864–1865.

While many Confederate deserters attempted to head back to their homes, thousands more made the simple choice of crossing no man's land and offering their surrender. Union reports of enemy desertion were typically low over the summer months, but as Northern victories piled up and conditions deteriorated in the Southern lines, a trickle of surrendering Confederates soon became a floodtide. Atlanta, as encouraging as it was for the Union army, was a severe setback for the Confederates, and its surrender brought a surge of deserters into the Union lines. Major Steve Clark of the 13th Ohio Cavalry described just such a response in a letter home in September, writing, "a good many are now deserting[,] almost every morning I have a squad to send to headQrs. They say these are a good deal discouraged since the fall of Atlanta."[35] The string of victories in the Shenandoah Valley by General Sheridan's forces proved equally demoralizing to Southerners and brought another surge in Confederate desertion. Discussing an area of the lines near the Bermuda Hundred, Corporal James Beard of the 142nd New York wrote in late October how "enemy diserters come in on those lines The[y] all report that Erleys defait in the Shanando Valley is the worst blow the[y] ever got."[36] While reports of desertion by soldiers like Beard and Clark were not uncommon over the summer and early fall months, Lincoln's reelection appeared to be the turning point that brought ever-increasing waves of Confederate deserters. Corporal William Ray of the 7th Wisconsin rarely commented on deserters prior to the election, but on November 8 Ray wrote in his journal, "there is many Deserters from the Rebs coming in. Most evryday some come into our Brigade."[37] In the days and months that followed, Ray would document in his diary frequent reports on the regularity and number of Confederate deserters crossing the lines.

As the raw conditions of winter set in and Confederates faced increasing hardship across the lines, one Union soldier declared that he expected Southern soldiers to "flock over tons."[38] These expectations were certainly met over the winter months and into spring 1865 as Confederate desertion became a constant element of Petersburg life. In December, Private John Arnold of the 49th Pennsylvania wrote to his wife and family of how "the Rebs are coming over into our lines Daily . . . Yester-Day the was a Brigadeer general came over . . . Captaines Privets lieutenants are coming Daily."[39] Sergeant Calvin Berry of the 1st Maine Veteran Infantry noted in his diary on February 24 that forty-one Confederates had surrendered the previous night, with many of them bringing their weapons with them, and the other day "a sleigh with 6 men and a mule came in with a load of wood."[40] "There is a good many deserters comes in to our lines everyday," Sergeant John Campbell of the 1st Rhode Island Light Artillery wrote to his father in March, "I guess that the rebs ar not as fast for fighting as they used to be it is getting plaid out."[41] For Private Henry Metzger of the 184th Pennsylvania, it was apparent that the desertions were affecting the deployment of Confederate troops along the trench lines. Writing in February, he explained that rebel pickets "are not thirty yards from their works. they cant trust them out of sight of the officers on account of desertions. they are coming in our lines faster at present than anny time during the war."[42]

The limitations of the Confederate war effort provided plenty of motivations for Southerners to desert, but reports by Union soldiers indicate that efforts were being made to actively induce Confederates to abandon their posts and cross the lines. Several Northern men offered comments similar to those of Private James Nugent of the 5th Wisconsin, who wrote to his father late in the campaign describing how Confederates would go about surrendering to Federal pickets. Noting that most deserters were coming into Northern lines with their weapons, Nugent explained that "Gen. Grant let them know in some way that he would pay them 18 dollars apiece for them, so now every man brings in his gun, and goes north with some Yank money in his pockets, a happy man."[43] First Lieutenant John Brincklé of the 5th United States Artillery noted a group of deserters coming over in February with a mule team and their weapons, receiving $18 and $16 for them, respectively.[44] Appealing to the desperation of Confederate soldiers through monetary rewards was a clever means by which to induce desertion in the enemy forces. The wartime letters of Theodore Lyman, a member of General George Meade's staff in the Army of the Potomac, suggests the success of this policy. Writing to his wife around the same time that Private Nugent told his tale, Lyman noted passing several Confederates being marched to the rear with loaded muskets in their hands, and stated that "they bring them in, all loaded, and we pay them so much for each weapon."[45] Lyman appears to verify Private Nugent's story, but the relatively few soldiers who commented on such a policy indicates that while a monetary exchange for enemy weapons may have occurred, it was initiated late in the siege and was not widespread.

Regardless of whether Southerners were being pushed or pulled across no man's land, the desertion of Confederates was one of the more popular subjects in the journals and correspondence of Union men in the trenches. Of particular interest to those documenting the phenomenon was the precise number of those who crossed the lines. At first, deserters came over individually or in small groups, and Federal troops kept track of the weekly or monthly totals. As the siege entered its final months, desertion dramatically increased as enemy soldiers crossed the lines by the dozen on a daily basis. The diary entries of Sergeant Henry Keiser of the 95th Pennsylvania offer typical examples of the precise recordkeeping undertaken by Northern witnesses to Confederate desertion in the winter and spring of the siege:

February 7, 1865:   "About eighty Rebs came over into our lines on the left last night."
February 20, 1865:   "Thirty-two Rebs came over through the picket line"
February 23, 1865:   "Nineteen Jonnies came into our lines in front of our brigade last night, bringing their arms with them."[46]

Other soldiers were less exact, instead offering estimates of the total number of deserters over a certain period of time. Describing a typical day in the trenches, Lieutenant Colonel Albert Rogall of the 118th United States Colored

Troops noted in his diary that "last night came in 300 Reb deserters on the lines of the 24th Corps."[47] In mid-March, Sergeant Joseph Young of the 184th Pennsylvania declared with unusual precision that 1,780 Confederates had surrendered over the previous month.[48] While many of the totals from soldiers were no doubt inflated through the rumor mill of exaggeration, the prevalence of these reports from the trenches makes it clear that enemy deserters were a ubiquitous occurrence, especially in the finals months of the siege in 1865.

What elicited more fascination than the actual number of deserters coming into the Union lines each day or week was the type of men who were surrendering. Despite the abundance of truces along the lines, for many Federal soldiers this was their first opportunity to see the enemy up close, and they did not hesitate to examine those coming in and report what they saw. The one common element in the descriptions of Confederate deserters was the impoverished, distressed appearance they presented as they crossed the lines. Their physical state alone demonstrated to Union soldiers why the Southerners were surrendering in such numbers. "The rebs are deserting every night in squads," wrote Corporal Daniel Chisholm of the 116th Pennsylvania in January, "they are a miserable looking set, with scarcely enough clothes to cover their nakedness. I don't think they will hold out much longer."[49] Sergeant Young of the 184th Pennsylvania echoed the comments of his fellow Pennsylvanian, with a hint of pity creeping into his words as he wrote his family, "thare was 60 Rebels came in last night thay all came in to our Regt thay look very hard and half starved thay have nothing to eat half of the time."[50] Seeing their enemy in such an up-close fashion was an education for Union soldiers as they began to truly appreciate the dire state of the Confederate cause.

Their education continued when Northern men actually conversed with the Confederate deserters who found their way into the Federal lines. As with truces, these conversations revealed the challenges faced by Southerners and the effect that Union victories were having on the Confederate home front. The accounts of hardship related by Confederates more than equaled their ragged appearance, as Union men increasingly heard "tales of distress, woe, and demoralization."[51] "There are a good many coming in to our lines," one Union soldier wrote to his brother in October. "They get in they say they are very bad off in the way of something to eat and that whole companys would come in if they could."[52] Meeting with some Southern deserters early in August, Lieutenant Colonel William Tilton of the 22nd Massachusetts noted in his diary: "They give a gloomy account of affairs on their side. All able bodied men are already in the army. they are on short allowance and their families are suffering at home."[53] Tilton's story indicates the growing effect that the Union blockade and the stresses of wartime were having on Confederate soldiers and the Southern populace, pressures that would only increase over the winter months. Some deserters offered specific details of the challenges that Confederates, both civilian and military, were facing. Speaking with a couple of Southern soldiers who had recently surrendered, Colonel Robert McAllister, a brigade commander in the 2nd Corps, related to his wife how "they told me that a good meal in Petersburg will cost them $36 in their money. They only get $11 a month, which, in our money, is about ten cents on the dollar. . . . Think of working three months for one meal!"[54] McAllister, like many Union soldiers who heard such tales of misery, expressed surprise at the problems that the Confederates were facing, but simultaneously realized that such difficulties indicated the success of the Northern war effort.

As an increasing number of Confederate soldiers deserted to the lines of the Army of the Potomac, Federal troops came to the unavoidable conclusion that this was a sign of rapidly approaching victory. This conclusion was only reinforced by the deserters themselves, who indicated their intense level of demoralization by relating to their captors the hopelessness that they and others now felt for the Southern cause. Writing to his sister in February, Private Daniel Sawtelle of the 8th Maine addressed the desertion issue by noting, "one regt (the 33rd N.C.) have all come over, so they say, leaving not enough for a color guard. Besides, their deserters say that twenty desert to the rear of their army to one here. Now what prospect is there for an army so demorilized as that?"[55] The idea that they were only seeing the tip of the desertion iceberg certainly would have been appealing to Northern soldiers, but even more attractive was the notion that Southerners were ready to admit their defeat and return to the Union. At Christmas, Lieutenant Ward Frothingham of the 59th Massachusetts noted a large surge of deserters and how they "seem much pleased to find themselves safe and sound in the land of freedom."[56] Men like Captain Mason Tyler of the 37th Massachusetts reported that Southern deserters, in this case North Carolinians, "say that their State and their soldiers want to come back into the Union, and they individually believe it their duty to encourage it by setting the example."[57] While the motive behind many of these declarations of loyalty may have been an effort by deserters to secure better treatment from their captors, their comments were welcomed by those who heard them and only reinforced the notion that the Confederacy was doomed. As Corporal William Ray of the 7th Wisconsin concluded, "The Rebellion is still on the wane & Treason's going down."[58]

The belief that the Southern cause was on the verge of extinction proved of immense benefit to Northern soldiers besieging Petersburg in the final months of the war. The appearance, numbers, and words of Confederate deserters all indicated this to be true, and Union soldiers used this as a reason to carry on in the trenches. For most, like Private Samuel Brooks of the 37th Massachusetts, it was the simple understanding that numbers were moving rapidly to the side of the Army of the Potomac, since "the more that come in the less we shall have to fight."[59] For others, the rapid crumbling of the Army of Northern Virginia suggested that there may no longer be a need for fighting; the Confederates might surrender without further hostilities. "Rebels are deserting and coming into our lines very rapidly," Private James Horrocks of the 5th New Jersey Light Artillery proudly declared in a letter to his parents back home in England, confidently proclaiming that "I think this war will be over very soon, and then we shall have a gay old time."[60] For the veterans of the Army of the Potomac, who had been in the service too long and seen too many defeats to give in to flights of fancy, Confederate desertion at the very least gave them hope to carry on and see the war through. Writing in his diary in late February 1865, Major Elisha Hunt Rhodes of the 2nd Rhode Island stated, "the enemy still continues to desert to our lines. Last night ten came. They all tell the same story—that the Southern cause is hopeless. I begin to feel that the war is really drawing to a close, but we shall have some severe fighting yet."[61] While Major Rhodes and others may not have fully understood the significance of the rising tide of Confederate deserters in the final months of the war, they did comprehend that it signaled a weakened Confederacy, and they used this as a means of maintaining their faith in the Union cause while continuing to live day by day in the trenches.

The comments of First Lieutenant Jacob Seibert of the 93rd Pennsylvania encapsulate many of the reactions that Union men felt toward the deserting Confederates as the Petersburg campaign progressed into 1865. Lieutenant

Seibert was a true veteran, being a shoemaker from Lebanon, Pennsylvania who enlisted originally in 1861 and received a bullet wound in the leg at the battle of Winchester in 1864. He returned to his unit shortly thereafter, but the wound would linger and continue to impede his service.[62] In February, only days before he would resign his commission due to complications from his leg wound, he proudly wrote home, "Father! I think war is nearly over." After rattling off the recent triumphs by Union arms across the country, Seibert continued:

> The capture of the above places has a powerful effect on the rebels. they desert by the hundred. During the past eight days, the Desertions from the rebel Army—from the Army of the James on the Extreme right and the cavalry front on the left of the Potomac Army—have averaged ten every hour each twenty-four hours makeing in Eight days nearly 2000 men. . . . The rebels come close to our picket lines to fetch wood and in that way they escape with teams and all. The rebels are paid for everything they bring with them. The rebels that came in last night say that they are now drilling Negroes in Petersburg for their Army, if they go to depend on them they will soon explode the Bogus shell of the Confederacy.[63]

For Seibert, the last-ditch effort to mobilize Southern slaves to fight for the Confederacy appeared to be the clearest indication of all that the South was finished.

Though the epidemic of Confederate desertion during the final months of the Petersburg campaign deserves recognition, it is important to note that not only Confederates abandoned their posts and surrendered. Some Union soldiers, precisely how many is not known, took it upon themselves to cross over to the enemy. The lack of data pertaining to the specific number of deserters within the Army of the Potomac impedes any definitive judgment on desertions to the enemy, let alone any numbers for total deserters. However, the comments of Federal soldiers themselves offer some insight into the prevalence and effect of desertion within the forces surrounding Petersburg. Their testimony indicates that it was not uncommon for Northern men along the line to desert, either to the enemy or to the rear. Writing to his father in February, Alpheus Packard, the Assistant Surgeon for the 1st Veteran Maine regiment, commented, "you say we hear nothing of deserters from our side . . . They are pretty rare . . . We have men in this regiment who are not sent out on picket for fear they shall leave."[64] Many soldiers reported a typical characteristic of Union deserters being that they were draftees or men who had signed up purely to gain financially from the high bounties being offered in the North (e.g., substitutes), not veterans who were devoted to the cause. "Desertions of conscript and bounty seekers from this part of our lines have become so frequent that an order has been issued from division headquarters offering twenty day furloughes to those who will arrest or shoot deserters," explained Private Wightman in a November letter.[65] "I am sorry to say we lose a good many from our army deserting to the enemy," Brigadier General Robert McAllister explained to his wife that same month as he contemptuously described the "poor miserable conscripts, bounty jumpers, and forigners who have no interest in our Government, country or cause. One native-born is worth a dozen of them."[66] Desertion was not a rare occurrence in the Army of the Potomac, but the words of these men suggest that they perceived it as limited to a small segment of the fighting force.

A factor that may have been effective in keeping Union desertions to a minimum was the widespread use of capital punishment for convicted deserters. While relatively few deserters were actually executed, the impact on Union soldiers was enormous since they were often called out by the hundreds to witness such death sentences. Executions appeared to spike over the winter months of December and January, indicating a corresponding increase in desertions. Private Alexander Rose of the 11th New York Light Artillery recorded in his diary the "solemn scene" of witnessing eleven men hung for desertion over the course of one week in December 1864.[67] Captain George Bowen of the 12th New Jersey witnessed a man shot for desertion in January, concluding that it "seems hard but presume it is necessary to prevent desertion."[68] In his memoirs, Private Robert McBride of the 11th Pennsylvania provided the most matter-of-fact description of a soldier execution during the Petersburg campaign:

> A military execution took place not long after our return from the Welden raid. A man had deserted to the enemy from a Maryland regiment, was captured, tried, and sentenced to be hung. The troops were ordered out to witness the execution. A hollow square was formed around the scaffold, and in due time the doomed man was led forth, accompanied by a guard, provost-marshal, and chaplain. The prisoner promptly ascended the scaffold, the sentence was read,

and prayer was offered by the chaplain. The rope was placed about his neck, and an attempt was made to draw the cap over his head. It was found that the cap should have been put on first, and they loosed the rope to change it. At this point the trap-door gave way, and precipitated them all to the ground. The straps with which the prisoner's knees had been bound were now loosed, so that he could again ascend the scaffold. He sat on the steps while repairs were made. When all was ready he took his place on the trap-door, first testing it with his weight, to see whether it might again give way prematurely. The cap was now drawn over his head, the noose adjusted, and the trap sprung. After he had hung for some time, we marched back to camp.[69]

Many eyewitnesses felt that such death sentences were deserved, especially if the victims had crossed the lines to surrender or join with the enemy. "Thare is three men hung hear evry Friday," Sergeant Londus Haskell of the 11th Vermont wrote to his mother on New Year's Day 1865, "thay are Diserters we cot most of the[m] up in the Valley thay was fighting against Uncle Sam thay dont get much pity hear."[70] Most soldiers were more sympathetic than Sergeant Haskell, yet still wrestled with how they should respond to the sight of fellow Northerners being executed. Another fighting man from the 11th Vermont, Captain Darius Safford, seemed conflicted when he described the execution of three men who had deserted to the enemy in December. Writing to his sister, Captain Safford explained, "I have seen death in many forms on the battle field but never anything so horrible as to see those men swinging in the air giving their lives as a penalty for their treason I could only say it is just, but deliver me from ever seeing anything of the kind again as long as I live."[71] Surgeon Henry Millard of the 34th Massachusetts appeared shocked by the extent of the executions: "The Discipline of the while army is very strict, scarcely a day passes without some solder being executed by either hanging or shooting. Saw last wek two hung near Div. HdQrs. they were from the 10th Connecticut Regt. They were quickly and coolly hung for a half hour then cut down and put under the Va. Soil beside the scaffold."[72] While the success of public executions at deterring Northern desertion is impossible to measure, the words of men like Safford and Millard indicate that the ceremonies had a tremendous effect on those who witnessed them. Many reached the conclusion that the executions were serving as a successful deterrent to Union desertion. Assistant Surgeon Packard of the 1st Veteran Maine believed that the executions were effective, writing to his father in March that "desertions from our army are not so numerous . . . hanging has stopped much of it."[73]

From the limited numerical evidence available, the eyewitness accounts of soldiers, and the methods deployed against it by the Union command structure, desertion remained limited and never became a critical issue within the Army of the Potomac. However, even if there was a desertion crisis occurring within the Federal forces surrounding Petersburg, Northern soldiers did not perceive it as such. Their accounts during the campaign suggest that men viewed desertion as a far greater problem for the Confederate than for Union forces. "Every day we stay here adds vastly to our strength and takes away from theirs," reported Colonel Edward Ripley from his vantage point as brigade commander within the 18th Corps. "We are getting strong reinforcements of recruits, and convalescents, while their men are actually and positively deserting by hundreds."[74] Even those who recognized the problem of desertion, such as Brigadier General Robert McAllister, seemed upbeat about the status of the Army of the Potomac in the face of the enemy. Two months after complaining to his wife about conscripts and "forigners" deserting to the Confederates, McAllister reported, "we have no desertions from us now. That seems to be stoped and I am glad of it."[75] In the weeks following, General McAllister would focus more on deserting Southerners than those who left from within his own lines, proclaiming in March, "if we lay here long enough we will have a large part of Lee's army on this side."[76] From the standpoint of these Union men positioned in the trenches around Petersburg in the winter and spring months of the campaign, their own Army of the Potomac was not only staying together but growing more powerful, while the legendary Army of Northern Virginia disintegrated in front of them.

———

"My health is good," declared Private John Steward of the 1st Maine Heavy Artillery in a letter to his wife Abby from the Petersburg lines on March 10.[77] A farmer from Minson, Maine, Steward had enlisted in December 1863, possibly because of what the $300 bounty could do for his wife and three children. Steward survived the 1st Maine's bloody attack against the Petersburg trenches in June 1864, but came out of the experience demoralized and declaring "it makes me sick of war." Steward still regarded himself a "union man" though, and kept his spirits up despite suffering from a recurring bout of diarrhea through the fall and winter months.[78] By March 1865, he was expressing positive thoughts about the future due to what he perceived as the abundant evidence provided by his enemy of their imminent defeat. In his letter from March 10, which also contained five dollars for his family, he described the growing number of deserters coming into his lines, including his personal experience with some a few days earlier. "Thare were three came in at my post the other night[,] two privets and a Coperel and I had the pleasure to take them in to head quarters," he wrote, explaining how the units in his sector were receiving more than a hundred deserters a week who "take the oath of alegance at Citty point and are sent whare thay choose to go." The plight of Southern deserters became clear to Steward as he chatted with his prisoners, who informed him that "thay think that the war is most over . . . say that their men will not fight any more if thay can help it."[79]

Little did Private Steward and the men of the Army of the Potomac know, but the large number of deserters was deceptive since the Confederate force facing them on the eve of the last campaign of the war in April 1865 was at least the same size as the one they had faced when Union forces first arrived near Petersburg the previous June.[80] This fact was irrelevant to the Federal troops preparing for what would become the Appomattox campaign, since in their eyes they had spent the previous nine months witnessing the Army of Northern Virginia teeter on the brink of disaster and the Confederacy edge closer to defeat. After a string of failures and setbacks over the summer of 1864, the Union war effort had rebounded, bringing forth blow after blow against the Confederate cause. This prompted much hopeful speculation for the future around the campfires and in the trenches of those stationed before Petersburg. However, the members of the Army of the Potomac were not passive eyewitnesses to the end of the war; Union soldiers believed that they were playing a significant, if not the most significant, role in bringing about the downfall of the Confederacy. "We are still before Petersburgh perhaps doing more than if we had taken Richmond," was the analysis of one soldier who stated openly what so many more were thinking: that the Army of the Potomac, by pinning down the most dangerous force in the Confederacy at Petersburg, allowed Union forces to gain victories in other sectors.[81] From their communications with the enemy between the lines and those deserters who crossed no man's land, Federal troops learned of the increasing desperation of the Southern military and populace. The crumbling of the Army of Northern Virginia before their eyes provided soldiers with proof of not only the imminent defeat of the Confederacy, but also their personal role in its demise.

Recognition of the important role they were playing in the final act of the Civil War served as a tremendous boost to the morale of the men of the Army of the Potomac for most of the Petersburg campaign. The trench lines, which served as a home for Union men for most of the campaign, were not conducive to maintaining a soldier's morale for extended periods of time. However, the resurrection of hope in the cause that occurred over the course of their time at Petersburg helped to counteract the destructive elements of trench life. While comrades, adrenalin, and God are key in helping a soldier rush across an open field on the assault against an enemy position, hope for the impending and certain success of one's cause is one factor that aids a soldier in the long periods of time between actual high-intensity combat operations. In an age of large armies composed of citizen soldiers who need to be convinced to fight for a reason, a soldier who has lost hope in his cause or nation will not last long in the ranks. Fortunately, this did not prove to be a concern for the Army of the Potomac during the Petersburg campaign. There were some reasons to doubt the Union war effort over the summer months of 1864, but as Northern fortunes rose dramatically in the fall, Federal troops quickly came to the conclusion that "there is something wrong over in rebeldom."[82] The recognition of approaching Northern victory, coupled with the soldiers' own personal methods for enduring the rigors of trench life, ensured that morale in the Army of the Potomac actually improved as the spring campaign approached in 1865. This guaranteed that, after nine months of trench warfare and all of the degrading conditions that it entailed, an animated, cohesive military force stepped off against the Army of Northern Virginia in early April and promptly brought about its defeat.

Conclusion

SPRING 1865

You may expect to hear great news.
—Lieutenant Thomas Owen, 50th New York Engineers

For those Union soldiers surrounding Petersburg, the first sign of spring in 1865 was a party. Given the large immigrant population within the Union armies, it was no surprise that St. Patrick's Day proved a welcome experience for not only Irish soldiers but nearly everyone who chose to take part in the festivities. The Irish Brigade led the way, of course, holding equestrian events in their camp on March 17 that attracted soldiers from all across the Union lines.[1] The result was "a Day of pleasure in the Army, Racing and Games," according to Private Alexander Rose of the 11th New York Light Artillery.[2] While it appears that there may not have been much in the way of specialty foods and alcohol at the celebration, eyewitnesses to the event still reported a rather exciting affair as some of the competitions got out of hand.[3] "On they went, horses flying the track, running over the spectators, falling over the hurdles, into the ditches, breaking arms, legs &c," was the assessment of Sergeant Samuel Clear of the 116th Pennsylvania in his diary, concluding that "never did I see such a crazy time. I will have to alter my mind if I ever go to see another Irish fair."[4] Lt. Col. Elisha Hunt Rhodes of the 2nd Rhode Island agreed with Sergeant Clear's conclusion, remarking that "Irish celebrations are dangerous amusements . . . I like a good horse and a good run, but such sport as I saw today is not to my liking."[5] Thousands of Union soldiers like Clear and Rhodes attended these events and, despite the "crazy" nature of the occasion, all found St. Patrick's Day a welcome escape from their daily life in the trenches.

Despite the at times surprising ability to keep up their spirits throughout the extended exposure to siege warfare, Northern soldiers had faced a remarkably unpleasant experience for much of the winter months. Their protective fortifications, full stomachs, and the visual assurances of approaching victory did not change the fact that the men still had to endure the foul elements and threat of enemy fire around Petersburg even when they were not in the trenches. Coupled with the stress of their everyday responsibilities and exposure to the enemy, life along the line could still prove rather destructive to Union men. After a particularly lengthy period in the trenches, Winthrop Phelps, the chaplain for the 2nd Connecticut Heavy Artillery, reported how at the last inspection the "Regiment looked poorly, so much rain, fatigue & guard duty, &c."[6] While inclement weather and the daily tasks of an army at war could take its toll on the soldier, nothing was more disturbing for those either at the front or to the rear than a reminder of the violent environment in which they all resided. Hostilities continued, and men were still dying at a steady, albeit comparatively lower, rate. Not all casualties were the result of the enemy, as evidenced by Private Daniel Sawtelle of the 8th Maine, who described in a March letter how a soldier in his unit accidentally shot himself. The man died, and Sawtelle solemnly concluded that "it seems hard here in camp, but thus it is in the midst of life we are in the midst of death."[7] Whatever methods soldiers used to maintain their morale in the face of the enemy, they could never forget that they were in a combat zone.

Thus, the arrival of spring was welcome to Federal troops since it brought an end to the foul weather that had virtually paralyzed active operations over the winter. In addition to exposing them to the elements and enemy for several months, this lack of activity had fueled the growth of a lethargic condition among the soldiers of the Army of the Potomac, as they found themselves manning the lines with little to distract them but the occasional incoming rifle shot or artillery round. Throughout February and early March, soldiers filled their diaries with their boredom, with the normal entry following the format of Sergeant Jacob Lyons of the 120th New York when he wrote on February 25, "still the same dull monotony of camp life."[8] Their commanders still managed to find activities for the men, having them drill and work on extending and strengthening fortifications, and the soldiers even found ways to fill out some days by tidying their camps and engaging in the perennial vices frequently associated with men in war. However, for Union soldiers the winter months were exasperating for the sheer lack of anything to distract them from their tortured surroundings. "We are lying here doing nothing but for what length of time it is to last I have no idea," noted Private William Hamilton of the 191st Pennsylvania in a March letter to his mother, adding, "it is dull enough I tell you."[9] While violence and discomfort were certainly problems over the winter, boredom was a factor that was equally, if not more, discouraging to those serving in the trench lines.

As spring approached, the boredom and subtle dismay of winter gave way to more upbeat feelings. By the time the games were played on St. Patrick's Day, a spirit was growing within the army that demonstrated just how successful the soldiers had been at maintaining their morale over the course of the campaign. They all realized that the improving weather meant that the army could move, and the odds were favorable that such a movement would include an advance against Lee's Army of Northern Virginia and the city of Petersburg. Rather than be discouraged by the possibility of renewed fighting, the men expressed enthusiasm for the upcoming campaign and confidently predicted success. As early as New Year's Day, Private John Haley of the 17th Maine, a usual pessimist when it came to war matters, spoke for his comrades when he wrote, "we expect peace shortly after the opening of the spring campaign."[10] Many soldiers lavished praise upon Grant, realizing that he was pulling the strings of the Union war effort and waiting for an opportunity to strike the coup de grâce. Seeing signs of a movement forward as early as late February, Surgeon William Watson of the 105th Pennsylvania assumed that "Genl. Grant is watching Lee very closely and is prepared to take immediate advantage of any movement Lee may hazard."[11] Confidence, bordering on buoyancy, increased as the days grew warmer and the roads dried; there was a pervasive notion that the next campaign would be the final one of the war. "I hope by next winter that we shall all go home in peace," wrote Alpheus Packard, an assistant surgeon with the 1st Maine, "everybody except Lee & Davis seem to think that the summer's campaign will close the war."[12]

Not only did Union soldiers predict that 1865 would bring peace, but also that the next campaign for the Army of the Potomac would be a quick, though possibly quite violent, experience. In mid-March, Captain George Bowen of the 12th New Jersey expressed the common feeling within the army when he referred to future operations and noted, "[a] Staff officer in my presence expressed it thus 'the next campaign will be short sharp and decisive' hurt it may."[13] Private Wilbur Fisk of the 2nd Vermont must have spoken to the same staff officer, since he emphasized in a letter the following week how "the coming conflict *must* be 'short, sharp and decisive,'" though he admitted that the prospect of bloodshed was likely, if not assured. Still confident of success, Fisk concluded his assessment of the upcoming campaign by noting, "while we prepare for the worst, we have much reason to hope for the best."[14] Obviously, veterans like Fisk and Bowen were using the Overland campaign as a frame of reference, which tempered their optimism. For soldiers like Sergeant Joseph Young of the 184th Pennsylvania, a recent recruit who had spent six months at Petersburg but no time in the Overland campaign, optimism was so boundless that it appeared to him that there would be no need for a resumption of active operations. Writing to his family in mid-March, Young boldly proclaimed, "the war is about played out I dont think we will have aney more fighting to do on this line."[15] While few were as sanguine in their hopes as Sergeant Young, there was a general feeling among the soldiers of the Army of the Potomac that, contrary to previous experience, the next campaign would actually be the decisive and crushing Confederate defeat that they had been seeking for several years.

As a corollary to this, the men realized that a final victory over Lee's army necessitated emerging from their protective entrenchments and once again crossing over the open field on the assault as they had done during the horrible days of the Overland campaign. Perhaps surprisingly, Union soldiers expressed their willingness and even enthusiasm to take the fight to the enemy once more. As he wrote to his mother from the Petersburg lines, Veteran Volunteer Sergeant Joseph Griner of the 8th Pennsylvania Cavalry looked forward to the next campaign and wrote, "I think Grant will use his best endeavors to wind up this affair this summer. I hope so, for what has got to be done must be, the sooner the better."[16] Assessing the men in his unit on March 15, Sergeant Clear conveyed a similar attitude when he wrote, "I hope the troops are all fat and hearty, and I think almost ready for anything Genl Grant asks at their hands."[17] Writing a couple of weeks later, Clear reiterated this idea and revealed the anxiety building among the men when he commented that "the Johnnies will get the devil soon or we will for the Army of the Potomac is getting in great earnest."[18] While the "or we will" comment reveals the lingering pessimism that most veterans of the Overland campaign felt at the prospect of another face-to-face exchange with the Confederates, Clear and Griner demonstrate how soldiers had overcome their fear of the assault and reawakened the faith in their commanders that had been nearly lost in June 1864.

Fighting was what they would have to do, and Lee's army would demonstrate that it still had some life left in it. At Petersburg, the spring campaigns began with a final Confederate effort to break the ring around the city and perhaps completely unseat the Union siege lines. In the predawn hours of March 25, a Confederate force of around 11,500 men under the command of General John Gordon attacked Fort Stedman, an earthen strongpoint along the eastern portion of the Union trench lines. The Confederate objective was City Point, the Union supply hub ten miles to the northeast on the James River. At first, thanks to some innovative assault techniques and the advantage of surprise, Confederate forces managed to seize the fort and several surrounding batteries. However, a delay in the arrival of Southern reinforcements rendered the Confederates unable to hold the position in the face of massed Union counterattacks, and Gordon's men were forced to retreat back to their original positions. Lee's army suffered thousands more casualties without achieving any major gains in what would turn out to be the last significant Confederate offensive operation in the East.[19]

The end of the Petersburg campaign actually began about fifteen miles west of the city at a place called Five Forks. It was there on April 1 that Union forces under Generals Philip Sheridan and G. K. Warren defeated a Confederate force under General George Pickett, gaining thousands of prisoners and effectively creating an open path to the Southside Railroad, which served as the last rail line into Petersburg.[20] Realizing the significance of this victory, Grant ordered multiple assaults on the Confederate positions surrounding Petersburg on April 2. By this point, Union forces around Petersburg were composed of the Army of the Potomac, the Army of the James, and portions of Philip Sheridan's Army of the Shenandoah, creating a host of manpower outnumbering the Confederate defenders more than 3 to 1. After nine months of recovering from the travails of the Overland campaign while enduring life in the trenches, the rested, refitted, and reinforced Union soldiers surged forward and rapidly achieved breakthroughs at multiple points of the Confederate lines. By the end of the day, Union forces were astride the Southside Railroad and Lee's position had become untenable. That night, Southern forces evacuated the city while the Confederate government prepared to leave Richmond. Finally driven from the earthworks that they had held for more than nine months, Lee's Army of Northern Virginia headed west and within a week was surrounded and forced into capitulation at Appomattox Court House.[21]

As Union soldiers prepared for these final operations of the war, their comments presented a stark contrast to the bleak mindset that followed the Overland campaign. However, their comments in spring 1865 were incredibly similar to the words written by many of these same men almost exactly a year earlier. Union soldiers displayed the same desire to end the boredom, the same hopes for the upcoming battles, and the same faith in their commander prior to the start of the 1865 campaigns as they had before the 1864 campaigns. While the enthusiasm may have been more muted than the year before, the spring of 1865 witnessed soldiers crawling out from under the shadow of Spotsylvania and expressing a desire to return to the open field and finish off a staggering enemy. They displayed a willingness to do Grant's bidding, even if that meant a repetition of the battles of the previous spring. They realized that this might mean many deaths, perhaps their own, but they accepted that risk just as they had come to accept the risk associated with life in the Petersburg trenches. The men had come full circle: the high hopes of spring giving way to the despair of summer turning to the rising hope and eventual enthusiasm of winter and spring. The men were prepared to once again take the offensive, as the Army of the Potomac did beginning on April 1, 1865. It came as a surprise to few observers, especially the soldiers themselves, when Petersburg fell two days later. The significance of that final victory at Petersburg and its effect on the veterans of the trenches was best captured by one of General Meade's staff officers, Colonel Theodore Lyman, as he advanced with Union forces toward the city:

> Turning to the left, on top of the crest, we passed a large cemetery, with an old ruined chapel, and, descending a little, we stood on the famous scene of the "Mine." It was this cemetery that our infantry should have gained that day. Thence the town is commanded. How changed these entrenchments! Not a soul

was there, and the few abandoned tents and cannon gave an additional air of solitude. Upon these parapets, whence the rifle-men have shot at each other, for nine long months, in heat and cold, by day and by night, you might now stand with impunity and overlook miles of deserted breastworks and covered ways! It was a sight only to be appreciated by those who have known the depression of waiting through summer, autumn, and winter for so goodly an event![22]

Parallels aside, the Army of the Potomac in the spring of 1865 bore little resemblance to the force that had kicked off the spring campaign one year earlier. Warfare had changed over the previous year, with the rapid succession of battles in May and June giving way to a protracted and low-intensity attritional campaign. The experience of the Overland campaign had been particularly difficult, with the harsh, unrelenting nature of the advance testing the abilities of even those hardy veterans who had witnessed previous horrors at places like Fredericksburg and Gettysburg. Six weeks of charging seemingly impregnable enemy works had nearly shattered those Union soldiers who were lucky enough to survive, and the effect was a profound state of demoralization that swept through the ranks. The buoyant hopes of April 1864 disappeared and were replaced by despair and a mounting hostility to authority, evidenced by the small but significant number of units refusing orders to attack. The effect of this despondency was obvious to enlisted men and commanding officers alike, with members of both groups commenting that soldier fatigue and demoralization contributed to the army's failure at taking Petersburg in mid-June. More importantly, many Union survivors of the Overland experience had reached a state where hopelessness was beginning to take over. It has been suggested that "the soldier is alone in his war with terror," and by June 1864 this appeared to be the case within the Army of the Potomac.[23] With the continual violence and defeats, coupled with the loss of so many comrades-in-arms, Union men certainly felt that theirs was a lonely task which only seemed to bring further suffering. No longer did the soldier view himself as an active participant on the battlefield, but rather a victim being led to the slaughter.

Fortunately, the Petersburg experience lowered the lethality of the battlefield and established conditions that contributed to the regeneration of those within the ranks of the Army of the Potomac. As one historian has noted, by the summer of 1864 "the battlefields of Virginia after three long years of war had become eerily empty," as armies in the field took to entrenching and utilizing field fortifications on a scale not previously witnessed in the East.[24] While the combat environment of the "empty battlefield" posed significant obstacles for Civil War soldiers, and would continue to do so for soldiers well into the twentieth century, Union men found ways to turn the mutilation of their surroundings to their benefit. They recognized and welcomed the change in tactics as the seemingly suicidal assaults of the Overland campaign gave way to the static nature of trench warfare. Throwing themselves into the mammoth task of constructing the army's fortified lines, Federal troops took pride in their work and embraced the opportunity to turn the tables on their opponents and hopefully blast incoming Confederate attacks from behind the protection of breastworks. More importantly, their life in the trenches, though dull and deadly, reestablished a valuable sense of independence within the ranks, as men exerted more control over their lives on the battlefield and no longer viewed themselves as helpless pawns under the control of their officers. On a more fundamental level, the nine-month investment of Petersburg allowed for a steady system of supply to be routed to the troops on the line. Keeping a constant chain of food and mail heading toward the front allowed Union soldiers one less thing to worry about, and provided a secure base from which to adapt to their lifestyle at the front. Significantly, this life was not monolithic, and the frequent escapes to the rear and even home from the main trenches kept the men from being overwhelmed by the Petersburg experience.

Such escapes from the front lines were also frequently employed by the Confederates, but unfortunately these trips were increasingly taken without the permission of their officers. Desertion became epidemic over the winter and spring months of the campaign as the war took a dramatic turn against the Confederate cause. The previous summer, in the first weeks and months spent near Petersburg, the reverse had been true, with large numbers of Union soldiers expressing discontent with the disasters striking Northern forces across the country. However, a series of Union victories culminating in the reelection of Abraham Lincoln in November simultaneously inspired the men of the Northern armies while demoralizing the Confederates. The evidence of this can be seen in the steady decline in Federal desertion while the Confederates faced quite the opposite, as hundreds of Southern soldiers crossed the siege lines and surrendered to their opponents. The sight of such Confederate demoralization, coupled with the stories of woe that often accompanied enemy deserters, served to augment the expectation of victory for Union soldiers and encourage them to hold on to see another campaign in the spring of 1865. The high hopes expressed by these men that spring reveal that, although the wounds and memories of the Overland campaign would never completely dissipate, the Petersburg experience had actually been beneficial to the morale of the Northern soldier and his willingness to see an end to the war.

There are several conclusions that may be drawn from the experience of these Union soldiers in the final year of the war. First, by successfully staying together as an operational force for the duration of the Petersburg campaign, the Army of the Potomac and the Army of the James were able to keep General Robert E. Lee's Army of Northern Virginia trapped in an increasingly distressing tactical situation. As one Union lieutenant astutely recognized in December,

> Grant is of course co-operating with Sherman & Lee is probably in as great a quandary as he has ever been in yet. If he determines to detach a force to oppose Sherman, it will be a *large* force (otherwise it will be of no avail) & Grant will take Richmond . . . if Lee decides not to move a large force from here to oppose Sherman he must make up his mind to let Sherman have Savannah, Charleston, Wilmington, Augusta, *everything*.[25]

Rather than viewing the campaign as a futile affair, Northern men quickly reached the accurate conclusion that their inactivity was playing a key role in the defeat of the Confederacy. Lee needed to keep the bulk of the Army of Northern Virginia at Petersburg as a guarantee for the safety of Richmond, but by doing so he opened a door into the heart of the South for Sherman and other Union forces. This "quandary" was made worse by the steady losses in personnel due to the rising numbers of deserters. While the Confederates were able to make good many of these losses through recruiting and conscription, the best they could accomplish was to maintain the size of their armies while the size of Union forces, the Army of the Potomac in particular, continued to increase. By avoiding the morale and desertion problems that plagued the Confederates throughout the Petersburg siege, Federal troops were able to outlast their opponents and ensure victories in other sectors of the war front.

Of greater significance for the Union soldiers surrounding Petersburg was their ability to carry on in the trenches and allow for the long awaited victory over the Army of Northern Virginia. While the armies of General Sherman and other Union commanders played instrumental roles in the overpowering of the Confederacy, there was perhaps no more significant victory during the war than the surrender of General Lee's Confederates at Appomattox on April 9, 1865. Such a triumph was made possible by the ability of Union men to survive their time before Petersburg in a combat-effective state. When the spring campaign began in the East in early April 1865, the Union armies were numerically superior to the opposing Confederate force, but such superiority had not prevented the repeated defeats suffered by Union armies in previous years. What added to the numerical preponderance of Union soldiers was their conviction that they were on the verge of bringing the long conflict to its conclusion. These were men who had endured the nightmarish battles of Spotsylvania and Cold Harbor, and then spent nine months exposed to some of the most violent and filthy conditions imaginable. Despite, and partially because of, these experiences, Northern men emerged after nine months in the trenches with their morale intact and a positive outlook on the end of the war. They quickly overran their Confederate foes that April and seized Petersburg and Richmond, along with more than 25,000 Southern prisoners at Appomattox, in a matter of days. These were some of the most significant victories of the Civil War, and they paved the way for a quick end to the conflict.

While the cohesion of the Army of the Potomac proved invaluable in a tactical and strategic sense during the war, the ability of Union soldiers to maintain their will to fight in the harsh conditions of trench warfare also illuminates some basic notions regarding the American soldier in battle. From the preceding chapters, one may conclude that Northern soldiers desired a sense of independence on the battlefield. Having been deprived of a feeling of control over their lives during the Overland campaign, Union men welcomed its return as they took command of their personal survival in the trenches. The Petersburg experience also reveals the value of a steady logistical network in maintaining those soldiers on the front lines. The United States usually enters into conflicts with an abundant economy and supply network ready to support its men in the field. Unfortunately, the case of the Overland campaign demonstrates that the "tail" of the American military structure did not always succeed in keeping up with its "teeth." At Petersburg, however, Union soldiers received the full benefit of Union largesse, and the positive effect of mitigating the trench experience reveals the necessity of keeping men provisioned to the fullest degree when in a theater of war. Another factor evident here was the level of exposure to combat conditions experienced by those at the front. While twentieth-century American armies would struggle with determining exactly how much combat a soldier could withstand before "breaking," those at both the top and bottom of the Army of the Potomac realized that men needed to escape from the front as often as possible.[26] The system of unit rotation and soldier furloughs implemented by Union officers had a tremendous positive effect by reducing the time that men spent in the trenches. This reveals some early, successful efforts at recognizing the physical and psychological limitations of the combat soldier.

On a more fundamental level, the experience of the Army of the Potomac from 1864 to 1865 demonstrates that, while soldiers may utilize a myriad of motivations on the battlefield, they are all governed by a simple desire to live to see the following day. As historian Marvin Cain has suggested, research into the Civil War soldier reveals that "the majority were driven by the most basic instinct in man—the will to survive."[27] This conclusion may seem like common sense, but it is an idea that is frequently overlooked by those who seek to ascribe noble intent and complex psychological paradigms to the American soldier. This is not meant to suggest the invalidity of such work, but merely to recommend that one appreciate how soldiers viewed the chances for their survival in combat and how differentiations between battlefields affected that perspective. What distinguished the Petersburg experience from most other campaigns of the war was that it provided soldiers on both sides an unprecedented level of protection on the battlefield, as the open linear tactics of earlier campaigns gave way to static trench warfare. Historian Bell Wiley has argued that Confederates rejected this form of warfare, claiming that "open fighting with all its dangers was immeasurably preferable to such existence as this."[28] However, the value of concealment on the battlefield had a particularly powerful effect on Union soldiers, who learned (perhaps before their commanders) the costs of an open-field assault during the devastation of the Overland campaign. By June, Northern men were no longer convinced that they would survive the war, and the result was a plunge in morale that threatened the cohesion of the Army of the Potomac. Despite an equally constant, yet generally less violent, level of hostilities at Petersburg, the trenches were comforting to those who had seen their value on the battlefield. Men once again became convinced that they had a chance to survive the war, and this, perhaps more than any other factor, played a decisive role in rebuilding the morale of Union soldiers in the East. Clearly, the Civil War soldier, as does any soldier in a primarily volunteer force, needed a certain level of faith in his ability to survive in order to prove effective on the battlefield, and the trenches provided that faith.

This emphasis on the survival instinct of Union soldiers should not detract from their most significant accomplishment during the investment of Petersburg. While the debate over the Civil War as a "modern" conflict continues in the academic community, it is clear that the Civil War exhibited developments that may at the very least be termed "transitional." The extent of trench warfare employed during the conflict falls under this heading. Even though the opposing trench lines and weaponry never reached the level and sophistication of those seen half a century later on the battlefields of Europe, the combat environment shifted during the war from the more Napoleonic tactics of concentration and maneuver at places like Chancellorsville to the more "modern," attritional tactics at places like Petersburg and Atlanta. While some may argue that this transition overwhelmed the soldiers of the war, the evidence presented in this study suggests otherwise. When faced with the challenges posed by the dawn of modern conflict, the men of the Army of the Potomac wavered but never broke. In this sense, these soldiers are the embodiment of the transitional argument. Their success in the Petersburg campaign arose from an ability to successfully shift from one form of warfare to another. Their story is the quintessential soldier's story of facing the incomprehensible experience of combat and finding a way to attain victory before succumbing to the physical and psychological destruction that accompanies life on the battlefield. Their legacy shaped not only the victory of the Union during the Civil War, but also the future of the American combat soldier as warfare entered its most destructive century.

Notes

INTRODUCTION

Note to epigraph: Epigraph taken from *Soldiers' Letters: From Camp, Battle-field, and Prison*, ed. Lydia Minturn Post (New York: Bunce & Huntington, 1865), 471. Manuscript housed at Massachusetts Historical Society, Boston, Massachusetts (MHS).

1. Diary entry, *The Rebel Yell and the Yankee Hurrah: The Civil War Journal of a Maine Volunteer*, ed. Ruth L. Silliker (Camden, ME: Down East Books, 1985), 133.

2. Diary entry, April 1, 1864, *The Civil War Notebook of Daniel Chisholm: A Chronicle of Daily Life in the Union Army 1864–1865*, ed. W. Springer Menge and J. August Shimrak (New York: Ballantine, 1989), 8. While the majority of this work is dedicated to the letters of Corporal Daniel Chisholm and his brother Alex, who both served in the 116th Pennsylvania, it also includes the diary of their sergeant, Samuel Clear.

3. Letter to Mother, April 15, 1864, Daniel Faust Papers, Harrisburg Civil War Round Table Collection, United States Army Heritage and Education Center, Carlisle, Pennsylvania (USAHEC).

4. Letter to Parents, April 22, 1864, *My Dear Parents: An Englishman's Letters Home from the American Civil War*, ed. A. S. Lewis (London: Gollancz, 1982), 74. Emphasis in original.

5. Diary entry, April 16, 1864, Francis Asbury Wallar (Waller) Papers, Civil War Document Collection, USAHEC. Emphasis in original.

6. Meade to Vincent, March 31, 1864, *The War of the Rebellion: A Compilation of the Official Records of the Union and Confederate Armies*, Series 1, Volume 33, 776. See also Noah Andre Trudeau, *Bloody Roads South: The Wilderness to Cold Harbor, May–June 1864* (Baton Rouge: Louisiana State University Press, 1989), 12. For a firsthand account of how men were motivated to enlist by the prospect of furloughs and bounties, at least in the 2nd Vermont Infantry regiment, see *Hard Marching Every Day: The Civil War Letters of Private Wilbur Fisk, 1861–1865*, ed. Emil Rosenblatt and Ruth Rosenblatt (Lawrence: University Press of Kansas, 1992), 208–11.

7. Diary entry, February 25, 1864, Menge and Shimrak, *The Civil War Notebook of Daniel Chisholm*, 3.

8. Letter to Mother, April 15, 1864, Daniel Faust Papers, Harrisburg Civil War Round Table Collection, USAHEC.

9. Diary entry, April 26, 1864, in *All for the Union: The Civil War Diary and Letters of Elisha Hunt Rhodes,* ed. Robert Hunt Rhodes (New York: Vintage Books, 1985), 135.

10. Diary entry of Corporal Cyrille Fountain, 77th New York Infantry, April 18, 1864, quoted in Donald Chipman, "An Essex County Soldier in the Civil War: The Diary of Cyrille Fountain," *New York History* 66 (July 1985): 289.

11. Letter to father, April 18, 1864, *Infantryman Pettit: The Civil War Letters of Corporal Frederick Pettit, Late of Company C, 100th Pennsylvania Veteran Volunteer Infantry Regiment, "The Roundheads," 1862–1864,* ed. William Gilfillan Gavin (Shippensburg, PA: White Mane Publishing, 1990), 142.

12. Diary entry, April 18, 1864, Rhodes, *All for the Union,* 134.

13. Letter to "Friend Hasbrouck," April 4, 1864, *This Regiment of Heroes: A Compilation of Primary Materials Pertaining to the 124th New York State Volunteers in the American Civil War,* ed. Charles J. LaRocca. Obtained at USAHEC; *Recollections of the Civil War, with Many Original Diary Entries and Letters Written from the Seat of War, and with Annotated References,* ed. William S. Tyler (New York: G. P. Putnam's Sons, 1912), 137.

14. Frank Wilkeson, *Turned Inside Out: Recollections of a Private Soldier in the Army of the Potomac* (Lincoln: University of Nebraska Press, 1997), 36.

15. Diary entry, May 2, 1864, in Silliker, *The Rebel Yell and the Yankee Hurrah,* 141.

16. Letter to Mary, April 3, 1864, Howard Malcolm Smith Papers, Library of Congress, Washington, D.C. (LOC).

17. General Orders Number 17, April 7, 1864, *Official Records,* Volume 33, 816–17. The intent of such an order was to provide for an advance as free of obstacles as possible, while also hopefully curtailing the spread of information among unauthorized personnel.

18. Letter to "Aunt Lydia," March 11, 1864, Julius Frederic Ramsdell Papers, Southern Historical Collection, University of North Carolina–Chapel Hill.

19. Robert Ekin McBride, *In the Ranks: From the Wilderness to Appomattox Court-House. The War, As Seen and Experienced by a Private Soldier in the Army of the Potomac* (Cincinnati: Walden & Stowe, 1881), 30.

20. Diary entry, April 12, 1864, James William Latta Papers LOC.

21. Diary entry, April 15, 1864, "Diary of Cyrille Fountain," 289.

22. Diary entry, May 1, 1864, Joseph J. Scroggs Diary, *Civil War Times Illustrated* Collection, USAHEC.

23. Gordon Rhea, *The Battle of the Wilderness, May 5–6, 1864* (Baton Rouge: Louisiana State University Press, 1994), 34. Rhea's total number includes the men of the 9th Corps, which, although operating in tandem with its movements, was technically an independent command from the Army of the Potomac. For a full breakdown of those who were present for duty in the Army of the Potomac, see *War of the Rebellion,* Volume 33, 1036.

24. Letter to "My Dear Sarah," April 6, 1864, Anson B. Shuey Letters, Civil War Document Collection, USAHEC.

25. Letter to "Brother Walt," April 22, 1864, in *Civil War Letters of George Washington Whitman*, ed. Jerome Loving (Durham, NC: Duke University Press, 1975), 118.

26. Sylvanus Cadwallader, *Three Years with Grant*, ed. Benjamin P. Thomas (New York: Knopf, 1955), 175.

27. Letter to "My dear Friends at Home," May 4, 1864, Austin J. Kendall Letters, Civil War Document Collection, USAHEC.

28. *Official Records*, Series 1, Volume 36, Part 1, 119–88.

29. Trudeau, *Bloody Roads South*, 317–18.

30. Gerald F. Linderman, *Embattled Courage: The Experience of Combat in the American Civil War* (New York: Free Press, 1987), 147.

31. John Keegan, *The Face of Battle* (New York: Penguin Books, 1976), 61. Gordon Rhea's work is perhaps the most detailed on the Overland campaign, but unfortunately his books follow the old trend of looking at individual battles rather than viewing them in the full context of the campaign. See *The Battle of the Wilderness, May 5–6, 1864* (Baton Rouge: Louisiana State University Press, 1994); *The Battles for Spotsylvania Court House and the Road to Yellow Tavern, May 7–12, 1864* (Baton Rouge: Louisiana State University Press, 1997); *To the North Anna River: Grant and Lee, May 13–25, 1864* (Baton Rouge: Louisiana State University Press, 2000); and *Cold Harbor: Grant and Lee, May 26–June 3, 1864* (Baton Rouge: Louisiana State University Press, 2002). For the Petersburg campaign, there are generalized treatments such as John Horn, *The Petersburg Campaign, June 1864–April 1865* (Conshohocken, PA: Combined Publishing, 1993); Edwin C. Bearss and Bryce A. Suderow, *The Petersburg Campaign, Volume 1: The Eastern Front Battles, June–August 1864* (El Dorado Hills, CA: Savas Beatie, 2011); and Bearss and Suderow, *The Petersburg Campaign, Volume 2: The Western Front Battles, September 1864–April 1865* (El Dorado Hills, CA: Savas Beatie, 2014). Richard Sommers provided a remarkably detailed battle study that effectively portrayed the operations of late September and early October 1864 while still capturing the multiple levels of battle and most of the nature of the campaign. Richard Sommers, *Richmond Redeemed: The Siege at Petersburg* (Garden City, NY: Doubleday, 1981). However, it has been Noah Trudeau who has made the greatest effort at portraying the Overland and Petersburg campaigns as the uniform experiences they were rather than the isolated battles they may have seemed. *Bloody Roads South* and *The Last Citadel: Petersburg, Virginia, June 1864–April 1865* (Baton Rouge: Louisiana State University Press, 1991).

32. Earl Hess, *Field Armies & Fortifications in the Civil War: The Eastern Campaigns, 1861–1864* (Chapel Hill: University of North Carolina Press, 2005); *Trench Warfare under Grant and Lee: Field Fortifications in the Overland Campaign* (Chapel Hill: University of North Carolina Press, 2007); and *In the Trenches at Petersburg: Field Fortifications and Confederate Defeat* (Chapel Hill: University of North Carolina Press, 2009).

33. Linderman, *Embattled Courage,* 155. Linderman offers a similarly bleak depiction of the American combat soldier in his later work *The World within War: America's Combat Experience in World War II* (New York: Free Press, 1997).

34. J. Tracy Power, *Lee's Miserables: Life in the Army of Northern Virginia from the Wilderness to Appomattox* (Chapel Hill: University of North Carolina Press, 1998), 303. Like Power, most

authors have noted the decline in the Army of Northern Virginia during the siege as short supplies began to take their toll. See Mark A. Weitz, *More Damning than Slaughter: Desertion in the Confederate Army* (Lincoln: University of Nebraska Press, 2005), 234–76. Edward Hagerman viewed the winter of 1864–1865 as the critical time for that army, when poor weather and living conditions led to "a growing belief among the troops that the Confederate cause was hopeless. Discipline began to collapse, and there were large-scale desertions." Edward Hagerman, *The American Civil War and the Origins of Modern Warfare: Ideas, Organization, and Field Command* (Bloomington: Indiana University Press, 1988), 272.

35. Power, *Lee's Miserables*, 268.

36. Ella Lonn, *Desertion during the Civil War* (Lincoln: University of Nebraska Press, 1998), 233, 236.

37. While there is no official tally of Confederate executions during the war, Bell Wiley suggested that there were 39 military executions of deserters in the last six months of the war. Bell Irvin Wiley, *The Life of Johnny Reb: The Common Soldier of the Confederacy* (Baton Rouge: Louisiana State University Press, 1943), 226. During this same time period, approximately forty-five Union deserters were executed by Northern military authorities. Robert Alotta, *Civil War Justice: Union Army Executions under Lincoln* (Shippensburg, PA: White Mane Publishing, 1989), 134–63. The wartime total for Union executions for desertion was at least 147. Barbara Long and E. B. Long, *The Civil War Day by Day: An Almanac, 1861–1865* (Garden City, NY: Doubleday, 1971), 714.

38. During the Civil War, line officers were generally those at the regimental command level, commissioned officers at the rank of colonel or below. The structure of nineteenth-century military forces dictated that those officers accompany their men into the combat zone, but notions of honor and chivalry often drove general officers across the battlefield as well.

39. Anthony Kellett, *Combat Motivation: The Behavior of Soldiers in Battle* (Boston: Kluwer-Nijhoff, 1982), 59–60. See Paddy Griffith, *Battle Tactics of the Civil War* (New Haven, CT: Yale University Press, 1989) for more on how Civil War armies reflect the nature of nineteenth-century warfare more than they offer a preview of the "modern" conflicts of the twentieth century.

40. Reid Mitchell, "The Infantryman in Combat," *North and South* 4 (August 2001): 21.

41. The American Civil War as a "modern" war debate dates back to the years following the First World War. See B. H. Liddell Hart, *Sherman: Soldier, Realist, American* (New York: Dodd, Mead, 1929); and J. F. C. Fuller, *The Generalship of Ulysses S. Grant* (Bloomington: Indiana University Press, 1929). For more recent work, see Herman Hattaway and Archer Jones, *How the North Won: A Military History of the Civil War* (Urbana: University of Illinois Press, 1983); and Edward Hagerman, *The American Civil War and the Origins of Modern Warfare: Ideas, Organization, and Field Command* (Bloomington: Indiana University Press, 1988). The current trend is to portray the Civil War as less of a "modern" war and more of a transitional conflict from the Napoleonic era of limited conflict to a more twentieth-century notion of "total war." See Paddy Griffith, *Battle Tactics of the Civil War;* Reid Mitchell, "The First Modern War, R.I.P.," *Reviews in American History* 17 (December 1989): 552–58; Keith Poulter, "The Civil War and the Evolution of Infantry Tactics," *North and South* 4 (August 2001): 78–84.

CHAPTER ONE

Note to epigraph: Diary entry, May 3, 1864, Samuel J. Gilpin Diary, E. N. Gilpin Papers, Library of Congress, Washington, D.C. (LOC).

1. Charles J. Stille, *History of the United States Sanitary Commission: Being the General of Its Work during the War of the Rebellion* (Philadelphia: J. B. Lippincott, 1866), 391–95. Manuscript housed at Massachusetts Historical Society, Boston, Massachusetts (MHS).

2. Carol Reardon, "A Hard Road to Travel: The Impact of Continuous Operations on the Army of the Potomac and the Army of Northern Virginia in May 1864," in *The Spotsylvania Campaign*, ed. Gary W. Gallagher (Chapel Hill: University of North Carolina Press, 1998), 177.

3. The new intensity of Civil War combat inaugurated by the Overland campaign has been well documented by historians. Edward Hagerman has argued that the first battle at the Wilderness signaled an end to "the familiar pattern of extended tactical and strategic stalemate in one position." Edward Hagerman, *The American Civil War and the Origins of Modern Warfare: Ideas, Organization, and Field Command* (Bloomington: Indiana University Press, 1988), 257. Earl Hess concurred, claiming that in 1864 "continuous campaigning was a new experience for American soldiers." Earl Hess, "Tactics, Trenches, and Men in the Civil War," in *On the Road to Total War: The American Civil War and the German Wars of Unification*, ed. Stig Förster and Jörg Nagler (Cambridge: Cambridge University Press, 1997), 485. For more on the intensity of the Overland campaign, and the role that field fortifications played in that intensity, see Earl J. Hess, *Trench Warfare under Grant and Lee: Field Fortifications in the Overland Campaign* (Chapel Hill: University of North Carolina Press, 2007).

4. Stephen Sears, *To the Gates of Richmond: The Peninsula Campaign* (New York: Mariner Books, 1992), 343–45.

5. Ulysses S. Grant, *Personal Memoirs of U.S. Grant, in Two Volumes*, Volume 2 (New York: Charles L. Webster, 1886), 141.

6. Noah Andre Trudeau, *Bloody Roads South: The Wilderness to Cold Harbor, May–June 1864* (Baton Rouge: Louisiana State University Press, 1989), 21.

7. Theodore Lyman, *With Grant and Meade from the Wilderness to Appomattox* (Lincoln: University of Nebraska Press, 1994), 83.

8. The returns for the Army of the Potomac for April 30, 1864 detail 97,273 officers and men present and equipped for duty. Although not part of the Army of the Potomac, General Ambrose Burnside's Ninth Corps would join it in the campaign and count 19,250 officers and men present for duty on April 30, 1864, for a total of 116,523 officers and men at the start of the campaign. United States War Department, *The War of the Rebellion: A Compilation of the Official Records of the Union and Confederate Armies* (Washington, D.C.: Government Printing Office), Series 1, Volume 33, 1036–46.

9. Gordon C. Rhea, *The Battle of the Wilderness, May 5–6, 1864* (Baton Rouge: Louisiana State University Press, 1994), 37–41.

10. Ibid., 48.

11. Diary entry, May 3, 1864, Samuel Gilpin Diary, E. N. Gilpin Papers, LOC.

12. Horace Porter, *Campaigning with Grant* (New York: Konecky & Konecky, 1992), 42.

13. Diary entry, May 4, 1864, *The Cormany Diaries: A Northern Family in the Civil War*, ed. James C. Mohr and Richard E. Winslow III (Pittsburgh: University of Pittsburgh Press, 1982), 418.

14. John J. Hennessy, "I Dread the Spring: The Army of the Potomac Prepares for the Overland Campaign," in *The Wilderness Campaign*, ed. Gary W. Gallagher (Chapel Hill: University of North Carolina Press, 1997), 78.

15. "Introduction," ibid., ix.

16. Diary entry, May 6, 1864, George A. Bowen Diary, Civil War Document Collection, United States Army Heritage and Education Center, Carlisle, Pennsylvania (USAHEC).

17. Letter to Mary, May 22, 1864, Howard Malcolm Smith Papers, LOC.

18. Union losses obtained from *Official Records*, Volume 36, Part 1, 119–33. Gordon Rhea estimates Confederates losses at more than 11,000. *The Battle of the Wilderness*, 440.

19. Robert E. McBride, *In the Ranks: From the Wilderness to Appomattox Court-House. The War, As Seen and Experienced by a Private Soldier in the Army of the Potomac* (Cincinnati: Walden & Stowe, 1881), 34.

20. Sylvanus Cadwallader, *Three Years with Grant*, ed. Benjamin Thomas (New York: Knopf, 1955), 176. While "unfavorable" for the offensive, the Wilderness could be very helpful for a defender, and this was obviously the reason why Lee used this location to strike at the Army of the Potomac, since the rough terrain would serve to nullify the numerical superiority that Grant had in both men and artillery.

21. Diary entry, May 5, 1864, Henry Keiser Diary, Gregory A. Coco Collection, Harrisburg Civil War Round Table Collection, USAHEC.

22. Diary entry, May 5, 1864, in *The Rebel Yell and the Yankee Hurrah: The Civil War Journal of a Maine Volunteer*, ed. Ruth L. Silliker (Camden, ME: Down East Books, 1985), 143.

23. Diary entry, May 6, 1864, in *The Civil War Notebook of Daniel Chisholm: A Chronicle of Daily Life in the Union Army, 1864–1865*, ed. W. Springer Menge and J. August Shimrak (New York: Ballantine Books, 1989), 13.

24. Diary entry, May 5, 1864, George A. Bowen Diary, Civil War Document Collection, USAHEC.

25. Letter from J. R. Pillings, May 29, 1864, in *Soldiers' Letters: From Camp, Battle-field, and Prison*, ed. Lydia Minturn Post (New York: Bunce & Huntington, 1865), 368. Manuscript housed at MHS. Compiled Military Service Record of John R. Pillings, Co. B, 86th New York Volunteer Regiment, National Archives and Records Administration, Washington, D.C. (NARA).

26. Frank Wilkeson, *Turned Inside Out: Recollections of a Private Soldier in the Army of the Potomac* (Lincoln: University of Nebraska Press, 1997), 57, 61, 64, 71.

27. Samuel Clear Diary entry, May 5, 1864, and Daniel Chisholm Letter to Father, May 19, 1864, in Menge and Shimrak, *The Civil War Notebook of Daniel Chisholm*, 13 and 113.

28. Diary entry, May 6, 1864, in Donald Chipman, "An Essex County Soldier in the Civil War: The Diary of Cyrille Fountain," *New York History* 66 (July 1985): 290.

29. Diary entry, May 6, 1864, Jacob Lyons Diary, Southern Historical Collection, University of North Carolina–Chapel Hill, NC.

30. Diary entry, May 7, 1864, William G. Hills Diary, LOC. Diary entry, May 8, 1864, in Frank Levstik, "The Civil War Diary of Colonel Albert Rogall," *Polish-American Studies* 27 (Spring/Autumn 1970): 37.

31. Diary entry, May 7, 1864, Charles E. Wood Diary, Civil War Document Collection, USA-HEC.

32. Rhea, *The Battle of the Wilderness,* 435–36, 440.

33. Grant to Halleck, May 11, 1864, *Official Records,* Volume 36, Part 2, 627–28.

34. Noah Andre Trudeau, "The Walls of 1864," in *With My Face to the Enemy: Perspectives on the Civil War,* ed. Robert Cowley (New York: G. P. Putnam's Sons, 2001), 413.

35. David Lowe, "Field Fortifications in the Civil War," *North and South* 4 (August 2001): 58.

36. Charles A. Dana, *Recollections of the Civil War: With the Leaders at Washington and in the Field in the Sixties* (Lincoln: University of Nebraska Press, 1996), 194.

37. Wilkeson, *Turned Inside Out,* 80. Abner Small, *The Road to Richmond: The Civil War Memoirs of Major Abner R. Small of the 16th Maine Vols.; with his Diary as a Prisoner of War,* ed. Harold Adams Small (Berkeley: University of California Press, 1957), 134.

38. Letter to Mother, May 20, 1864, in Wayne C. Temple, ed., "A Signal Officer with Grant: The Letters of Captain Charles L. Davis," *Civil War History* 7 (December 1961): 433–34.

39. Letter, May 17, 1864, *Letters to Eliza from a Union Soldier, 1862–1865,* ed. Margery Greenleaf (Chicago: Follett, 1963), 90.

40. Gordon C. Rhea, *The Battles for Spotsylvania Court House and the Road to Yellow Tavern, May 7–12, 1864* (Baton Rouge: Louisiana State University Press, 1997), 43–44.

41. Wilkeson, *Turned Inside Out,* 81–82.

42. Diary entry, May 8, 1864, in *Three Years with Company K: Sergt. Austin C. Stearns, Company K, 13th Mass. Infantry (Deceased),* ed. Arthur A. Kent (Rutherford, NJ: Fairleigh Dickinson University Press, 1976), 264.

43. Diary entry, May 10, 1864, in *Touched with Fire: Civil War Letters and Diary of Oliver Wendell Holmes, Jr., 1861–1864,* ed. Mark DeWolfe Howe (Cambridge, MA: Harvard University Press, 1946), 113; Letter, May 9, 1864, in *Hard Marching Every Day: The Civil War Letters of Private Wilbur Fisk, 1861–1865,* ed. Emil Rosenblatt and Ruth Rosenblatt (Lawrence: University Press of Kansas, 1992), 221. Though the Fisk letter is dated May 9, the events described in it clearly depict Upton's attack on the 10th and the Mule Shoe assault on the 12th.

44. Rhea, *The Battles for Spotsylvania Court House,* 176.

45. Mason Whiting Tyler, *Recollections of the Civil War, with Many Original Diary Entries and Letters Written from the Seat of War, and with Annotated References,* ed. William S. Tyler (New York: G. P. Putnam's Sons, 1912), 176. Tyler was a captain in the 37th Massachusetts Infantry by this point in the campaign.

46. Rhea, *The Battle of the Wilderness,* 436.

47. Trudeau, *Bloody Roads South,* 171.

48. Tyler, *Recollections,* 170.

49. Diary entry, May 12, 1864, in *Rebel Yell and Yankee Hurrah,* 157.

50. Diary entry, May 12, 1864, James William Latta Papers, LOC.

51. *Official Records,* Volume 36, Part 1, 119–88; Rhea, *The Battles for Spotsylvania Court House,* 311–12.

52. William Corby, *Memoirs of Chaplain Life: Three Years with the Irish Brigade in the Army of the Potomac,* ed. Lawrence Frederick Kohl (New York: Fordham University Press, 1992), 234.

53. Samuel Clear Diary entry, May 12, 1864, in Menge and Shimrak, *Civil War Notebook of Daniel Chisholm,* 15.

54. Tyler, *Recollections,* 195–96.

55. Diary entry, May 12, 1864, Charles C. Morey Diary, Stuart A. Goldman Collection, USA-HEC.

56. Letter to Mother, May 15, 1864, in *When This Cruel War Is Over: The Civil War Letters of Charles Harvey Brewster,* ed. David W. Blight (Amherst: University of Massachusetts Press, 1992), 298–99.

57. Diary entry, May 12, 1864, in "The Civil War Diary of Colonel Albert Rogall," 38.

58. Letter, May 9, 1864, in Rosenblatt and Rosenblatt, *Hard Marching Every Day,* 221.

59. McBride, *In the Ranks,* 38.

60. *Official Records,* Volume 36, Part 1, 136–50. Confederate casualties during this same period have been estimated to be 12,062. See Trudeau, *Bloody Roads South,* 213.

61. Robert Goldthwaite Carter, *Four Brothers in Blue, or Sunshine and Shadows of the War of the Rebellion: A Story of the Great War from Bull Run to Appomattox* (Austin: University of Texas Press, 1978), 396.

62. Diary entry, May 16, 1864, James William Latta Papers LOC.

63. Letter to "Ma," May 16, 1864, Curtis C. Pollock Correspondence, Civil War Document Collection, USAHEC. Compiled Military Service Record for Curtis Pollock, Co. G, 48th Pennsylvania Volunteer Regiment, NARA.

64. Gordon C. Rhea, *To the North Anna River: Grant and Lee, May 13–25, 1864* (Baton Rouge: Louisiana State University Press, 2000), 126–63.

65. Diary entry, May 18, 1864, Charles E. Wood Diary, Civil War Document Collection, USAHEC.

66. Diary entry, May 15, 1864, Charles H. Edgerly Diary, Northwest Corner Civil War Round Table Collection, USAHEC.

67. Wilkeson, *Turned Inside Out,* 120–21.

68. Rhea, *To the North Anna,* 280–324, and *Cold Harbor: Grant and Lee,* 114–60.

69. Letter to Mary, May 23, 1864, in *When This Cruel War Is Over,* 302.

70. Diary entry, May 23, 1864, in *Letters from a Sharpshooter: The Civil War Letters of Private William B. Greene, Co. G, 2nd United States Sharpshooters (Berdan's), Army of the Potomac, 1861–1865,* ed. William H. Hastings (Belleville, WI: Historic Publications, 1993), 211.

71. Rhea, *To the North Anna,* 325–26.

72. Trudeau, *Bloody Roads South,* 234.

73. Samuel Clear Diary entry, May 24, 1864, in Menge and Shimrak, *Civil War Notebook of Daniel Chisholm*, 19.

74. Diary entry, May 17, 1864, in Silliker, *The Rebel Yell and the Yankee Hurrah*, 159.

75. Letter to Eliza, May 17, 1864, in Greenleaf, *Letters to Eliza from a Union Soldier*, 90.

76. Letter to Mother, May 20, 1864, in *Civil War Letters of George Washington Whitman*, ed. Jerome M. Loving (Durham, NC: Duke University Press, 1975), 119.

77. Diary entry, May 20, 1864, in George A. Bowen Diary, Civil War Document Collection, USAHEC.

78. Trudeau, *Bloody Roads South*, 248–63.

79. *Official Records*, Volume 36, Part 1, 153–64.

80. William Glenn Robertson, *Back Door to Richmond: The Bermuda Hundred Campaign, April–June 1864* (Newark: University of Delaware Press, 1987), 58–62.

81. Diary entry, May 5, 1864, Joseph J. Scroggs Diary, *Civil War Times Illustrated* Collection, USAHEC.

82. Letter to Mother and Sister, May 7, 1864, Francis H. Woods Correspondence, David M. Rubenstein Rare Book & Manuscript Library, Duke University, Durham, NC.

83. Robertson, *Back Door to Richmond*, 90–91.

84. Letter to Mother, May 18, 1864, John B. Foote Correspondence, Rubenstein Library, Duke University.

85. Letter to Sister, May 17, 1864, in *All's for the Best: The Civil War Reminiscences and Letters of Daniel W. Sawtelle, Eighth Maine Volunteer Infantry*, ed. Peter H. Buckingham (Knoxville: University of Tennessee Press, 2001), 267.

86. Diary entry, May 16, 1864, John E. Bassett Diary, MHS.

87. Letter to Mother, May 18, 1864, John B. Foote Correspondence, Rubenstein Library, Duke University.

88. Letter to "Bro," May 26, 1864, in *From Antietam to Fort Fisher: The Civil War Letters of Edward King Wightman, 1862–1865*, ed. Edward G. Longacre (Rutherford, NJ: Fairleigh Dickinson University Press, 1985), 183.

89. Robertson, *Back Door to Richmond*, 205–19.

90. Letter to Wife, May 25, 1864, Joseph Barlow Papers, USAHEC; and Diary entry, May 10, 1864, Joseph J. Scroggs Diary, *Civil War Times Illustrated* Collection, USAHEC.

91. Letter to Dad, May 31, 1864, in *My Dear Parents: An Englishman's Letters Home from the American Civil War*, ed. A. S. Lewis (London: Gollancz, 1982), 85. Emphasis in original.

92. Grant to Halleck, May 22, 1864, in *Official Records*, Volume 36, Part 3, 77.

93. Rhea, *Cold Harbor*, 109–10.

94. Trudeau, *Bloody Roads South*, 224, 260; and ibid., 159–60.

95. Rhea, *Cold Harbor*, 191–93.

96. Smith to Meade, June 2, 1864, *Official Records*, Volume 36, Part 3, 506.

97. Grant to Meade, June 2, 1864, *Official Records*, Volume 36, Part 3, 478.

98. Rhea, *Cold Harbor*, 319; and Trudeau, "Walls of 1864," 426.

99. Wilkeson, *Turned Inside Out*, 127.

100. Letter to Mother, May 24, 1864, in Blight, *When This Cruel War is Over*, 303–04.

101. Letter to "Bro," June 1, 1864, in Longacre, *From Antietam to Fort Fisher*, 186–87.

102. *The Memoirs of Charles Henry Veil: A Soldier's Recollections of the Civil War and the Arizona Territory*, ed. Herman J. Viola (New York: Orion Books, 1993), 45; and Letter to Father, May 24, 1864, George M. Barnard Papers, MHS.

103. Diary entry, June 3, 1864, John E. Bassett Diary, MHS.

104. Diary entry, June 3, 1864, in Menge and Shimrak, *Civil War Notebook of Daniel Chisholm*, 20.

105. Diary entry, June 3, 1864, in Carter, *Four Brothers in Blue*, 424.

106. Buckingham, *All's for the Best*, 104.

107. *Official Records*, Volume 36, Part 1, 166–80.

108. Grant, *Personal Memoirs*, 276.

109. Diary entry, June 3, 1864, in *All for the Union: The Civil War Diary and Letters of Elisha Hunt Rhodes*, ed. Robert Hunt Rhodes (New York: Vintage Books, 1985), 150; and Letter to Father, June 8, 1864, in Menge and Shimrak, *Civil War Notebook of Daniel Chisholm*, 119.

110. "The Campaign," *New York Times*, June 6, 1864.

111. Diary entry, June 4, 1864, James William Latta Papers, LOC.

112. Diary entry, June 7, 1864, George A. Bowen Diary, Civil War Document Collection, USAHEC; and Tyler, *Recollections of the Civil War*, 214.

113. Buckingham, *All's for the Best*, 102.

114. Letter to Mother, June 6, 1864, in Hastings, *Letters from a Sharpshooter*, 216.

115. Letter to Sister, June 6, 1864, in Buckingham, *All's for the Best*, 274.

116. Letter to Father, May 31, 1864, in Lewis, *My Dear Parents*, 85.

117. Diary entry, June 12, 1864, John E. Bassett Diary, MHS.

118. Diary entry, June 13, 1864, James William Latta Papers, LOC.

119. Noah Andre Trudeau, *The Last Citadel: Petersburg, Virginia, June 1864–April 1865* (Baton Rouge: Louisiana State University Press, 1991), 22–24. See also Cadwallader, *Three Years with Grant*, 231.

120. Diary entry, June 14, 1864, in Menge and Shimrak, *Civil War Notebook of Daniel Chisholm*, 23.

121. *Official Records*, Volume 36, Part 1, 188. One hundred miles is merely an approximation of the linear distance traveled by the Army of the Potomac from its starting point near Brandy Station, Virginia in early May to its terminal destination of Petersburg, Virginia in mid-June. Given that there was no direct route between these two points, and that Grant's maneuvers involved units zigzagging and sometimes backtracking across the countryside, it is clear that the average soldier in either army had marched well over one hundred miles by the conclusion of the Overland campaign.

122. Rhea, *Cold Harbor*, 393.

123. Letter to Father, May 26, 1864, George M. Barnard Papers, MHS.

124. Trudeau, *Bloody Roads South*, 341.

125. Mark M. Boatner, *The Civil War Dictionary* (New York: David McKay, 1988), 935.

126. Allen C. Guelzo, *Gettysburg: The Last Invasion* (New York: Alfred A. Knopf, 2013), 444–45.

CHAPTER TWO

Note to epigraph: Frank Wilkeson, *Turned Inside Out: Recollections of a Private Soldier in the Army of the Potomac* (Lincoln: University of Nebraska Press, 1997), 178.

1. Details on Coon's background come from Compiled Military Service Record for Private David Coon, Co. A, 36th Wisconsin and Widow's Certificate for Isabel A. Coon, National Archives and Records Administration, Washington, D.C. (NARA). Letter, May 15, 1864, David Coon Papers, Library of Congress, Washington, D.C. (LOC).

2. Letter to "My dear daughter Emma," June 5, 1864, LOC.

3. Compiled Military Service Record for Private David Coon, Co. A, 36th Wisconsin, NARA. Coon is listed as having died at a Confederate prison in Salisbury, North Carolina on November 2, 1864.

4. Carol Reardon, "A Hard Road to Travel: The Impact of Continuous Operations on the Army of the Potomac and the Army of Northern Virginia in May 1864," in *The Spotsylvania Campaign*, ed. Gary W. Gallagher (Chapel Hill: University of North Carolina Press, 1998), 170–71.

5. Diary entry, May 6, 1864, Henry Keiser Diary, Gregory A. Coco Collection, Harrisburg Civil War Round Table Collection, United States Army Heritage and Education Center, Carlisle, Pennsylvania (USAHEC).

6. Compiled Military Service Record for Sergeant Henry Keiser, Co. G, 96th Pennsylvania, NARA. Keiser had reenlisted on February 15, 1864, earning him the designation "veteran volunteer."

7. Letter to Father, May 7, 1864, in *Letters of a Civil War Surgeon*, ed. Paul Fatout (West Lafayette, IN: Purdue University Press, 1996): 126; and Letter to "My Dear Sarah," May 7, 1864, Anson B. Shuey Letters, Civil War Document Collection, USAHEC.

8. Letter to Wife, in *Soldiers' Letters: From Camp, Battle-field, and Prison*, ed. Lydia Minturn Post (New York: Bunce & Huntington, 1865), 355. Manuscript housed at Massachusetts Historical Society, Boston, Massachusetts (MHS).

9. *Recollections of the Civil War, with Many Original Diary Entries and Letters Written from the Seat of War, and with Annotated References*, ed. William S. Tyler (New York: G. P. Putnam's Sons, 1912), 140.

10. Diary entry, May 10, 1864, in Frank Levstik, "The Civil War Diary of Colonel Albert Rogall," *Polish-American Studies* 27 (Spring/Autumn 1970): 37.

11. Diary entry, May 12, 1864, George A. Bowen Diary, Civil War Document Collection, USAHEC.

12. Letter, May 9, 1864, in *Hard Marching Every Day: The Civil War Letters of Private Wilbur Fisk, 1861–1865*, ed. Emil Rosenblatt and Ruth Rosenblatt (Lawrence: University Press of Kansas, 1992), 221. Although the Rosenblatt collection of Fisk's papers dates this letter as May 9, it is clear from his description of the fighting around Spotsylvania that this letter was written on or after May 12. Fisk's letters were intended for publication in *The Green Mountain Freeman* in Montpelier, Vermont.

13. Rogall had served in the 54th Ohio prior to taking a commission with the 27th USCT, and he had military experience dating back to service with the Prussian army in the 1850s. Compiled Military Service Record for Captain Albert Rogall, Co. G, 54th Ohio, NARA. George Bowen's enlistment dated to August 11, 1862. Compiled Military Service Record for Captain George Bowen, 12th New Jersey, NARA. Wilbur Fisk enlisted in May 1861. Compiled Military Service Record for Private Wilbur Fisk, 2nd Vermont, NARA.

14. Diary entry, May 12, 1864, in *The Rebel Yell and the Yankee Hurrah: The Civil War Journal of a Maine Volunteer,* ed. Ruth L. Silliker (Camden, ME: Down East Books, 1985), 155; and Howell Letter to Mother, May 14, 1864, in *This Regiment of Heroes: A Compilation of Primary Materials Pertaining to the 124th New York State Volunteers in the American Civil War,* ed. Charles J. LaRocca. Manuscript housed at USAHEC.

15. Letter from J. R. Pillings, June 10, 1864, in Post, *Soldiers' Letters: From Camp, Battle-field, and Prison,* 370; and Diary entry, May 12, 1864, Thomas Francis Galwey Papers, LOC.

16. Diary entries, May 12 & 13, 1864, James William Latta Papers, LOC.

17. Letter to Father, June 8, 1864, in *The Civil War Notebook of Daniel Chisholm: A Chronicle of Daily Life in the Union Army, 1864–65,* ed. W. Springer Menge and J. August Shimrak (New York: Ballantine Books, 1989), 118.

18. Letter to "Sallie," June 4, 1864, George L. Prescott Papers, MHS.

19. Letter to "parents, brothers, and sisters," June 13, 1864, in *Infantryman Pettit: The Civil War Letters of Corporal Frederick Pettit, Late of Company C, 100th Pennsylvania Veteran Volunteer Infantry Regiment, "The Roundheads," 1862–1864,* ed. William Gilfillan Gavin (Shippensburg, PA: White Mane Publishing, 1990), 158.

20. Ibid.; and Diary entry, May 5, 1864, in *Four Years with the Iron Brigade: The Civil War Journals of William R. Ray, Co. F, Seventh Wisconsin Volunteers,* ed. Lance Herdegen and Sherry Murphy (Cambridge, MA: Da Capo Press, 2002), 270–72.

21. Letter to Wife, May 15, 1864, in *A War of the People: Vermont Civil War Letters,* ed. Jeffrey D. Marshall (Hanover, NH: University Press of New England, 1999), 228.

22. Diary entry, May 20, 1864, in Menge and Shimrak, *Civil War Notebook,* 18.

23. Letter to "Wife and family," May 19, 1864, John Carvel Arnold Papers, LOC.

24. *All's for the Best: The Civil War Reminiscences and Letters of Daniel. W. Sawtelle, Eighth Maine Volunteer Infantry,* ed. Peter H. Buckingham (Knoxville: University of Tennessee Press, 2001), 86.

25. Robert E. McBride, *In the Ranks: From the Wilderness to Appomattox Court-House. The War, as Seen and Experienced by a Private Soldier in the Army of the Potomac* (Cincinnati: Walden & Stowe, 1881), 38.

26. Ibid., 39–40.

27. Diary entry, May 18, 1864, Lewis Luckenbill Diary, Northwest Corner Civil War Round Table Collection, USAHEC.

28. Diary entry, May 22, 1864, in Donald Chipman, "An Essex County Soldier in the Civil War: The Diary of Cyrille Fountain," *New York History* 66 (July 1985): 293; Diary entry, May 27–28, 1864, ibid.

29. Letter to Father, May 14, 1864, George M. Barnard Papers, MHS.

30. Diary entry, May 11, 1864, in Menge and Shimrak, *Civil War Notebook,* 15; and Diary entry, May 14, 1864, in *Touched with Fire: Civil War Letters and Diary of Oliver Wendell Holmes, Jr., 1861–1864,* ed. Mark DeWolfe Howe (Cambridge, MA: Harvard University Press, 1946), 118–19.

31. Letter to Sister, June 1, 1864, in Gavin, *Infantryman Pettit,* 150–52.

32. Diary entry, June 1, 1864, Timothy Bateman Diary, Civil War Document Collection, USAHEC.

33. Robert Krick, *Civil War Weather in Virginia* (Tuscaloosa: University of Alabama Press, 2007), 124–25.

34. Letter, May 11, 1864, in *From Antietam to Fort Fisher: The Civil War Letters of Edward King Wightman, 1862–1865,* ed. Edward G. Longacre (Rutherford, NJ: Fairleigh Dickinson University Press, 1985), 176.

35. Letter, May 17, 1864, in *Letters to Eliza from a Union Soldier, 1862–1865,* ed. Margery Greenleaf (Chicago: Follett, 1963), 89.

36. Diary entry, May 8, 1864, in *Three Years with Company K: Sergt. Austin C. Stearns, Company K, 13th Mass. Infantry (Deceased),* ed. Arthur A. Kent (Rutherford, NJ: Fairleigh Dickinson University Press, 1976), 264.

37. Diary entry, May 23, 1864, Thomas Francis Galwey Papers, LOC.

38. Diary entry, June 14, 1864, in *All for the Union: The Civil War Diary and Letters of Elisha Hunt Rhodes,* ed. Robert Hunt Rhodes (New York: Vintage Books, 1985), 153.

39. Buckingham, *All's for the Best,* 74.

40. William Corby, *Memoirs of Chaplain Life: Three Years with the Irish Brigade in the Army of the Potomac,* ed. Lawrence Frederick Kohl (New York: Fordham University Press, 1992), 240.

41. Sergeant Keiser commented in his diary on the lack of water on May 29, June 20, and June 24, 1864. Henry Keiser Diary, Gregory A. Coco Collection, Harrisburg Civil War Round Table Collection, USAHEC.

42. Kent, *Three Years with Company K,* 285.

43. Wilkeson, *Turned Inside Out,* 153–54.

44. Letter, May 17, 1864, in Greenleaf, *Letters to Eliza,* 90; and Diary entry, May 13, 1864, in Rhodes, *All for the Union,* 145.

45. Kent, *Three Years with Company K,* 267.

46. Diary entry, May 14, 1864, ibid., 267.

47. Diary entry, June 5, 1864, Thomas Francis Galwey Papers, LOC.

48. For more information on the logistical network of the Army of the Potomac in the Overland campaign, see Edward Hagerman, *The American Civil War and the Origins of Modern Warfare: Ideas, Organization, and Field Command* (Bloomington: Indiana University Press, 1988), 245–51.

49. Diary entry, May 14, 1864, in *The Cormany Diaries: A Northern Family in the Civil War,* ed. James C. Mohr and Richard E. Winslow III (Pittsburgh: University of Pittsburgh Press, 1982), 425.

50. Diary entry, June 15, 1864, in Menge and Shimrak, *Notebook of Daniel Chisholm,* 23. It would be another twenty-four hours before Clear and his men obtained rations, and then only because they "borrowed" some from a neighboring unit.

51. Letter to "Doctor," May 19, 1864, in Fatout, *Letters of a Civil War Surgeon,* 127.

52. Diary entry, May 29, 1864, Henry Keiser Diary, Gregory A. Coco Collection, Harrisburg Civil War Round Table Collection, USAHEC.

53. Diary entry, May 29, 1864, Lewis Luckenbill Diary, Northwest Corner Civil War Round Table Collection, USAHEC.

54. Letter to Mary, May 28, 1864, in *When This Cruel War Is Over: The Civil War Letters of Charles Harvey Brewster,* ed. David W. Blight (Amherst: University of Massachusetts Press, 1992), 309; and Diary entry, May 30, 1864, in Robert Goldthwaite Carter, *Four Brothers in Blue, or Sunshine and Shadows of the War of Rebellion: A Story of the Great Civil War from Bull Run to Appomattox* (Austin: University of Texas Press, 1978), 420.

55. McBride, *In the Ranks,* 79.

56. Letter to Parents, May 16, 1864, in Gavin, *Infantryman Pettit,* 144.

57. Letter, May 30, 1864, in *"Dear Friends at Home": The Letters and Diary of Thomas Jane Owen, Fiftieth New York Volunteer Engineer Regiment during the Civil War,* ed. Dale E. Floyd (Washington, D.C.: Office of the Chief of Engineers, 1985), 40.

58. Letter to M. F. Dickinson, June 20, 1864, in Tyler, *Recollections,* 230.

59. Letter from "Howard" to "My Dear Friend," June 23, 1864. Civil War Document Collection, USAHEC.

60. Diary entry, May 15, 1864, William S. Tilton Diaries, MHS.

61. For a thorough examination of the evolution of field fortifications during the war, see Earl Hess, *Field Armies & Fortifications in the Civil War: The Eastern Campaigns, 1861–1864* (Chapel Hill: University of North Carolina Press, 2005); *Trench Warfare under Grant and Lee: Field Fortifications in the Overland Campaign* (Chapel Hill: University of North Carolina Press, 2007); and *In the Trenches at Petersburg: Field Fortifications and Confederate Defeat* (Chapel Hill: University of North Carolina Press, 2009).

62. Diary entry, May 29, 1864, George A. Bowen Diary, Civil War Document Collection, USAHEC.

63. Letter, June 5, 1864, in Greenleaf, *Letters to Eliza,* 96.

64. Letter to "My Dear Ellen & family," May 25, 1864, in *The Civil War Letters of General Robert McAllister,* ed. James I. Robertson, Jr. (New Brunswick, NJ: Rutgers University Press, 1965), 426.

65. Letter, June 15, 1864, in Greenleaf, *Letters to Eliza,* 103.

66. Diary entry, June 18, 1864, in Kent, *Three Years with Company K,* 287.

67. Diary entry, June 3, 1864, in Silliker, *The Rebel Yell and the Yankee Hurrah,* 165. Emphasis in original.

68. *The Road to Richmond: The Civil War Memoirs of Major Abner R. Small of the 16th Maine Vols.; with his Diary as a Prisoner of War,* ed. Harold Adams Small (Berkeley: University of California Press, 1957), 137.

69. Letter to "Dearest Mother," May 29, 1864, Charles J. Mills Papers, Gregory A. Coco Collection, Harrisburg Civil War Round Table Collection, USAHEC.

70. Letter to "My dear Wife and Children," May 26, 1864, David Coon Papers, LOC.

71. Letter to Father, May 11, 1864, George M. Barnard Papers, MHS; Diary entry, May 13, 1864, in Howe, *Touched with Fire,* 118; Letter to "My dear Ellen & family," May 20, 1864, in Robertson, *Civil War Letters of General Robert McAllister,* 424.

72. Diary entry, June 16, 1864, Charles H. Edgerly Diary, Northwest Corner Civil War Round Table Collection, USAHEC.

73. Tyler, *Recollections of the Civil War*, 203, 206; Letter to Mother, June 2, 1864, in Blight, *When This Cruel War Is Over*, 311.

74. Letter to "My dear absent one," May 15, 1864, Frank C. Morse Papers, MHS.

75. Diary entry, May 13, 1864, in Rhodes, *All for the Union*, 145; Diary entry, June 17, 1864, in Carter, *Four Brothers in Blue*, 437. Emphasis in original.

76. Letter to Father, May 24, 1864, George M. Barnard Papers, MHS; Letter to "Ellen & family," May 20, 1864, in *Civil War Letters of General Robert McAllister*, 424.

77. Letter, May 17, 1864, in Greenleaf, *Letters to Eliza*, 90.

78. Lord Charles Moran, *The Anatomy of Courage* (London: Constable, 1945), 75.

79. Letter to Father, May 11, 1864, George M. Barnard Papers, MHS.

80. Letter to Mother, May 17, 1864, Charles J. Mills Papers, Gregory A. Coco Collection, Harrisburg Civil War Round Table Collection, USAHEC.

81. Letter to "Annie," June 5, 1864, William Penn Oberlin Letters, Civil War Document Collection, USAHEC.

82. Letter to Mother, May 15, 1864, in Blight, *When This Cruel War Is Over*, 298.

83. Letter to "Mary," May 23, 1864, ibid., 300.

84. Maurus Oestreich Diary, Harrisburg Civil War Round Table Collection, USAHEC. There are few dates listed in Private Oestreich's diary to guide the reader, but it clear that Oestreich was writing on the same day that Sedgwick was killed.

85. Letter to Mother, May 11, 1864, in Blight, *When This Cruel War Is Over*, 294.

86. The issue of "primary group cohesion" is well documented in the field of military history. See Anthony Kellett, *Combat Motivation: The Behavior of Soldiers in Battle* (Boston: Kluwer-Nijhoff, 1982). Historians of the Civil War have also seen fit to apply the modern concept of primary groups to America's greatest conflict. See James M. McPherson, *For Cause and Comrades: Why Men Fought in the Civil War* (New York: Oxford University Press, 1997).

87. Letter, May 9, 1864, in Rosenblatt and Rosenblatt, *Hard Marching Every Day*, 219.

88. Letter to Father, May 22, 1864, Nathan Hayward Letters, MHS; Letter to Wife and Family, June 5, 1864, John Carvel Arnold Papers, LOC; Diary entry, June 30, 1864, in Herdegen and Murphy, *Four Years with the Iron Brigade*, 285.

89. Carter, *Four Brothers in Blue*, 427. Emphasis in original.

90. Letter to "Abby," June 27, 1864, John M. Steward Correspondence, Civil War Document Collection, USAHEC.

91. Maurus Oestreich Diary, Harrisburg Civil War Round Table Collection, USAHEC.

92. Tyler, *Recollections*, 196.

93. Letter to "Dear Ones at Home," June 21, 1864, Austin J. Kendall Letters, Civil War Document Collection, USAHEC.

94. Letter to Father, June 4, 1864, George M. Barnard Papers, MHS.

95. Letter to Brother and Sister, May 23, 1864, James Beard Correspondence, Civil War Document Collection, USAHEC.

96. Diary entry, May 24, 1864, Horatio S. Soule Diary, Civil War Document Collection, USAHEC.

97. Letter, June 10, 1864, in *Soldiers' Letters: From Camp, Battle-field, and Prison*, ed. Lydia Minturn Post (New York: Bunce & Huntington, 1865), 371. Manuscript housed at MHS.

98. Diary entry, June 6, 1864, James William Latta Papers, LOC.

99. Letter to "My dear daughter Henrietta," June 8, 1864, in Robertson, *Civil War Letters of General Robert McAllister*, 436.

100. Letter to "My dear Ellen," June 8, 1864, ibid., 437.

101. Letter to Sister, June 1, 1864, in Gavin, *Infantryman Pettit*, 150.

102. Letter to "Abby," June 6, 1864, John M. Steward Correspondence, Civil War Document Collection, USAHEC.

103. Letter to Mother, May 24, 1864, Charles J. Mills Papers, Gregory A. Coco Collection, Harrisburg Civil War Round Table Collection, USAHEC.

104. Carter, *Four Brothers in Blue*, 413, 439.

105. Letter to Father, May 31, 1864, John B. Foote Correspondence, David M. Rubenstein Rare Book & Manuscript Library, Duke University, Durham, North Carolina.

106. Letter to Sister, June 26, 1864, in Buckingham, *All's for the Best*, 282.

107. While no references to this legendary story of man's courage in the face of imminent death were uncovered in the letters and diaries examined for this project, the most frequently cited source for this Cold Harbor tale is Horace Porter, *Campaigning with Grant* (New York: Konecky and Konecky, 1992), 174–75.

108. Letter to Mother, May 15, 1864, in Blight, *When This Cruel War Is Over*, 298.

109. Diary entry, June 5, 1864, in Silliker, *The Rebel Yell and the Yankee Hurrah*, 166.

110. Corby, *Memoirs of Chaplain Life*, 238.

111. Letter to Mother, May 11, 1864, in Blight, *When This Cruel War Is Over*, 295.

112. Diary entry, May 20, 1864, in Silliker, *The Rebel Yell and the Yankee Hurrah*, 160.

113. Small, *The Road to Richmond*, 147–48.

114. Diary entry, May 15, 1864, Timothy Bateman Diary, Civil War Document Collection, USAHEC; Letter, June 10, 1864, in Post, *Soldiers' Letters: From Camp, Battle-field, and Prison*, 373. Manuscript housed at MHS.

115. Letter to Parents, May 16, 1864, in Gavin, *Infantryman Pettit*, 144.

116. Letter to Sister, June 1, 1864, ibid., 152. Compiled Military Service Record for Corporal Frederick Pettit, Co. C, 100th Pennsylvania, NARA.

117. Ibid., 163–65.

118. Ibid., 166.

CHAPTER THREE

Note to epigraph: Letter from unknown Union soldier, "Before Petersburg," 1864, in *Soldier's Letters: From Camp, Battle-field, and Prison*, ed. Lydia Minturn Post (New York: Bunce & Huntington, 1865), 452. Manuscript housed at Massachusetts Historical Society, Boston, Massachusetts (MHS).

1. Sylvanus Cadwallader, *Three Years with Grant,* ed. Benjamin P. Thomas (New York: Knopf, 1955), 215–17.

2. Robert Goldthwaite Carter, *Four Brothers in Blue, or Sunshine and Shadows of the War of Rebellion: A Story of the Great Civil War from Bull Run to Appomattox* (Austin: University of Texas Press, 1978), 437.

3. The concept of "trauma" as it applies to Civil War combat is an under-studied one, but one work that offers some excellent preliminary work on the subject is Eric T. Dean, Jr., *Shook Over Hell: Post-Traumatic Stress, Vietnam and the Civil War* (Cambridge, MA: Harvard University Press, 1997).

4. Diary entry, May 15, 1864, Henry C. Carr Diary, Civil War Document Collection, United States Army Heritage and Education Center, Carlisle, Pennsylvania (USAHEC).

5. Letter to Wife, June 6, 1864, Charles H. Smith Correspondence, Civil War Document Collection, USAHEC.

6. Letter to "Bro," June 11, 1864, in *From Antietam to Fort Fisher: The Civil War Letters of Edward King Wightman, 1862–1865,* ed. Edward Longacre (Rutherford, NJ: Fairleigh Dickinson University Press, 1985), 189.

7. Letter, May 25, 1864, in *Hard Marching Every Day: The Civil War Letters of Private Wilbur Fisk, 1861–1865,* ed. Emil Rosenblatt and Ruth Rosenblatt (Lawrence: University Press of Kansas, 1992), 222.

8. Letter to "Brother Charles," June 11, 1864, Theodore Vaill Papers, Northwest Corner Civil War Round Table Collection, USAHEC.

9. Letter to "Abby," June 7, 1864, John M. Steward Correspondence, Civil War Document Collection, USAHEC; Letter to "Ma," May 15, 1864, Curtis C. Pollock Correspondence, ibid.

10. Frank Wilkeson, *Turned Inside Out: Recollections of a Private Soldier in the Army of the Potomac* (Lincoln: University of Nebraska Press, 1997), 52–53.

11. For returns illustrating the starting number of the Army of the Potomac (plus the 9th Corps) prior to the Overland campaign, see United States War Department, *The War of the Rebellion: A Compilation of the Official Records of the Union and Confederate Armies,* Series 1, Volume 33, 1036–46. For the casualties reported by the army during the Overland campaign, see ibid., Series 1, Volume 36, Part 1, 119–88.

12. Noah Andre Trudeau, *The Last Citadel: Petersburg, Virginia, June 1864–April 1865* (Baton Rouge: Louisiana State University Press, 1991), 20–25. For a lengthier treatment of this movement, including an assessment of its limitations, see Gordon C. Rhea, "Grant's Disengagement from Cold Harbor, June 12–13, 1864," *Cold Harbor to the Crater: The End of the Overland Campaign,* ed. Gary W. Gallagher and Caroline E. Janney (Chapel Hill: University of North Carolina Press, 2015), 176–209.

13. Trudeau, *The Last Citadel,* 29–55.

14. Diary entry, June 18, 1864, Thomas Francis Galwey Papers, Library of Congress, Washington, D.C. (LOC).

15. Ulysses S. Grant, *Personal Memoirs of U.S. Grant in Two Volumes,* Volume 2 (New York: Charles L. Webster, 1886), 298–99.

16. Letter to "Gren," July 15, 1864, Frederic Winthrop Papers, MHS.

17. Letter to Mother, June 25, 1864, Charles J. Mills Papers, Gregory A. Coco Collection, Harrisburg Civil War Round Table Collection, USAHEC.

18. Horace Porter, *Campaigning with Grant* (New York: Konecky & Konecky, 1992), 210.

19. Letter, June 18, 1864, in Theodore Lyman, *With Grant and Meade from the Wilderness to Appomattox* (Lincoln: University of Nebraska Press, 1994), 170.

20. Wilkeson, *Turned Inside Out,* 181.

21. Bell Irvin Wiley, *The Life of Billy Yank: The Common Soldier of the Union* (Baton Rouge: Louisiana State University Press, 1952), 223.

22. Charles A. Dana, *Recollections of the Civil War: With the Leaders at Washington and in the Field in the Sixties* (Lincoln: University of Nebraska Press, 1996), 221–22.

23. Letter to Father, June 4, 1864, George M. Barnard Papers, MHS. Emphasis in original. Barnard also noted the loss of officers in letters dated May 11, May 13, and May 26.

24. Carol Reardon references the Vietnam conflict when identifying these incidents of men disobeying orders during the Overland campaign as "combat refusal," "Hard Road to Travel" in *The Spotsylvania Campaign,* ed. Gary W. Gallagher (Chapel Hill: University of North Carolina Press, 1998), 189. Examples of such "combat refusals" can be found in Noah Andre Trudeau, *Bloody Roads South: The Wilderness to Cold Harbor, May–June 1864* (Baton Rouge: Louisiana State University Press, 1989), 294; and Wilkeson, *Turned Inside Out,* 134–35.

25. David Lowe, "Field Fortifications in the Civil War," *North and South* 4 (August 2001): 70.

26. Diary entry, June 3, 1864, George A. Bowen Diary, Civil War Document Collection, USAHEC.

27. Gordon Rhea, *Cold Harbor: Grant and Lee, May 26–June 3* (Baton Rouge: Louisiana State University Press, 2002), 341–42.

28. Diary entry, June 18, 1864, George A. Bowen Diary, Civil War Document Collection, USAHEC.

29. Grant, *Personal Memoirs,* 293–94.

30. Robert Ekin McBride, *In the Ranks: From the Wilderness to Appomattox Court-House. The War, As Seen and Experienced by a Private Soldier in the Army of the Potomac* (Cincinnati: Walden & Stowe, 1881), 100–01.

31. There has been abundant discussion of the American citizen soldier in the historical field. See Russell Weigley, *Towards an American Army: Military Thought from Washington to Marshall* (New York: Columbia University Press, 1962); James McPherson, *For Cause and Comrades: Why Men Fought in the Civil War* (New York: Oxford University Press, 1997); Edward Coffman, "The Duality of the American Military Tradition: A Commentary," *Journal of Military History* 64 (October 2000): 967–80; Ricardo A. Herrera, "Self-Governance and the American Citizen as Soldier, 1775–1861," *Journal of Military History* 65 (January 2001): 21–52; and Elizabeth Samet, *Willing Obedience: Citizens, Soldiers, and the Progress of Consent in America, 1776–1898* (Stanford, CA: Stanford University Press, 2004).

32. Diary entry, May 10, 1864, in *The Rebel Yell and the Yankee Hurrah: The Civil War Journal of a Maine Volunteer,* ed. Ruth Silliker (Camden, ME: Down East Books, 1985), 150–51.

33. Diary entry, May 17, 1864, in *The Cormany Diaries: A Northern Family in the Civil War,* ed. James C. Mohr and Richard E. Winslow III (Pittsburgh: University of Pittsburgh Press, 1982), 426.

34. Letters May 17, May 31, and June 16, 1864, in *From Antietam to Fort Fisher: The Civil War Letters of Edward King Wightman, 1862–1865,* ed. Edward G. Longacre (Rutherford, NJ: Fairleigh Dickinson University Press, 1985), 179, 185, and 193.

35. *The Road to Richmond: The Civil War Memoirs of Major Abner R. Small of the 16th Maine Vols.; with his Diary as a Prisoner of War,* ed. Harold Adams Small (Berkeley: University of California Press, 1957), 147; Letter to Father, June 4, 1864, George M. Barnard Papers, MHS.

36. Wilkeson, *Turned Inside Out,* 121–22.

37. Letter, May 25, 1864, in Rosenblatt and Rosenblatt, *Hard Marching Every Day,* 225.

38. Diary entry, May 8, 1864, in Silliker, *The Rebel Yell and the Yankee Hurrah,* 148.

39. Carter, *Four Brothers in Blue,* 428.

40. Letter to Parents, June 24, 1864, in *Touched with Fire: Civil War Letters and Diary of Oliver Wendell Holmes, Jr., 1861–1864,* ed. Mark DeWolfe Howe (Cambridge, MA: Harvard University Press, 1946), 149–50.

41. Small, *The Road to Richmond,* 147.

42. Letter to Father, June 20, 1864, Nathan Hayward Letters, MHS.

43. Letter to Father, June 4, 1864, George M. Barnard Papers, MHS.

44. Letter to Father, June 19, 1864, Ibid.

45. Letter to Sister, May 13, 1864, John Rumsey Brincklé Papers, LOC.

46. Wilkeson, *Turned Inside Out,* 193.

47. Diary entry, June 15, 1864, in Frank Levstik, "The Civil War Diary of Colonel Albert Rogall," *Polish-American Studies* 27 (Spring/Autumn 1970): 33, 44.

48. Wilkeson, *Turned Inside Out,* 142–45.

49. Bruce Catton, "Union Discipline and Leadership in the Civil War," *Marine Corps Gazette* 40 (1956): 20.

50. Ibid., 21. See also Bell Irvin Wiley, *The Life of Billy Yank: The Common Soldier of the Union* (Baton Rouge: Louisiana State University Press, 1952), 223.

51. Reid Mitchell, *The Vacant Chair: The Northern Soldier Leaves Home* (New York: Oxford University Press, 1993), 54. Herrera's piece also confirms the notion that, at least early in the war, soldiers on both sides voluntarily submitted themselves to military discipline. Herrera, "Self-Governance," 40. See also Fred Shannon, *The Organization and Administration of the Union Army, 1861–65,* 2 vols. (Gloucester, MA: Arthur H. Clark Company, 1928), Volume 1, 151–67; and McPherson, *For Cause and Comrades,* 53–57.

52. Stephen Ramold, *Baring the Iron Hand: Discipline in the Union Army* (DeKalb: Northern Illinois University Press, 2009), 6–7.

53. United States War Department, *Revised United States Army Regulations of 1861, with an appendix containing the changes and laws affecting Army regulations and Articles of War to June 25, 1863* (Ann Arbor: University of Michigan Library, 2005), 9.

54. Frederic S. Klein, "On Trial," *Civil War Times Illustrated* 10 (1969): 40.

55. Catton, "Union Discipline and Leadership during the Civil War," 19.

56. Shannon, *Organization and Administration*, Volume 1, 182–89. See also Catton, "Union Discipline and Leadership," 25; McPherson, *For Cause and Comrades*, 48; and Wiley, *Life of Billy Yank*, 200.

57. United States War Department, *Revised Regulations*, 124–27. For more on the structure and procedures of the army's court-martial system, see Ramold, *Baring the Iron Hand*, 316–26; Thomas Lowry, *Don't Shoot That Boy!: Abraham Lincoln and Military Justice* (Mason City, IA: Savas Publishing, 1999), 10–11; and General Francois Du Chanal, "How Soldiers Were Tried," *Civil War Times Illustrated* 7 (1969): 10–15.

58. General Court Martial held near Petersburg, HQ of 2nd Division, 9th Corps, July 7, 1864. Case NN-2359, Record Group 153: Records of the Office of the Judge Advocate General, National Archives and Records Administration, Washington, D.C. (NARA).

59. General Court Martial, HQ of 1st Division, 2nd Corps, July 18, 1864. Case LL-2520, NARA.

60. Ramold, *Baring the Iron Hand*, 328.

61. General Court Martial held on September 12, 1864. Case NN-2559, NARA.

62. Hearing held on July 22, 1864. Case LL-2203, NARA.

63. General Court Martial held near Petersburg at the HQ of 1st Division, 5th Corps, June 29, 1864. Case NN-2095, NARA.

64. General Court Martial held at HQ of the 1st Division, 2nd Corps, June 29, 1864. Case NN-2010, NARA.

65. Ibid. By the time of his court-martial, Lacey was only two months shy of concluding his three-year enlistment, rising in rank from First Sergeant to First Lieutenant over the course of his service. Perhaps his time in the service, coupled with the praise from the victim in the case, Major Hogg, contributed to Lacey's conviction being overturned in December 1864. Compiled Military Service Record for 1st Lieutenant George Lacey, 2nd New York Heavy Artillery, NARA.

66. General Courts Martial held near Petersburg, HQ of 2nd Division, 9th Corps, June 25 & June 27, 1864. Case NN-2015, NARA. Interestingly, some of the testimony indicated that such self-wounding cases were not unfamiliar to those at the court-martial. Dr. Emmerson, the assistant surgeon of the 9th New Hampshire who examined both of the defendants, testified, "We usually examine both hands in a case like this, to see if the hands are stained with powder." One other case of self-inflicted wounding was found in the research for this project, that of Private Joshua Pheasant of the 45th Pennsylvania, who was accused of leaving his regiment and "running a rammer through his hand during the battle at Cold Harbor, Va." Pheasant put forward a solid defense, however, and was acquitted of all charges. General Court Martial held near Petersburg, HQ of 2nd Division, 9th Corps, July 13, 1864. Case NN-2359, NARA. For more on self-inflicted wounding, see Ramold, *Baring the Iron Hand*, 199–200.

67. See Robertson, "Military Executions," 34–39, and Ramold, *Baring the Iron Hand*, 219–63.

68. Ella Lonn, *Desertion during the Civil War* (New York: Century Company, 1928), 233. Lonn's numbers indicate that regimental reports of desertion peaked at 10,692 in October. This number had been cut almost in half by the last full month of the Petersburg campaign, with desertion at only 5,621 for March.

69. Ibid., 236. The peak for arrests of deserters in the Union armies during the last year of the war was 3,824 for December 1864.

70. General Court Martial held near Petersburg, HQ of 3rd Division, 5th Corps, August 1, 1864. Case NN-3094, NARA.

71. General Court Martial held near Weldon Railroad, HQ of 2nd Division, 9th Corps, September 24, 1864. Case LL-2484, NARA.

72. Ibid.

73. General Court Martial in the field, HQ of 3rd Division, 2nd Corps, July 9, 1864. Case NN-2282, NARA.

74. General Court Martial, HQ of 1st Division, 2nd Corps, January 1865. Case LL-3105, NARA.

75. General Court Martial held on September 24, 1864. Case NN-2559, NARA.

76. General Court Martial held in the field, August 9, 1864. Case LL-2343, NARA. Emphasis in original.

77. For example, see Wiley, *Life of Billy Yank,* 209–10; and Robertson, "Military Executions," 34–39. Ramold is the exception to this, but he does not identify leniency to the scale seen here. Ramold, *Baring the Iron Hand,* 328.

78. General Court Martial, HQ of 1st Division, 2nd Corps, July 18, 1864. Case LL-2520, NARA. That same day Miles also reduced the sentence of Sergeant John Higgins of the 63rd New York Regiment, court martial held at the HQ of the 1st Division, 2nd Corps, July 18, 1864. Case LL-2520, NARA. Higgins was convicted of drunkenness on duty and offering violence to his superior officer. Miles commuted the hard labor, but sustained the sentences of loss of pay and reduction in rank. Thus, as with Private Black, Higgins was punished but remained in the trenches.

79. The cases in question were those of Privates James Moore, John Miles, and John Floyd of the 61st New York Regiment. General Court Martial, HQ of 1st Division, 2nd Corps, November 19, 1864. Cases NN-3143 & NN-3165. Miles's comments are dated November 26, 1864.

80. General Court Martial, Headquarters of the 2nd Division, 6th Corps, January 13, 1865. Case NN-3552, NARA.

81. Anthony Kellett, *Combat Motivation: The Behavior of Soldiers in Battle* (Boston: Kluwer-Nijhoff, 1982), 329.

CHAPTER FOUR

Note to epigraph: Letter to "Friend Cranston," June 27, 1864, George Tate Papers, Rudolph Haerle Collection, United States Army Heritage and Education Center, Carlisle, Pennsylvania (USAHEC).

1. Letter to "Miss Sarah," July 27, 1864, John C. Hackhiser Letters, Earl M. Hess Collection, USAHEC. Compiled Military Service Record for Captain John Hackhiser, 28th United States Colored Troops, and Pension Certificate for George Heckhiser, National Archives and Records Administration, Washington, D.C. (NARA).

2. Earl Hess, *In the Trenches at Petersburg: Field Fortifications and Confederate Defeat* (Chapel Hill: University of North Carolina Press, 2009), xv. Hess notes that it is wrong to label the Petersburg campaign a "siege," since Grant's men never truly surrounded the town and lacked the capability to do so. Rather, a more accurate description would be "a traditional field campaign with some limited aspects of siege warfare."

3. David Lowe, "Field Fortifications in the Civil War," *North and South* 4 (August 2001), 72.

4. Sergeant George Fowle, 39th Massachusetts, Letter, June 9, 1864, in *Letters to Eliza from a Union Soldier, 1862–1865*, ed. Margery Greenleaf (Chicago: Follett, 1963), 99.

5. Paddy Griffith, *Battle Tactics of the Civil War* (New Haven, CT: Yale University Press, 1989), 124–26. Griffith identifies men like Dennis Hart Mahan and Henry Halleck, both of whom were strongly influenced by the seventeenth-century French engineer Sébastien Vauban, as propagating the study and use of scientifically engineered fortification networks at West Point before the war. This was at least partly because they "had no faith in the ability of militia armies to hold their own in the complex manoeuvres of regular warfare."

6. Earl Hess's series of works on this subject provides ample evidence of the prevalence of field entrenchments during the war. See *Field Armies & Fortifications in the Civil War: The Eastern Campaigns, 1861–1864* (Chapel Hill: University of North Carolina Press, 2005); *Trench Warfare under Grant and Lee: Field Fortifications in the Overland Campaign* (Chapel Hill: University of North Carolina Press, 2007); and *In the Trenches at Petersburg*.

7. Edward Hagerman, *The American Civil War and the Origins of Modern Warfare: Ideas, Organization, and Field Command* (Bloomington: Indiana University Press, 1988), 262.

8. While the siege of Petersburg was certainly the most advanced experiment with trench warfare in American history by the middle of the nineteenth century, Europeans had faced the horrors of the fortified battlefield for decades, if not centuries. Only ten years earlier, the siege of Sevastopol during the Crimean War revealed to Europeans, and American observers, the power of trench lines and fortified positions when Russian defenders held off French and British forces for a full year. For more on the Crimean War, and specifically how the American Civil War was affected by its course, see Trevor Royle, *Crimea: The Great Crimean War, 1854–1856* (New York: St. Martin's, 2000), 503–06.

9. Dave Grossman, *On Killing: The Psychological Cost of Learning to Kill in War and Society* (Boston: Little, Brown, 1995), 44. Emphasis in original.

10. John Ellis, *Eye-Deep in Hell: Trench Warfare in World War I* (Baltimore: Johns Hopkins University Press, 1976), 183. For more on the destructive effect of trench warfare during the First World War and how it shaped those exposed to it, see Eric J. Leed, *No Man's Land: Combat and Identity in World War I* (Cambridge: Cambridge University Press, 1979). For more on the French Mutiny of 1917, see Richard Watt, *Dare Call It Treason: The True Story of the French Mutinies of 1917* (New York: Dorset Press, 2001).

11. James Stokesbury, *A Short History of World War I* (New York: HarperCollins, 1981), 235.

12. Ellis, *Eye-Deep in Hell*, 180.

13. In particular, the technology of artillery had advanced dramatically by the time of the First World War. The use of high-explosive rounds and rapid-fire artillery significantly increased the rigors of trench life in World War I. See Leed, *No Man's Land*, 97–98.

14. Griffith, *Battle Tactics*, 72. Griffith's claims are certainly valid when campaigns from the two wars are placed numerically side by side. For example, the Petersburg campaign involved a few hundred thousand men and resulted in approximately 70,000 casualties over a ten-month period. See Mark Boatner, *The Civil War Dictionary* (New York: David McKay, 1988), 644–47. The Allied offensive that began near the Somme in July 1916 involved several million men and resulted in 620,000 casualties on the Allied side alone over a four-month period. See John Keegan, *The Face of Battle* (New York: Penguin, 1976), 207–89.

15. Anthony Kellett, *Combat Motivation: The Behavior of Soldiers in Battle* (Boston: Kluwer-Nijhoff, 1982), 59. Kellett notes that by 1954, almost one hundred years following the Civil War, the breakdown of American military forces went as follows: 28.8 percent combat-related tasks, 20.3 percent mechanical or maintenance, 17.5 percent administrative or clerical, and 14.5 percent technical and scientific. The balance of forces in both conflicts was made up of service workers and laborers (60).

16. Ellis, *Eye-Deep in Hell*, 190.

17. Lord Charles Moran, *The Anatomy of Courage* (London: Constable, 1945), x.

18. Hagerman, *Origins of Modern Warfare*, 266.

19. First Lieutenant Charles F. Stinson, Letter, September 11, 1864, Charles Stinson Papers, Lewis Leigh Collection, USAHEC. Stinson was a member of the 19th United States Colored Troops.

20. Diary entries, June 23 and June 20, 1864, Charles E. Wood Diary, Civil War Document Collection, USAHEC.

21. Letter to Sister, July 29, 1864, Henry Clay Heisler Papers, Library of Congress, Washington, D.C. (LOC).

22. Letter to "Del," July 11, 1864, Steve R. Clark Correspondence, Jay Luvaas Collection, USAHEC.

23. Letter to Brother, September 15, 1864, John Rumsey Brincklé Papers, LOC. Emphasis in original.

24. Letter to "Abby," June 27, 1864, John M. Steward Correspondence, Civil War Document Collection, USAHEC.

25. Letter to Mother, June 25, 1864, Charles J. Mills Papers, Gregory A. Coco Collection, Harrisburg Civil War Round Table Collection, USAHEC.

26. What follows is a brief description of the physical characteristics of the Union lines around Petersburg, and is drawn from the overview of trench networks provided in Hess, *In the Trenches at Petersburg*, 295–316; Noah Andre Trudeau, *The Last Citadel: Petersburg, Virginia, June 1864–April 1865* (Baton Rouge: Louisiana State University Press, 1991), 286–99; and Griffith, *Battle Tactics of the Civil War*, 127–35.

27. Letter, July 9, 1864, in *Infantryman Pettit: The Civil War Letters of Corporal Frederick Pettit, Late of Company C, 100th Pennsylvania Veteran Volunteer Infantry Regiment, "The Roundheads," 1862–1864*, ed. William Gilfillan Gavin (Shippensburg, PA: White Mane Publishing, 1990), 164.

28. Letter to Mother, August 16, 1864, Edwin W. Bearse Letters, MHS.

29. Letter, November 11, 1864, James Horrocks, *My Dear Parents: An Englishman's Letters Home from the American Civil War*, ed. A. S. Lewis (London: Gollancz, 1982), 102.

30. Letter, July 2, 1864, George Hopper Papers, USAHEC.

31. Letter, July 29, 1864, Robert Goldthwaite Carter, *Four Brothers in Blue, or Sunshine and Shadows of the War of Rebellion: A Story of the Great Civil War from Bull Run to Appomattox* (Austin: University of Texas Press, 1978), 464.

32. Diary entry, July 21, 1864, Joseph J. Scroggs Diary, *Civil War Times Illustrated* Collection, USAHEC. Emphasis in original.

33. Letter, October 15, 1864, M. T. Haderman Papers, David M. Rubenstein Rare Book & Manuscript Library, Duke University, Durham, North Carolina.

34. Diary entry, August 19, 1864, Francis Asbury Wallar (Waller) Papers, Civil War Document Collection, USAHEC.

35. Diary entry, June 30, 1864, Julius Frederic Ramsdell Papers, Southern Historical Collection, University of North Carolina–Chapel Hill.

36. Letter, June 23, 1864, Harrison Montague Correspondence, Civil War Document Collection, USAHEC.

37. Diary entry, October 19, 1864, Alexander Grant Rose Diary, Civil War Document Collection, USAHEC.

38. Diary entry, September 3, 1864, in *The Civil War Notebook of Daniel Chisholm: A Chronicle of Daily Life in the Union Army, 1864–1865,* ed. W. Springer Menge and J. August Shimrak (New York: Ballantine Books, 1989), 38.

39. Eric Dean, Jr., *Shook Over Hell: Post-Traumatic Stress, Vietnam, and the Civil War* (Cambridge, MA: Harvard University Press, 1997), 66.

40. Diary entry, July 10, 1864, Charles E. Wood Diary, Civil War Document Collection, USAHEC.

41. Diary entry, June 30, 1864, John E. Bassett Diary, MHS.

42. Letter, August 25, 1864, Thomas G. Bennett Correspondence, Civil War Document Collection, USAHEC.

43. Letter to Sister, December 20, 1864, Henry Clay Heisler Papers, LOC.

44. Letter, September 4, 1864, Thomas G. Bennett Correspondence, Civil War Document Collection, USAHEC.

45. Letter, October 8, 1864, in Edward Hastings Ripley, *Vermont General: The Unusual War Experiences of Edward Hastings Ripley, 1862–1865,* ed. Otto Eisenschiml (New York: Devin-Adair, 1960), 244. Emphasis in original.

46. Letter, July 25, 1864, Charles Chipman Papers, Wendall W. Lang, Jr. Collection, USAHEC. In this letter to "Lissie," Chipman included a rough diagram to demonstrate the high vertical trajectory of mortar shells. He followed it with the comment, "You will see that men in trenches can protect themselves against bullets and common artillery but a mortar shell can be dropped right into our works." For details of his death, see Compiled Military Service Record of Major Charles Chipman, 29th Massachusetts Infantry and 14th New York Heavy Artillery, NARA.

47. Diary entry, June 24, 1864, Charles E. Wood Diary, Civil War Document Collection, USAHEC.

48. Letter, September 18, 1864, A. H. Sanger, Jr. Papers, Gregory A. Coco Collection, Harrisburg Civil War Round Table Collection, USAHEC.

49. Diary entry, June 20, 1864, in *The Rebel Yell and the Yankee Hurrah: The Civil War Journal of a Maine Volunteer,* ed. Ruth L. Silliker (Camden, ME: Down East Books, 1985), 174.

50. *All's for the Best: The Civil War Reminiscences and Letters of Daniel W. Sawtelle, Eighth Maine Volunteer Infantry,* ed. Peter H. Buckingham (Knoxville: University of Tennessee Press, 2001), 116.

51. Diary entry, July 6, 1864, Joseph J. Scroggs Diary, *Civil War Times Illustrated* Collection, USAHEC.

52. Buckingham, *All's for the Best,* 120.

53. Ibid., 116.

54. Trudeau, *The Last Citadel,* 98–127. Earl Hess figures a total of 3,798 casualties for the Union assault on July 30. Hess, *Into the Crater: The Mine Attack at Petersburg* (Columbia: University of South Carolina Press, 2010), 200–01. See also John Cannan, *The Crater: Petersburg* (Cambridge: Da Capo Press, 2002).

55. Hess, *Into the Crater,* 221–26.

56. Letter, August 7, 1864, Austin J. Kendall Letters, Civil War Document Collection, USAHEC.

57. Letter, August 7, 1864, James Beard Correspondence, Civil War Document Collection, USAHEC.

58. Diary entry, June 24, 1864, Horatio S. Soule Diary, Civil War Document Collection, USAHEC.

59. *Three Years with Company K: Sergt. Austin C. Stearns, Company K, 13th Mass. Infantry (Deceased),* ed. Arthur A. Kent (Rutherford, NJ: Fairleigh Dickinson University Press, 1976), 291. Emphasis in original.

60. Diary entry, July 2, 1864, in *All for the Union: The Civil War Diary and Letters of Elisha Hunt Rhodes,* ed. Robert Hunt Rhodes (New York: Vintage Books, 1985), 158.

61. Letter, June 24, 1864, in *The Civil War Letters of General Robert McAllister,* ed. James I. Robertson, Jr. (New Brunswick, NJ: Rutgers University Press, 1965), 450.

62. Letter, June 24, 1864, in Carter, *Four Brothers in Blue,* 446.

63. Letter to "Friend Cranston," June 27, 1864, George Tate Papers, Rudolph Haerle Collection, USAHEC.

64. Letter, July 10, 1864, in Buckingham, *All's for the Best,* 288.

65. Letter, November 26, 1864, John B. Foote Correspondence, David M. Rubenstein Rare Book & Manuscript Library, Duke University, Durham, North Carolina.

66. Diary entry, February 7, 1865, in Rhodes, *All for the Union,* 204. Things only got worse for Rhodes and his men as they tried to dig themselves out of the snow that day, as he noted in this entry that "to make it still more uncomfortable the Rebels opened fire upon us and pitched one shell almost into my fire."

67. Diary entry, August 19, 1864, in Springer and Shimrak, *Civil War Notebook,* 33.

68. Diary entry, July 24, 1864, Charles H. Edgerly Diary, Northwest Corner Civil War Round Table Collection, USAHEC; Letter, July 25, 1864, Charles Chipman Papers, Wendall W. Lang, Jr. Collection, USAHEC.

69. Diary entry, September 6, 1864, in Silliker, *Rebel Yell and Yankee Hurrah,* 197.

70. Letter, September 15, 1864, Thomas G. Bennett Correspondence, Civil War Document Collection, USAHEC.

71. Letter, July 16, 1864, Henry Metzger Papers, Harrisburg Civil War Round Table Collection, USAHEC.

72. Letter to Brother, July 6, 1864, John Rumsey Brincklé Papers, LOC.

73. Diary entry, September 28, 1864, in *The Cormany Diaries: A Northern Family in the Civil War,* ed. James Mohr and Richard E. Winslow III (Pittsburgh: University of Pittsburgh Press, 1982), 480.

74. Based on the reports of medical personnel during the war, Frank Freemon has calculated that approximately 70 percent of the Union army suffered from some form of diarrhea or dysentery in the final year of the war. Of those diagnosed, 3.6 percent died. Frank R. Freemon, *Gangrene and Glory: Medical Care during the American Civil War* (Madison, NJ: Fairleigh Dickinson University Press, 1998), 219.

75. Freemon noted that while typhoid was not as prevalent as other ailments, "about one in four Civil War soldiers who received the diagnosis of typhoid fever died." On the contrary, due to its transmission through the bite of a mosquito, malaria was more prevalent during the war but not as deadly. Freemon calculated that in the final year of the war, only about 1.3 percent of those who contracted malaria died from it. Ibid., 206, 219.

76. Letter, June 30, 1864, in Carter, *Four Brothers in Blue,* 450.

77. Compiled Military Service Record of 1st Lieutenant John Cook, Co. E, 57th Massachusetts Infantry, NARA.

78. Undated Letter, published in *Soldiers' Letters: From Camp, Battle-field, and Prison,* ed. Lydia Minturn Post (New York: Bunce & Huntington, 1865), 423–24. Manuscript housed at MHS.

CHAPTER FIVE

Note to epigraph: Diary entry, May 28, 1864, in *All for the Union: The Civil War Diary and Letters of Elisha Hunt Rhodes,* ed. Robert Hunt Rhodes (New York: Vintage Books, 1985), 147.

1. Robert Ekin McBride, *In the Ranks: From the Wilderness to Appomattox Court-House. The War, As Seen and Experienced by a Private Soldier in the Army of the Potomac* (Cincinnati: Walden & Stowe, 1881), 94–95. Emphasis in original.

2. Letter to Parents, May 19, 1864, Allen Landis and Aaron J. Landis Correspondence, Library of Congress, Washington, D.C. (LOC).

3. For more on desensitization in a twentieth-century conflict (Vietnam), see Dave Grossman, *On Killing: The Psychological Cost of Learning to Kill in War and Society* (Boston: Little, Brown, 1995), 249–61.

4. Letter, June 11, 186, in *When This Cruel War Is Over: The Civil War Letters of Charles Harvey Brewster,* ed. David W. Blight (Amherst: University of Massachusetts Press, 1992), 314.

5. Letter, August 5, 1864, Harrison Montague Correspondence, Civil War Document Collection, United States Army Heritage and Education Center (USAHEC).

6. Letter, undated. *Soldiers' Letters,* 460–61. Manuscript housed at Massachusetts Historical Society, Boston, Massachusetts (MHS).

7. Letter, July 9, 1864, in *From Antietam to Fort Fisher: The Civil War Letters of Edward King Wightman, 1862–1865,* ed. Edward G. Longacre (Rutherford, NJ: Fairleigh Dickinson University Press, 1985), 199.

8. Letter, July 5, 1864, Howard Malcolm Smith Papers, LOC.

9. Letter to Brother and Sister, July 25, 1864, James Beard Correspondence, Civil War Document Collection, USAHEC.

10. Theodore Lyman, *With Grant and Meade from the Wilderness to Appomattox* (Lincoln: University of Nebraska Press, 1994), 186.

11. Letter, December 19, 1864, George C. Chandler Letters, Civil War Document Collection, USAHEC.

12. Diary entry, October 21, 1864, Francis Asbury Wallar (Waller) Papers, Civil War Document Collection, USAHEC.

13. Diary entry, September 1, 1864, in *The Civil War Notebook of Daniel Chisholm: A Chronicle of Daily Life in the Union Army 1864–1865,* ed. W. Springer Menge and J. August Shimrak (New York: Ballantine Books, 1989), 38.

14. Diary entry, July 26, 1864, in *Four Years with the Iron Brigade: The Civil War Journals of William R. Ray, Co. F., Seventh Wisconsin Infantry,* ed. Lance Herdegen and Sherry Murphy (Cambridge, MA: Da Capo Press, 2002), 295.

15. Letter, September 8, 1864, Thomas G. Bennett Correspondence, Civil War Document Collection, USAHEC.

16. Letter, July 12, 1864, Howard Malcolm Smith Papers, LOC.

17. Diary entry, July 9, 1864, Joseph J. Scroggs Diary, *Civil War Times Illustrated* Collection, USAHEC.

18. Diary entry, August 1, 1864, in *The Rebel Yell and the Yankee Hurrah: The Civil War Journal of a Maine Volunteer,* ed. Ruth L. Silliker (Camden, ME: Down East Books, 1985), 187.

19. Diary entry, July 30, 1864, in Frank Levstik, "The Civil War Diary of Colonel Albert Rogall," *Polish American Studies* 27 (Spring/Autumn 1970): 51. The heat continued and so did Rogall's drinking; less than a week later, he noted in his diary on August 3 that "Whiskey punch in water" was one of the highlights of his day.

20. Diary entry, February 26, 1865, in *All's for the Best: The Civil War Reminiscences and Letters of Daniel W. Sawtelle, Eighth Maine Volunteer Infantry,* ed. Peter H. Buckingham (Knoxville: University of Tennessee Press, 2001), 329.

21. Ricardo A. Herrera, "Self-Governance and the American Citizen as Soldier, 1775–1861," *Journal of Military History* 65 (January 2001): 21. Herrera was trying to touch upon the frequently overlooked enlisted men of the early republic, but it is the works of William Skelton and Edward

Coffman that still offer important, detailed analyses of the development and motivations of the early Army officer corps. See William Skelton, *An American Profession of Arms: The Army Officer Corps, 1784–1861* (Lawrence: University Press of Kansas, 1992), and Edward Coffman, *The Old Army: A Portrait of the American Army in Peacetime, 1784–1898* (New York: Oxford University Press, 1986). See also Russell Weigley, *Towards an American Army: Military Thought from Washington to Marshall* (New York: Columbia University Press, 1962); James McPherson, *For Cause and Comrades: Why Men Fought in the Civil War* (New York: Oxford University Press, 1997); Edward Coffman, "The Duality of the American Military Tradition: A Commentary," *Journal of Military History* 64 (October 2000): 967–80; and Elizabeth Samet, *Willing Obedience: Citizens, Soldiers, and the Progress of Consent in America, 1776–1898* (Stanford, CA: Stanford University Press, 2004).

22. Herrera, "Self-Governance," 51.

23. Ibid., 40.

24. Diary entry, September 22, 1864, in *The Cormany Diaries: A Northern Family in the Civil War*, ed. James C. Mohr and Richard E. Winslow III (Pittsburgh: University of Pittsburgh Press, 1982), 479.

25. For more on the disciplining of the Army of the Potomac under McClellan, see Mark A. Weitz, "Drill, Training and the Combat Performance of the Civil War Soldier: Dispelling the Myth of the Poor Soldier, Great Fighter," *Journal of Military History* 62 (April 1999): 263–90.

26. Anthony Kellett, *Combat Motivation: The Behavior of Soldiers in Battle* (Boston: Kluwer-Nijhoff, 1982), 331.

27. Letter, July 8, 1864, in *Letters to Eliza from a Union Soldier, 1862–1865*, ed. Margery Greenleaf (Chicago: Follett, 1963), 117.

28. Paddy Griffith, *Battle Tactics of the Civil War* (New Haven, CT: Yale University Press, 1989), 39.

29. Letter, July 2, 1864, George Hopper Papers, USAHEC.

30. Letter, October 6, 1864, in *The Civil War Letters of General Robert McAllister*, ed. James I. Robertson, Jr. (New Brunswick, NJ: Rutgers University Press, 1965), 513.

31. Noah Andre Trudeau, "Walls of 1864," in *With My Face to the Enemy: Perspectives on the Civil War*, ed. Robert Cowley (New York: G. P. Putnam's Sons, 2001), 428.

32. Edward Hagerman, *The American Civil War and the Origins of Modern Warfare: Ideas, Organization, and Field Command* (Bloomington: Indiana University Press, 1988), 264. Grant does not deserve all of the blame here; few Civil War commanders found effective means of defeating a well-entrenched enemy other than through the use of a massed infantry assault. For decades following the war, the US Army would wrestle with the demonstration of the power of fortified positions in the hands of well-trained infantry. For more on the army's struggle with this issue and its search for "no more Cold Harbors," see Perry Jamieson, *Crossing the Deadly Ground: United States Army Tactics, 1865–1899* (Tuscaloosa: University of Alabama Press, 1994).

33. Frank Wilkeson, *Turned Inside Out: Recollections of a Private Soldier in the Army of the Potomac* (Lincoln: University of Nebraska Press, 1997), 105.

34. Letter to Mother, May 8, 1864, in *This Regiment of Heroes: A Compilation of Primary Materials Pertaining to the 124th New York State Volunteers in the American Civil War*, ed. Charles J. LaRocca, 204. Manuscript housed at USAHEC.

35. Diary entry, June 3, 1864, in *The Rebel Yell and the Yankee Hurrah,* 165. Emphasis in original.

36. Letter to "Brother Joe & Sister Lizzie," June 21, 1864, Theodore Vaill Papers, Northwest Corner Civil War Round Table Collection, USAHEC. Emphasis in original.

37. Letter to "Friends at home," October 3, 1864, Theodore W. Skinner Correspondence, Civil War Document Collection, USAHEC.

38. Letter to Mother, August 16, 1864, Edwin W. Bearse Letters, MHS.

39. Letter to "Maurice," July 9, 1864, Henry Jacobs Letter, Civil War Document Collection, USAHEC.

40. Griffith, *Battle Tactics,* 132.

41. Letter, July 11, 1864, in *Hard Marching Every Day: The Civil War Letters of Private Wilbur Fisk, 1861–1865,* ed. Emil Rosenblatt and Ruth Rosenblatt (Lawrence: University Press of Kansas, 1992), 237.

42. Letter, July 11, 1864, Steve R. Clark Correspondence, Jay Luvaas Collection, USAHEC.

43. Letter, July 17, 1864, in Robert Goldthwaite Carter, *Four Brothers in Blue, or Sunshine and Shadows of the War of Rebellion: A Story of the Great Civil War from Bull Run to Appomattox* (Austin: University of Texas Press, 1978), 459.

44. Letter, October 21, 1864, Bayard Taylor Cooper Letters, Civil War Document Collection, USAHEC.

45. Diary entry, July 26, 1864, in Herdegen and Murphy, *Four Years with the Iron Brigade,* 295.

46. Diary entry, July 25, 1864, ibid.

47. Letter, July 16, 1864, Julius Frederic Ramsdell Papers, Southern Historical Collection, University of North Carolina–Chapel Hill.

48. Letter, July 20, 1864, in Robertson, *Civil War Letters of Robert McAllister,* 465.

49. Diary entry, July 15, 1864, Julius Frederic Ramsdell Papers, Southern Historical Collection, University of North Carolina–Chapel Hill.

50. Letter, October 24, 1864, Bayard Taylor Cooper Letters, Civil War Document Collection, USAHEC.

51. Earl Hess, *The Union Soldier in Battle: Enduring the Ordeal of Combat* (Lawrence: University Press of Kansas, 1997), 136. Hess also suggested that the uneducated, working-class nature of the Union soldier gave him "a phlegmatic insensitivity toward danger and a pragmatic acceptance of whatever the battle experience had to offer its participants" (135). In so doing, Hess concurs with Lord Moran's claim that most of the armies of the nineteenth century contained uneducated "yokel soldiers" and that "their courage seems to have had its roots in a vacant mind." Lord Charles Moran, *The Anatomy of Courage* (London: Constable, 1945), 6.

52. Hess, *The Union Soldier in Battle,* 138.

53. Letter, July 15, 1864, in Greenleaf, *Letters to Eliza,* 103.

54. Letter, July 20, 1864, Clarence H. Bell Correspondence, Civil War Document Collection, USAHEC.

55. Letter, September 15, 1864, in *Civil War Letters of Robert McAllister,* 503.

56. Letter, September 17, 1864, in George Washington Whitman, *Civil War Letters of George Washington Whitman,* ed. Jerome Loving (Durham, NC: Duke University Press, 1975), 131.

57. Letter, August 5, 1864, Harrison Montague Correspondence, Civil War Document Collection, USAHEC.

58. Letter to Sister, September 2, 1864, Henry Clay Heisler Papers, LOC.

59. Diary entry, November 1, 1864, in Silliker, *The Rebel Yell and the Yankee Hurrah,* 216.

60. Diary entry, June 22, 1864, in Menge and Shimrak, *Civil War Notebook,* 25.

61. Letter, October 26, 1864, in Longacre, *From Antietam to Fort Fisher,* 212.

62. Letter, August 19, 1864, in *Letters of a Civil War Surgeon,* ed. Paul Fatout (West Lafayette, IN: Purdue University Press, 1996), 130.

63. Letter, July 20, 1864, Clarence H. Bell Correspondence, Civil War Document Collection, USAHEC.

64. Letter, January 11, 1865, Alexander Adams Papers, Northwest Corner Civil War Round Table Collection, USAHEC. Adams probably missed the final fight; he was accidentally shot in the hip less than two weeks after this letter. There is no indication that he was killed, though. In fact, a comrade who described the incident in a January 24, 1865, letter to Adams's mother noted that Corporal Adams "was in the best of spirits and laughed and talked while they extracted the ball." Ibid.

CHAPTER SIX

Note to epigraph: Letter, July 13, 1864, in Robert Goldthwaite Carter, *Four Brothers in Blue, or Sunshine and Shadows of the War of the Rebellion: A Story of the Great Civil War from Bull Run to Appomattox* (Austin: University of Texas Press, 1978), 458.

1. Letter to "Friend Daelhouser," July 5, 1864, Fred Ployer Papers, Harrisburg Civil War Round Table Collection, United States Army Heritage and Education Center, Carlisle, Pennsylvania (USAHEC). Compiled Military Service Record for Private Frederick K. Ployer, Co. D, 187th Pennsylvania Infantry, National Archives and Records Administration, Washington, D.C. (NARA).

2. Sergeant George Fowle, 39th Massachusetts, Letter to "Eliza," June 21, 1864, in *Letters to Eliza from a Union Soldier, 1862–1865,* ed. Margery Greenleaf (Chicago: Follett, 1963), 105; Second Lieutenant John Rumsey Brincklé, 5th United States Artillery, Letter to Brother, October 4, 1864, John Rumsey Brincklé Papers, Library of Congress, Washington, D.C. (LOC).

3. Letter to "Jany," June 1864, in "The Civil War Letters of James Rush Holmes," ed. Ida Bright Adams, *Western Pennsylvania Historical Magazine* 44 (June 1961): 126.

4. Letter to Brother, September 1, 1864, William Coffee Correspondence, LOC.

5. For general treatments of the Petersburg campaign that offer more detail on the engagements and maneuvers involved, see Noah Andre Trudeau, *The Last Citadel: Petersburg, Virginia, June 1864–April 1865* (Baton Rouge: Louisiana State University Press, 1991); John Horn, *The Petersburg Campaign, June 1864–April 1865* (Conshohocken, PA: Combined Publishing, 1993); and Charles Bowery, Jr. and Ethan Rafuse, *Guide to the Richmond-Petersburg Campaign (U.S. Army War College Guides to Civil War Battles)* (Lawrence: University Press of Kansas, 2014). For information on Grant's efforts in the Deep Bottom region, along with an excellent treatment of the strategy

employed on both sides during the siege, see Richard Sommers, *Richmond Redeemed: The Siege at Petersburg* (Garden City, NY: Doubleday, 1981).

6. Trudeau, *The Last Citadel,* 142–91.

7. Ibid., 202–17.

8. Ibid., 218–54.

9. Letter, August 28, 1864, in *From Antietam to Fort Fisher: The Civil War Letters of Edward King Wightman, 1862–1865,* ed. Edward G. Longacre (Rutherford, NJ: Fairleigh Dickinson University Press, 1985), 206.

10. Letter, July 5, 1864, Fred Ployer Papers, Harrisburg Civil War Round Table Collection, USAHEC.

11. Letter to Wife, September 2, 1864, Charles H. Smith Correspondence, Civil War Document Collection, USAHEC.

12. Letter to "Friend Hattie," July 2, 1864, Martin Connally Letter, Hattie Burleigh Papers, USAHEC.

13. Edward Hagerman has stressed the growth of technology as a modern element, claiming that during the war "the industrial technology of railroads and steam-powered water transportation, combined with the technological anomaly of animal-drawn field transportation and supply, shaped the logistics of land maneuver through World War II." *The American Civil War and the Origins of Modern Warfare: Ideas, Organization, and Field Command* (Bloomington: Indiana University Press, 1988), xii. For more on the use of railroads during the war, see Christopher R. Gabel, *Railroad Generalship: Foundations of Civil War Strategy* (Fort Leavenworth, KS: Combat Studies Institute Press, 1997). For a broader overview of how industrialization transformed warfare in the nineteenth century, see Brian Holden Reid, *The Civil War and the Wars of the Nineteenth Century* (New York: HarperCollins, 2006).

14. For more detail on the use and efficiency of wagons as instruments of supply during the war, see James A. Huston, "Logistical Support of Federal Armies in the Field," *Civil War History* 7 (March 1961): 36–47.

15. Hagerman, *Origins of Modern Warfare,* 248.

16. Diary entry, June 15, 1864, George A. Bowen Diary, Civil War Document Collection, USAHEC.

17. Huston, "Logistical Support," 46. Huston painted a vivid picture of the bustling port at City Point, describing how "over 1,800 men were employed on the wharves and in the warehouses, repair shops, and bakery. During the year over 3,600 carriages and 2,400 ambulances were repaired, and over 50,000 horse and mules were shod. Twenty large ovens could turn out 110,000 bread rations a day. . . . Almost no supplies could be obtained locally; practically everything had to be imported. On the average 40 steamboats and tugs, 75 sailing ships, and 100 barges were used to transport stores" to City Point.

18. Quoted in Robert Bruce Sylvester, "The U.S. Military Railroad and the Siege of Petersburg," *Civil War History* 10 (September 1964): 311.

19. Letter to "Annie," July 31, 1864, William Penn Oberlin Letters, Civil War Document Collection, USAHEC.

20. Diary entry, October 10, 1864, Alexander Grant Rose Diary, Civil War Document Collection, USAHEC.

21. Sylvester, "U.S. Military Railroad," 310–11.

22. Ibid., 312–13.

23. Private Charles E. Field, 108th New York, Letter to "Friend Hattie," September 11, 1864, Charles E. Field Letters, Hattie Burleigh Papers, USAHEC.

24. Horace Porter, *Campaigning with Grant* (New York: Konecky and Konecky, 1992), 212.

25. Gabel, *Railroad Generalship,* 21. For more on the use of railroads during both the Petersburg campaign and the war in general, see George Edgar Turner, *Victory Rode the Rails: The Strategic Place of the Railroads in the Civil War* (Westport, CT: Greenwood Press, 1953).

26. Diary entry, October 10, 1864, Alexander Grant Rose Diary, Civil War Document Collection, USAHEC.

27. Letter, December 22, 1864, in *Hard Marching Every Day: The Civil War Letters of Private Wilbur Fisk, 1861–1865,* ed. Emil and Ruth Rosenblatt (Lawrence: University Press of Kansas, 1992), 294.

28. Letter to Mother, October 26, 1864, William Hamilton Papers, LOC.

29. Letter to "Sis. Sarah," September 11, 1864, Charles Stinson Papers, Lewis Leigh Collection, USAHEC.

30. For more on the difficulties faced by medical personnel during the Overland campaign, see Mary C. Gillett, *The Army Medical Department, 1818–1865* (Washington, D.C.: Center of Military History, 1987), 232–43.

31. George Worthington Adams, *Doctors in Blue: The Medical History of the Union Army in the Civil War* (New York: Henry Schuman, 1952), 103. See also Gillett, *Army Medical Department,* 239–41.

32. The exact numbers were 19,607 sick soldiers in July 1864 and 13,659 men in March 1865. Frank Freemon, *Gangrene and Glory: Medical Care during the American Civil War* (Madison, NJ: Fairleigh Dickinson University Press, 1998), 177. The high number of ill soldiers in July can be attributed to the spread of malaria in the mosquito-infested Tidewater region of Virginia.

33. For more on the improvement of sanitary conditions during the war and the work of charitable organizations, see Adams, *Doctors in Blue,* and Gillett, *Army Medical Department.*

34. Adams, *Doctors in Blue,* 226. Adams also commented that, during this time period, "the average daily sick report was only 4 per cent—then considered phenomenal—and most of the cases were relatively mild."

35. Letter to Mother, July 4, 1864, John Owen, Jr. Papers, Massachusetts Historical Society, Boston, Massachusetts (MHS).

36. Letter to "Father and Friends at Home," August 28, 1864, in *"Dear Friends at Home": The Letters and Diary of Thomas Jane Owen, Fiftieth New York Volunteer Engineer Regiment during the Civil War,* ed. Dale Floyd (Washington, D.C.: Office of the Chief of Engineers, 1985), 53.

37. Letter to "Brother Joseph," in *My Dear Parents: An Englishman's Letters Home from the American Civil War,* ed. A. S. Lewis (London: Gollancz, 1982), 91. There is no date on this letter, but its comments suggest that it was written sometime during the summer of 1864.

38. Letter to "Wife and Little Daughter," November 22, 1864, Joseph H. Young Papers, Southern Historical Collection, University of North Carolina–Chapel Hill.

39. Diary entry, June 26, 1864, William S. Tilton Diaries, MHS.

40. Letter to Father and Mother, July 27, 1864, John B. Foote Correspondence, David M. Rubenstein Rare Book & Manuscript Library, Duke University, Durham, North Carolina.

41. Letter to "dear Wife and Children," July 4, 1864, David Coon Papers, LOC.

42. Diary entry, August 24, 1864, in *The Civil War Notebook of Daniel Chisholm: A Chronicle of Daily Life in the Union Army, 1864–1865,* ed. W. Springer Menge and J. August Shimrak (New York: Ballantine Books, 1989), 34–35.

43. Letter to Wife, October 13, 1864, Steve R. Clark Correspondence, Jay Luvaas Collection, USAHEC.

44. Letter to "dear Wife and Children," July 4, 1864, David Coon Papers, LOC. Diary entry, August 21, 1864, Christian A. Fleetwood Papers, LOC.

45. Letter to Mother, August 9, 1864, in *Letters from a Sharpshooter: The Civil War Letters of Private William B. Greene, Co. G, 2nd United States Sharpshooters (Berdan's), Army of the Potomac, 1861–1865,* ed. William H. Hastings (Belleville, WI: Historic Publications, 1993), 244. Emphasis in original. By "cow," Private Greene meant milk, a delicacy he had not had for a long while.

46. Letter to Parents, August 7, 1864, Andrew R. Linscott Papers, MHS.

47. Letter to Uncle, November 11, 1864, Caleb H. Beal Papers, MHS.

48. Diary entry, November 24, 1864, in Frank Levstik, "The Civil War Diary of Colonel Albert Rogall," *Polish American Studies* 27 (Spring/Autumn 1970): 62–63.

49. Diary entry, November 24, 1864, Joseph J. Scroggs Diary, *Civil War Times Illustrated* Collection, USAHEC.

50. Letter to Father, November 26, 1864, James F. Goodwin Correspondence, Civil War Document Collection, USAHEC; Letter to Uncle, December 19, 1864, George C. Chandler Letters, Civil War Document Collection, USAHEC; Letter to "Friends at home," December 1, 1864, Theodore W. Skinner Correspondence, Civil War Document Collection, USAHEC.

51. Letter to Parents, November 30, 1864, Caleb H. Beal Papers, MHS.

52. Letter to "Sister Mary," November 26, 1864, John B. Foote Correspondence, David M. Rubenstein Rare Book & Manuscript Library, Duke University, Durham, North Carolina.

53. Letter to Sister, July 2, 1864, in *All's for the Best: The Civil War Reminiscences and Letters of Daniel W. Sawtelle, Eighth Maine Volunteer Infantry,* ed. Peter H. Buckingham (Knoxville: University of Tennessee Press, 2001), 285. The ethical implications of foraging did not seem to bother Private Sawtelle, who justified his gathering of food from the countryside by stating, "I think that there is no harm in making these rebels feed us when they have something for us to eat. They were the cause of our coming out here and according to the old saying 'Those that dance must pay the fidler'" 286.

54. Letter to Elizabeth Smith, February 15, 1865, in Robert F. Crawford, "The Civil War Letters of S. Rodman and Linton Smith," *Delaware History* 21 (Fall/Winter 1984): 111. Emphasis in original.

55. Robert Ekin McBride, *In the Ranks: From the Wilderness to Appomattox Court-House. The War, as Seen and Experienced by a Private Soldier in the Army of the Potomac* (Cincinnati: Walden & Stowe, 1881), 135.

56. Ibid., 139.

57. Diary entry, November 25, 1865, Horatio S. Soule Diary, Civil War Document Collection, USAHEC. Soule was a surgeon attached to the 56th Massachusetts.

58. Letter to "Friend Hattie," September 16, 1864, Charles E. Field Letters, Hattie Burleigh Papers, USAHEC.

59. Diary entry, September 18, 1864, Francis Asbury Wallar (Waller) Papers, Civil War Document Collection, USAHEC.

60. Letter to "Abby," June 27, 1864, John M. Steward Correspondence, Civil War Document Collection, USAHEC.

61. General Court Martial, Headquarters of 1st Division, 2nd Corps, September 24, 1864. Case NN-2559, Record Group 153: Records of the Office of the Judge Advocate General, NARA.

62. David Raney, "In the Lord's Army: The United States Christian Commission, Soldiers, and the Union War Effort," in *Union Soldiers and the Northern Home Front: Wartime Experiences, Postwar Adjustments,* ed. Paul A. Cimbala and Randall M. Miller (New York: Fordham University Press, 2002): 263–92. In this study Raney praised the work of both commissions, but acknowledged that "the two groups routinely competed with each other for resources and quarreled incessantly over ideology and methods for solving problems" (287).

63. Charles J. Stille, *History of the United States Sanitary Commission: Being the General of Its Work during the War of the Rebellion* (Philadelphia: J. B. Lippincott, 1866), 398. Manuscript housed at the MHS.

64. Ibid., 399.

65. United States Sanitary Commission, *The Soldier's Friend* (Philadelphia: Perkinpine & Higgins, 1865). Emphasis in original. Manuscript housed at MHS.

66. Raney, "In the Lord's Army," 292.

67. Andrew B. Cross, *The War and the Christian Commission* (1865), 48. Manuscript at MHS.

68. Ibid.

69. Diary entry, July 29, 1864, Charles Edward Bolton Diary, MHS.

70. Diary entry, August 15, 1864, ibid. Emphasis in original.

71. Diary entry, August 16, 1864, ibid.

72. Letter to "Ellen," July 19, 1864, in *The Civil War Letters of General Robert McAllister,* ed. James I. Robertson, Jr. (New Brunswick, NJ: Rutgers University Press, 1965), 465.

73. Letter, July 9, 1864, in Carter, *Four Brothers in Blue,* 454–55. Emphasis in original.

74. For more on the successes and failures of charitable organizations during the war, see David Raney, "In the Lord's Army."

75. Letter to Mother, March 20, 1865, Solomon D. Rose Correspondence, LOC. There is no unit specified for Private Rose, but the details of this letter suggest that he was in an artillery unit.

76. Letter to Mother, September, 1864, Andrew Robeson Letters, MHS.

77. Letter to Wife, July 9, 1864, Anson B. Shuey Letters, Civil War Document Collection, USAHEC; Letter to Father, August 3, 1864, Nathan Hayward Letters, MHS.

78. Letter to "Aunt Lydia," July 16, 1864, Julius Frederic Ramsdell Papers, Southern Historical Collection, University of North Carolina–Chapel Hill.

79. Letter to "Old Dad," July 10, 1864, in Lewis, *My Dear Parents,* 89. Emphasis in original.

80. Letter to Sister, July 20, 1864, Clarence H. Bell Correspondence, Civil War Document Collection, USAHEC.

81. Diary entry, July 17, 1864, in *The Rebel Yell and the Yankee Hurrah: The Civil War Journal of a Maine Volunteer,* ed. Ruth L. Silliker (Camden, ME: Down East Books, 1985), 182. Emphasis in original.

82. Ibid., 205.

83. Ibid., 228.

84. Historian Edward Hagerman has performed extensive research on the development of logistical structures during the war. He gave both Union and Confederate armies high marks on the subject, arguing that "beginning the war with inadequate French logistical models, [Civil War armies] quickly improvised a realistic standard for mid-nineteenth century America." Hagerman, *Origins of Modern Warfare,* xiii.

85. *The Road to Richmond: The Civil War Memoirs of Major Abner R. Small of the 16th Maine Vols.; with his Diary as a Prisoner of War,* ed. Harold Adams Small (Berkeley: University of California Press, 1957), 153.

CHAPTER SEVEN

Note to epigraph: Diary entry, March 6, 1865, in *All for the Union: The Civil War Diary and Letters of Elisha Hunt Rhodes,* ed. Robert Hunt Rhodes (New York: Vintage Books, 1985), 210.

1. Letter to Uncle, November 5, 1864, George C. Chandler Letters, Civil War Document Collection, United States Army Heritage and Education Center, Carlisle, Pennsylvania (USAHEC).

2. Letter to Uncle, December 19, 1864, ibid. While the heading of the letter is dated December 19, the homesickness comments are included in a section of the letter dated December 25.

3. James M. McPherson, *For Cause and Comrades: Why Men Fought in the Civil War* (New York: Oxford University Press, 1997), 133.

4. Anthony Kellett, *Combat Motivation: The Behavior of Soldiers in Battle* (Boston: Kluwer-Nijhoff, 1982), 184.

5. Letter to "Wife and family," June 24, 1864, John Carvel Arnold Papers, Library of Congress, Washington, D.C. (LOC).

6. Diary entry, June 26, 1864, William S. Tilton Diaries, Massachusetts Historical Society, Boston, Massachusetts (MHS).

7. Letter to Mother, November 6, 1864, Andrew Robeson Letters, MHS.

8. Letter to Brother, July 6, 1864, John Rumsey Brincklé Papers, LOC.

9. Letters to Mother, June 11 and June 25, 1864, Charles J. Mills Papers, Gregory A. Coco Collection, Harrisburg Civil War Round Table Collection, USAHEC.

10. Diary entry, August 21, 1864, Joseph J. Scroggs Diary, *Civil War Times Illustrated* Collection, USAHEC.

11. Diary entry, August 4, 1864, Julius Frederic Ramsdell Papers, Southern Historical Collection, University of North Carolina–Chapel Hill; Compiled Military Service Record of Private Julius Frederic Ramsdell, Co. K, 39th Massachusetts Infantry, National Archives and Records Administration, Washington, D.C. (NARA).

12. Letter to "Abby," March 10, 1865, John M. Steward Correspondence, Civil War Document Collection, USAHEC.

13. Letter to Parents, August 7, 1864, Andrew R. Linscott Papers, MHS. It is in this letter that Linscott refers to Julius Ramsdell being his bunkmate in the 39th Massachusetts.

14. Sylvanus Cadwallader, *Three Years with Grant*, ed. Benjamin P. Thomas (New York: Knopf, 1955), 296.

15. Letter to Brother, July 7, 1864, in *Letters from a Sharpshooter: The Civil War Letters of Private William B. Greene, Co. G, 2nd United States Sharpshooters (Berdan's), Army of the Potomac, 1861–1865*, ed. William H. Hastings (Belleville, WI: Historic Publications, 1993), 230.

16. Letter to Children, November 11, 1864, Warren Goodale Papers, MHS.

17. *All's for the Best: The Civil War Reminiscences and Letters of Daniel W. Sawtelle, Eighth Maine Volunteer Infantry*, ed. Peter H. Buckingham (Knoxville: University of Tennessee Press, 2001), 114. Sawtelle was with the 8th Maine before he joined a sharpshooting unit in the 1st Division of the 18th Corps.

18. Letter to "Father and Friends," August 28, 1864, in *"Dear Friends at Home": The Letters and Diary of Thomas Jane Owen, Fiftieth New York Volunteer Engineer Regiment during the Civil War*, ed. Dale E. Floyd (Washington, D.C.: Office of the Chief of Engineers, 1985), 53.

19. Letter to Sister, July 16, 1864, Henry Metzger Papers, Harrisburg Civil War Round Table Collection, USAHEC.

20. Letter to Sister, June 20, 186, John B. Foote Correspondence, David M. Rubenstein Rare Books & Manuscript Library, Duke University, Durham, North Carolina.

21. Letter to Wife and Children, June 24, 1864, John Carvel Arnold Papers, LOC.

22. Letter to "Dear Friend," June 23, 1864, Civil War Document Collection, USAHEC. This is the only letter from "Howard" at the USAHEC, and there is no further information available as to his rank or unit.

23. Letter to Cousin, November 30, 1864, John O'Brien Correspondence, Civil War Document Collection, USAHEC.

24. Such regular access to pen and paper may have stemmed from the pay of enlisted men in the Union army, which had reached sixteen dollars per month by 1864. See Bell Irvin Wiley, *The Life of Billy Yank: The Common Soldier of the Union* (Baton Rouge: Louisiana State University Press, 1952), 48–49. While Union soldiers did not get excellent wages for the time period, they still received money that had greater buying power than that of their Confederate counterparts, who faced rising inflation as the war turned against the Southern states. For more on the Confederate pay situation, see Bell Irvin Wiley, *The Life of Johnny Reb: The Common Soldier of the Confederacy* (Baton Rouge: Louisiana State University Press, 1943), 136.

25. Letter to "Dearest Wife and Famlie," December 28, 1864, John Carvel Arnold Papers, LOC.

26. Kellett, *Combat Motivation,* 323.

27. Letter to "Dear Friends at Home," July 2, 1864, Austin J. Kendall Letters, Civil War Document Collection, USAHEC.

28. Letter to Sister, July 6, 1864, John B. Foote Correspondence, David M. Rubenstein Library, Duke University.

29. Letter to Uncle, August 25, 1864, Caleb H. Beal Papers, MHS.

30. Gerald Linderman, *Embattled Courage: The Experience of Combat in the American Civil War* (New York: Free Press, 1987), 153.

31. Letter to Parents, September 18, 1864, A. H. Sanger, Jr. Papers, Gregory A. Coco Collection, Harrisburg Civil War Round Table Collection, USAHEC.

32. Letter to Sister, July 6, 1864, John B. Foote Correspondence, David M. Rubenstein Library, Duke University.

33. Robert Ekin McBride, *In the Ranks: From the Wilderness to Appomattox Court-House. The War, As Seen and Experienced by a Private Soldier in the Army of the Potomac* (Cincinnati: Walden & Stowe, 1881), 143.

34. Letter, July 1, 1864, in *Letters to Eliza from a Union Soldier, 1862–1865,* ed. Margery Greenleaf (Chicago: Follett, 1963), 112.

35. Letter to "My Dear and Loving Wife," August 27, 1864, Charles H. Smith Correspondence, Civil War Document Collection, USAHEC.

36. Letter to Mother, October 8, 1864, John Owen, Jr. Papers, MHS.

37. Diary entry, August 29, 1864, Joseph J. Scroggs Diary, *Civil War Times Illustrated* Collection, USAHEC.

38. Letter to "Sister Ellen & Bro. Jim," December 16, 1864, George Hopper Papers, USAHEC.

39. Diary entry, March 3, 1865, in Rhodes, *All for the Union,* 209.

40. Letter, December 14, 1864, in Theodore Lyman, *With Grant and Meade from the Wilderness to Appomattox* (Lincoln: University of Nebraska Press, 1994), 302.

41. Diary entry, December 20, 1864, George A. Bowen Diary, Civil War Document Collection, USAHEC.

42. Letter to Parents, November 20, 1864, in *My Dear Parents: An Englishman's Letters Home from the American Civil War,* ed. A. S. Lewis (London: Gollancz, 1982), 108.

43. Letter to Brother, January 19, 1865, in *Recollections of the Civil War, with Many Original Diary Entries and Letters Written from the Seat of War, and with Annotated References,* ed. William S. Tyler (New York: G. P. Putnam's Sons, 1912), 319.

44. Letter to Mother, January 17, 1865, William Hamilton Papers, LOC.

45. McBride, *In the Ranks,* 132–33.

46. Letter to "Ellen," December 20, 1864, in *The Civil War Letters of General Robert McAllister,* ed. James I. Robertson, Jr. (New Brunswick, NJ: Rutgers University Press, 1965), 559.

47. Diary entry, September 15, 1864, Timothy Bateman Diary, Civil War Document Collection, USAHEC.

48. Letter to Mother, January 26, 1865, Edwin W. Bearse Letters, MHS.

49. Letter to Father, January 23, 1865, Henry J. Millard Letters, MHS.

50. Diary entry, January 8, 1865, Winthrop Henry Phelps Papers, LOC.

51. Letter to Parents, January 12, 1865, in Lewis, *My Dear Parents,* 115–16.

52. Letter to Sister, February 28, 1865, Henry Clay Heisler Papers, LOC.

53. Compiled Military Service Records of Lieutenant Colonel George Hopper, 10th New York Infantry and Captain James William Latta, 119th Pennsylvania Infantry, NARA.

54. McBride, *In the Ranks,* 110.

55. Diary entry, February 1, 1865, in *The Rebel Yell and the Yankee Hurrah: The Civil War Journal of a Maine Volunteer,* ed. Ruth L. Silliker (Camden, ME: Down East Books, 1985), 239.

56. Letter to Mother, February 7, 1865, in *Vermont General: The Unusual War Experiences of Edward Hastings Ripley, 1862–1865,* ed. Otto Eisenschiml (New York: Devin-Adair, 1960), 284.

57. Diary entry, December 11, 1864, in *The Cormany Diaries: A Northern Family in the Civil War,* ed. James C. Mohr and Richard E. Winslow III (Pittsburgh: University of Pittsburgh Press, 1982), 505.

58. Diary entry, July 9, 1864, in Donald Chipman, "An Essex County Soldier in the Civil War: The Diary of Cyrille Fountain," *New York History* 66 (July 1985): 299.

59. For more on Sheridan's Valley Campaign, see Jeffrey Wert, *From Winchester to Cedar Creek: The Shenandoah Campaign of 1864* (Mechanicsburg, PA: Stackpole Books, 1997).

60. Letter to Sister, September 14, 1864, Daniel Faust Papers, Harrisburg Civil War Round Table Collection, USAHEC.

61. Letter to Wife, July 9, 1864, Anson B. Shuey Letters, Civil War Document Collection, USAHEC. Compiled Military Service Record of Corporal Anson B. Shuey, Co. C, 93rd Pennsylvania Infantry, NARA.

62. Letter, December 15, 1864, in *Hard Marching Every Day: The Civil War Letters of Private Wilbur Fisk, 1861–1865,* ed. Emil Rosenblatt and Ruth Rosenblatt (Lawrence: University Press of Kansas, 1992), 287.

63. Diary entry, December 4, 1864, in Rhodes, *All for the Union,* 191.

64. Letter, December 15, 1864, in Rosenblatt and Rosenblatt, *Hard Marching Every Day,* 288.

65. The men of the Sixth Corps were not the only Federal forces to escape the trench lines during the siege. The expeditions against Fort Fisher in North Carolina in late 1864 and early 1865 were another example of forces being redeployed to other sectors. In this case, portions of three corps were sent southward before Fort Fisher finally fell in January 1865. See Rod Gragg, *Confederate Goliath: The Battle of Fort Fisher* (Baton Rouge: Louisiana State University Press, 2006). However, since most of the men on these expeditions never returned to Virginia before the end of the war, it is not possible to determine the before-and-after effect described with the Sixth Corps' experience in the Valley.

66. Letter to "Ellen," November 2, 1864, in Robertson, *The Civil War Letters of General Robert McAllister,* 533. At this point in the campaign, McAllister was in command of the 1st Brigade, 4th Division, 2nd Corps.

67. November Diary entries, George A. Bowen Diary, Civil War Document Collection, USAHEC.

68. Letter to "friends at home," November 19, 1864, Theodore W. Skinner Correspondence, Civil War Document Collection, USAHEC. When referring to "Chapins Farm," Skinner probably

meant the area near Chaffin's Bluff, in the Deep Bottom region of the Federal line. Despite the poor treatment on his journey northward, the satisfaction that Skinner displayed in this letter over Lincoln's reelection suggests that he offered his vote in support of Lincoln's electoral victory.

69. Corporal William Ray, 7th Wisconsin. Diary entry, September 6, 1864, in *Four Years with the Iron Brigade: The Civil War Journals of William R. Ray, Company F, Seventh Wisconsin Volunteers,* ed. Lance Herdegen and Sherry Murphy (Cambridge, MA: Da Capo Press, 2002), 317.

CHAPTER EIGHT

Note to epigraph: Letter to "Mary Lizzie," October 15, 1864, M. T. Haderman Papers, David M. Rubenstein Rare Book & Manuscript Library, Duke University, Durham, North Carolina.

1. Letter to Wife, September 2, 1864, Charles H. Smith Papers, Civil War Document Collection, United States Army Heritage and Education Center, Carlisle, Pennsylvania (USAHEC).

2. Letter to Wife, October 20, 1864, ibid.

3. Compiled Military Service Record of Private Charles H. Smith, Co. F, 8th Maine Infantry, National Archives and Records Administration, Washington, D.C. (NARA).

4. Historian Earl Hess has explored this issue of Civil War soldiers calculating their odds of survival. See Earl Hess, *The Union Soldier in Battle: Enduring the Ordeal of Combat* (Lawrence: University Press of Kansas, 1997), 150–51.

5. Horatio Soule, assistant surgeon for the 56th Massachusetts, diary entry, July 14, 1864, Horatio S. Soule Diary, Civil War Document Collection, USAHEC.

6. Letter to "Bro Chris," June 28, 1864, Theodore Vaill Papers, Northwest Corner Civil War Round Table Collection, USAHEC.

7. Letter to Mother, September 25, 1864, Edwin W. Bearse Letters, Massachusetts Historical Society, Boston, Massachusetts (MHS).

8. Letter to Wife, June 26, 1864, Joseph Barlow Papers, USAHEC.

9. For a detailed treatment of the Atlanta campaign, see Albert Castel, *Decision in the West: The Atlanta Campaign of 1864* (Lawrence: University Press of Kansas, 1992).

10. For more on the Confederate invasion of Maryland, see Frank Vandiver, *Jubal's Raid* (New York: McGraw-Hill, 1960).

11. Diary entry, July 13, 1864, Joseph J. Scroggs Diary, *Civil War Times Illustrated* Collection, USAHEC.

12. Letter to Brother, July 20, 1864, John Rumsey Brincklé Papers, Library of Congress, Washington, D.C. (LOC). Emphasis in original.

13. Letter to Mother, July 15, 1864, Francis C. Barlow Letters, MHS. For more on how far General Barlow's morale sank during the summer following the Overland campaign, see Joan Waugh, "Francis Channing Barlow's Civil War," *Cold Harbor to the Crater: The End of the Overland Campaign,* ed. Gary W. Gallagher and Caroline Janney (Chapel Hill: University of North Carolina Press, 2015), 138–75.

14. Letter to Wife, July 14, 1864, Joseph Barlow Papers, USAHEC.

15. Letter to "Gren," July 15, 1864, Frederic Winthrop Papers, MHS.

16. For more on the Mobile campaign, see Paul Calore, *Naval Campaigns of the Civil War* (Jefferson, NC: McFarland, 2002).

17. Letter to Mother and Sister, August 13, 1864, Francis H. Woods Correspondence, David M. Rubenstein Library, Duke University.

18. Letter to Wife, August 30, 1864, Joseph Barlow Papers, USAHEC.

19. Diary entry, August 8, 1864, Joseph J. Scroggs Diary, *Civil War Times Illustrated* Collection, USAHEC.

20. Diary entry, September 6, 1864, in *The Cormany Diaries: A Northern Family in the Civil War,* ed. James Mohr (Pittsburgh: University of Pittsburgh Press, 1982), 475.

21. Letter, September 8, 1864, Thomas G. Bennett Correspondence, Civil War Document Collection, USAHEC; Letter to Mother, September 10, 1864, Austin J. Kendall Letters, Civil War Document Collection, USAHEC.

22. Diary entry, September 2, 1864, Joseph J. Scroggs Diary, *Civil War Times Illustrated* Collection, USAHEC.

23. Letter to Mother, September 12, 1864, John B. Foote Correspondence, David M. Rubenstein Library, Duke University.

24. Letter to Brother and Sister, September 5, 1864, George Hopper Papers, USAHEC.

25. For more on Sheridan's efforts in the Valley, see Jeffrey Wert, *From Winchester to Cedar Creek: The Shenandoah Campaign of 1864* (Mechanicsburg, PA: Stackpole Books, 1997).

26. Diary entry, October 20, 1864, Christian A. Fleetwood Papers, LOC, and Letter to "Mother and All," September 23, 1864, Austin J. Kendall Letters, Civil War Document Collection, USAHEC.

27. Diary entry, September 24, 1864, in *The Rebel Yell and the Yankee Hurrah: The Civil War Journal of a Maine Volunteer,* ed. Ruth Silliker (Camden, ME: Down East Books, 1985), 202.

28. Diary entry, September 23, 1864, William S. Tilton Diaries, MHS.

29. Letter to Wife, September 25, 1864, Charles H. Smith Correspondence, Civil War Document Collection, USAHEC.

30. Letter to "Ellen," September 24, 1864, in *The Civil War Letters of General Robert McAllister,* ed. James I. Robertson, Jr. (New Brunswick, NJ: Rutgers University Press, 1965), 509. Although he fluctuated between regimental and brigade command, at this point Colonel McAllister was in command of the First Brigade, Fourth Division, Second Corps.

31. *The War of the Rebellion: A Compilation of the Official Records of the Union and Confederate Armies,* Series 1, Volume 42, Part 2, 939. Ibid., 280.

32. Letter to "My Friend Hattie," September 16, 1864, Charles E. Field Letters, Hattie Burleigh Papers, USAHEC.

33. Letter to "Father and Friends at Home," September 15, 1864, in *"Dear Friends at Home": The Letters and Diary of Thomas Jane Owen, Fiftieth New York Volunteer Engineer Regiment during the Civil War,* ed. Dale Floyd (Washington, D.C.: Office of the Chief of Engineers, 1985), 58.

34. Letter to Mother, October 25, 1864, Alexander Adams Papers, Northwest Corner Civil War Round Table Collection, USAHEC.

35. Letter to "Friend Cranston," October 1, 1864, George Tate Papers, Rudolph Haerle Collection, USAHEC.

36. Diary entry, October 11, 1864, in *The Civil War Notebook of Daniel Chisholm: A Chronicle of Daily Life in the Union Army, 1864–1865,* ed. W. Springer Menge and J. August Shimrak (New York: Ballantine Books, 1989), 43. Despite his support for the incumbent, Sergeant Clear noted that the men in his unit split in their voting, with Lincoln only winning the regiment by three votes. Ibid.

37. Letter to Brother, September 6, 1864, in *Letters from a Sharpshooter: The Civil War Letters of Private William B. Greene, Co. G, 2nd United States Sharpshooters (Berdan's), Army of the Potomac, 1861–1865,* ed. William H. Hastings (Belleville, WI: Historic Publications, 1993), 252–53.

38. Letter to "Hattie," October 10, 1864, Charles E. Field Letters, Hattie Burleigh Papers, USAHEC.

39. Letter to Wife, July 23, 1864, Joseph Barlow Papers, USAHEC.

40. Diary entry, October 11, 1864, in *Civil War Notebook,* 43.

41. Letter to Mother, October 12, 1864, in "The Civil War of a Pennsylvania Trooper," ed. Daniel Woodward, *Pennsylvania Magazine of History and Biography* 87 (January 1963): 57.

42. Letter to Brother and Sister, September 5, 1864, George Hopper Papers, USAHEC.

43. Letter to Father, October 16, 1864, Andrew Robeson Letters, MHS.

44. Letter to Brother and Sister, October 23, 1864, James Beard Correspondence, Civil War Document Collection, USAHEC.

45. Letters to Mother, October 29 and November 12, 1864, Alexander Adams Papers, Northwest Corner Civil War Round Table Collection, USAHEC.

46. Out of approximately 150,000 votes cast by Union soldiers in the 1864 presidential election, 116,887 went to Lincoln, with the remainder going to McClellan. Barbara Long and E. B. Long, *The Civil War Day by Day: An Almanac, 1861–1865* (Garden City, NY: Doubleday, 1971), 594. Given that there were more than four million votes cast and that Lincoln won both the popular and electoral vote by significant margins, it is clear that the soldier vote did not win the election for Lincoln. However, it demonstrated the tremendous amount of enthusiasm and support for the incumbent within the ranks of the army despite the reverses and bloodshed of the summer. For more on the breakdown of the soldier vote and its significance, see Josiah H. Benton, *Voting in the Field: A Forgotten Chapter of the Civil War* (Boston: Plimpton Press, 1915).

47. Letter to Mother, October 14, 1864, Bayard Taylor Cooper Letters, Civil War Document Collection, USAHEC.

48. Diary entry, November 8, 1864, Charles H. Edgerly Diary, Northwest Corner Civil War Round Table Collection, USAHEC.

49. Letter to "Sister Mary," October 20, 1864, John B. Foote Correspondence, David M. Rubenstein Library, Duke University. Emphasis in original.

50. Letter to "Friend Henry," October 18, 1864, in *This Regiment of Heroes: A Compilation of Primary Materials Pertaining to the 124th New York State Volunteers in the American Civil War,* ed. Charles J. LaRocca, 236. Manuscript at USAHEC.

51. Diary entries, November 5 & 8, 1864, Francis Asbury Wallar (Waller) Papers, Civil War Document Collection, USAHEC.

52. Letter to Mother, November 7, 1864, William Hamilton Papers, LOC.

53. Letter to "Father and Friends at Home," November 13, 1864, in Floyd, *"Dear Friends at Home,"* 62.

54. Letter to "Ellen," November 12, 1864, in *Civil War Letters of Robert McAllister,* 540.

55. Letter to Brother and Sister, November 12, 1864, George Hopper Papers, USAHEC.

56. For more on the campaigns in Tennessee at the end of 1864, see Wiley Sword, *The Confederacy's Last Hurrah: Spring Hill, Franklin, and Nashville* (Lawrence: University Press of Kansas, 1993).

57. For General Meade's order for the salute, see *Official Records,* Series 1, Volume 42, Part 3, 1024.

58. Diary entry, December 25, 1864, in *Four Years with the Iron Brigade: The Civil War Journals of William R. Ray, Company F, Seventh Wisconsin Infantry,* ed. Lance Herdegen and Sherry Murphy (Cambridge, MA: Da Capo Press, 2002), 346.

59. Letter, December 22, 1864, in *Hard Marching Every Day: The Civil War Letters of Private Wilbur Fisk, 1861–1865,* ed. Emil Rosenblatt and Ruth Rosenblatt (Lawrence: University Press of Kansas, 1992), 295.

60. Sherman's movements following the fall of Atlanta have received a great deal of attention from historians. For a general account of Sherman's march, see Noah Andre Trudeau, *Southern Storm: Sherman's March to the Sea* (New York: Harper Perennial, 2008). For an excellent work that places Sherman's campaign in the context of similar actions during the war, see Charles Royster, *The Destructive War: William Tecumseh Sherman, Stonewall Jackson, and the Americans* (New York: Alfred A. Knopf, 1991).

61. Letter to "Friend Cranston," December 3, 1864, George Tate Papers, Rudolph Haerle Collection, USAHEC.

62. Letter to Mother, December 3, 1864, Alexander Adams Papers, Northwest Corner Civil War Round Table Collection, USAHEC.

63. Letter to "Brother Charles," December 6, 1864, Theodore Vaill Papers, ibid.

64. Letter to Sister, December 27, 1864, in *All's for the Best: The Civil War Reminiscences and Letters of Daniel W. Sawtelle, Eighth Maine Volunteer Infantry,* ed. Peter Buckingham (Knoxville: University of Tennessee Press, 2001), 319. As with previous Union victories, a one hundred gun salute was fired into the Confederate lines following the fall of Savannah to signal success to both the Army of the Potomac and their Southern opponents. *Official Records,* Series 1, Volume 42, Part 3, 1073.

65. Letter to Wife, December 26, 1864, Samuel Brooks Correspondence, Civil War Document Collection, USAHEC.

66. Letter to "Abby," December 24, 1864, John M. Steward Correspondence, Civil War Document Collection, USAHEC.

67. Letter to Brother and Sister, January 23, 1865, George Hopper Papers, USAHEC.

68. Letter to Father, January 23, 1865, Henry J. Millard Letters, MHS.

69. Diary entry, February 25, 1865, James William Latta Papers, LOC.

70. Letter to "Aunt Lydia," February 24, 1865, Julius Frederic Ramsdell Papers, Southern Historical Collection, University of North Carolina–Chapel Hill.

71. Letter to Mother, March 20, 1865, William Hamilton Papers, LOC.

72. Diary entry, February 21, 1865, Alexander Grant Rose Diary, Civil War Document Collec-
tion, USAHEC. Letter to Parents, February 23, 1865, in *My Dear Parents: An Englishman's Letters Home from the American Civil War,* ed. A. S. Lewis (London: Gollancz, 1982), 124.

73. Letter to Father, February 24, 1865, Jacob Seibert Letters, Seibert Family Papers, USAHEC.

74. Letter to Father and Mother, February 4, 1865, J. Chapin Warner Papers, MHS.

75. Letter to Father and Mother, February 22, 1865, ibid.

76. Letter to Father and Mother, March 17, 1865, ibid.

77. Letter to Father, September 26, 1864, in *Vermont General: The Unusual War Experiences of Edward Hastings Ripley, 1862–1865,* ed. Otto Eisenschiml (New York: Devin-Adair, 1960), 242. At this point, Colonel Ripley was in command of the 1st Brigade, 2nd Division, 18th Corps.

CHAPTER NINE

Note to epigraph: Letter to "Sis. Sarah," September 11, 1864, Charles Stinson Papers, Lewis Leigh Collection, United States Army Heritage and Education Center, Carlisle, Pennsylvania (USAHEC).

1. Letter to Brother, June 25, 1864, in *From Antietam to Fort Fisher: The Civil War Letters of Edward King Wightman, 1862–1865,* ed. Edward Longacre (Rutherford, NJ: Fairleigh Dickinson University Press, 1985), 196.

2. Letter to Brother, June 29, 1864, ibid., 198.

3. For an excellent treatment of this operation, see Richard Sommers, *Richmond Redeemed: The Siege of Petersburg* (Garden City, NY: Doubleday, 1981).

4. Noah Andre Trudeau, *The Last Citadel: Petersburg, Virginia, June 1864–April 1865* (Baton Rouge: Louisiana State University Press, 1991), 262–85.

5. Ibid., 300–25.

6. Letter to Father, September 17, 1864, in *Vermont General: The Unusual War Experiences of Edward Hastings Ripley, 1862–1865,* ed. Otto Eisenschiml (New York: Devin-Adair, 1960), 238.

7. Letter to Sister, September 19, 1864, in *Letters of a Civil War Surgeon,* ed. Paul Fatout (West Lafayette, IN: Purdue University Press, 1996), 131.

8. Diary entry, July 1, 1864, in *Four Years with the Iron Brigade: The Civil War Journals of William R. Ray, Company F, Seventh Wisconsin Infantry,* ed. Lance Herdegen and Sherry Murphy (Cambridge, MA: Da Capo Press, 2002), 286.

9. Letter, September 15, 1864, Thomas G. Bennett Correspondence, Civil War Document Collection, USAHEC.

10. *The Road to Richmond: The Civil War Memoirs of Major Abner R. Small of the 16th Maine Vols.; with his Diary as a Prisoner of War,* ed. Harold Adams Small (Berkeley: University of California Press, 1957), 153.

11. *Three Years with Company K: Sergt. Austin C. Stearns, Company K, 13th Mass. Infantry (Deceased),* ed. Arthur A. Kent (Rutherford, NJ: Fairleigh Dickinson University Press, 1976), 297.

Although appearing like a journal, Stearns's work is actually a memoir with dated entries. The date for these comments is identified as July 8, 1864.

12. Tony Ashworth, *Trench Warfare, 1914–1918: The Live and Let Live System* (New York: Holmes & Meier, 1980), 24–47.

13. Diary entry, August 28, 1864, Jacob Lyons Diary, Southern Historical Collection, University of North Carolina–Chapel Hill.

14. Small, *The Road to Richmond,* 153.

15. It appears that some soldiers took steps to prevent their enemy from receiving too much information from this type of exchange. As Small notes, when newspapers were traded, "the Johnnies were careful to cut out some of their news, and the Yanks, equally cautious, clipped the papers which they gave into Southern hands." Ibid.

16. Letter to Brother, August, 17, 1864, James Beard Correspondence, Civil War Document Collection, USAHEC.

17. Unknown Soldier, Letter dated 1864, in *Soldiers' Letters: From Camp, Battle-field, and Prison,* ed. Lydia Minturn Post (New York: Bunce & Huntington, 1865), 452. Manuscript housed at Massachusetts Historical Society, Boston, Massachusetts (MHS).

18. Diary entry, August 27, 1864, in *The Rebel Yell and the Yankee Hurrah: The Civil War Journal of a Maine Volunteer,* ed. Ruth L. Silliker (Camden, ME: Down East Books, 1985), 194.

19. Letter to Father, March 22, 1865, James H. Nugent Letters, Civil War Document Collection, USAHEC.

20. See Ashworth, *Trench Warfare.*

21. Diary entry, December 6, 1864, in Henry Morrow, "The Last of the Iron Brigade," *Civil War Times Illustrated* 14 (February 1976): 13–14. Emphasis in original.

22. Diary entry, October 16, 1864, in Silliker, *Rebel Yell and the Yankee Hurrah,* 210. The next day, when another Union soldier was shot while trading with Confederate pickets, Haley proclaimed that "shooting the man was deliberate *murder*" (210). Emphasis in original. Once again, this closely parallels Tony Ashworth's portrayal of truces, their violations, and "escalated aggression" in the First World War. Ashworth, *Trench Warfare,* 147–52.

23. Diary entry, June 26, 1864, in *Letters from a Sharpshooter: The Civil War Letters of Private William B. Greene, Co. G, 2nd United States Sharpshooters (Berdan's), Army of the Potomac, 1861–1865,* ed. William H. Hastings (Belleville, WI: Historic Publications, 1993), 228.

24. Letter to "Brother Marl," September 1, 1864, ibid., 250.

25. General Court Martial in the field, HQ of 3rd Division, 2nd Corps, July 7, 1864. Case NN-2282, Record Group 153: Records of the Office of the Judge Advocate General, National Archives and Records Administration, Washington, D.C. (NARA).

26. General Court Martial, HQ of 1st Division, 18th Corps, July 7, 1864. Case LL-2233, NARA.

27. Diary entry, July 8, 1864, Julius Frederic Ramsdell Papers, Southern Historical Collection, University of North Carolina–Chapel Hill.

28. Diary entry, July 6, 1864, ibid.

29. Letter to "Friend Daelhouser," July 5, 1864, Fred Ployer Papers, Harrisburg Civil War Round Table Collection, USAHEC.

30. Diary entry, August 30, 1864, in Silliker, *Rebel Yell and the Yankee Hurrah*, 195.

31. For more on the Christmas truce of 1914, see Stanley Weintraub, *Silent Night: The Story of the World War I Christmas Truce* (New York: Free Press, 2001). Lord Moran, who was an eyewitness to the truce, described the event as "unreal" when British and German soldiers met between the lines on the most civil of terms. His commentary on the subject bears some similarity to the behavior of the Civil War soldiers described above. Looking back on it, Moran commented that "the men of course were like children; they dearly loved a new game; they were glad to get out of the water for a little and to stretch their stiff limbs." Lord Charles Moran, *The Anatomy of Courage* (London: Constable, 1945), 54–56. See also Ashworth, *Trench Warfare*, 24–28.

32. J. Tracey Power, *Lee's Miserables: Life in the Army of Northern Virginia from the Wilderness to Appomattox* (Chapel Hill: University of North Carolina Press, 1998), 223–25. For a thorough study of Confederate desertion during the war, see Mark A. Weitz, *More Damning than Slaughter: Desertion in the Confederate Army* (Lincoln: University of Nebraska Press, 2005).

33. Power, *Lee's Miserables*, 212; Earl Hess, "Tactics, Trenches, and Men in the Civil War," in *On the Road to Total War: The American Civil War and the German Wars of Unification, 1861–1871*, ed. Stig Forster and Jorg Nagler (Cambridge: Cambridge University Press, 1997), 492.

34. Power, *Lee's Miserables*, 307. Power argued that while the Confederates did a reasonable job of using conscription to maintain the size of the Army of Northern Virginia during the siege, the quality was greatly diminished as the veteran core deserted to their homes or the Union lines.

35. Letter to "Del," September 10, 1864, Steve R. Clark Correspondence, Jay Luvaas Collection, USAHEC.

36. Letter to Brother and Sister, October 23, 1864, James Beard Correspondence, Civil War Document Collection, USAHEC.

37. Diary entry, November 8, 1864, in Herdegen and Murphy, *Four Years with the Iron Brigade*, 336.

38. Letter to "Parents Mother & Sisters," November 1, 1864, Bayard Taylor Cooper Letters, Civil War Document Collection, USAHEC.

39. Letter to "Wife and Famlie," December 28, 1864, John Carvel Arnold Papers, Library of Congress, Washington, D.C. (LOC).

40. Diary entry, February 24, 1864, Calvin Berry Diary, Civil War Document Collection, USAHEC.

41. Letter to Father, March 11, 1865, John Preston Campbell Correspondence, Civil War Document Collection, USAHEC.

42. Letter to Sister, February 20, 1865, Henry Metzger Papers, Harrisburg Civil War Round Table Collection, USAHEC.

43. Letter to Father, March 22, 1865, James H. Nugent Letters, Civil War Document Collection, USAHEC.

44. Letter to Brother, February 20, 1865, John Rumsey Brincklé Papers, LOC.

45. Letter to Wife, March 4, 1865, in Theodore Lyman, *With Grant and Meade from the Wilderness to Appomattox* (Lincoln: University of Nebraska Press, 1994), 309–10. Horace Porter, a member of General Grant's staff, confirms Lyman's comment regarding compensation for enemy

rifles, noting in his memoirs that Confederates were given "a fair price" for their weapons. Horace Porter, *Campaigning with Grant* (New York: Konecky & Konecky, 1992), 405.

46. Henry Keiser Diary, Gregory A. Coco Collection, Harrisburg Civil War Round Table Collection, USAHEC.

47. Diary entry, January 18, 1865, in "The Civil War Diary of Colonel Robert Rogall," ed. Frank Levstik, *Polish-American Studies* 27 (Spring/Autumn 1970): 69.

48. Letter to "My Dear and affecate Wife and Little Daughter," March 13, 1865, Joseph H. Young Papers, Southern Historical Collection, University of North Carolina–Chapel Hill.

49. Letter to Father, January 20, 1865, in *The Civil War Notebook of Daniel Chisholm: A Chronicle of Daily Life in the Union Army, 1864–1865*, ed. W. Springer Menge and J. August Shimrak (New York: Ballantine Books, 1989), 145.

50. Letter to Wife and Daughter, March 18, 1865, Joseph H. Young Papers, Southern Historical Collection, University of North Carolina–Chapel Hill.

51. Diary entry, February 19, 1864, James William Latta Papers, LOC.

52. Letter from Phineas Cooper to "Respected Brother," October 21, 1864, Bayard Taylor Cooper Letters, Civil War Document Collection, USAHEC. Phineas was Bayard Cooper's uncle.

53. Diary entry, August 4, 1864, William S. Tilton Diaries, MHS.

54. Letter to "My Dear Ellen & Family," October 8, 1864, in *The Civil War Letters of General Robert McAllister,* ed. James I. Robertson, Jr. (New Brunswick, NJ: Rutgers University Press, 1965), 517.

55. Letter to "Sister Cull," February 4, 1865, in *All's for the Best: The Civil War Reminiscences and Letters of Daniel W. Sawtelle, Eighth Maine Volunteer Infantry,* ed. Peter H. Buckingham (Knoxville: University of Tennessee Press, 2001), 326.

56. Letter, 1864, in *Soldiers' Letters: From Camp, Battle-field, and Prison,* ed. Lydia Minturn Post (New York: Bunce & Huntington, 1865), 462–63. Manuscript housed at MHS.

57. Letter to Mother, February 15, 1865, in *Recollections of the Civil War, with Many Original Diary Entries and Letters Written from the Seat of War, and with Annotated References,* ed. William S. Tyler (New York: G. P. Putnam's Sons, 1912), 332.

58. Diary entry, January 13, 1865, in Herdegen and Murphy, *Four Years with the Iron Brigade,* 353.

59. Letter to Wife, January 18, 1865, Samuel Brooks Correspondence, Civil War Document Collection, USAHEC.

60. Letter to Parents, February 23, 1865, in *My Dear Parents: An Englishman's Letters Home from the American Civil War,* ed. A. S. Lewis (London: Gollancz, 1982), 124.

61. Diary entry, February 21, 1865, in *All for the Union: The Civil War Diary and Letters of Elisha Hunt Rhodes,* ed. Robert Hunt Rhodes (New York: Vintage Books, 1985), 206.

62. Compiled Military Service Record of Jacob M. Seibert, Co. F, 93rd Pennsylvania Infantry, NARA. During his convalescence in the hospital following Winchester, Seibert contracted syphilis, which would combine with the lingering effects of his gunshot wound to force him to resign on February 28, 1865.

63. Letter to Father, February 24, 1865, in Jacob Seibert Letters, Seibert Family Papers, USAHEC.

64. Letter to Father, February 27, 1865, Alpheus Packard Papers, Civil War Document Collection, USAHEC.

65. Letter to "Bro," November 28, 1864, in Longacre, *From Antietam to Fort Fisher,* 215.

66. Letter to "Ellen," November 28, 1864, in Robertson, *Civil War Letters of General Robert McAllister,* 549.

67. Diary entries for December 16, December 23, and December 24, 1864, Alexander Grant Rose Diary, Civil War Document Collection, USAHEC. Ella Lonn also identified a spike in Union executions over the winter of 1864–1865. She claimed that during that time "executions were taking place almost daily in the Army of the Potomac." Ella Lonn, *Desertion during the Civil War* (New York: Century Company, 1928), 146.

68. Diary entry, January 6, 1865, George A. Bowen Diary, Civil War Document Collection, USAHEC.

69. Robert Ekin McBride, *In the Ranks: From the Wilderness to Appomattox Court-House. The War, As Seen and Experienced by a Private Soldier in the Army of the Potomac* (Cincinnati: Walden & Stowe, 1881), 133–34.

70. Letter to Mother, January 1, 1865, in *A War of the People: Vermont Civil War Letters,* ed. Jeffrey D. Marshall (Hanover, NH: University Press of New England, 1999), 285.

71. Letter to Sister, December 17, 1864, ibid., 280. Safford's comment seems to validate some of the ideas set forth by author Eric Dean in his study on the effects of combat on Civil War soldiers. Dean noted that the public execution of deserters during the Civil War, a factor not present in the American armies of the twentieth century, added to the stress placed upon combat soldiers and contributed to the postwar problems they experienced. Eric Dean, Jr., *Shook over Hell: Post-Traumatic Stress, Vietnam, and the Civil War* (Cambridge, MA: Harvard University Press, 1997), 68–69.

72. Letter to Parents, February 25, 1865, Henry J. Millard Letters, MHS.

73. Letter to Father, March 1865, Alpheus Packard Papers, Civil War Document Collection, USAHEC. Ella Lonn concurs, claiming that after the army's winter executions, "a diminution of the evil was perceptible on that part of the fighting front." Lonn, *Desertion during the Civil War,* 146.

74. Letter to Brother, October 12, 1864, in Eisenschiml, *Vermont General,* 257.

75. Letter to "Ellen," January 19, 1865, in Robertson, *Civil War Letters of General Robert McAllister,* 568.

76. Letter to "Ellen," March 22, 1865, ibid., 595.

77. Letter to "Abby," March 10, 1865, John M. Steward Correspondence, Civil War Document Collection, USAHEC.

78. Letter to "Abby," June 27, 1864, ibid. Compiled Military Service Record of Private John Steward, Co. A, 1st Maine Heavy Artillery, NARA.

79. Letter to "Abby," March 10, 1865, John M. Steward Correspondence, Civil War Document Collection, USAHEC.

80. J. Tracey Power argued that the Army of Northern Virginia numbered approximately 40,000 men after the casualties of the Overland campaign, and was still between 35,000 and 40,000 men when it evacuated Petersburg in early April 1865. Power, *Lee's Miserables,* 79, 275. The figures presented by Noah Trudeau were more generous, showing Lee's army at 35,000

men at the end of August 1864, but rising to more than 58,000 by the following April. Trudeau, *The Last Citadel,* 418. Both authors agree, however, that despite widespread Confederate desertion, the Army of Northern Virginia managed to keep up its numbers during the siege thanks to the expansion and enforcement of conscription in the Confederacy.

81. Lieutenant Colonel George Hopper, Letter to "Sister Ellen & Bro. John," December 16, 1864, George Hopper Papers, USAHEC. This was also the conclusion reached by those in command. Theodore Lyman, a member of General Meade's staff, praised the Petersburg strategy of Grant and Meade by asking rhetorically in a letter, "suppose there had been no army capable of clinging thus for months in a death-grapple and still clinging and meaning to cling; what would have become of Sherman and his great work?" Lyman, *With Grant and Meade,* 271.

82. Corporal Daniel Chisholm, 116th Pennsylvania. Letter to Father, February 24, 1865, in Menge and Shimrak, *Civil War Notebook,* 148.

CONCLUSION

Note to epigraph: Letter, March 30, 1865, in Thomas Jane Owen, *"Dear Friends at Home": The Letters and Diary of Thomas Jane Owen, Fiftieth New York Volunteer Engineer Regiment during the Civil War,* ed. Dale Floyd (Washington, D.C.: Officer of the Chief of Engineers, 1985), 80.

1. The Irish Brigade was made up of several regiments from northeastern states (primarily New York) and was part of the 1st Division, 2nd Corps.

2. Diary entry, March 17, 1865, Alexander Grant Rose Diary, Civil War Document Collection, United States Army Heritage and Education Center, Carlisle, Pennsylvania (USAHEC).

3. Meade's staff officer Colonel Theodore Lyman noted that the day before the St. Patrick's Day gala was held, a supply boat carrying the "fine collation" for the event had run aground and did not arrive until the day after. Despite the soldier claims that follow, Lyman's synopsis of the day was that "everything was extremely quiet and orderly, and no tipsy people about." Letter, March 18, 1865, in Theodore Lyman, *With Grant and Meade from the Wilderness to Appomattox* (Lincoln: University of Nebraska Press, 1994), 321–22.

4. Diary entry, March 17, 1865, in *The Civil War Notebook of Daniel Chisholm: A Chronicle of Daily Life in the Union Army, 1864–1865,* ed. W. Springer Menge and J. August Shimrak (New York: Ballantine Books, 1989), 69.

5. Diary entry, March 17, 1865, in *All for the Union: The Civil War Diary and Letters of Elisha Hunt Rhodes,* ed. Robert Hunt Rhodes (New York: Vintage Books, 1985), 212. Rhodes suggested in this entry that some men had been killed due to the events of the day.

6. Diary entry, February 26, 1865, Winthrop Henry Phelps Papers, Library of Congress, Washington, D.C. (LOC).

7. Letter to Sister, March 14, 1865, in *All's for the Best: The Civil War Reminiscences and Letters of Daniel W. Sawtelle, Eighth Maine Volunteer Infantry,* ed. Peter Buckingham (Knoxville: University of Tennessee Press, 2001), 331.

8. Diary entry, February 25, 1865, Jacob Lyons Diary, Southern Historical Collection, University of North Carolina–Chapel Hill.

9. Letter to Mother, March 11, 1865, William Hamilton Papers, LOC.

10. Diary entry, January 1, 1865, in *The Rebel Yell and the Yankee Hurrah: The Civil War Journal of a Maine Volunteer*, ed. Ruth Silliker (Camden, ME: Down East Books, 1985), 233.

11. Letter to Father, February 25, 1865, in *Letters of a Civil War Surgeon*, ed. Paul Fatout (West Lafayette, IN: Purdue University Press, 1996), 142.

12. Letter to Father, February 27, 1865, Alpheus Packard Papers, Civil War Document Collection, USAHEC.

13. Diary entry, March 19, 1865, George A. Bowen Diary, ibid.

14. Letter, March 24, 1865, in *Hard Marching Every Day: The Civil War Letters of Private Wilbur Fisk, 1861–1865*, ed. Emil Rosenblatt and Ruth Rosenblatt (Lawrence: University Press of Kansas, 1992), 318–19. Emphasis in original.

15. Letter to Wife and Daughter, March 16, 1865, Joseph H. Young Papers, Southern Historical Collection, University of North Carolina–Chapel Hill.

16. Letter to Mother, March 19, 1865, in "The Civil War of a Pennsylvania Trooper," ed. Daniel Woodward, *Pennsylvania Magazine of History and Biography* 87 (1963): 60. Sergeant Griner's comments in this letter also reveal a very positive assessment of the Army of the Potomac on the eve of the spring campaign. Commenting on the state of his comrades, Griner wrote, "the army has improved greatly this winter, notwithstanding their several severe marches, and I do not think was ever in better condition." Ibid. Unfortunately, as willing as Griner was to take to the field once more, he would pay the ultimate price for such enthusiasm. He was killed in the fighting around Petersburg on March 31, only days before the end of the siege and the defeat of the Army of Northern Virginia. Compiled Military Service Record for Joseph A. Griner, Co. D, 8th Pennsylvania Cavalry, National Archives and Records Administration, Washington, D.C. (NARA).

17. Diary entry, March 15, 1865, in Menge and Shimrak, *Civil War Notebook*, 68.

18. Diary entry, March 28, 1865, ibid., 71.

19. Noah Andre Trudeau, *The Last Citadel: Petersburg, Virginia, June 1864–April 1865* (Baton Rouge: Louisiana State University Press, 1991), 329–54.

20. Noah Andre Trudeau, *Out of the Storm: The End of the Civil War, April–June 1865* (Boston: Little, Brown, 1994), 14–48.

21. For the most thorough treatment of the fall of Petersburg, see A. Wilson Greene, *The Final Battles of the Petersburg Campaign: Breaking the Backbone of the Rebellion*, 2nd edition (Knoxville: University of Tennessee Press, 2008).

22. Letter, April 3, 1865, in Lyman, *With Grant and Meade*, 341.

23. Lord Charles Moran, *The Anatomy of Courage* (London: Constable, 1945), ix.

24. David Lowe, "Field Fortifications in the Civil War," *North and South* 4 (August 2001): 58.

25. First Lieutenant Theodore Vaill, 2nd Connecticut Heavy Artillery. Letter to "Brother Charles," December 6, 1864, Theodore Vaill Papers, Northwest Corner Civil War Round Table Collection, USAHEC. Emphasis in original.

26. For the most noteworthy study on the ability of twentieth-century soldiers to sustain themselves in combat, see Roy Swank and Walter Marchand, "Combat Neuroses: Development of Combat Exhaustion," *Archives of Neurology and Psychology* 55 (1946): 236–47.

27. Marvin R. Cain, "A 'Face of Battle' Needed: An Assessment of Motives and Men in Civil War Historiography," *Civil War History* 28 (1982): 27.

28. Bell Irvin Wiley, *The Life of Johnny Reb: The Common Soldier of the Confederacy* (Baton Rouge: Louisiana State University Press, 1943), 80.

Bibliography

MANUSCRIPT SOURCES

Library of Congress, Washington, D.C.

John Carvel Arnold Papers, 1856–1937
John Rumsey Brincklé Papers, 1859–1936
William Coffee Correspondence, 1864
David Coon Papers, 1864
Christian A. Fleetwood Papers, 1797–1945
Thomas Francis Galwey Papers, 1861–1908
E. N. Gilpin Papers, 1861–1911
William Hamilton Papers, 1838–1896
Henry Clay Heisler Papers, 1861–1865
William G. Hills Diary, 1864
Allen Landis and Aaron J. Landis Correspondence, 1862–1864
James William Latta Papers, 1854–1913
Winthrop Henry Phelps Papers, 1864–1865
Solomon D. Rose Correspondence, 1865
Howard Malcolm Smith Papers, 1862–1914

Massachusetts Historical Society, Boston, MA

Francis C. Barlow Letters, 1861–1865
George M. Barnard Papers, 1848–1891
John E. Bassett Diary, 1861–1883
Caleb H. Beal Papers, 1861–1865
Edwin W. Bearse Letters, 1862–1865

Charles Edward Bolton Diary, 1864

Andrew B. Cross, *The War and the Christian Commission*, 1865

Warren Goodale Papers, 1847–1892

Nathan Hayward Letters, 1861–1864

Andrew R. Linscott Papers, 1819–1926

Henry J. Millard Letters, 1865

Frank C. Morse Papers, 1825–1941

John Owen, Jr. Papers, 1863–1865

Lydia Minturn Post, ed., *Soldiers' Letters: From Camp, Battle-field, and Prison*, New York: Bunce & Huntington, 1865

    James Ayres

    J. T. Conolly

    John H. Cook

    Charles De Mott

    Ward Frothingham

    John R. Pillings

    Charlie White

George L. Prescott Papers, 1861–1904

Andrew Robeson Letters, 1864–1865

Charles J. Stille, *History of the United States Sanitary Commission: Being the General of Its Work during the War of the Rebellion*, Philadelphia: J. B. Lippincott, 1866*

William S. Tilton Diaries, 1862–1864

United States Sanitary Commission, *The Soldier's Friend*, Philadelphia: Perkinpine & Higgins, 1865

J. Chapin Warner Papers, 1861–1905

Frederic Winthrop Papers, 1861–1867

National Archives and Record Administration, Washington, D.C.

Record Group 94: Records of the Adjutant General's Office, 1780s–1917

Compiled Military Service Records

    George Bowen

    Charles Chipman

    John Cook

    David Coon

    Wilbur Fisk

    Joseph Griner

    John Hackhiser

George Hopper
Henry Keiser
George Lacey
James Latta
John Pillings
Frederick Ployer
Curtis Pollock
Julius Ramsdell
Albert Rogall
Jacob Seibert
Charles H. Smith
John Steward

Record Group 153: Records of the Office of the Judge Advocate General

Case #LL-2203
Case #LL-2233
Case #LL-2343
Case #LL-2484
Case #LL-2520
Case #LL-3105
Case #NN-2010
Case #NN-2015
Case #NN-2095
Case #NN-2282
Case #NN-2359
Case #NN-2369
Case #NN-2559
Case #NN-3094
Case #NN-3143
Case #NN-3165
Case #NN-3552

David M. Rubenstein Rare Book & Manuscript Library, Duke University, Durham, NC

John B. Foote Correspondence, 1862–1865
M. T. Haderman Papers, 1864–1865
Francis H. Woods Correspondence, 1863–1865

Southern Historical Collection, University of North Carolina–Chapel Hill, NC

Jacob Lyons Diary, 1862–1865
Julius Frederic Ramsdell Papers, 1864–1869, 1910–1911
Joseph H. Young Papers, 1864–1865

United States Army Heritage and Education Center, Carlisle, Pennsylvania

Joseph Barlow Papers, 1861–1865

Hattie Burleigh Papers, 1862–1865
Martin Connally Letter
Charles E. Field Letters

Civil War Document Collection, 1839–2003

Timothy Bateman Diary
James Beard Correspondence
Clarence H. Bell Correspondence
Thomas G. Bennett Correspondence
Calvin Berry Diary
George A. Bowen Diary
Samuel Brooks Correspondence
John Preston Campbell Correspondence
Henry C. Carr Diary
George C. Chandler Letters
Bayard Taylor Cooper Letters
James F. Goodwin Correspondence
Letter from "Howard"
Henry Jacobs Letter
Austin J. Kendall Letters
Harrison Montague Correspondence
James H. Nugent Letters
William Penn Oberlin Letters
John O'Brien Correspondence
Alpheus Packard Papers
Curtis C. Pollock Correspondence
Alexander Grant Rose Diary
Anson B. Shuey Letters
Theodore W. Skinner Correspondence
Charles H. Smith Correspondence
Horatio S. Soule Diary

John M. Steward Correspondence

Francis Asbury Wallar (Waller) Papers

Charles E. Wood Diary

Civil War Times Illustrated Collection, 1861–1865

Joseph J. Scroggs Diary

Stuart A. Goldman Collection, 1772–1865

Charles C. Morey Diary

Rudolph Haerle Collection, 1860–1944

George Tate Papers

Harrisburg Civil War Round Table Collection, 1861–1865

Gregory A. Coco Collection

Henry Keiser Diary

Charles J. Mills Papers

A. H. Sanger, Jr. Papers

Daniel Faust Papers

Henry Metzger Papers

Maurus Oestreich Diary

Fred Ployer Papers

Earl M. Hess Collection, 1861–1909

John C. Hackhiser Letters

George Hopper Papers, 1860–1892

Charles J. LaRocca, ed., *This Regiment of Heroes: A Compilation of Primary Materials Pertaining to the 124th New York State Volunteers in the American Civil War,* 1991

Lewis Leigh Collection, 1861–1865

Charles Stinson Papers

Wendall W. Lang, Jr. Collection, 1861–1913

Charles Chipman Papers

Jay Luvaas Collection, 1861–1877

Steve R. Clark Correspondence

Northwest Corner Civil War Round Table Collection, 1861–1896

Alexander Adams Papers

Charles H. Edgerly Diary

Lewis Luckenbill Diary

Theodore Vaill Papers

Seibert Family Papers

Periodicals

The New York Times

PUBLISHED PRIMARY SOURCES

Adams, Ida Bright, ed. "The Civil War Letters of James Rush Holmes." *Western Pennsylvania Historical Magazine* 44 (June 1961): 105–27.

Blight, David W., ed. *When This Cruel War Is Over: The Civil War Letters of Charles Harvey Brewster.* Amherst: University of Massachusetts Press, 1992.

Buckingham, Peter H., ed. *All's for the Best: The Civil War Reminiscences and Letters of Daniel W. Sawtelle, Eighth Maine Volunteer Infantry.* Knoxville: University of Tennessee Press, 2001.

Cadwallader, Sylvanus. *Three Years with Grant.* Edited by Benjamin P. Thomas. New York: Knopf, 1955.

Carter, Robert Goldthwaite. *Four Brothers in Blue, or Sunshine and Shadows of the War of the Rebellion: A Story of the Great Civil War from Bull Run to Appomattox.* Austin: University of Texas Press, 1978.

Chipman, Donald. "An Essex County Soldier in the Civil War: The Diary of Cyrille Fountain." *New York History* 66 (July 1985): 281–317.

Crawford, Robert F. "The Civil War Letters of S. Rodman and Linton Smith." *Delaware History* 21 (Fall/Winter 1984): 86–116.

Dana, Charles A. *Recollections of the Civil War: With the Leaders at Washington and in the Field in the Sixties.* Lincoln: University of Nebraska Press, 1996.

Eisenschiml, Otto, ed. *Vermont General: The Unusual War Experiences of Edward Hastings Ripley, 1862–1865.* New York: Devin-Adair, 1960.

Fatout, Paul, ed. *Letters of a Civil War Surgeon.* West Lafayette, IN: Purdue University Press, 1996.

Floyd, Dale E., ed. *"Dear Friends at Home": The Letters and Diary of Thomas Jane Owen, Fiftieth New York Volunteer Engineer Regiment during the Civil War.* Washington, D.C.: Office of the Chief of Engineers, 1985.

Gavin, William Gilfillan, ed. *Infantryman Pettit: The Civil War Letters of Corporal Frederick Pettit, Late of Company C, 100th Pennsylvania Veteran Volunteer Infantry Regiment, "The Roundheads," 1862–1864.* Shippensburg, PA: White Mane Publishing, 1990.

Grant, Ulysses S. *Personal Memoirs of U.S. Grant, in Two Volumes.* New York: Charles L. Webster, 1886.

Greenleaf, Margery, ed. *Letters to Eliza from a Union Soldier, 1862–1865.* Chicago: Follett, 1963.

Hastings, William H., ed. *Letters from a Sharpshooter: The Civil War Letters of Private William B. Greene, Co. G, 2nd United States Sharpshooters (Berdan's), Army of the Potomac, 1861–1865.* Belleville, WI: Historic Publications, 1993.

Herdegen, Lance, and Sherry Murphy, eds. *Four Years with the Iron Brigade: The Civil War Journals of William R. Ray, Company F, Seventh Wisconsin Volunteers.* Cambridge, MA: Da Capo Press, 2002.

Howe, Mark DeWolfe, ed. *Touched with Fire: Civil War Letters and Diary of Oliver Wendell Holmes, Jr., 1861–1864.* Cambridge, MA: Harvard University Press, 1946.

Kent, Arthur A., ed. *Three Years with Company K: Sergt. Austin C. Stearns, Company K, 13th Mass. Infantry (Deceased).* Rutherford, NJ: Fairleigh Dickinson University Press, 1976.

Kohl, Lawrence Frederick, ed. *Memoirs of Chaplain Life: Three Years with the Irish Brigade in the Army of the Potomac.* New York: Fordham University Press, 1992.

Levstik, Frank. "The Civil War Diary of Colonel Albert Rogall." *Polish American Studies* 27 (Spring/Autumn 1970): 33–79.

Lewis, A. S., ed. *My Dear Parents: An Englishman's Letters Home from the American Civil War.* London: Gollancz, 1982.

Longacre, Edward G, ed. *From Antietam to Fort Fisher: The Civil War Letters of Edward King Wightman, 1862–1865.* Rutherford, NJ: Fairleigh Dickinson University Press, 1985.

Loving, Jerome, ed. *Civil War Letters of George Washington Whitman.* Durham, NC: Duke University Press, 1975.

Lyman, Theodore. *With Grant and Meade from the Wilderness to Appomattox.* Lincoln: University of Nebraska Press, 1994.

Marshall, Jeffrey D., ed. *A War of the People: Vermont Civil War Letters.* Hanover, NH: University Press of New England, 1999.

McBride, Robert Ekin. *In the Ranks: From the Wilderness to Appomattox Court-House. The War, As Seen and Experienced by a Private Soldier in the Army of the Potomac.* Cincinnati: Walden & Stowe, 1881.

Menge, W. Springer, and J. August Shimrak, eds. *The Civil War Notebook of Daniel Chisholm: A Chronicle of Daily Life in the Union Army, 1864–1865.* New York: Ballantine Books, 1989.

Mohr, James C., and Richard E. Winslow III, eds. *The Cormany Diaries: A Northern Family in the Civil War.* Pittsburgh: University of Pittsburgh Press, 1982.

Morrow, Henry. "The Last of the Iron Brigade." *Civil War Times Illustrated* 14 (February 1976): 10–21.

Porter, Horace. *Campaigning with Grant.* New York: Konecky and Konecky, 1992.

Rhodes, Robert Hunt, ed. *All for the Union: The Civil War Diary and Letters of Elisha Hunt Rhodes.* New York: Vintage Books, 1985.

Robertson, James I., Jr., ed. *The Civil War Letters of General Robert McAllister.* New Brunswick, NJ: Rutgers University Press, 1965.

Rosenblatt, Emil, and Ruth Rosenblatt, eds. *Hard Marching Every Day: The Civil War Letters of Private Wilbur Fisk, 1861–1865.* Lawrence: University Press of Kansas, 1992.

Silliker, Ruth L., ed. *The Rebel Yell and the Yankee Hurrah: The Civil War Journal of a Maine Volunteer.* Camden, ME: Down East Books, 1985.

Small, Harold Adams, ed. *The Road to Richmond: The Civil War Memoirs of Major Abner R. Small of the 16th Maine Vols.; with his Diary as a Prisoner of War.* Berkeley: University of California Press, 1957.

Temple, Wayne C., ed. "A Signal Officer with Grant: The Letters of Captain Charles L. Davis." *Civil War History* 7 (December 1961): 428–37.

Tyler, William S, ed. *Recollections of the Civil War, with Many Original Diary Entries and Letters Written from the Seat of War, and with Annotated References.* New York: G. P. Putnam's Sons, 1912.

United States War Department. *Revised United States Army Regulations of 1861, with an appendix containing the changes and laws affecting Army regulations and Articles of War to June 25, 1863.* Ann Arbor: University of Michigan Library, 2005.

———. *The War of the Rebellion: A Compilation of the Official Records of the Union and Confederate Armies.* Washington, D.C.: Government Printing Office, 1880–1901.

Viola, Herman J., ed. *The Memoirs of Charles Henry Veil: A Soldier's Recollections of the Civil War and the Arizona Territory.* New York: Orion Books, 1993.

Wilkeson, Frank. *Turned Inside Out: Recollections of a Private Soldier in the Army of the Potomac.* Lincoln: University of Nebraska Press, 1997.

Woodward, Daniel, ed. "The Civil War of a Pennsylvania Trooper." *Pennsylvania Magazine of History and Biography* 87 (January 1963): 39–62.

SECONDARY SOURCES

Adams, George Worthington. *Doctors in Blue: The Medical History of the Union Army in the Civil War.* New York: Henry Schuman, 1952.

Adams, Michael C. C. *Our Masters the Rebels: A Speculation on Union Military Failure in the East, 1861–1865.* Cambridge, MA: Harvard University Press, 1978.

Alotta, Robert I. *Civil War Justice: Union Army Executions under Lincoln.* Shippensburg, PA: White Mane Publishing, 1989.

Ashworth, Tony. *Trench Warfare, 1914–1918: The Live and Let Live System.* New York: Holmes & Meier, 1980.

Bearss, Edwin C., and Bryce A. Suderow. *The Petersburg Campaign, Volume 1: The Eastern Front Battles, June–August 1864*. El Dorado Hills, CA: Savas Beatie, 2011.

———, *The Petersburg Campaign, Volume 2: The Western Front Battles, September 1864–April 1865*. El Dorado Hills, CA: Savas Beatie, 2014.

Benton, Josiah H. *Voting in the Field: A Forgotten Chapter of the Civil War*. Boston: Plimpton Press, 1915.

Boatner, Mark M. *The Civil War Dictionary*. Rev. ed. New York: David McKay, 1988.

Bowery, Charles R., Jr., and Ethan S. Rafuse. *Guide to the Richmond-Petersburg Campaign (U.S. Army War College Guides to Civil War Battles)*. Lawrence: University Press of Kansas, 2014.

Cain, Marvin R. "A 'Face of Battle' Needed: An Assessment of Motives and Men in Civil War Historiography." *Civil War History* 28 (1982): 5–27.

Calore, Paul. *Naval Campaigns of the Civil War*. Jefferson, NC: McFarland, 2002.

Cannan, John. *The Crater: Petersburg*. Cambridge: Da Capo Press, 2002.

Castel, Albert. *Decision in the West: The Atlanta Campaign of 1864*. Lawrence: University Press of Kansas, 1992.

Catton, Bruce. "Union Discipline and Leadership in the Civil War." *Marine Corps Gazette* 40 (1956): 18–25.

Cimbala, Paul A., and Randall M. Miller, eds. *Union Soldiers and the Northern Home Front: Wartime Experiences, Postwar Adjustments*. New York: Fordham University Press, 2002.

Coffman, Edward M. "The Duality of the American Military Tradition: A Commentary." *Journal of Military History* 64 (October 2000): 967–80.

———. *The Old Army: A Portrait of the American Army in Peacetime, 1784–1898*. New York: Oxford University Press, 1986.

Cole, Garold L. *Civil War Eyewitnesses: An Annotated Bibliography of Books and Articles, 1955–1986*. Columbia: University of South Carolina Press, 1988.

———. *Civil War Eyewitnesses: An Annotated Bibliography of Books and Articles, 1986–1996*. Columbia: University of South Carolina Press, 2000.

Cowley, Robert, ed. *With My Face to the Enemy: Perspectives on the Civil War*. New York: G. P. Putnam's Sons, 2001.

Dean, Eric T., Jr. *Shook over Hell: Post-Traumatic Stress, Vietnam, and the Civil War*. Cambridge, MA: Harvard University Press, 1997.

Du Chanal, General Francois. "How Soldiers were Tried." *Civil War Times Illustrated* 7 (1969): 10–15.

Ellis, John. *Eye-Deep in Hell: Trench Warfare in World War I*. Baltimore: Johns Hopkins University Press, 1976.

Förster, Stig, and Jörg Nagler, eds. *On the Road to Total War: The American Civil War and the German Wars of Unification, 1861–1871.* Cambridge: Cambridge University Press, 1997.

Frassanito, William A. *Grant and Lee: The Virginia Campaigns, 1864–1865.* New York: Scribner's, 1983.

Freemon, Frank R. *Gangrene and Glory: Medical Care during the American Civil War.* Madison, NJ: Fairleigh Dickinson University Press, 1998.

Fuller, J. F. C. *The Generalship of Ulysses S. Grant.* Bloomington: Indiana University Press, 1929.

———. *Grant and Lee: A Study in Personality and Generalship.* Bloomington: Indiana University Press, 1957.

Gabel, Christoper R. *Railroad Generalship: Foundations of Civil War Strategy.* Fort Leavenworth, KS: Combat Studies Institute Press, 1997.

Gallagher, Gary W., ed. *The Spotsylvania Campaign.* Chapel Hill: University of North Carolina Press, 1998.

———, ed. *The Wilderness Campaign.* Chapel Hill: University of North Carolina Press, 1997.

Gallagher, Gary W., and Caroline E. Janney, eds. *Cold Harbor to the Crater: The End of the Overland Campaign.* Chapel Hill: University of North Carolina Press, 2015.

Gillett, Mary C. *The Army Medical Department, 1818–1865.* Washington, D.C.: Center of Military History, 1987.

Gragg, Rod. *Confederate Goliath: The Battle of Fort Fisher.* Baton Rouge: Louisiana State University Press, 2006.

Greene, A. Wilson. *The Final Battles of the Petersburg Campaign: Breaking the Backbone of the Rebellion.* 2nd edition. Knoxville: University of Tennessee Press, 2008.

Griffith, Paddy. *Battle Tactics of the Civil War.* New Haven, CT: Yale University Press, 1989.

Grimsley, Mark. *And Keep Moving On: The Virginia Campaign, May–June 1864.* Lincoln, NE: University of Nebraska Press, 2002.

Grossman, Dave. *On Killing: The Psychological Cost of Learning to Kill in War and Society.* Boston: Little, Brown, 1995.

Guelzo, Allen C. *Gettysburg: The Last Invasion.* New York: Alfred A. Knopf, 2013.

Hagerman, Edward. *The American Civil War and the Origins of Modern Warfare: Ideas, Organization, and Field Command.* Bloomington: Indiana University Press, 1988.

Hattaway, Herman. "The Changing Face of Battle." *North and South* 4 (August 2001): 34–43.

Hattaway, Herman, and Archer Jones. *How the North Won: A Military History of the Civil War.* Urbana: University of Illinois Press, 1983.

Herrera, Ricardo A. "Self-Governance and the American Citizen as Soldier, 1775–1861." *Journal of Military History* 65 (January 2001): 21–52.

Hess, Earl J. *Field Armies & Fortifications in the Civil War: The Eastern Campaigns, 1861–1864*. Chapel Hill: University of North Carolina Press, 2005.

———. *In the Trenches at Petersburg: Field Fortifications and Confederate Defeat*. Chapel Hill: University of North Carolina Press, 2009.

———. *Into the Crater: The Mine Attack at Petersburg*. Columbia: University of South Carolina Press, 2010.

———. *Trench Warfare under Grant and Lee: Field Fortifications in the Overland Campaign*. Chapel Hill: University of North Carolina Press, 2009.

———. *The Union Soldier in Battle: Enduring the Ordeal of Combat*. Lawrence: University Press of Kansas, 1997.

Horn, John. *The Petersburg Campaign, June 1864–April 1865*. Conshohocken, PA: Combined Publishing, 1993.

Howe, Thomas J. *The Petersburg Campaign: Wasted Valor, June 15–18, 1864*. Lynchburg, VA: H. E. Howard, 1988.

Huston, James A. "Logistical Support of Federal Armies in the Field." *Civil War History* 7 (March 1961): 36–47.

Jamieson, Perry D. *Crossing the Deadly Ground: United States Army Tactics, 1865–1899*. Tuscaloosa: University of Alabama Press, 1994.

Keegan, John. *The Face of Battle*. New York: Penguin Books, 1976.

Kellett, Anthony. *Combat Motivation: The Behavior of Soldiers in Battle*. Boston: Kluwer-Nijhoff, 1982.

Klein, Frederic S. "On Trial." *Civil War Times Illustrated* 10 (1969): 40–46.

Kohn, Richard H. "The Social History of the American Soldier: A Review and Prospectus for Research." *The American Historical Review* 86 (June 1981): 553–67.

Krick, Robert. *Civil War Weather in Virginia*. Tuscaloosa: University of Alabama Press, 2007.

Leed, Eric J. *No Man's Land: Combat and Identity in World War I*. Cambridge: Cambridge University Press, 1979.

Liddell Hart, B. H. *Sherman: Soldier, Realist, American*. New York: Dodd, Mead, 1929.

Linderman, Gerald F. *Embattled Courage: The Experience of Combat in the American Civil War*. New York: Free Press, 1987.

———. *The Mirror of War: American Society and the Spanish-American War*. Ann Arbor: University of Michigan Press, 1974.

———. *The World within War: America's Combat Experience in World War II*. New York: Free Press, 1997.

Long, Barbara, and E. B. Long. *The Civil War Day by Day: An Almanac, 1861–1865*. Garden City, NY: Doubleday, 1971.

Lonn, Ella. *Desertion during the Civil War.* Lincoln: University of Nebraska Press, 1998.

Lowe, David. "Field Fortifications in the Civil War." *North and South* 4 (August 2001): 58–73.

Lowry, Thomas. *Don't Shoot That Boy!: Abraham Lincoln and Military Justice.* Mason City, IA: Savas Publishing, 1999.

Mahon, John. "Civil War Infantry Assault Tactics." *Military Affairs* 25 (Summer 1961): 57–68.

McPherson, James M. *For Cause and Comrades: Why Men Fought in the Civil War.* New York: Oxford University Press, 1997.

———. *What They Fought For, 1861–1865.* Baton Rouge: Louisiana State University Press, 1994.

Mitchell, Reid. *Civil War Soldiers.* New York: Penguin, 1997.

———. "The First Modern War, R.I.P." *Reviews in American History* 17 (December 1989): 552–58.

———. "The Infantryman in Combat," *North and South* 4 (August 2001): 12–21.

———. *The Vacant Chair: The Northern Soldier Leaves Home.* New York: Oxford University Press, 1993.

Moran, Lord Charles. *The Anatomy of Courage.* London: Constable, 1945.

Novick, Peter. *That Noble Dream: The "Objectivity Question" and the American Historical Profession.* Cambridge: Cambridge University Press, 1998.

Phisterer, Frederick. *Statistical Record of the Armies of the United States.* New York: Charles Scribner's Sons, 1883.

Poulter, Keith. "The Civil War and the Evolution of Infantry Tactics." *North and South* 4 (August 2001): 78–84.

Power, J. Tracy. *Lee's Miserables: Life in the Army of Northern Virginia from the Wilderness to Appomattox.* Chapel Hill: University of North Carolina Press, 1998.

Ramold, Stephen J. *Baring the Iron Hand: Discipline in the Union Army.* DeKalb: Northern Illinois University Press, 2009.

Reid, Brian Holden. *The Civil War and the Wars of the Nineteenth Century.* New York: HarperCollins, 2006.

Rhea, Gordon. *The Battle of the Wilderness, May 5–6, 1864.* Baton Rouge: Louisiana State University Press, 1994.

———. *The Battles for Spotsylvania Court House and the Road to Yellow Tavern, May 7–12, 1864.* Baton Rouge: Louisiana State University Press, 1997.

———. *Cold Harbor: Grant and Lee, May 26–June 3, 1864.* Baton Rouge: Louisiana State University Press, 2002.

———. *To the North Anna River: Grant and Lee, May 13–25, 1864.* Baton Rouge: Louisiana State University Press, 2000.

Robertson, James I. "Military Executions in the Civil War." *Civil War Times Illustrated* 5 (1966): 34–39.

Robertson, William Glenn. *Back Door to Richmond: The Bermuda Hundred Campaign, April–June 1864.* Newark: University of Delaware Press, 1987.

Rodgers, Thomas. "Billy Yank and G.I. Joe: An Exploratory Essay on the Sociopolitical Dimensions of Soldier Motivation." *The Journal of Military History* 69 (January 2005): 93–121.

Royle, Trevor. *Crimea: The Great Crimean War, 1854–1856.* New York: St. Martin's, 2000.

Royster, Charles. *The Destructive War: William Tecumseh Sherman, Stonewall Jackson, and the Americans.* New York: Alfred A. Knopf, 1991.

Samet, Elizabeth. *Willing Obedience: Citizens, Soldiers, and the Progress of Consent in America, 1776–1898.* Stanford, CA: Stanford University Press, 2004.

Sears, Stephen. *To the Gates of Richmond: The Peninsula Campaign.* New York: Mariner Books, 1992.

Shannon, Fred. *The Organization and Administration of the Union Army, 1861–65.* 2 volumes. Gloucester, MA: Arthur H. Clark Company, 1928.

Skelton, William B. *An American Profession of Arms: The Army Officer Corps, 1784–1861.* Lawrence: University Press of Kansas, 1992.

Slotkin, Richard. *No Quarter: The Battle of the Crater, 1864.* New York: Random House, 2009.

Sommers, Richard J. *Richmond Redeemed: The Siege at Petersburg.* Garden City, NY: Doubleday, 1981.

Stokesbury, James L. *A Short History of World War I.* New York: HarperCollins, 1981.

Swank, Roy, and Walter Marchand. "Combat Neuroses: Development of Combat Exhaustion," *Archives of Neurology and Psychology* 55 (1946): 236–47.

Sword, Wiley. *The Confederacy's Last Hurrah: Spring Hill, Franklin, and Nashville.* Lawrence: University Press of Kansas, 1993.

Sylvester, Robert Bruce. "The U.S. Military Railroad and the Siege of Petersburg." *Civil War History* 10 (September 1964): 309–16.

Trudeau, Noah Andre. *Bloody Roads South: The Wilderness to Cold Harbor, May–June 1864.* Baton Rouge: Louisiana State University Press, 1989.

———. *The Last Citadel: Petersburg, Virginia, June 1864–April 1865.* Baton Rouge: Louisiana State University Press, 1991.

———. *Out of the Storm: The End of the Civil War, April–June 1865.* Boston: Little, Brown, 1994.

———. *Southern Storm: Sherman's March to the Sea.* New York: Harper Perennial, 2008.

Turner, George Edgar. *Victory Rode the Rails: The Strategic Place of the Railroads in the Civil War.* Westport, CT: Greenwood Press, 1953.

Vandiver, Frank. *Jubal's Raid*. New York: McGraw-Hill, 1960.

Watt, Richard. *Dare Call It Treason: The True Story of the French Mutinies of 1917*. New York: Dorset Press, 2001.

Weigley, Russell. *Towards an American Army: Military Thought from Washington to Marshall*. New York: Columbia University Press, 1962.

Weintraub, Stanley. *Silent Night: The Story of the World War I Christmas Truce*. New York: Free Press, 2001.

Weitz, Mark A. "Drill, Training and the Combat Performance of the Civil War Soldier: Dispelling the Myth of the Poor Soldier, Great Fighter." *Journal of Military History* 62 (April 1999): 263–90.

———. *More Damning than Slaughter: Desertion in the Confederate Army*. Lincoln: University of Nebraska Press, 2005.

Wert, Jeffrey. *From Winchester to Cedar Creek: The Shenandoah Campaign of 1864*. Mechanicsburg, PA: Stackpole Books, 1997.

Wiley, Bell Irvin. *The Life of Billy Yank: The Common Soldier of the Union*. Baton Rouge: Louisiana State University Press, 1952.

———. *The Life of Johnny Reb: The Common Soldier of the Confederacy*. Baton Rouge: Louisiana State University Press, 1943.

Index

Abbott, Charles, 78

Adams, Alexander, 144–45, 198, 201, 204, 272n64

African American troops, 30, 164, 168

American Civil War (1864–1865), 1, 6–7; general lack of discipline in the armies of, 77; growth of technology during, 273n13; as a "modern" conflict, 12, 40, 87, 91, 151, 242, 246n41, 273n13; percentage of uniformed personnel that held combat-related tasks during, 9, 92

Anatomy of Courage (Moran), 53

Army of the James, 5, 30–31, 67, 102, 235

Army of Northern Virginia, 1, 147, 148, 184, 192, 219; capitulation of at Appomattox, 236, 240; decline and disintegration of, 8, 228, 229, 230, 245–46n34; pessimism and anxiety in, 9; size of, 289–90n80; stymying of Grant's flanking movements by, 133; use of conscription to maintain the size of, 239, 287n34, 289–90n80. *See also* Overland campaign; Petersburg campaign

Army of the Potomac, 1, 29–30, 67, 192, 239, 291n16; anger of some soldiers in toward those on the home front, 150–51; benefits to of better food, medical care, and sanitation, 155; better morale of compared to that of the Army of Northern Virginia, 9, 12, 147–48; crippling effect of the Overland campaign on, 11, 14–15, 50–51,

86–87, 89; fifth drive of on Richmond, 5–6; indiscipline in, 69–71; medical and logistical support agencies for, 13–14; number of troops serving in (1864), 5, 17, 244n23, 247n8; outmarching of its supply lines by, 49, 152; reenlistment policies of, 2–3; support of from the Army of the James, 30; survival instinct of the soldiers in, 241–42; transfer of Smith's Eighteenth Corps to, 32, 66. *See also* Army of the Potomac, and the 1864 presidential election; desertion, problem of in the Army of the Potomac; Overland campaign; Petersburg campaign

Army of the Potomac, and the 1864 presidential election, 197–98; distrust of the Democratic Party and the "Copperheads," 198–99; support among the troops for Lincoln, 187–88, 189–90, 200–202, 283n46; support among the troops for McClellan, 199–202

Army of the Shenandoah, 235

Army of Tennessee, defeat of, 202–3

Arnold, John, 44, 55, 170, 174, 220

Ashworth, Tony, 212

Atlanta campaign, 6, 195–96

Baltimore, antiwar riots in, 194

Banks, Nathaniel, 14

Barlow, Francis, 193–94